Dominant Symbols in Popular Culture

Dominant Symbols in Popular Culture

Edited
by
Ray B. Browne
Marshall W. Fishwick
Kevin O. Browne

Bowling Green State University Popular Press
Bowling Green, Ohio 43403

Library of Congress Catalogue Card No.: 89-082333
ISBN: 0-87972-481-1 Clothbound
0-87972-482-X Paperback

Cover design by Laura Darnell Dumm

Contents

Introduction

You demonstrate nothing to anybody but those who understand your symbols.

Thomas Hobbes, 1669

A symbol stands for, represents, or denotes something else—the cross for Christianity, the crescent for Islam, Old Glory for the United States, the clenched fist for protest.

Symbols surround and engulf us as emblems, tokens, signs, images. They are part of the hidden language that makes the spoken language possible. Civilization depends on symbols to supply meaning.

Yet symbols don't *stand*—they move, elude, transform, die. Old meanings and interpretations fade away. Symbology—the study of symbols—is along with ideology on the cutting edge of contemporary thought. Life itself can be seen as symbolic and, in a deeply mystical sense, always is. In *A Machine That Would Go By Itself: The Constitution in American Culture,* Michael Kammen treats the Constitution "in the symbolic life of the American people." A symbol inside a symbol: wheels within wheels.

Then there are the writers who seek to express ideas or emotions through symbols, using words and even word-sounds to convey meanings which are often mystical or vague (Verlaine, Mallarme, and Maeterlinck). Artists may try to make colors symbolic, musicians, sounds.

Max Frisch called technology the knack of so arranging the world that you don't have to experience it. Does this mean that the symbols of technology—which glut our lives, advertisements, dreams—are not so much about experience as fantasy?

How and why do we invent symbols? Why do some last and others disappear? And how do we convey them through space and preserve them in time?

Consider our prominent symbolic lady, the Statue of Liberty. She has aroused more intense emotion than any other work of art in the New World. There is the symbolism in the torch, the history of female figures of liberty (like Joan of Arc, or the central personage in Delacroix's celebrated "Liberty Leading the People"), and the placement of the statue just when the floodgates of immigration were opened. Her power and immediacy was symbolized in May 1989 when the Chinese students raised her in Tiananmen Square in Beijing as a symbol around which to create a threat to totalitarian rule. Alas, their Lady, without a real tradition of democracy to stand on, was a less substantial symbol than the original extending greeting to oppressed people from other oppressive tyrannies.

"If the significance of the Statue of Liberty has in our day again been altered," Marvin Trachtenberg notes, "it still symbolizes America's grandeur as Mother of Exiles."[1] Restoration for the 1986 Centennial gave it new life, and projected revitalized symbolic value into the Electronic Age.

In the '60s our rhetoric and symbols choked in their own fumes. We have had trouble finding new ones. We seem to be at the tail-end of modernism and defiant individualism. What next? We still labor under the pseudo-shadow of the Frankfurt School, especially Adorno, Horkheimer and Marcuse, who saw little hope for "the masses" and their symbols. For them and their academic followers, mass culture reconciled consumers to the status quo and capitalism. Only "high art" with its special symbols could keep alive the utopian promises once fostered by religion. These scholars refused to admit that there is a mass sensibility and vitality, crucial for understanding our world.

They turned their back, for example, on television's bardic functions: to restore personal autonomy to ordinary people; to supply the social and symbolic conditions which make specific messages meaningful, as with lost storytellers, wise old men, and elders. They were part of, but could not recognize, a new organic community of listeners.[2]

But the Frankfurt School, and their contemporaries in France, did show us that symbols do not exist in a vacuum, and are not mere individual preferences. Symbols grow out of structure, and out of community. Others had hinted at this much earlier. In *Endymion,* John Keats urges us to explore all forms and substances "to their symbol-essences." We can hardly hope to do that; but this essay and those that follow hope to move in that direction.

"Symbol" is derived from the Greek (symbolon). When two people in ancient Greece made an agreement, they often sealed it by breaking something (a tablet, vase, or ring) into two pieces, each keeping one half. Later on either party could identify himself or herself by fitting one part of the broken object into the other's. The two pieces were called *symbola,* which gradually came to mean "recognition sign." Hence a symbol was originally a thing, sign, or word used for mutual recognition. Over the centuries "symbol" has come to mean any such sign, or form of recognition—linguistic or nonlinguistic, intentional or unintentional; a device or an image representing one thing but meaning something else.

From baptism to burial symbols permeate our lives; our conventions, clothes, and conversations. Above all we are surrounded by symbolic images, in big things and small, on matchbooks and billboards, in kindergarten and cathedral, in war and peace. "It seems clear that we cannot distinguish reality from our symbolization of it," Robert Bellah writes. "Being human, we can think only in symbols, only make sense of any experience in symbols." "To live symbolically," Thomas Mann observed, "spells true freedom."

One of the most famous definitions of modern times appears in Alfred North Whitehead's book *Symbolism:*

> The human mind is functioning symbolically when some components of its experience elicit consciousness, beliefs, emotions and images respecting other components of its experience. The former set of components are the 'symbols' and the latter the 'meaning' of the symbols.

A century earlier Goethe had noted that "in true symbolism the particular represents the universal not as a dream or shadow, but as a living, momentary revelation of the unfathomable." Coleridge wrote that a symbol "partakes of the reality which it renders intelligible." Thus a symbol is in Louis Macneice's words, "a signature of God's imminence."[3]

If to a theologian symbol means "creed," to a computer operator it might mean "disc." There is no mental connection, either rational or logical, between the symbol and its meaning. One may *know* that an apple symbolizes our fall or that a horseshoe stands for luck; but one could not deduce this by studying an apple or horseshoe.

Hence related terms must be examined as we begin our symbolic journey. Allegory in a way means the same thing as symbol, with an important difference. A symbol is simple, uncomplicated, known only to the initiated; an allegory is complex, often complicated, the reverse of secret and has extension, the narrative quality.

A "pictogram" reflects meaning as directly and unmistakably as possible—as with road and tourist signs. If a picture of a fish means "Buy fish here," it's a pictogram; if it means "I am a Christian," it's a symbol.

An "attribute" is an accessory; a predetermined identification. Neptune has his trident, Mary her halo, the Pope his keys. There are collective attributes—the martyrs' palm branches and the knights' armour. "Insignias" are indications of the power or dignity of an office or function. The actress has her Oscar, the field marshal his baton, the mayor his chain. Crown and scepter are *insignias* of royalty; coats of arms and flags of nations. The borderline between terms is not clear. A device belonging to any of these categories may lose its connotation and end up merely as an *ornament*. In the world of symbols, as in that of the humans who use them, success may lead first to popularity, then to oblivion.

Before examining specific ones, we might review briefly the chief work of five philosophers and anthropologists who have specialized in this area. The most famous is Ernst Cassirer, whose *Philosophy of Symbolic Forms* was first published in 1923. He argued that symbolism is an essential function of the human consciousness—basic to our understanding of language, history, science, art, myth and religion. He was convinced that only our use of symbolic forms had allowed humans to advance to their present eminence in the world—and that only by constructing new symbolic forms could we maintain that eminence. On this foundation most subsequent scholarship has been built. Cassirer went on to offer frameworks for handling problems of symbol definition and classification. We have been using them for over sixty years.[4]

Carl Jung developed the idea of "natural symbols," which grow out of the human psyche. One example is the Cross, representing the basic principle of order or stability. Another is the circle, or *mandala,* which appears in many different cultures. Such symbols reach down to and express the unconsciousness of primitivism, while corresponding to the highest intuitions of consciousness. Today Jungian disciples abound.

Mary Douglas, building on Jung, held that natural symbols were derived not from nature in the wild but from the human body—flesh, breath, blood, orifices, excretions. She centers on the intimate relationship between the human body and human society, at all times and in all places:

> The physical body can have universal meaning only as a system which responds to the social system, expressing it as a system. What it symbolizes naturally is the relation of parts of an organism to the whole...The two bodies are the self and society. The tension between them allows the elaboration of meaning.

Mircea Eliade is widely regarded as the most informed twentieth-century historian of religion. He directs his attention to *particular* objects and events, stressing what he calls "hierophanies"—manifestations of the sacred in the secular world which are represented and remembered by symbols. For Eliade symbolism is a language which connects humans with society and the cosmos; makes clear our deepest identity and social status; brings us into harmony with the rhythms of nature:

> What we call *symbolic thought* makes it possible for man to move freely from one level of reality to another. Symbols identify, assimilate and unify diverse levels and realities that are to all appearance incompatible. Magico-religious experience makes it possible for man himself to be transformed into a symbol.[5]

The most revolutionary of recent writers on symbolism is Clifford Geertz, who discards all theories of primitive mentality or of cultural evolution. For him there is no magic key to unlock the secret meaning of symbolic forms. Symbols function to synthesize our ethos—the tone, character, and quality of our life, its moral and aesthetic style and mood, the picture we have of the way things actually are, and how the world is ordered. A symbol is an object, act, event, quality or relation which serves as a vehicle for a conception. This conception is the meaning of symbol.[6]

Geertz' symbols are tangible, public, popular, concrete. To interpret a culture one must interpret its symbols. Since our book hopes to interpret American culture by concentrating on its perceptible and popular symbols, we are Geertzians. Under his banner we shall explore roads, automobiles, politics, pornography, cartoons, folk art, movie palaces, ethnicity, regionalism.

We believe, as does Geertz, that in today's world people can and do become symbols. Elvis Presley, James Dean, and Marilyn Monroe may be physically dead (are we *sure* about Elvis? In 1988 A.D. he, like June, was "bustin' out all over") but they are symbolically alive. And so are their symbolic successors. Have we moved, at the end of the twentieth century, into the Era of Symbol-Think? We look at Nixon and *think* about Watergate; or at Jimmy Swaggart, and *think* about downtown prostitutes. Our political candidates appear not so much thinkers as symbols. (Bush vs. Dukakis—the Wimp vs. the Shrimp). The great sociologist Emile Durkheim foresaw this a decade ago: "It is well known that the sentiments around us are simultaneously attached to the symbols which represent them."

Meaning is a perception in symbolic value space. When we speak of meaning, we are referring to "seeing" within the world of human symbols—not just grammars and syntaxes. Like taxes, and like God, symbols are always there. And if (as Einstein says) God does not play dice with the universe, the student who wishes to deal with symbolism must enter a floating crap game with definitions. Just what do such units as money, atoms, or symbols *mean?*[8]

Symbols are closely related to metaphor. But just what do astrophysicists imply when they say the Black Hole (source of the universe's creation) "has no hair?" If metaphors are listed, tallied, analyzed, annotated, do we really know what they *mean?*[9] Metaphors and symbols are the translation of the numinous into consciousness, the transcendent Divine into the immanent. If there is not a numinous quality to the metaphor or symbol, then it is merely a relatively lifeless comparison. Can the same question be raised about symbols? Does our quest lead us not just to structure but to *deep* structure—to the very creation of the universe? Deep structure is the primal pattern created by eons of the unconscious projections—values, fears and aspirations—of human beings. The resulting energy patterns in our unconscious are the archetypes which Jung spoke of, which serve as vehicles to communicate our symbols and metaphors. Archetypes such as the Wise Woman and the Wild Man evoke the numinous qualities which nourish our psyche.

Concern with "deep structure" goes back far beyond the ancient Greeks; but the linking of structure with subconscious mental processes is post-Freudian. Tracing this process through Freud and Jung goes beyond the theme of this introduction. But we can single out a landmark study that directly affected symbolism: Claude Levi-Strauss' *Structural Anthropology* (1963). History, Levi-Strauss argued, is not a succession of events, but a discernible pattern working according to discoverable laws. Social structures (and the symbols they generate) aren't visible to the eye; they are like molecular substances which can be seen only under an electron microscope. They determine how we act. What *appears* to be acts of human will are results of structure. Symbols and structure are Siamese twins. Long-term history and short-term perception are both controlled by such structure. In the long term, symbolism and religion were synonymous. The distinguishing mark of all symbol-systems we know about until the seventeenth century was that they were set in an essentially religious context. The world and society were dependent on a transcendent Being or beings. Hence symbols were reflections of a given manifestation of divine reality. All things partook of the sacred. Human's own systems reflected the realm of divine order. But revolutionary changes in Western Society have diminished the sacred and the hierophony (manifestation of sacred reality). We have built imposing national signs and symbols to assist us in controlling nature and society. For the first time in history, so far as we know, we have a symbolic system in a religious vacuum—in a desacralized world. To be desacralized means to accept no model for humanity outside the human condition as seen in history.[10] Most parts of the world still have a very hierophanic reality. Even in the West, though organized religion is mostly bankrupt, there is a subconscious sacred sense, albeit at a greater psychical distance, which operates in the same way as always, nurturing our human need for the numinous.

For western culture the results have been ominous—existentialism, alienation, narcissism. "Hard Edge" painting and "Primary Structures" sculpture have left art works without images and references—and viewers without any sense of attachment. The Theatre of the Absurd, which peaked in the 60's, gloried in chaos and contradiction. "We get," wrote critic Richard Barr, "a distorted picture of a world gone mad—in order to break the old mold of language and symbol."

Hence Arthur Kopit wrote *Oh Dad, Poor Dad, Mamma's Hung You in the Closet and I'm Feeling So Sad.* The Butcher in Arnold Weinstein's *The Red Eye of Love* builds a skyscraper out of rotten meat. The subject of Eugene Ionesco's *The Chairs* is "the absence of people, the absence of the emperor, the absence of God. The theme is nothingness."

Such works and attitudes demonstrated that symbols, once powerful, can become empty shells of fragmentary memories. The notorious obscurity of modern poetry, for example, stems from the absence in our lives of commonly accepted symbols to represent and house our deepest feelings. Once the church spire was the eminent symbols of uplift for a community, topped by a cross. Now it is a skyscraper, topped by a cooling tower.

Thirty years ago Anthony Bridges wrote a seminal article called "The Life and Death of Symbols." A style, he maintained, lives just as long as the symbols continue to be used as symbols pointing to something beyond themselves. Once a symbol is used for its own sake, treated as a *fact,* fundamentalists—who regard the recorded *fact* as the reality—emerge. At that moment symbolism dies.[11]

Symbols are sturdy, but they cannot survive a fixed, restricted, confined interpretation. Literalism, which removes overtones and imaginative suggestion, is lethal. Symbols must be constantly re-adapted and re-interpreted within fresh contexts. A new form—be it verbal, visual, aural—must "catch on," stir us to action, thrill the popular imagination. That is a basic premise of popular culture.

In place of the Sacred City we have fashioned the Secular City, and theologians like Harvey Cox have sung its praises. But creating a new symbology can be extremely difficult, as the Soviets discovered when they outlawed the Russian Orthodox Church and made agnosticism the new "creed." When Ronald Reagan visited Moscow in 1988, it was not to the Museum of Agnosticism but the officially revived Orthodox church that he went for a state visit. The revival of religious fervor is one of the astonishing features of our time.

Still it is science and not religion that rules both our hearts and our minds. The sacred priest in black has been replaced by the scientist in white. Woody Allen summed up the situation succinctly: "Not only is God dead, but try getting a plumber on the weekend."

Whatever happened to God, symbols reshaped, regrouped, and flourished. Space age scientific change was not only technological but symbolic. Secularism, individualism, capitalism, imperialism, and socialism all have their roots in the symbolic dynamic of production. Production and quantity became ends in themselves, fostering not only the plurality of mass production but ultimately of mass and popular culture—the area on which we concentrate in this book.[12] A new Age of Symbolism is upon us. The argonauts have become astronauts.

Basic Symbols will not be diminished, and certainly not dismissed. As soon as the child confronts the outside world—and school—he or she must translate his or her experience immediately into discrete SYMBOLS—a remarkable feat, the reduction of reality to a code. No changes in theology or ontology can alter this.

Surely symbolic thinking comes before language and discursive reason. Symbols still reveal the deepest aspect of reality; images, symbols and myths still fulfill a function, bringing to light the most hidden modalities of being. We must beware of supposing that symbols refer only to "spiritual" realities. To archaic thinking the separation of "spiritual" and "material" has no meaning; the two planes are complimentary. Symbolism adds a new value to an object or activity without any prejudice whatever to its own immediate value.[13]

In the world of advertising, symbols are now called trademarks. But they go back far into the past, having been used by ancient potters and stonemasons in Egypt dating from about 4000 B.C., as have marks on early Chinese porcelain. Livestock brands were used in Egyptian wall paintings and European wall paintings. The ancient world abounded with such symbolic marks. In the Middle Ages scribes's marks, watermarks, bread marks, and various craft guild symbols were added. A 1226 English law required bakers to put their mark on every loaf of bread sold. In 1597 two goldsmiths convicted of putting false marks on their wares were nailed to the pillory by their ears. (Anyone thinking of cribbing from our essays, take note.)

We see trademarks today on wrappers, boxes, and labels. Many were invented in the nineteenth century. Patent medicine led the way. Names like Swaim's Panacea, Fahnestock's Vermifuge, Mug-Wump Specific (For All Venereal Diseases), and Perry Davis' Vegetable Pain Killer were widely known and used. Times change, pain persists. How many symbolic ads have you recently seen for Bayer's, Tylenol, and Excedrin? The subject has been carefully explored and illustrated in Hal Morgan's *Symbols of America* (1986), "A Lavish Celebration of America's Best-Loved Trademarks and the Products They Symbolize."[14] We intend to augment and extend that Celebration.

Any collection of essays covering American symboland is bound to be partial, incomplete and merely suggestive. Any other commentator on the American scene could supply his own list. But our collection of nineteen essays serves as a big tent with some of the ribs showing. The canopy is meant to be suggestive.

Marshall Fishwick's essay, "Symbols: America's 'Natural Facts'," serves as a beginning. In many ways it is a symbol of a symbol, hinting at the number of symbols lying all around us.

"Evolution of the Book as Symbol," by Ray Browne, seizes one of America's most important symbol-icons and suggests how as icon the book has been used to keep people away from democratic learning yet how as symbol it has been used perhaps more than any other medium to spread the notion of the equality of communication and access to information.

In the third essay, James Combs' "The Political Meaning of Popular Symbolic Activity," the author works through for new insights into the use of political significance and purpose, in the broad sense of the word, in various forms of popular symbolism. As usual the implications are far-reaching.

In "The Goblin Child: Folktale Symbolism in Popular Art," the authors reach back for their symbolism to the essence of folklore and demonstrate how integral an understanding of folk symbolism is in the study of all arts and humanities.

Love and seduction, televangelical style, are the subject of Richard Peterson's essay, "Symbolism's 'New Spin'," and Peterson looks closely into the machinations and devices of one of the latest and most powerful spin groups whose device is falsification and whose goal is untold wealth and power.

If televangelism represents one kind of mobility in America, land travel symbolizes one of the oldest and most powerful lures of mankind, especially in the United States. In "Mobility in America," Michael Aaron Rockland gets at the very heart of what makes Americans *Americans* in his study of the mobility of people of this vast continent.

In the world of mobility there must be workers who make all things possible. Just as transportation facilities change, so does the concept and image of the worker, as Tom Juravich points out in his incisive essay "The Changing Image of Workers in Popular Culture."

Two concepts of the general nature of forces that drive popular culture are studied in John Cawelti's two essays "Symbols of Ethnicity and Popular Culture" and "Regionalism and Popular Culture: From Social Force to Symbolism." In Cawelti's mind regionalism—long a powerful force in society—has been replaced by ethnicity, which for any of several reasons now constitutes one of the most powerful drives and controlling forces in society. The consequences of this force are yet to be fully appreciated, and the end is by no means predictable.

Another powerful force in popular culture is, of course, pornography. Long recognized as one of the most powerful drives among people, sex has been for centuries distorted, exaggerated and centralized into art, power, impulse and inspiration. It has been cursed by many people, exploited by many others, feared by others. Whatever the feeling about it and reaction to pornography, Cawelti and Flannery are correct in recognizing that it is one of the world's great drives.

Another great—and seemingly cleansing—force is, of course, the notion or reality of wilderness, as Philip Terrie explains in his article "Wilderness: Ambiguous Symbol of the American Past." But wilderness and its creatures is not a dead or dying issue, as we recognize in the large number of examples of our reawakened interest in physical and creature environment. Thus, Elizabeth Lawrence's essay, "The Tamed Wild: Symbolic Bears in American Culture," is particularly pertinent and revealing.

Another aspect of environment, that of the architecture of building, is revealingly discussed by Gary Edgerton in his essay "Recreational Architecture as Popular Culture: The Symbolic Design of the American Movie Theater." The role of the movie-palace of the past is, perhaps, now being sought in an effort to recreate by-gone days by restoring the environment that we have tried so hard and casually to destroy. But the movie-palace of the past was an idealized, not a real, escape from reality.

Three aspects of humor—one of which is a kind of grim humor—are discussed in the following three essays. Marc Baldwin's essay on "Discourse of the Deal: The Car Salesman as Symbol" may or may not cast light on the dark side of our society, but at least it does reveal some spark of humor. Sam Riley's "Symbolism in Humor" is a more general and categorical approach to the subject, and probes the meaning and uses of humor in society. Roger Fischer's essay, "Political Cartoon Art as Symbol of Divergence of Popular and Traditional

Cultures in the United States," discusses the particular political cartoon humor of the last generation.

"Pink Flamingoes: Symbols and Symbolism in Yard Art," by Anthony Synnott, approaches an aspect of American society which constitutes a large force in society today and undoubtedly with the democratization of art and the determination of people to exercise the right of self-expression in all media will continue to grow. Already people are what they display in their gardens, as they are what they eat and what they wear. Who is to say nay to this form of self-expression?

Finally, this collection of dominant symbols in popular culture centers on two expressions of one of many ethnic groups in the U.S., the Italians. The Harvey Levenstein-Joseph R. Conlin essay, "The Food Habits of Italian Immigrants to America: An Examination of the Persistence of a Food Culture and the Rise of 'Fast Food' in America," cuts to the very bone of one of the great foodways of the country. And the J. Michael Ferri essay, "Deaths, Wakes, Funerals: Italian American Style," completes symbolically the life cycle. Thus the picture is complete.

Symbols are the heartbeat of society, the forces that we live and die by, that hold us apart and pull us together. They drive us forward, they inhibit our motion. They make us prosper or force us to languish. They are the fiber of a civilization. The more we know about symbols, what makes them and what keeps them alive, the more we know about ourselves, our society and our nation. We cannot know too much.

Notes

[1]See Marvin Trachtenberg, *The Statue of Liberty* (New York, Viking, 1976), p. 156.

[2]For a fuller development of these points see John Fiske and John Hartley, *Reading Television* (London, Methuen, 1978); and Michael Parenti, *Inventing Reality* (New York, St. Martin's Press, 1986).

[3]Quoted by F.W. Dillistone, *The Power of Symbols in Religion and Culture* (New York, Crossroad, 1986), p. 11.

[4]Ernest Cassirer, *Philosophy of Symbolic Forms* (1923).

[5]Mircea Eliade, *Patterns in Comparative Religion* (Princeton, Bollingen Series, 1970), p. 455.

[6]Michael Banton, ed., *Anthropological Approaches to the Study of Religion* (London, Methuen, 1968), p. 5.

[7]Emile Durkheim, *The Elementary Forms of the Religious Life* (London, Allen & Unwin, 1926), p. 219.

[8]For more on this approach, see Roy Wagner, *Symbols That Stand for Themselves* (Chicago, University of Chicago Press, 1986), chapter 1.

[9]Paul Ricoeur thinks a metaphoric utterance can "redescribe a reality inaccessible to direct description." See his *Time and Narrative,* translated by K. McLaughlin and D. Pellbauer (Chicago, University of Chicago Press, 1984), xl.

[10]Paul Tillich elaborates on this in *The Shaking of the Foundations* (1950). He finds nothing so irritating as the phrase "merely a symbol." Tillich regards symbols as the supreme media through which the human mind can be opened up to reality. So do I.

[11]See Chapter 11, "The Life and Death of Symbols," in F.W. Dillistone, *The Power of Symbols in Religion and Culture* (New York, Crossroad, 1986).

[12]The symbolic statement implied here is explored in David Schneider's provocative study of *American Kinship* (Chicago, University of Chicago Press, 1980). See also Schneider's "Notes toward a Theory of Culture" in K. Basso and H. Selby, eds. *Meaning in Anthropology* (Alburquerque, University of New Mexico Press, 1976).

[13]See Mircea Eliade, *Images and Symbols* (New York, Sheed and Ward, 1961), ch. V.

[14]The best source of information is of course the Commission of Patents and Trademarks in Washington. There are even two pertinent journals: *Trademark* Bulletin and *Trademark Reporter*.

Bibliography

Covering many disciplines, cultures, and periods, books on symbolism form a library of their own. In addition to titles already quoted, these provide a basis for further exploration and study; most have bibliographies of their own:

Achen, Tito Sven, *Symbols Around Us* (New York: Van Nostrand, 1978)

Bowra, B.M., *The Heritage of Symbolism* (London: Macmillan, 1943)

Bridge, Anthony, "The Life and Death of Symbols," *Theology*, January 1958, pp. 8f.

Dunbar, H.F., *Symbolism in Mediavel Thought* (New Haven: Yale University Press, 1929)

Dillistone, F.W., *Traditional Symbols and the Contemporary World* (London: Epworth Press, 1973)

Eliade, Mircea, *Images and Symbols,* translated by P. Mairet (New York: Sheed and Ward, 1969)

Firth, Raymond, *Symbols: Public and Private* (Ithica: Cornell University Press, 1973)

Girard, René, *Violence and the Sacred,* translated by Patrick Gregory (Baltimore: The Johns Hopkins Press, 1972)

Jantzen, Grace, *God's World: God's Body* (London: Darton, Longman, 1984)

Kripke, Saul, *Naming and Necessity* (Cambridge: Harvard University Press, 1980)

Levi-Strauss, Claude, *Structural Anthropology* (New York: Basic Books, 1963)

——. *Tristes Tropiques* (New York: Basic Books, 1975)

Olson, Alan M., ed., *Myth, Symbol, and Reality* (Notre Dame: University Press, 1980)

Radcliffe-Browne, A.R., *Structure and Function in Primitive Society* (New York: Free Press, 1964)

Sperber, Dan, *Rethinking Symbolism.* Translated by A.L. Morton. (Cambridge: Cambridge University Press, 1975)

Swiatecka, Jadwiga, *The Idea of the Symbol* (Cambridge: Cambridge University Press, 1980)

Whitehead, Alfred N., *Symbolism, Its Meaning and Effect* (New York: Macmillan, 1927)

Zuckerkandl, Victor, *Sound and Symbol,* translated by W.R. Trask. (Princeton: Bolligen Series XLIV, 1969)

Symbols: America's "Natural Facts"

Marshall Fishwick

Every natural fact is a symbol of some spiritual fact.

Ralph Waldo Emerson

Emerson was right: symbols are both our natural and spiritual "facts." That is what our history is all about—and that is why we are publishing yet another book on symbolism.

Our Founding Fathers knew this. They agreed with Jefferson: we would rather die free men than live slaves. We rejected Old World symbolism—hereditary monarchy, established church, class structure, entrenched military, and wrote a Constitution which began: "We the people..."

This, and more. A French visitor, the Duc de Liancourt, wrote in 1790 that "the wit, imagination, and genius of Europe are already in decrepitude." To American patriots, lightening the ship of state was the reward, not the price, of sailing out in unchartered waters. Years later Carl Sandburg put the whole thing in Mid-West idiom: the past is but a bucket of ashes.

That was the essential symbolic meaning of our Revolution. Souls were tried and not found wanting. Lord Cornwallis surrendered; we sent his Redcoats packing. His band played, "The World Turned Upside Down."

Having humbled mighty Albion, zealous nationalists demanded a cultural instauration. That we ought instantly to have a national literature was obvious. To speed up the arrival of the new Augustan Age, James Northmore wrote *Washington: or, Liberty Restored,* which was said to rival Milton. "Hasten, o come quickly, thou season of expectation!" was Dr. Samuel Mitchill's fervent plea. "Let our writers emulate the ambition, diligence, and zeal that have characterized our gentlemen of the sword," said Robert Treat Paine, "and the object for which they contend must inevitably be attained." Perhaps inevitably, but not instantly. Political freedom is easier won than cultural independence. Addressing "The American Scholar" half a century later, Emerson would still be complaining: "We have listened too long to the courtly muses of Europe."

The new Republic was long on enthusiasm and short on symbols: those tangible manifestations of the intangible; those short circuits of thought that compress and convey emotions. To endure, a nation needs not only authority, but the symbolic means of generating and expressing it. Sound symbols are as indispensable as sound currency; and for a while, it looked as if neither might be worth a Continental.

Rattlesnakes, turkeys, tobacco leaves, pine trees, liberty bells, Lockean phrases, and bisons were thrown into the symbolic void. None of these adequately symbolized abstractions like liberty, equality, and justice. It is simpler to dispose of crowns, crests, and mitres than to replace them. America's eagle seemed less wise than Athena's owl. There was a notable difference between the Oracle at Delphi and Liberty holding a mob cap on a stick; between Galas the man-headed bull and the American bison; between the high-altar cherubim and the cigar-store Indian.

How, in the Age of Reason, could one endow objects with the extra-physical and irrational power called *mana?* Our surest course was to substitute rather than invent. Thus, "My Country Tis of Thee" doubled for "God Save the King;" Old Glory used the same color scheme as the Union Jack. The cult of the new flag flourished. But who, then or now, could sing the second verse of "The Star-Spangled Banner"?

Fortunately, we had George Washington, *pater patriae,* who proved to be more effective as a symbol than as a general. "He personally was ninety per cent of the force which made the American Revolution a successful issue," writes William Carlos Williams. "America has furnished the world the character of Washington," said Daniel Webster. "If our institutions had done nothing else, that alone would have entitled them to the respect of mankind." Washington's inexhaustible patience and tenacity best symbolized our cause. After Yorktown, his prestige surpassed that of the United States government.[1]

Like Cincinnatus, he returned to his ploughshare (which soon became a major American symbol) when the war was won. But his country needed him again, and as first president Washington set the pattern for that crucial office. When he died, Napoleon ordered a week of mourning for France, and had his eulogy delivered in the Temple of Mars. To Europeans, Washington was the human embodiment of resistance to despotism and tyranny.

Apotheosized in his own lifetime, the squire of Mount Vernon was (as we shall see in a later chapter) eventually turned into the Man in the White Marble Toga. He is first in everything. His Olympian face still greets us on dollar bills, postage stamps, school tablets, and granite mountains. When the Southern states left the Union, they took Washington's image with them, and used it on the Confederate Great Seal. The man who became a super-human symbolic force. Cryptic Gertrude Stein put it neatly: "She is very sleepy, George Washington."

But there was nothing sleepy about the Connecticut Wits, the most self-conscious school of early nationalist writers. David Humphrey's *Poem on the Industry of the United States of America* foretold wordy Chamber of Commerce reports to come, and John Trumbull's *McFingal* was a verbose satire on Tory sympathizers. Timothy Dwight's *Conquest,* with eleven books of ponderous pentameter couplets, was so well received that the Wits tried a joint effort, the *Anarchiad.* Having written a new version of the Psalms, Joel Barlow came forth with Columbia's answer to the *Iliad. The Columbiad* was enough to bring Columbus' whole venture into question. "The Wits were," Vernon Parrington has said, "rather tedious fellows, who substituted fustion for creative thought, and blew up their verses with flatulent rhetoric."

Still, we must be impressed by their terrible sincerity and their success in preparing the way for Irving, Cooper, Longfellow, and Simms. With this quartet American literature won a European audience. They, in turn, laid the groundwork for the nineteenth century American Renaissance in symbolic literature, and for the successful fusion of appearance and reality.[2]

Ralph Waldo Emerson's wise words peppered American intellectual circles like buckshot. He saw nature as the symbol of spirit, and words as signs of natural facts. "What would we really know the meaning of?" he asked. "The meal in the firkin; the milk in the pan; the ballad in the street..." He preached self-reliance (a trait known today as inner-direction) and became a transparent eyeball through which the currents of the Universal Being circulated.

For Henry David Thoreau one single veil hung over the past, present, and future; the historian should find out not only what was, but what is. Thoreau could hear in the atmosphere aeolian harp-music, and he insisted on marching to the beat of a distant drummer. He went to the woods because he wished to live deliberately, to front only the essential facts of life; and the account of that trip, *Walden,* abounds with organic symbolism. The scythe with which he cuts becomes time; the snake he uncovers, temptation. Tangible natural objects always point beyond themselves, to the intangible.

So too with Nathaniel Hawthorne, who said: "Everything has its spiritual meaning, which to the literal meaning is what the soul is to the body." In books like *The Marble Faun,* the symbolism becomes so central that it interferes with the story. Herman Melville's cosmic hero, Captain Ahab, "tears the pasteboard masks off appearance" to reveal the truth underneath. The *Pequod* sails on symbolic seas.

"Do you guess I have some intricate purpose?" Walt Whitman asks, and gives a blunt answer: "Well, I have." That intricate purpose is brilliantly articulated in *Leaves of Grass.* He would convince us that a leaf of grass—the handkerchief of the Lord—is no less than the journey-work of the stars; that running blackberry would adorn the parlors of heaven. Whitman is a poet who finds "letters from God dropt in the street, and everyone signed by God's name." With him and his contemporaries, symbolic expression and realization reached literary maturity.

Yet no one would argue that the wellspring of American symbolism is poetry or fiction. The matter goes much deeper than that. The primary American symbols are a folk product, shaped later by leaders and manipulators, but springing from the grassroots mentality. The chief source of New World symbolism is landscape.

Free land was the magnet which set off the largest folk-wandering in modern times, and made the United States. To men in old and tired lands, it seemed that the human race had not had such an opportunity since Eden. The main American folk symbol is the Garden. Around it, notes Henry Nash Smith, "clusters a whole galaxy of lesser ones, expressing fecundity, growth, increase, and blissful labor in the earth, all centering around the heroic figure of the idealized frontier farmer armed with that supreme agrarian weapon, the sacred plow."[3]

Whereas primitive men saw nature teeming with evil demons, and medieval men saw nature aspiring to the Redemption, Americans saw it as inviting the Good Society. Countless examples can be cited as evidence, none more interesting than Crevecoeur's 1782 letter. "Here nature opens her broad lap to receive the perpetual accession of new comers," he wrote in *Letters from an American Farmer*. "The spectacle afforded by these pleasing scenes must be more entertaining, and more philosophical, than that which arises from beholding the musty ruins of Rome."

In symbol and in saga, as in sinew and fact, the American story has from the beginning been one of painful separation and slow adjustment; the recurring tale of caravans leaving citadels. "What will we do with the land?" pioneers asked. A question seldom raised was: "What will the land do to us?" Being strong medicine, it did and does much.

Landscape and culture are siamese twins. The earth is the womb of life. On it men leave their bounties, bodies, and histories. Landscape is more than a place; it is the state of being of that place—a totality of aspect.

Different people approach it differently. They see what they are prepared to see. The mind trains the eye. The Indians' approach was religious, the white man's, economic. Rich in symbol and myth, Indian culture flowered long before Jamestown. In the dance, hunt, and sacrifice, the Red Men re-enacted symbolically the spiritual drama of existence.[4]

The violence which characterizes so much American Literature and action parallels the continental waywardness of rampaging nature. Hurricanes, typhoons, line storms, and flash floods abound in our wild, bone-breaking landscape, fit for uncouth exiled gods.

Beyond the coastal plains were foothills and blue mountains, and beyond that vast forests which stretched west to lakes that were inland oceans, and a river that drained half the continent. Beyond the Mississippi were unmeasured miles of grass so high you could tie it over a horse's saddle. Still further were canyons, mesas, valleys, Rocky Mountains; and another majestic forest, reaching northwards indefinitely. Here were millions of virgin acres ready for a single slogan; Manifest Destiny.

The things Americans grew, built, imagined, on that two billion acres filled up their empty symbol storehouse.

Start with an obvious example: corn. Basic to American life, as wheat is to Europe and rice to Asia, this giant grass cannot reproduce itself; there is no such thing as a wild ear of corn. When the tiller dies, the field decays with him. But the corn fields have lived, and expanded. They symbolize the land which has been our breadbasket for generations, and that of the free world in this one. No wonder the red men staged corn dances and the white men husking bees. Stand in a corn field in August, and hear the corn growing in the blazing sun that scorches a hole in the sky. Then you can say: *this* is America.

Not only the crops, but the special devices that have made them possible in the west (the six-shooter, barbed wire, combine, tractor, cotton sled, for example) come to mind. They were more than technological achievements. They were, and remain, symbols of American "know-how" and adaptability. A western hero without a six-shooter is as unthinkable as a knight without a sword, or a sailor without a ship.

A large segment of our symbol storehouse is reserved for architecture. In organizing and utilizing space, we (like others before us) have created the most enduring national symbols. We remember Egypt for her pyramids, China for her walls, Greece for her Acropolis, Rome for her Forum, France for her cathedrals—and America for her log cabins, skyscrapers, and factories.

Few Americans know that the log cabin stems from Swedish, not British, culture. The first ones were built in the Delaware Bay area, two centuries before this simple structure became a "sacred" American symbol.[5] If log cabins were built and revised by the common people, that fact was dramatized by an election and a book of the 1840s. The Rev. Alexander Young's *Chronicles of the Pilgrim Fathers* made the unhistorical claim that the log cabin "had come straight down to us from the immortal hands of the Pilgrim fathers." A Democratic newspaper, meanwhile, foolishly suggested that for the Whig candidate, William Henry Harrison, a log cabin and hard cider would suffice. The Whigs turned the taunt into a battle cry, swept into power, and nationalized the log cabin symbol. So have American politicians, ever since.

Daniel Webster apologized for *not* having been born in one. He told of the remains of an earlier Webster cabin, which he visited on pilgrimages. "I carry my children to it to teach them the hardships endured by the generations which have gone before them," he said. He and many others also knew that the New England "salt box" house, with its small windows, plain facade, and steep roof, was a splendid symbol of Puritanical New England. Dutch and Flemish settlers in New York and New Jersey built more decorative houses with "corbie steps," double transome windows, and roofs flared at the eves with the "Dutch kick"—a different style with different cultural and symbolic implications. Further South, the Tidewater planters came not to reject but to project British culture. They adapted the Georgian style, and imitated the British aristocracy. Williamsburg, with its elegant Governor's Palace and Capitol, had a special symbolic role in the eighteenth century. It re-assumed that role again in the twentieth, thanks to millions of Rockefeller dollars.

Isolated from the English colonies, the Spanish in Florida and the Southwest developed their own style, just as did the French in Louisiana. Semi-tropicaer del Bac are as "American" as the Boston State House, the Leendert Bronk House, and Westover, and just as important as regional symbols.[6]

The Republic acquired a national architectural style with the Classical Revival. Anxious to exhibit the antique virtues, Americans built their new capital, and many lesser places in the Roman manner, expressive of the ruggedness and energetic materialism of Jacksonian America. The Classical Revival was a modified version of the age-old search for an Eldorado of the mind. It tied in with the psychic force which drove men westward. Though related to a world-wide trend, America's buildings reflected native materials and methods. Bundles of corn appeared on columns, and tobacco leaves flowered on cappings. Workaday buildings like Philadelphia's pump house sported Roman columns and domes. So did churches, banks, state capitols, and colleges.

In addition to being architectural symbols, the courthouses were the setting of the most elaborate symbolic behavior of the nineteenth century. Based on the fundamental belief in the certainty of law, prescribed rituals sprang up around the judicial activities held in them. This condition prevailed in the twentieth century, when the Supreme Court was moved to a Greek temple that outshone any of those in Athens. That matchless politician, Franklin D. Roosevelt, found the Court one thing which could not be tampered with. The Supreme Court has taken over the church's preeminence as the national symbol of social stability—despite the fact that (in such instances as the 1954 desegregation case) its rulings stir up social revolutions.

Few nineteenth century Americans walked before the Supreme Court, but many had reason to walk down Main Street and view two significant structures. At one end was the church, its steeple pointing upward to unlimited bliss. At the other was the saloon, its door swinging inward to unlimited iniquity. The struggle of good and evil was no dry abstraction; it was a wet option.

After the Civil War an advancing technology uprooted men, methods, and symbols. In architecture was given the skyscraper. The term, derived from the top spar of a sailing ship, has become so symbolic of our culture (despite the fact that the first skyscrapers appeared only in the 1880s) that George Mikes calls his recent satire of the United States *How to Scrape Skies*. In these structures the direct, simple thinking of the engineer is wedded to the vision and ingenuity of the artist-architect. When after World War II the Archbishop of Canterbury opposed the erection of a London skyscraper, he stated his case in overtly symbolic fashion. "The building would be out of place here," he said. "The small steps of a tubby John Bull should not be lengthened to compete with the stride of Uncle Sam."

Readers knew what he meant, because Uncle Sam is the cartoon symbol par excellence of our nation. He began as flesh and blood, but became more than that—the world-wide embodiment of all that is American. Uncle Sam looks like a Vermont farmer, but he speaks for us all.

So, in a very different way, does Ronald McDonald. A leading theologian, Henri Nouwen, notes the deep symbolic significance of clowns:

> Clowns remind us that we share the same human weaknesses. Psychologists have found in the clown a powerful image to help us understand contemporary society.[7]

Ronald lives in the very American McDonaldland, but is at home anywhere in the world—a new global symbol. He loves hamburgers, jokes, and children. He can do almost anything, and defies the laws of gravity. Ronald, dubbed "official spokesman" of the McDonald Corporation in 1967, has become a living entity, a *ding an sich,* for millions. His creators proclaim him "more famous than Lassie or the Easter Bunny."

Ronald has made not only children, but adults who run McDonald's very happy too. He chronicles a commercial bonanza, powered by a mighty munching army consuming billions of hamburgers. But there is much more to it than that. As Professor Conrad P. Kottack, an anthropologist has noted, Ronald heads a kind of secular religion, the shelter between the Golden Arches, a sacred place. "One finds here spirituality without theological doctrine."

For most people, however, the most powerful symbolic figures are not clowns but president, generals, champions. Yet some of those we admire most today were reviled and rejected in their own. Consider Jefferson. Three states flatly refused to be named "Jefferson," even though he had acquired the Louisiana Territory and laid out the Northwest. When the convention met to name what is now Louisiana, a delegate threatened to blow up the building if Jefferson's name were debated on the floor; and sentiment in what would be Colorado was just as strong. But half a century later the New Dealers up-graded Jefferson to rank with Washington and Lincoln as one of the trinity. His face was put on the three-cent stamp, the nickel, and Mount Rushmore. Having approved a Jefferson Memorial to stand with Washington and Lincoln's in the capital, Roosevelt took care to make his "stab in the back" speech at Monticello. In World War II Jefferson was the symbol of an endangered democracy—and of the Democratic party that was guiding its destiny.

Some symbols have two sides, like a coin. So it is with the man Daniel Boone, and the object, the covered wagon. Boone (not only in fact, but in Cooper's novels) was ingenious, independent, liberty-loving: the embodiment of our frontier, and prototype of manner, lesser frontier favorites. Some of these, like Davy Crockett and Mike Fink, are grotesque parodies. The material part of the symbol is the covered wagon, in which the Western trek was effected. Not until Henry Ford produced the Model T, and his contemporaries Lizzie Lore, would there be an American item of transport so dear to the nation's heart.

This is only one example of what we mean when we say heroes and symbols are related to the climate of opinion. The nation that yearned for "normalcy" in 1920 could hardly have idolized Thomas Jefferson—any more than the nations that voted for a New Deal in 1934 could have venerated Hamilton. For the generation after World War I, Lindbergh seemed like the hero of heroes in the air age. But when Hollywood made a major movie about him after World War II, a new generation asked, "Who's Lindbergh?"

By rising from symbol to symbol (log-cabin to White House), preserving the Union, and freeing the Negro, Abraham Lincoln became the leading symbol of the American democratic dream. His martyred death added the crowning touch. Had it not been for the printing press, said Emerson, Lincoln would have been mythological in a few years. Actually the printing press only speeded up the process. In 1872 D.B. Turney published *The Mythifying Theory, Or Abraham Lincoln a Myth,* and three generations later Lloyd Lewis made a collection of *Myths After Lincoln.*

His symbolism smacks of the religious. Consider his national Memorial in Washington: a white Greek temple, in which sits a graven image. On the wall the sports-shirted pilgrims read:

> In this temple as in the hearts of the people for whom he saved the Union the memory of Abraham Lincoln is enshrined forever.

So did the Greeks venerate Zeus, and the Italians St. Francis. Styles change, but sentiment endures.

So do the golden calves which have attracted sizable audiences for centuries. A list of American symbols which included only heroes, documents, buildings, and beliefs would be a naive one. America is full of attractive godlets. Mammon need not be venerated on a high hill. He can do very well, for example, in the Rose Bowl.

This could be predicted. After all, Americans are human beings, and all cultures set up symbols which are taken so seriously that they become idols. (One good definition of religion might be: those things at which people refuse to laugh.) Such a list for America would surely include success, money, power, racial exclusiveness, creature comfort, speed, and scientism. There is also the urge to publish books about America—but never mind about that.

If the symbolic function is to compress and convey emotion, our sports contests are far more than past times. This was brought home to me vividly when recently I heard a professor at the University of Hamburg comment on American character to his German students.

"If you want to understand the American, watch one of their infielders play baseball," he said. "They seem half asleep as the batter steps up, relaxed, slouching forward, kicking the dirt with their shoes. You'd think anyone could knock the ball past them. Then comes the pitch, the crack of the bat on the ball. Suddenly our infielder is alive. He leaps into the air, like a giant steel spring; grabs the ball; and throws it across the field too fast for the eye to follow. The play is over. He is asleep again. You would hardly think he realized that they were playing a game."

Football, too has begun to have its serious cultural analysts, such as David Riesman.[8] Any "big" football game is a uniquely American combination of ritual, pageantry, and symbolic action; with no more deer or buffalo to chase, the rugged American male chases the pigskin. To assist him hundreds of students yell and bend to preconceived patterns, guided by cultic "cheerleaders." A good friend of mine who is an Episcopal clergyman and expert on religious liturgy has stopped going to "Big Ten" football games. "They're too high church for me," he explains.

At many such games "queens" reign. In fact, it is apparent that the production curve for queens is one of the fastest rising in America. It is a poor school indeed that doesn't have a May Queen, and a poor Chamber of Commerce that doesn't elect an Onion Queen for Jones County. Having been selected and crowned by an Important Person, the young and buxom queen holds court in the minimum attire. (One is not always sure just what product she is glorifying.) Her court of slightly less buxom competitors look on, as maids in waiting. If they can still look down on their Republic, what must her monarchy-hating Founding Fathers say to all *this?*

The simple truth is that we need queens, just as we need flags and documents and heroes and shrines. We love them because they are ours, and we need them because they are symbolic. As we celebrated the bicentennial of our nation, our Constitution, our first Presidency in the 1980s, they seemed to have gained, not lost, in symbolic importance. If we are to have and to hold onto a common culture, symbols will be the essential glue.[9] Symbols are more precious than gold, yea much fine gold. They are us.

Notes

[1]See Ralph Gabriel's chapter on "Pre-Sumter Symbolism" in *The Course of American Democratic Faith* (New York, 1940); and Sydney Fisher's *The Legendary and Mythmaking Process of the American Revolution* (Philadelphia, 1912).

[2]These matters are fully discussed in F.O. Mattheissen's *American Renaissance* (New York, 1941) and in more current books by Daniel Boorstin.

[3]Henry Nash Smith, *Virgin Land: The American West as Symbol and Myth* (Boston, 1950), p. 138.

[4]A good one-volume introduction to this subject is John Collier's *Indians of the Americas* (New York, 1947). The reawakened interest in Amerinds is a major movement of the 1980s.

[5]See Harold Shurtliff's *Log Cabin Myth* (Cambridge, Mass., 1939).

[6]See Hugh Morrison's *Early American Architecture from the First Colonial Settlements to the National Period* (New York, 1952).

[7]Henry Nouwen, *Clowning in Rome* (New York, 1979). See also my book on *The World of Ronald McDonald* (Bowling Green: Popular Press, 1982).

[8]See Riesman's essay on the socio-cultural implications of football in *Individualism Reconsidered* (New York, 1955) and in Robert Bellah's *Habits of the Heart* (New York, 1986).

[9]For more on this, see my book *Common Culture and the Great Tradition* (Westport: Greenwood Press, 1986): and Hal Morgan, *Symbols of America* (New York: Penguin Books, 1987). Recent world events raise new questions about the "essential glue" which is symbolism. Will the policy of *glasnost* proclaimed by the Soviet Union affect the symbols not only of Eastern Europe but the whole world? How will the dramatic changes in the Eastern Bloc, including the removal of the Berlin Wall, change our symbols and our thinking? Can the Global Village alter and amend old national symbols, or will new ones emerge? Can and will the media manipulate Emerson's "natural facts?" The essays that follow give us clues, but only time will give us answers.

Evolution of the Book as Symbol

Ray B. Browne

The symbol of the book is one of the most powerful in American culture and has been since the days of the earliest settlers. The English who moved to this country in the seventeenth and eighteenth centuries brought with them the concept of the book as a symbol of great importance. They read exactly what, and to the same extent, their counterparts who stayed in England read. The lists of books sold by John Usher, a bookseller in Boston during the 1680s, as reported by Russel Nye, indicates "fairly well what his patrons bought and in what proportion—a thousand religious books, four hundred Bibles, a thousand schoolbooks...but also a hundred and sixty-two 'romances,' eighty one books of poetry, and twenty-eight jest books." Distribution of books depended, of course, on bookstores. Boston had fifty in the 1770s; both Philadelphia and New York had more than half that number. The feeling gathered by English travellers in America in the eighteenth century was that in the new country *everybody* read books. Easy access to booksellers has continued down to our day, though bookstores seem not to be so numerous, per capita, now as they used to be. Few people, nevertheless, cannot get at books when they want to.

The book has always signified knowledge, a sign of "education," what people wanted to know, and the agent of transmission, as well as the guarantor of the power of civilization. Throughout history a nation of book readers has been accounted a "civilized" nation. Thomas Jefferson, as an example of the people who respected books, prided himself on the books he owned, and continually imported them from England. In 1800 he sold his library of 20,000 books to the U.S. Government because he knew that there should be a Library of Congress to serve both as a place where Congressmen might pick up some learning and also as a symbol of the value of learning in the new country. On the American frontier, by the end of the eighteenth century, peddlers sold books from their pouches, and pioneers held them as symbols almost magical in their power. Throughout the early nineteenth century, for example, Johnny Appleseed wandered for forty years through western Pennsylvania and the present states of Ohio and Indiana distributing apple trees and circulating books chapter by chapter from one settler to another—and became a folk hero for his efforts. From the eastern frontier to the West Coast through the nineteenth century two "books," Shakespeare and the Bible, were memorized by many adults because they represented the epitome of knowledge and religion. The persons who knew these "books" had invaluable knowledge and wisdom in their grasp.

Through the years the "book" has lost little if any of the magic of its symbolism in the United States, and that symbolism has expanded and changed as people's knowledge and needs have enlarged. Now the conventional book represents every possible kind of knowledge and experience from the frivolous to the profound, from the instructive to the pleasurable. Its importance seems not to be challenged. But now, since the book is only one of several media of communication, its role and significance are being opened to other forces.

The book as medium for the transmission of information, nevertheless, continues to increase in importance even as other media saturate society. In 1947, for example, when no more than one-half of one percent of American homes had television sets, 487 million books were sold nationwide. By 1985 nearly every American home had at least one television set and more than two *billion* books, of some 50,000 titles, were sold in the U.S. yearly.

These books were bought to be read, and read they were, sometimes only once by a single individual, often several times by the same or different persons. Counting the multiple readings and the books that were supplied by libraries, the figure of two billion might be raised to four or five billion to represent the number of yearly book readings in this country. The number is mind-boggling, and does not include an even larger number of people who read magazines and newspapers, which are kinds of books.

The degree of importance ascribed to a book varies from its unassailable religious importance to its purely pleasurable. Sometimes religious books take on the magic of the Ark of the Covenant and become icons themselves, not for the message contained but simply because they contain the message. The degree of attention that a particular book or author can command is amazing. Certain books are treasures, storehouses of experience, that some segments of society seem to demand—Shakespeare, Melville, Mark Twain; sometimes these "treasures" are, to be sure, more owned than read; nevertheless they are duly respected and revered. In other cases certain authors are to be read assiduously every time they publish a book; it is the author, not the book, that is appreciated. The number of readers an author can command is sometimes staggering. Western writer Louis L'Amour, for example, is now translated into twenty different languages and has some 200 million copies of his books in print, making him without question the leading writer of western fiction of all times. Crime fiction, of the fastest-growing genres, is represented by hundreds of authors. Romances are widely distributed, and main-line bestsellers, such as Sidney Sheldon, Irving Wallace, John Irving, Andrew Greeley, Stephen King and Clive Barker break the backs of bookshelves in the thickness and number of their novels.

The publishing business is obviously not in trouble despite the increasing gobbling up of the old publishing houses by faceless would-be monopolies, the escalation of prices of books and the cries of Armageddon. Paperbacks, which are as old as this country and which originally could be bought for next to nothing now run to $5-$20, and clothbound books, which earlier in this century could be bought for a dollar now run $15-$100. Clothbound books are so expensive that libraries generally constitute the bulk of the buying trade. Publishing houses in America are doing everything they can to promote the sale and reading of books. They obviously have vested interests in the continued sales, and they plug books to develop their own profit. According to present-day advertising blurbs books will do everything for a reader that any other good product will do—keep him/her happy, clean, entertained, well informed, out of trouble, weight reduced, and success guaranteed. Publishers promote the sales of books for their own selfish interests, of course, but then so do authors. If it is good for a book to be read, then it is good for the book to be bought; purchasing books keeps authors and publishers and booksellers alive and viable.

Publishers generally in the last quarter of the twentieth century may have other media in which they have financial interests—movies, TV, videos, even musicals and circuses. So they may promote books as one of several media, and not necessarily the most important. Such multiple recognition of the various media which perform the same roles that books do is frightening and threatening to some bibliophiles. Such people are afraid that the other forms of the media will devour and destroy the books and the book trade. History has demonstrated, however, that such fears are shortsighted and groundless. The early introduction of movies in the first third of the twentieth century seemed to threaten the life of books. It was feared that if people could see the images on a screen before them they would not go to the printed work for the more arduous task of reading up the images. More recently, it has been assumed that a nation dedicated to watching television could not be a nation that read books—a people obsessively hooked on the hedonistic pursuit of sensuous self-indulgence could not be a nation dedicated to what some people would call a spartan pleasure in reading.

All such fears have been proven without foundation. Apparently all media are cross-fertilizing. Many people who watch movies and television also read, often while watching the television. They are stimulated by the experience of the visual image to want to experience it through the printed word because they recognize that one medium enriches another; all media are not and cannot be the same. Each enters the psyche through its own channels, and for the full enrichment of all the senses, every medium should be utilized. Therefore for the full impact of the experience and the wisdom to be gained, one should use all the various media. For the fullness of its potential, for example, one should see the movie or TV version of a work of fiction, say *Moby-Dick,* hear a musical rendition, read Peter Benchley's *Jaws* for whatever enrichment it can cast on the total experience, eat the food that whalers ate in 1850, wear their clothes, sing their songs and otherwise live fully the life of the men in the American fleet of whalers in the nineteenth century who slaughtered whales. Few readers experience the full learning potential to this extent, but they should if they would understand the novel completely. It is surely an incomplete experience to read *Moby-Dick* as self-contained novel and art form. Recognizing this, increasingly people are, in fact, interested in understanding the full range of a book's impact. But millions—and billions—begin with the book. So the future of the book as medium seems assured.

Although the fate of the book medium seems safe, nevertheless many concerned people, with the best interests at heart, are genuinely worried about the fate of the book *qua* book.

Daniel Boorstin, for example, in 1977, when he was head of the Library of Congress, created the Center for the Book on the assumption that there is a community of people in the United States for whom the printed word as it appears in books is of the utmost importance. "As the national library of a great free republic," Boorstin said, "The Library of Congress has a special duty and a special interest to see that books do not go unread, that they are read by all ages and conditions, that they are not buried in their own excess...here we shape planes for a grand national effort to make all people eager, avid, understanding, critical readers." The community belonging to this Center includes authors, editors, publishers, printers, book designers, booksellers, librarians, book wholesalers and distributors, literary agents and critics, book reviewers, journalists, translators, book collectors, educators, scholars and readers—most important of all, readers. All recognize that Thomas Jefferson was right when he said that a people cannot have a viable democracy when the citizenry is illiterate. The citizenry must read. Luckily, Boorstin did not designate that he was interested in only "good" books and not "bad" books, but *books,* all kinds of books. Literacy is vital. Books are useful. Libraries are helpful. Everybody benefits from the publication and reading of books. Boorstin's interest and faith seems to be in the book, regardless of what is in the book.

Other vested interest groups, however, do not feel that way. To certain elitists there are "bad" books—or non-books—and "good" books. Lynne Cheney, for example, Chairman of the National Endowment for the Humanities, in her 1988 publication *Humanities in America: A Report to the President, the Congress, and the American People,* drives a wedge between so-called "good" books and the others:

> Anyone who has spent time in a bookstore recently knows that many of the books available are what some have called 'Non-books'—collections of statistics or cartoons, for example, that one dips into here and there, but seldom reads sequentially. It is also obvious that the print medium is as capable of producing trash as the video medium is. But in the vast outpouring of books that has occurred in the television age, there is also much of quality. Classics are amazingly easy to obtain. In neighborhood bookstores, one can find volumes of Aeschylus and Sophocles, Dickens and Shakespeare selling for under five dollars.

Alas, how gravely does Ms. Cheney misread the world of literature. Anyone who is promoting the importance of reading and the value of books with such an attitude is missing the point and has a different and hidden agenda. Books to such a person are subtle propaganda, a means of promoting an elitism which if not anathema to universal literacy is surely a deterrent. To such a person, books are not to be used as a medium to transmit knowledge but a means to transmit only approved knowledge and appreciation sanctioned by a group of self-appointed priest-critics who have their own purposes. Books are used as a club to beat particular people and to exclude them from certain benefits derived from participation in the club of books. Imagine speaking to the person who has just discovered how delightful reading can be: "Yes, dear, rush down to B. Dalton's and see if you can't get copies of *Prometheus Bound* and *Oedipus Rex*. I believe I saw some there yesterday when I bought my latest translations!" Imagine the bee-line the newly-literate enthusiast will make to B. Dalton's and the treasures of the ancient Greeks! Perhaps he will buy dozens of copies.

The assumption that only canonical books are worth reading is based upon a silent and willful misreading of literary history. In English literature, for example, it is interesting that Shakespeare, now the elitists' fountain of wisdom, was originally condemned by one of England's early scholars, Ben Jonson, for having "little Latin and less Greek." Is it possible that an elitist classical scholar can have been proved wrong through the ages! That somebody ignorant of Latin and Greek could have become a classic! Further, anybody who has followed the Charles Dickens canon from the nineteenth century must admit that his works that are not considered elite classics began as humble magazine publications condemned by everybody but the reading public, prized by the humble and barely literate and soundly condemned by the elitist. Can it be that the critics have again been proved wrong and the general public right! If so is there some message for those who are now choosing between the "good" and the "bad" literature, the worthwhile and the worthless? Are such people not only merely trying to perpetuate their own role and function but in doing it actually performing a kind of mischief that damages the society and function of books that they profess they want to improve? The word "trash" that the elitists like to pin on some mediated culture is a negative and inappropriate adjective to be used in describing media communication. Books are like the air we breathe. Some are more health-giving than others, but nearly all support life.

The feeling of elitist advocates of the book seems to be that there is only so much time to be allotted to the book and therefore only "good"—that is *approved*—books should be read. Such an attitude insults the human potential and the intelligence of those people who want to read what they desire even if those books are not on the "approved" list. Such negativism can do much harm. Critic Jacques Barzun, for example, interested mainly in the *"literary"* thriller insists that only "good" books be read, and is afraid that in the great number of books pouring from publishers the "great" books will get buried. It is indeed a strange complaint from somebody interested in books that there are too many being published! Gresham's law may or may not apply to economics but it surely does not apply to books. "Bad" books do not drive out "good." There is plenty of room in the reading habits of 250 million Americans for the pet literary diets of all. One reader's caviar is another's fish eggs. One person's perfect cure for society's ills is another's snake-oil. Someone who is a self-installed gate-keeper of culture and value is another person's scold. What delights one person's fancy merely irritates another's.

Further, in gate-keeping there is the implied effort to censor books and to disallow the First Amendment to the U.S. Constitution, with all the long-lasting threats implied therein. Just as democracy can exist only when every person has the right to vote his preferences, literature can flourish only when everybody has access to all kinds of books and each is his own critic and guide. The flourishing or languishing of certain types of books perhaps depends on the role that people want books to perform.

The experience of the book phenomenon in Japan seems to contradict the apprehensions of U.S. elitists. In that country, which claims virtually 100 percent literacy, all books seem to be created equal, or at least all should be granted equality before the bar of accessibility. The most widely read and appreciated books are pornography, romance, crime fiction and comic-books—all books that are on the proscribed list of U.S. elitists. These books are read widely in Japan, by all segments of society, and accomplish at least the primary, though not the gate-keepers', function in society—transmitting information, entertainment and encouraging literacy.

In this way did "popular" books work in the nineteenth century when prerevolutionary Russians were trying to become literate. As Jeffrey Brooks (in *When Russia Learned to Read: Literacy and Popular Literature, 1861-1917)* demonstrates, it was the humble literature of chapbooks, detective stories, newspapers serials and women's fiction on which the illiterate cut their teeth when they were trying to learn to read, and which shaped the lives of the lowly as well as the well-to-do. In other words, the popular fiction—the "trash" literature—became the voice of Russia which everybody could hear. Strange indeed that the elitists of prerevolutionary Russia cried out against the vulgarization of culture!

Lynne Cheney's *Report,* mentioned earlier, is filled with ironies that issue from the philosophy and actions of the National Endowment for the Humanities, a tax-supported government institution that supposedly is trying to encourage the growth and influence of the humanities on all society, the democratization of a force in the lives of Americans which is supposed to make us all the more human but is in fact perpetuating an artificial schism between the privileged few who are trying in every way to maintain their separate and superior status. Prof. Maynard Mack, director of the American Studies Programs at Yale University, once demonstrated this effort starkly. In commenting on the democratization of the humanities he said: "The humanities are like surgery. Who would want a man in off the street to perform surgery on him?" Who would want anybody in off the streets to participate in and benefit from the humanities? Robert Coles, psychologist and Pulitzer Prize winner, stated a point which serves as answer to Mack and his school of thinking: "The humanities," he said, "belong to no one kind of person; they are part of the lives of ordinary people, who have their own various ways of struggling for coherence, for a compelling faith, for social vision, for an ethical position, for a sense of historical perspective." But perhaps the greatest irony in Cheney's *Report* is that fact that it, replete with elitist sentiments, was presented to President Ronald Reagan, who has never been known for the "good" literature he reads or the "good" movies he played in while a movie star! He and his crowd might not be the persons who constitute the best guides to future American literature. But elitists will call upon and use any ally when they are preening their feathers to improve their own looks.

In the role that they might appropriately play, the directors of the National Endowment for the Humanities, and people in similar positions of power, need to rethink the purpose and role of the book historically. Originally a book was a succession of words and sentences with a beginning and ending rolled or wrapped into an entity which could have some purpose. Historically books were the second or third form of communication, coming after oral words and maybe crude pictures. As such, books were miniaturizations and nuggets of hard reality abstracted into a different form of communication. Thus the gigantic library of scrolls at Alexandria, Egypt, represented to a certain extent abstractions of the world known at that time. Cut into sheets and sewn together after the 2nd century A.D. books came more and more to represent separate and distinct entities, a tendency which continued to grow until the development of the practice of binding books in "paper covers," which in effect because of the fragility of the binding reduced the "separateness" and returned books at least partially to the everyday world. Books with paper coverings were something—at least symbolically—less than traditional books.

But throughout history books have essentially been aspects of the world abstracted and reduced to a convenient and manageable size and medium of communication. They were and are accumulations of signs and symbols and as such have themselves become symbols. As symbols they may have been divided into certain descriptive and evaluated categories, as most useful, useful, least useful; most treasured, least treasured; loved, unloved, despised. But they were not classified as elite and trash. In the last two hundred years or so self-appointed gate-keepers have tried to separate books into "good" and "bad." The sloppiness of such thinking in using these two umbrella categories reveals the imprecision of the distinctions. The terms "good" and "bad" have scores of meanings, none of which actually means such things as "effective, ineffective"; "pleasurable, painful"; "strong, weak"; "correct, incorrect"; "desirable, undesirable." "Good" and "bad" are moralistic generalizations which are meaningless when applied to books. The really "good" books are generally those which suggest and effect change in the status quo, generate new ways of thinking, precipitate subversion and revolution. How can they still be "good"? The concept is a contradiction in terms. Yet the concept is a cave-man's club of evaluation that the elitists continue to use to beat humanity over the head.

In so doing, they have not done the image of the book any favor. In trying to encourage the production and consumption of one kind of book and to discourage the production and use of others, elitists have tried to warp the image of the book. They have imposed a conservative static image on a medium which has never been static but has always responded to the latest innovations of technology. Despite their fulminations, however, elitists have no influence on the progress of the book, only on some readers. Elitists persuade many readers to deny themselves the benefits of reading all kinds of books. But the book business continues to serve its purposes and to respond to new technologies just as though the elitists did not exist, or are at best mere irritants.

Technologically, hand-written scrolls and pages gave way to hand-printed sheets, which in turn gave way to movable type and fast presses that turn out millions of copies of a title. These have in turn been augmented by electronic pages and books which make *them*—and whole libraries—instantly accessible. Pages with nothing but printed words have given way to pages mixed with pictures and line-drawings. Words have given way to line-drawings and photographs with or without words. Two-dimensional pages have given way to three-dimensional holographic pages that move before the readers' very eyes. All kinds of books are created instantly on the computer.

Where the printed page goes next nobody knows. But as the printed page has changed, so has the notion of what a book is. Already there are a score of meanings for the term. One is, according to Webster, "something regarded as a subject of study." If a book, in the strict meaning of the term, is a subject of study and a technological medium of communication not limited to the printed work or picture, then we are in the middle of the transformation of the concept of the book into all kinds of new forms. With introduction of the holograph the book has gone three-dimensional. It is therefore only a short step from the printed page to the movie or TV video as book. Then the present-day and future concept of the image of "book" becomes clearer.

Objects, then, which are other forms of "books" take on new importance. As Jules David Prown says ("Mind in Matter" An Introduction to Material Culture Theories and Method," in *Material Life in America: 1600-1860,* edited by Robert Blair St. George), "They offer the possibility of a way to understand the mind of the great majority of non-literate people, past and present, who remain otherwise inaccessible except through impersonal records and the dictating view of a contemporary library elite."

In *Documenting America, 1935-1943* (edited by Carl Fleishchnauer and Beverly W. Brannan), Alan Trachtenberg, a leading interpreter of photographs as documents, recognized that photos are "words" in a dictionary or facts in an encyclopedia, which, used together, become literature and books. Individual photos strung together become sentences just as words grow into sentences. As Trachtenberg says: "To recognize that an image is a kind of writing prepares us for the larger challenge of reading or making sense of (a group of photos)." "A film is a kind of book, a kind of language, a kind of speech-act...an expressive cultural act," says Lawrence W. Levine (*Folklore Forum,* Vol. 21, No. 1, 1988, p. 52). To recognize that any kind of artifact is a form of writing and thus a part of a book is the first step in doing that artifact justice in placing it in the larger context of the body of literature and books.

From that concept it is only logical to take the short step from the conventional book on a subject, say architecture, to the artifact itself: the book on architecture to architecture as the book, the book about a building to the building as book. "Objects are signs that convey meaning, a mode of communication, a form of language," correctly says Jules David Prown, in "Mind in Matter: An Introduction to Material Culture Theory and Method," p.32). "The buildings which a society constructs convey information at a symbolic level," says Phyllis Lambert, in "The Record of Buildings as Evidence" (in Richard Pare's *Court House: A Photographic Document,* pp. 10-13). Individually and collectively, Lambert goes on, "They are a formal expression of its needs, values, and aspirations." Likewise with other constructions: the mall, for example, and the logicality of moving from the book on a mall to the mall as a book. So too with such subjects as the automobile as book, the highway, and thousands of other phenomena as books.

In his delightful book *In Small Things Forgotten,* James Deetz comments on the many kinds of "books" which most people ignore or despise: "In ways great and small, gravestones, grave pits, houses, refuse, cuts of meat, recipes, ceramics, furniture, and cutlery inform us that a great change was worked between 1760 and 1800 on the world view of most Anglo-Americans." In somewhat greater details, Robert Blair St. George, in his introduction to the book *Material Life in America 1600-1860,* names other artifacts: "Houses, furniture, teacups, probate inventories, diaries, account books, newspaper and tax lists may all warrant investigation in the course of a single topic." "Everything," says French historian Fernand Broudel, "is connected."

The list is almost endless, as further elaborated by Henry Glassie in his essay "Meaningful Things and Appropriate Myths: The Artifact's Place in American Studies" (St. George, *Material Life in America 1600-1860),* with a considerably different thrust: "Plowing, strip mining, laying brick upon brick in mortar, weeding, bulldozing: these are as much historical acts as scratching a pen over paper. The shapes of fields, the wrecked faces of hills, the houses and bridges, corrals, docks, temples, factories, prisons, switchyards, junkyards, graveyards, the highways on the plains, the paths in the woods—all are historical texts, overlaid, opposed, related into a single perfect structure, simultaneously spatial and temporal, qualitative, quantitative, as incluse as the planet, as deep as time itself; a universal memory, a democratic historian's dream." In other words a veritable library of "books" waiting to be read, he might have added, by people who comprehend their language. On the most basic of all levels, we should never forget that human excrement, as found in various forms of the historically familiar outhouse or other dung heap, is now recognized as an invaluable storehouse of the "books" of human behavior of the past.

As Alan Gowans, one of the leading interpreters of history revealed by art, comments, if one can read a single work of art, or artifact, fully and properly, he/she will find a whole book of culture spread before him/her. "The mere smell of cooking can evoke a whole civilization," said French historian Fernand Broudel, in *Capitalism and Material life 1400-1800,* perhaps barely overstating the case to all but the most romantic nostril. But his point is well made. Both Broudel and Gowans might have added that unless people can read the artifacts properly, can sniff out the odors discriminatingly, they will miss significant points and nuances of culture.

Generally conventional book libraries have recognized the changing format of the book. They have introduced videos, movies, record collections, toys and games—anything that the public wants and uses. As such they are inching over toward some of the functions of the museum. In fact the ideal library is a mixture of the library and the museum. The Library of Congress represents a major step toward the ideal library—with its mixture of photograph displays, various kinds of exhibits, artifacts relating to individuals, lectures, etc. The Smithsonian Institution, with its various kinds of displays of printed materials, is reaching toward the center where the two concepts would merge into the proper library, especially if they could be more thoroughly integrated with the concept of the "living museum" with its articulated and living reenactments of life. The roles of books have indeed expanded vastly.

Conventional libraries have nothing to fear from the expanded mission of books. They have always collected and preserved the "books" in whatever form available. Some academic librarians may resist the expansion of their role. Others, however, especially public librarians, will see the recognized expansion of their collections as opportunities to enhance their own roles and missions, and in so doing insure their future. It would be far too expensive to translate or transliterate all "books" into the new media. Therefore all the media will exist concurrently in the library, as they do in life. Anyone wanting to enjoy the numerous kinds of books available will have to understand the many languages they are in. But everybody knows—or thinks he knows—most of those already.

So the "book"—whatever its form—will continue to serve as a dominant symbol in American life. The form will change. The changes will continue to reach out toward universal coverage of American life. As such the changes will further democratize the book and the democratization will further universalize the role of the book. Some people may resist because of personal proclivities or personal purposes to serve. Some people who see some virtue in the tension created in the stress between old and new forms of "books" will continue to exacerbate that tension.

Probably that tension could be more profitably expended in the creative mastery of the contents of the books than in the legitimization of the form. There is less substance in the name of the medium than in its content. Elite books are not people's books. They are private. In many ways their publication is not really a public event. But books that are publicly published for the public respond to the public demand. As such they both reflect and influence the public and change as the technology of societies change. They are a slowly but surely changing symbol of the accumulation and medium of transmission of knowledge. Books should educate us at least enough to prompt us to realize their dual roles and many modifications and to appreciate them. Without that realization, books of all kinds will continue to be fragmented into different media, and as such will fail to reach the full potential of their possibilities. And readers will ultimately be the ones who suffer.

In a recent publication (*Current,* May 1989) Carl Gershman, President of the National Endowment for Democracy, cogently argues that democracy is overwhelming authoritarian governments and philosophies throughout the world and is becoming the wave of the political future. But, he points out, in order for a political democracy to evolve there must be democracy in culture. Democratic culture depends on the free interchange of ideas. The free interchange of ideas depends, of course, upon a free and multiple communication—in other words a vast library of all kinds of "books." If, as John Stuart Mill thought, "What men think...determines how they act," then what men and women read determines what they think. Some critics want to interrupt the free and full communication of culture. To do so runs against democracy and is an effort that cannot prevail. Books in all their forms and symbols should flow freely as the culture they serve and the books themselves evolve into ever new symbols. The evolution is without end but not without consequence.

The Political Meaning of Popular Symbolic Activity

James Combs

The study of symbols and the symbolic is now common in the social sciences. Figures such as George Herbert Mead and Kenneth Burke are taken seriously, and a literature has developed dealing with "significant symbols" utilized by the "symbol-using animal." In particular, there has been a great deal of work on political symbols, "those symbols of relevance to the exercise of political authority and to the management of social conflict."[1] All too often those "symbols of relevance" are delimited to the more apparent and recognizable forms of political communication—the symbols attached to political rituals, the invocation of national myth, the manipulation of ideological symbols. However, if we take an expansionary and speculative view of symbol-making and symbol-using to include symbols of popular relevance, it may be the case that the study of political symbols can be enhanced by inquiry into activities that at first glance do not seem to have anything to do with politics. It is our objective here to explore the political meaning of some commonly observable forms of popular symbolic activity with a view to stimulating new work in areas of popular life with implicit symbolic relevance to politics.

Such an inquiry is in accord with the conviction held, one would think, by most students of American popular culture that popular activities hold a symbolic significance beyond the mundane quality of common pursuits. At both work and play, popular communication is a source of learning that gives direction and meaning to many forms of social thought and activity in what has been called "covert culture."[2] A better term might be "implicit culture," in that social choices as to what to believe and do are often affected by the suggestions inherent in the flow of popular discourse. There has been a tendency to regard symbolic activity as something that elites communicate to masses, to which the latter then obediently response. Since people interpret and use symbolic communication, elites are not entirely free to manipulate masses, and indeed, may have to respond themselves to messages from "below." It is true that power does tend to concentrate among the few at the top in a formal sense, but this view must be complemented by the fact that the many exercise a form of popular power and ultimate control through sheer numbers in their opinions and choices. Especially in a political order with democratic and populist values and pretensions, there is a strong sense in which the decisions of elites are constrained by the desires and whims of the mass, or at least organized and vocal segments of the populace. This is not to say that the few do not often have the power to manipulate the many, only that what often happens is a matter not so much of conspiracy among secret councils of power as it is complicity with the many in the formation and communication of both material and symbolic values and habits. This is consistent with the Tocquevillian "logic of a popular society," which suggests an inherent and often implicit "socio-logic" in the preference and honor given to the activities of the many. A popular society may be dominated by elites who control the preponderance of what there is to get, but it can only do so if it accords the many proper deference through convincing them of elite efficiency in "giving them what they want." If it is the case that elite and mass understand the complicit bargain, then a modicum of material rewards, always unevenly distributed in a country committed to accumulative rather than distributive justice, must be heavily complemented, and even substituted, by the creation and accessibility of agencies of popular symbolic expression. A bank or bureaucratic building communicates elite power and mass inaccessibility. But in a popular society, there must be settings or vehicles of popular power that convince us of the validity of widely held values and habits, and not by chance the benevolence of elites who provide us the opportunity for expressions of popular symbolic activity.

This vision of a popular society lets us admit the existence of elite structures on the one hand combined with the "convergent selectivity" of masses onto popular activities and objects.[3] There is nothing explicitly political about these activities and objects, nor the elite motives that provide the context of their expression. Yet there is an implicit and highly subtle complicity here that communicates something profoundly political, at least in terms of the satisfaction of popular symbolic activity in settings that provide ritual outlets for personal and social validation. If those ritual expressions were to be denied, there might be negative economic and political consequences. At this level, we are talking about something more inclusive and cosmic than the familiar "referential" and "condensation" symbols of Sapir, what we will call "representational" symbols.[4] A referential symbol refers to a denotative relationship of self to a sign or image (a street sign or photograph); a condensational symbol refers to a connotative relationship of self to another (a family tree or a diagram such as a map); but a representational symbol refers to a metaphorical relationship of self to a generalized other (to "society" and "state" or spectacular metaworlds of popular valuation and validation such as the movies). Symbols at base involve something that stands for or suggests something else, so what we have in mind here is that the level of complexity and scope of meaning that a populace may attribute to a symbol will range up to the most inclusive and deepest symbolic form. Representational symbols do not condense but rather expand meaning, serving as a virtual metaphor for the common experience of we as a people by dramatizing the multiplicity and significance of what we are all about and what we live for. A condensation symbol by definition "condenses" experience and emotion into an identifiable form ("Watergate," "President Bush," "rock 'n'roll"). But a representational symbol "re-presents" us at the most mythic or valued level, validating our very continuity and purpose as a people. Perhaps "American democracy" and "Divine Providence" are political and religious representational symbols, but if we are searching for deep structures of popular meaning, we may turn to those symbolic objects specifically created as a forum of such expression.

Let us go to the mall. With the growth of suburbia over the past forty years, this modal lifestyle was accompanied by the advent first of the shopping center and now the enclosed shopping mall. A mall is a major representational symbol of popular meaning, a multiple, expansive, and dramatic world of valid consumption. The "people of plenty" are not moved so much by a will to power as they are by a will to consume. The "pursuit of happiness" and the "freedom of choice" are their birthright, so they walk the malls as if they were in a magic kingdom, the cornucopia of goods and services which they use as validating objects of their happiness and freedom. The mall is designed by elites in order to facilitate and encourage purchase, but for the many who wander and browse and socialize the mall represents the validation of a popular way of life. Malls are a stage of popular theater in which we, the people are the principle actors, seeing everywhere the pluralistic metareality of choice and the primacy of the individual as the agent of choice. The actors in this popular drama of "malling" do not worry about "commodity fetishism" or the Protestant ethic of frugality and thrift. The mall exists as the representational symbol of a consumer culture, offering us the opulent setting for the enactment of a ritual drama of individual self-enhancement that validates not only individual self-worth but also one's participation in the collective faith of the American Dream. If it is the case that malls are public arenas for the popular dramaturgy of self-expression, then the mall itself exists as a representational symbol of inclusive and pervasive myth, a linkage between ourselves and our highest meanings. A mall is a popular shrine, a joyous celebration of self-indulgence made so by converting the vulgar exchange of the marketplace into a transaction sanctified as a votive ritual whereby one acquires not merely a thing but also a symbolic ornament of self-worth. Consumption in a mall setting is not really "conspicuous" since everyone there is doing it; it is rather more a communal act graced by the sanctuary of the setting and the credit-card denial of the filth of lucre. A shopping mall is after all a spiritual place, wherein the individual is linked to mythic values that are the "property" of the larger community.

Let us move on to the theme park. Like the enclosed shopping mall, the theme park is a universe unto itself. But it is a universe created as a representative symbol—a model universe that stands for something of value—of community myths and aspirations. The theme park is typically a pastiche of experiences including the past, present, and future in a Barnumian "sinless carnival" that validates the "oughtness" and destiny of a people through the representation of popularly valued objects. When we enter a Disneyworld or Greenfield Village or Six Flags, we have gone into a metaworld that is a simulation of historical or social objects and values. Theme parks are places of play, but not merely meaningless diversion and amusement. Rather they are places of ritual play designed for the cultural edification of populaces through the representation of symbolic "referentials" that simulate a metaworld of idealized or mythic referents. In the celebration of technology, for example, the emphasis is on the power and majesty of technology to the point of idolatry. Technology is the magic available to the high priests of the scientific temple that will open the doors to the future. Behind the manifest celebration of the fruits of technology as a "theme" is the exaltation of technique itself in the "myth of method," and underlying that is the "master myth" of progress.[5] Further, theme parks mobilize anticipation of the past and nostalgia for the future, by re-creating a mythic past that is represented as the key to our vitality that we must now regain, and an image of the future that is both wonderful and totally at odds with what we expect. Greenfield Village replicates a mythic past (such as Edison's boyhood home) of individual craftsmanship as the vital precursor of technological capitalism, while Epcot Center simulates a "high-tech" future beyond the economic reach of most. But theme parks are by definition "thematic," in the presentation of cultural mythemes that sustain or reinvigorate faith at a time when fears and doubts develop about political values and goals. Theme parks invite ritual play with representational symbols as a way of popular self-persuasion, wherein the playful populace that frequent such parks convince themselves anew of the benevolence of what we are supposed to be and to believe.

Let us go to the stadium. As we watch the contest unfold before us on the playing field below, we become aware again of the importance of that metaphorical world. We sit in a monumental edifice worthy of the Roman Colosseum or a medieval cathedral and immerse ourselves in a play-universe that enacts the canons of popular folklore and the mythology of heroic endeavor. Those who gather at the stadium, or attend it through radio and television, participate in a cultural metaevent, an event that is above and beyond the ordinary and involves the clash of titans. The Super Bowl, the World Series, the NCAA Final Four—all are metaevents that involve the celebration and communication of representational symbols. A metaevent symbolizes things of popular value, not only in the drama of the event itself, but also by the fact that it is attended by multitudes who implicitly attest to its importance as a bearer of value. The heroics of the playing field evoke vicarious enjoyment, accompanied by a sense that our most cherished beliefs in the power of individual and collective effort to achieve success on the "level playing field" of life are being represented in the unfolding drama on the plain below. Sports include a plethora of meanings for the many millions that attend to them, and exist in political rhetoric as metaphor and exemplar of everything from model relationships to the holy fun of warfare. If we regard sports as meaningful social play conducted in a ritual setting, we can see the extent to which sports are "a representation of the sacred which mediates between the individual and the moral order" in symbolic form.[6]

Let us hit the road. We drive where we wish in an automobile, the symbol of our belief in our own freedom of choice and the right to roam. The automobile represents national and individual promise and aspiration, as a vehicle not only of transportation but also of symbolic meaning. We think that the very selection of a car is an expression of choice, that we have a right to the comfort and privacy of a singular vehicle as a bastion of individualism, that luxury or fashion in cars is an inherent part of our success or lifestyle, and like the mythic cowboy with his horse, we are free to ride the range of American roads to anywhere. We no longer have the Chisholm Trail, but we do have the corollary object that supports our wanderlust, the superhighway, monumental outlets for our restless spirit and anxiety about the extent to which we are free. We are willing to endure enormous social risks—large death tolls on the highways, traffic jams and delays, taxes for road infrastructure maintenance, destructive air pollution, and dependence on foreign sources of oil—in order to sustain the illusions that the car has come to symbolize for us. When we drive our favorite automobile onto a superhighway, we may experience an exhilarating sense of popular power, that both car and road are material creations that symbolize the extent to which public policy must cater to the sovereignty of the popular desire to drive at will.

Let us exit off the ramp to the suburban development. As we drive through the endless antiseptic streets of similar tract houses, we are reminded as to the extent that the American Dream is symbolized by the single family dwelling. Such developments will or have names such as "Heritage Valley," although they are devoid of heritage or history, tradition or diversity, intellect or funkiness. No matter how expensive, the dwellings (houses, town houses, condominium, and so on) simulate rather than conserve style and grace. But they exist as representations of self-worth, serving as a symbol of achieved status and as a museum for the display of the symbolic objects of self-conferral. The objects of social rank—silver and china, wedding pictures, fashionable furniture and clothes, and so on—are not merely the playthings of conspicuous consumption and leisure, but rather more the outward and visible signs of the absence of an inward and spiritual grace. More precisely, they shore up our conviction that the price we have paid to achieve a place in the sun we thought distinctive and comfortable was not too costly. But if such anxieties exist about the worth of upward social mobility and the acquisition of things, then it may often be the case that one seeks political vindication of affluent lifestyle through political symbols (ideologies, candidates) that defend the legitimacy of our enjoyment of status. In a subtle and unrecognized way, the domestic self-assertion of a lifestyle makes a political as well as a social statement. As we surround ourselves with representative symbols of how we have chosen to live, we imply or infer a way of life with political meanings.

The patterns of symbolic action we have pointed to all seem a part of the American "expressive culture," whereby we express our sense of ourselves as seekers of cultural and political meaning. More and more, we seek out "designed experiences"—theme restaurants, fantasy vacations, "total television" with interactive holograms projected into your living room—in which we temporarily immerse ourselves for purposes of self-expression.[7] Malls, stadii, highways, and so forth exist precisely for the collective expression of popular will and vivid experience. In terms of the expression of popular power by the many who feel the necessity for self-vindication, the arenas of ritual action we have mentioned seem typical of the process of symbolic representation. But we may wonder if there is not something profoundly historical about our insistence on such expressive behavior and symbolic reassurance. Representational symbols are what we might call "first-order," central to our cosmic sense of ourselves as a people and political entity. Since they are so important to so many among the populace, we expect elites to provide settings for ritual play that revalidates their meaning for us. Yet in examining the extent to which our public behavior is directed toward such validation, we appear both defensive and desperate about our desire for the sovereign voice of the people to be exalted in public gatherings. The infamous "Pledge of Allegiance" pseudo-issue of the 1988 Presidential campaign may have spoken to a mass feeling that even the most fundamental things were somehow in question. But our widespread desire for predictable and ritualized experiences that reassure us of both the power and rectitude of the common life may well belie anxious doubts beneath the surface.

In all the areas of popular action we have addressed, there was the creation of an analogical universe in which the symbols of popular representation could be safely celebrated. There is nothing new about people seeking the validation of basic symbols in arenas of ritual play. But the suspicion lingers that our pursuit of symbolic expression in such analogues to reality means that we don't trust reality anymore to pay anything but lip service to our most cherished popular myths. Despite all of the earnest reaffirmations of Ronald Reagan and George Bush, their rhetoric took on a hollow ring when it was clear that their actions were totally at variance with their words, and that the nation continued its downward drift in the array of world power and wealth. Thus as the "imperial Presidency" and the conduct of government, not to mention giant and multinational corporations, become more remote from people's lives and control, this makes arenas of play all the more important in the sustenance of fundamental representational symbols. The expansion of evangelical religion, for instance, is likely part of the same large-scale historical process. But if this is the case, it makes our immersion in sports and automobility and theme parks and domestic dramaturgy all the more crucial in sustaining the edifice of first-order symbols that undergird the entire mythic structure of our lives. Such symbols lend themselves to dramatic representation, so perhaps now we believe that the only places we can trust to adequately celebrate our most profound faiths are in metaworlds separate from decaying reality.

Our intense attention to popular symbols, then, may stem not from a sense of the continuity of popular power but rather from a fear of the onset of popular powerlessness. Our active engagement in play increasingly occurs in settings characterized by gigantism, places of such magnitude that they dwarf the individual by their megalopic scale. Not only the dinosaur size of malls and stadii diminish the stature of the individual, but also the mass media, which tends to emphasize the magnitude of the events they broadcast. In the near future, it is predicted, shopping malls and theme parks will be combined in "megacenters" that include hotels, entertainment facilities, high-tech shopping experiences, and even condominiums.[8] But there may be a point in the elevation of these analogical universes to a height of social magnitude wherein they no longer can be viewed as a symbol of popular power. They may then be seen as bastions of elite elegance and wealthy play inaccessible to the tastes and pocketbooks of the populace. At that juncture, what had been a benevolent symbol of popular power is transformed into a potentially malevolent symbol of elite power and popular powerlessness. If shopping malls and vacation sites and Super Bowls become unrelentently upscale, then they may cease to serve the symbolic function of dramatizing the validity, and even the possibility, of the common American life. Along with the current trends towards mass inaccessibility to housing, higher education, health care, an increasing standard of living, and national politics, now it may be that ordinary people will find little validation of representational symbols in which they desperately want to continue to believe confirmed by common play experiences. If the political meaning of representational symbols is thought to be the province of elite and not populace, then not only the Super

Bowl and the Christmas shopping spree but also Presidential elections will occur in an atmosphere in which there will be fewer people left to care.

If this thesis is correct, then the interplay of images of great power and widespread powerlessness might proliferate in various levels and contexts of culture. When people acquire a sense that institutions of both work and play are not for them, then their subsequent responses include feelings of exclusion and alienation. And if it is the case that the arts, popular and otherwise, capture and represent the mood and spirit of an age, then we might expect to see negative and discordant sensibilities about the present and the future. Important clues can be found in what is loosely called "post-modernism" in the arts, with the pervasive sense of discontinuity and pointlessness, eclecticism and pastiche, cultural "lateness" and hopelessness, favoring farcical and even cynical creations and stances and eliminating, or making fun of, traditional canons such as the integrity of text or the necessity of narrative. The arts converge and comment, but they do so without expecting to continue, or create anew, meaning. The "deconstruction" of texts can be construed as an attack on the possibility of meaning, not to mention integrity and narration. The works that are labeled post-modern usually describe a random and unknowable universe where rational cosmos has been superceded by bleak chaos, and the familiar dimensions of reality disappear, leaving us with the manipulation of appearances. Such a world is, in short, bereft of representational symbols with expansive and inclusive content and expressive form identifiable to large populations.[9]

It has been one of the major functions of popular culture in modern society to provide symbolic expressions and explanations. But if the post-modernist movement is anything more than a passing intellectual fashion, then it may be the case that societies such as the United States are changing into a "post-popular" or "non-popular" condition that is as yet unnamed and unknowable. If we are witnessing the evolution of those dramatic settings for the expression of popular faith into something remote, inaccessible, and exclusive, then we will have to interpret what's happening. We may be in an interim or "liminal" period of historical change that includes the breakdown of the meaning of representational symbols and the transformation of the analogical metaworlds of play we have discussed into something completely different. Yet aspects of the present are not so unique as to be beyond historical comparison or precedent. The political culture of contemporary America resembles in many ways previous periods of imperial decline, characterized by the perpetuation of a static social and political hierarchy, great inequalities of wealth and access, the awesome power of praetorian forces and military adventurers, the growth of insoluble social problems and restless populations, and the shift of power and initiative to other peoples. (Perhaps the "Rome analogy" is more apt than we are willing to admit, if we are indeed witnessing the transformation of the republic into an imperial State characterized by god-like executive power, palace corruption and intrigues, and a succession of emperors who preside over the demise of republican institutions and virtues. Perhaps then Richard Nixon was our Julius Caesar, making the initial moves to suspend constitutional rule and failing, but setting in motion the historical change that eventually sticks; Barry Goldwater was Brutus, joining the senatorial revolt against executive fiat and dispensing the would-be dictator; Gerald Ford and Jimmy Carter, like Marc Antony and

Cassius, attempted to rule in the interregnum, but were finally dispensed by the accession of our Augustus, Ronald Reagan; Reagan, like the stolid and popular Caesar Augustus, presided over the facade of the restored republic but furthered its descent into imperial corruption; Nancy Reagan was remarkably similar to Livia, with her palace intrigues and personal ambitions. It may be then that George Bush will turn out to be our Tiberius, the emperor with the resume who will attempt to rule in an increasingly impossible situation, but retreat in dismay to his Capri, Kennebunkport; perhaps too, Oliver North will turn out to be our Sejanus, attempting a praetorian coup to restore order and faith; Dan Quayle might be our own golf-playing Caligula, Sam Nunn our Claudius, and Donald Trump our Nero). Although such historical analogies are limited, nevertheless there is a very real popular sense now that we are in an irreversible decline and that no one seems to be able to do very much about it. If we follow the classical pattern, popular art will express that political sensibility, reinforcing further the deluge mentality that resigns itself to historical apocalypse and oblivion. Students of popular culture should take seriously over the next decades popular expressions that seem to be appropriate to such an age. The "imperial theme" in the movies actually includes a cluster of related themes associated with periods of political loss of energy and control—nostalgia for the prelapsarian age, the celebration of praetorian daring, doubts about the burden of empire, criticism of the decadence and ineptitude of elites, the conservative defense of fundamental virtues and institutions as timeless truths at precisely the time they are deteriorating, and an imagination of the future that is bleak and hopeless.

This is a cosmic idea, to be sure, but popular culture such as the movies may be the analogical universe wherein we can still play out our fears and fancies about what is happening to us as a nation and civilization. But if in the many forms of popular culture used for learning, we see the absence of the validation of representational symbols, then we may be witnessing the preface to a political crisis, a crisis of meaning. Rudolf Arnheim has noted the relationship between entropy and art.[10] We may expand on this idea by asserting that popular culture is a source of political learning, even if in often implicit and oblique ways. But political learning from popular culture can either be energizing, wherein popular experience validates representational symbols, or entropic, wherein popular experience gives credence to the feeling that the old values don't work and that things are coming apart and mere anarchy is loosed upon the world. If such popular activities as malling and driving and gaming become exclusionary, they may be disallowed as meaningless. And if people begin to entertain notions of disenchantment and anomie, they will seek out popular creations, such as movies, that validate that creeping sense of political meaninglessness. Eventually, they may seek out alternative representational symbols on which to believe and hope will supercede myths and values that have been rendered exclusive and obsolete. One can try to make sense out of political entropy, but the sense of decline and hopelessness is not something people can live with forever. As the United States careens towards its historical fate, we are all becoming aware that there just isn't as much time as there used to be.

Notes

[1]Charles D. Elder and Roger W. Cobb, *The Political Uses of Symbols* (New York: Longman, 1983) 30.

[2]Bernard Bowron, Leo Marx and Arnold Rose, "Literature and Covert Culture," *American Quarterly* IX (Winter 1957): 377-386.

[3]William Stephenson, *The Play Theory of Mass Communication* (Chicago: University of Chicago Press, 1967): 2.

[4]Edward Sapir, "Symbolism," *Encyclopedia of the Social Sciences,* Vol. 14 (1934): 492-495.

[5]Jean Baurdillard, *Simulations* (New York: Semiotext, 1983); Jacques Ellul, *Propagandy* (New York: Vintage, 1973).

[6]Susan Birrell, "The Rituals of Sports," *Social Forces,* Vol. 60, no. 2 (December 1981): 354-376.

[7]Robert Bellah, et. al., *Habits of the Heart* (Berkeley: University of California Press, 1985).

[8]Elizabeth Hopp-Peters, "New Theme for Malls: Creativity," Chicago *Tribune,* February 6, 1989, Business section, 1, 3.

[9]Charles Newman, *The Post-Modern Aura* (Evanston: Northwestern University Press, 1987).

[10]Rudolf Arnheim, *Entropy and Art* (Berkeley: University of California Press, 1971).

The Goblin Child: Folktale Symbolism in Popular Art

Harold Schechter and Jonna G. Semeiks

By an ironic paradox of time, the playful symbolism of the folk tale—a product of the vacant hour—today seems to us more true, more powerful to survive, than the might and weight of myth.

Joseph Campbell

The rather highfalutin Jungian notion that the mere presence of archetypal symbols in an imaginative work automatically endows it with a "curiously compulsive power" over "the minds of multitudes"[1] is clearly in need of serious rethinking. After all, what could be more archetypal than the 1982 drive-in epic *Mad Monkey Kung Fu,* a Grade-Z martial arts movie which features a Wise Old Man, a Helpful Animal, an Evil Shadow, and a Heroic Quest, and whose entire nationwide audience seems to have consisted of Joe Bob Briggs and his best friend, Bobo Rodriguez?

Still, at a time when *Advertising Age* magazine runs articles on the mythic significance of Speedy Alka-Seltzer and Joseph Campbell appears on public TV to elucidate the religious symbolism of *Star Wars,*[2] the idea that the popular arts embody archetypal themes would seem to have gained widespread acceptance. Analyzing popular works in terms of their archetypal content, however, presents the critic with a number of problems, one of which is identified by Ursula K. Le Guin, who deplores the application of the "noble" term myth to the "grotty" creations of the American entertainment industry, to characters like Superman, "the blond heroes of sword and sorcery...detectives who find out who done it, brave starship captains, evil aliens, good aliens" and so on—fantasy figures who, though "vigorously alive and powerful," possess "no religious or moral resonance and no intellectual or aesthetic value." "It hurts to call these creatures mythological," Le Guin protests.[3]

While her language smacks somewhat of intellectual snobbery (a defensive reaction, perhaps, to her own long years of labor in the critically despised—"grotty"—genre of science fiction), there is undeniable validity to Le Guin's point, though to our minds the real critical issue is not pain—how much it "hurts" to describe, say, Bomba the Jungle Boy as a mythological figure—but pretentiousness. Indeed, it is precisely this kind of critical pomposity—so bitingly parodied in Frederick Crews' *The Pooh Perplex* ("*Winnie-the-Pooh* as Myth, Symbol, Ritual, and Archetype")—that has given the field of popular culture studies its bad name in more conservative academic circles.

Le Guin's solution is to invent a new term for pop archetypes—"submyths," she calls them, by which she means those "images, figures and motifs" which "have the vitality of the collective unconscious but nothing else, no ethical, aesthetic, or intellectual value."[4] But Le Guin's coinage is both unwieldy and unnecessary, since there already exists a far more precise and felicitous term for those vulgar but vital and psychologically resonant fantasies embodied by the popular arts. The term we're referring to is folktales—those unassuming (even crude) but perennially appealing fictions that contain the same narrative archetypes as myths but perform a much less exalted social function, being told (as Northrop Frye puts it) not "to explain certain features in [a] society's religion, laws, social structure, environment, history or cosmology" but simply "to entertain or amuse," to "meet the imaginative needs of the community."[5]

Since folk stories achieve their comparatively modest aim by taking stock motifs—characters and situations which, for whatever reason, have pleased unsophisticated audiences throughout the centuries—and adapting them to the conditions and concerns of a particular time and place, they tend to be simple stories with complex social and psychological meanings. As a result, the folkloric approach to the popular arts (i.e., seeing movies, television shows, bestsellers and so on as our modernday, technologically transmitted form of traditional folk narrative) helps the critic avoid the traps of pretentiousness, on the one hand—of making exaggerated aesthetic claims for the material—and, on the other, of Jungian (or, for that matter, Freudian) reductionism, of simply translating pop symbols into the jargon of his or her preferred methodology.

This essay is being written, for example, shortly after Labor Day, 1988, when the annual summertime race for box office megabucks—Hollywood's equivalent of the Indy 500—is officially over. This year's major winners are *Big, Crocodile Dundee II, Coming to America,* and *Who Framed Roger Rabbit,* a quartet of slick entertainments which, precisely because they aspire to nothing higher than short-term escapism, offer the culture critic a prime opportunity for considering the question of the nature, function, and meaning of pop symbolism.

At first glance, these four films would seem to have little in common. *Big* is an affable comedy about a twelve-year-old boy who, fed up with the indignities of preadolescence, makes a wish upon an amusement park fortune-telling machine and wakes up the next morning reincarnated in the thirty-year-old body of Tom Hanks. *Crocodile Dundee II* concerns the further adventures of the unflappable Aussie backwoodsman who, in his first screen appearance, was transported to Manhattan, where his rugged frontier ways made him an instant folk hero to the jaded New York natives. In *Coming to America,* Eddie Murphy plays the pampered prince of a mythical African nation who travels into the heart of darkest Queens in search of the perfect bride. And—as anyone who didn't spend the summer of '88 sunk in a coma undoubtedly knows—*Who Framed Roger Rabbit* is a technically breathtaking, burlesque film noir in which a down-and-out gumshoe gets drawn into the case of a cuckolded cartoon critter—a living, three-dimensional, loony Toon who's been set up for the murder of his wife's prank-playing sugar daddy.

Though this past summer was notable for the number of grownup films which did well at the box office—from the sophisticated sex-and-sports comedy, *Bull Durham,* to *Midnight Run,* the thinking man's buddy movie—what is immediately striking about the season's top four moneymakers is that they are all, in essence, fairy tales, full of fabulous elements: magic wishes, miraculous transformations, mythic kingdoms, legendary heroes, talking beasts. More significantly (and here we come to the crux of the matter) the plot lines and protagonists of each of these films are precise cinematic analogues of traditional folktale motifs—which is to say that, for all their technical sophistication and modernday trappings, these motion pictures achieve their effects by exploiting the same types of folktale symbols that have beguiled human beings for centuries.

The overgrown naif played by Tom Hanks in *Big,* for example—who consumes a baby corn at a fancy buffet by nibbling off each separate kernal and who (in his absolute innocence) comically misconstrues every sexual remark or reference—is a Yuppie-era version of a well-known folk character variously known as the Dummling, Numskull or Simpleton. Indeed, the movie's visual and verbal gags correspond closely to such widely distributed motifs as "Absurd Ignorance of Food" (J 1732) and "Absurd Ignorance of Sex" (J 1745), both of them catalogued by Stith Thompson in his standard folklore index under the general category, "Fools and Other Unwise Persons."[6] Similarly, the *Crocodile Dundee* films are nothing more than contemporary reworkings of a favorite American folk theme, involving a cocksure backwoodsman or country bumpkin on his first visit to the big city—a type of story which is itself a particular cultural variant of a universal folk motif that Thompson labels "The Countryman in the Great World" (J 1742). Underlying Eddie Murphy's *Coming to America* is a folk motif known as "The Incognito Prince" (K 1812.2). And *Who Framed Roger Rabbit* is part of an age-old and worldwide tradition of so-called "Animal Tales." In its dazzling evocation of a mythical Hollywood where animated creatures and humans coexist, *Roger Rabbit* offers striking confirmation of Stith Thompson's observation that, "for the teller of folktales today as in the past, and in our western culture as well as in the most primitive tribes, the world of the human and of the animal are never far apart."[7]

Of course, to apply the term "folktale" to a state-of-the-art product of the Hollywood fun-factory like *Who Framed Roger Rabbit* might seem to be stretching the meaning of that word beyond all reasonable limits. And it's certainly true that a $45 million motion picture that required two years and the services of seven hundred or so technicians to create is a far cry from a medieval beast fable or the tall tales of an Appalachian yarn-spinner. Nevertheless, as various culture critics have observed, popular works in general (not only movies but paperback potboilers, superhero comics, soap operas and the like) possess many of the essential features of traditional folk story—so many, in fact, that it's possible to see our modernday, mass-produced entertainments as serving the same narrative function performed in earlier times by orally transmitted folk tales and legends.

According to S. S. Prawer, the resemblance between folktales and genre films, "with their strictly defined character-types and limited situations," was pointed out as early as 1927 by the Russian critic A. Piotrovsky.[8] Seven years later, in 1934, Erwin Panofsky drew a similar connection in his pioneering essay, "Style and Medium in the Motion Pictures." Tracing the origins of film to various "folkloristic" pastimes, Panofsky argued that—with their powerful appeal to certain basic emotions and impulses (a "primitive sense of justice", "plain sentimentality," a "primordial instinct for bloodshed and cruelty," a "taste for mild pornography," and a "crude sense of humor")—the movies both derive from and continue to reflect the "folk-art mentality."[9] More recently, critics like Northrop Frye, Leslie Fielder, and Marshall McCluhan have commented on the close affinities between modernday, commercial "mass art" and "the folk entertainments of the illiterate poor."[10]

Some of these similarities are immediately apparent. Both pop art and folklore, for example, achieve their effects through the repetition of time-tested, sure-fire formulas, which are continually varied and revised to fit the communal concerns of the moment. Both depend on strong storylines and stock characters to elicit very basic responses—laughter, tears, wonder, suspense, terror, erotic titillation. Besides displaying what Stith Thompson describes as an absolute "disregard for originality of plot," they share an equally profound indifference to individual expression.[11] One of the favorite insults deployed by highbrow critics in their attacks on things like blockbuster movies and pop bestsellers is to say that these works are created "by committee," meaning that, unlike serious art, the popular narrative is not the embodiment of a unique sensibility but merely a concoction of crowd-pleasing ingredients. But much the same can be said of the typical folk story, which is every bit as impersonal as, say, the average episode of "Dynasty," being the end result of a collaborative process involving generations of listeners and storytellers—storytellers whose success depends on their ability to adapt their inherited materials to the psychic and social needs of the audience.

But the relationship between pop art and folklore extends beyond these structural and functional similarities. To see B-movies, sitcoms, supermarket tabloids and the like as a kind of mass-produced folklore—as the form of narrative entertainment that has taken the place of traditional oral storytelling in our technological world—makes it clear that when we talk about pop symbolism we are really dealing with the archetypes of the folktale, with the same age-old, universally appealing character types and story motifs collected and catalogued by scholars like Antii Aarne, Stith Thompson, and Ernest Baughman. Seen in this light, pop culture, particularly in its least pretentious manifestations, takes on a new and larger significance. For example, once we become aware of the widespread popularity of the kind of folk story known as "The Monster in the Bridal Chamber" (Type 507 B), then a poverty-row picture like *I Married a Monster from Outer Space* or a tabloid article headlined MY HUSBAND IS A UFO ALIEN can be looked at as something more than simply a piece of "schlock" or "camp." Rather, it can be recognized as a contemporary, space-age analogue of a peculiarly compelling fantasy that has formed the basis of countless wondertales throughout the world.

Of course, the fact that *I Married a Monster from Outer Space* is a cut-rate, commercialized, sci-fi version of that fantasy is significant. What it signifies is that, although there is a universal or archetypal aspect to every folk story, there is a culturally specific dimension to it as well—which is to say that every folktale, being the product of a particular historical moment, is a reflection not only of "the unchanging operations of man's inner being" (as Robert Darnton puts it) but also of the prevailing values, concerns, and anxieties of the period in which it appears.[12] Thus, analyzing a popular work (a recent Hollywood comedy, for example) as a contemporary, technologically transmitted folk story requires the critic not simply to classify the film according to type or motif—to identify the folktale category it belongs to—but to consider the social implications of the variations it works on its archetypal themes.

Once again, a look at the top four movie moneymakers of the summer of 1988 is instructive. What, if any, connection is there between the popularity of these films (each of which has already earned more than $100 million) and the social climate of the country? Certainly, the megasuccess of these movies was not a foregone conclusion. *Big*, for example, was preceded by a trio of films about youngsters who take over grown-up bodies—*Vice Versa, 18 Again, Like Father, Like Son*—all of them major flops. *Crocodile Dundee II* was, of course, a follow-up to one of the major sleepers of recent years. But being a sequel to a blockbuster is no guarantee of success, as the poor box-office showing of *Croc's* main macho-movie competitor, *Ramboo III*, attests. *Who Framed Roger Rabbit* was not only Hollywood's biggest summer hit but also its biggest gamble, since the movie it most closely resembles—1985s *Howard the Duck* (another comedy-adventure about a cartoony character who gets mixed up with humans)—was a fiasco from which George Lucas is still trying to recover. And, though putting Eddie Murphy in a movie is probably the closest thing to a sure bet that Hollywood has yet come up with, even he couldn't attract paying customers to the 1984 bomb, *Best Defense*.

That each of the four movies in question contains a popular folktale motif that has delighted audiences throughout the ages would certainly seem to be a factor in their success. Still, the mere existence of such a motif in a movie is not enough to make for a hit. Indeed, it would be possible to cite dozens of totally obscure exploitation movies—movies which have been viewed only by the most ardent aficionados of schlock—that are especially rich in folktale symbols. *Voyage to the Planet of Prehistoric Women* (a cinematic variant of Motif F 112, "Journey to the Land of Women") and *They Saved Hitler's Brain* (an analogue of the widely distributed tale type known as "The Severed-But-Living Head") are only two of many examples.

Clearly, the key issue has to do not with the simple presence of a folktale symbol in a popular work but with a society's readiness to respond to—its need to hear—a specific story at a particular time. And in looking more closely at the folkloric content of this past summer's four top-grossing films, we are struck by a significant fact. All of them use folktale protagonists of timeless and seemingly universal appeal (the simpleton, the backwoodsman-in-the-big-city, the anthropomorphic animal, and the disguised prince) to tell what is essentially the same story—i.e., that of a hero who journeys from an Edenic Never-Land into the modern world of money, greed, and corruption and defeats the forces of rapacity through the power of his own invincible innocence.

The hero of the *Crocodile Dundee* movies—part Tarzan, part Davy Crockett, part Aussie good-ol'-boy—is a modernday noble savage: lord of the outback but, in Manhattan, a mere babe in the woods. It is precisely his childlike simplicity, however—as well as his close kinship with Nature—that allows him to prevail over his infinitely more sophisticated adversaries (an insufferably pretentious

Yuppie in the first film and, in the second, a Columbian drug lord). Eddie Murphy's Prince Akeem starts out in the impossibly lush realm of Zamunda, a fairytale land that seems to be located not in Africa but in Disney's Magic Kingdom (among the gentle jungle beasts that roam freely over the royal grounds is a baby elephant named Babar). Coming to the States, Akeem must contend with a particularly obnoxious son of American capitalism, the self-centered heir of a beauty-products entrepreneur. Roger Rabbit emerges from the magical precincts of Toontown—an enchanted land of perpetual sunshine, where visitors are greeted by a choir of singing bluebirds and a chorus line of dancing trees—to grapple with the nefarious Judge Doom, the heartless personification of runaway urban development. And in *Big,* the hero is transported from the paradise of childhood to the aggressive world of corporate Manhattan, where he finds himself vying with a ruthlessly ambitious young executive. What we see in each of these films, in short, is a traditional folktale motif reinvented in terms that speak directly to the concerns of the time, a fantasy in which an incarnation of Reagan-era avarice—of the moneygrubbing, "greed is good" ethic epitomized by the insider-trading scandals of the late 1980s—is put to rout by a figure of natural, childlike innocence and virtue.

Though each of these movies is, in important ways, a very calculated product of the Hollywood entertainment factory, it is impossible to believe that they were created with a full awareness of the powerful fantasy that exists at their core and that accounts, we would argue, for a large part of their appeal to a mass audience troubled, on some deep (perhaps not wholly acknowledged) level, by the narrowly mercenary values of the Reagan years. But this very lack of awareness is one of the distinctive traits of popular art, which tends—like all true folk narrative—to communicate its symbolic messages in the most artless and unselfconscious ways, as opposed to "high" literature, which, when it does make use of folktale symbolism, generally manipulates it for the sake of an aesthetic effect or thematic end. Serious artists have frequently turned to folklore as a source of inspiration and raw material. Commenting on *The Canterbury Tales* and the comedies of Shakespeare, for example, Northrop Frye points out that, in both cases, "we notice an influence from folktale so pervasive as to make it clear that folktale is their direct literary ancestor. There are hardly any comedies of Shakespeare, and few tales told on the Canterbury pilgrimage, that do not have some common folktale theme prominently featured in them."[13] The difference between the serious and the popular artist in this regard is that, whereas the former uses folktale motifs in the service of a unique aesthetic vision (and thus imposes a particular meaning on them), the latter, by aspiring to nothing more than mass entertainment, is content to transmit these narrative archetypes in the most crudely effective and impersonal forms and thus allows them to communicate their *own* meanings, to speak in their obscure but strangely resonant, symbolic language.

A look at how the same folktale symbol is represented in two radically different works—Doris Lessing's 1988 novella *The Fifth Child* and *It's Alive,* a 1968 low-budget horror movie produced, written, and directed by schlockmeister Larry Cohen—will help illustrate this crucial distinction. Underlying both these works is the archaic belief in changelings—the idea, as Edwin Sidney Hartland has written, "that fairies and other imaginary beings are on the watch for young children...that they may, if they can find them unguarded, seize and carry them off, leaving in their place one of themselves."[14] Though changeling babies bear a rough resemblance to their human counterparts, they possess several traits which make them immediately recognizable as the monstrous offspring of goblins, elves, or fairies: forbidding looks, formidable strength, a savage temper, a ferocious appetite (according to one commentator, "the mothers of such sort are sucked out, that afterwards they are able to give suck no more"),[15] and a furious bellow. "A fine child at Caerlaveroc, in Nithsdale," reports Thomas Keightley in his classic folklore compilation, *The Fairy Mythology,* "was observed on the second day after its birth, and before it was baptized, to have become quite ill-favored and deformed. Its yelling every night deprived the whole family of rest; it bit and tore its mother's breasts, and would lie still neither in the cradle nor the arms."[16] Creatures such as this are not merely disruptive but actively destructive, and unless prompt measures are taken to dispose of them, they will end by wreaking havoc on the families that have been cursed with their presence.

Just such a fate befalls the protagonists of Lessing's critically acclaimed novella. The book tells the story of Harriet and David Lovatt, a young couple whose old-fashioned notions of home and family make them analomies during the sexually freewheeling 1960s. Disdaining both the hedonism of their peers and the prudent advice of their parents, Harriet and David set about creating what they continually refer to as their own special "kingdom"—a sprawling Victorian house brimming with convivial guests and, increasingly (as Harriet proceeds to bear children at a pace that disconcerts everyone but her husband), with the happy offspring of the Lovatt's apparently ideal marriage:

> Around the great family table, where so many chairs could be comfortably accommodated, people sat through long pleasant meals, or found their way there between meals to drink coffee and tea, and to talk. And laugh...Listening to the laughter, the voices, the talk, the sounds of children playing, Harriet and David in their bedroom, or perhaps descending from the landing, would reach for each other's hand, and smile, and breathe happiness...There were twelve adults and ten children. Neighbors invited, did appear, but the sense of family togetherness was strong and excluded them. And Harriet and David exulted that they, their obstinacy, what everyone had criticized and laughed at, had succeeded in this miracle: they were able to unite all these so different people, and make them enjoy each other.[17]

This domestic idyll, however, comes to an abrupt end with the birth of the Lovatt's fifth child, a seemingly subhuman creature they call Ben, who emerges from Harriet's womb (after an agonizingly difficult pregnancy) looking not "like a baby at all. He had a heavy-shouldered hunched look...His forehead sloped from his eyebrows to his crown. His hair grew in an unusual pattern from the double crown where started a wedge or triangle that came low on the forehead, the hair lying forward in a thick yellowish stubble, while the side and back hair grew downwards. His hands were thick and heavy, with pads of muscle in the palms. He opened his eyes and looked straight up into his mother's face. They were focussed greeny-yellow eyes, like lumps of soapstone" (48-49). When the attending nurse places the newborn into its mothers arms, Harriet's first words are, "He's like a troll, or a goblin or something"—and at no point in the book does she budge from her conviction that the "nasty little brute" who has somehow been born to her is a member of an ancient and alien species: a hobgoblin, gnome, gremlin, or dwarf. In short, a changeling.

In a 1984 interview published in the *New York Times,* Lessing insisted that "what is happening in the world is so fantastic that it needs fantasy—a rebirth of the imagination...I am going back to the origins of storytelling 12,000 years ago, the way it all began, with fables, parables, legends and fairy tales."[18] And for the first half of the book, *The Fifth Child* does indeed function as a superior fantasy tale, a kind of highbrow *Rosemary's Baby.* Ben is a terrifying creation, a malevolent "little troll" possessed of an unappeasable hunger (placed at Harriet's breast, he fastens "like a leech to the nipple," and drains "every drop in two or three minutes") and a demoniac rage, which he expresses in an incessant, maddening roar. At six months old, he grabs his older brother's arm and tries to break it; at a year, he strangles the family dog. Eventually, he fragments the family, creates an irreparable rift between Harriet and David, and reduces the Lovatt's fairytale "kingdom" to a state of more or less complete ruin.

This is all very unnerving. As Lessing's story progresses, however, it turns into something other than a supernatural chiller—into a story with larger intellectual ambitions. Though Lessing (in the peculiarly disingenuous way of many serious writers with weighty messages on their minds) disclaims any higher significance for her book, insisting that it is nothing more nor less than "a horror story,"[19] it is impossible to avoid seeing Ben as an allegorical figure, since his birth and development are so blatantly tied to the coming of what Lessing describes as "the barbarous eighties" (107). By the end of the novel—when Ben has become the ringleader of a gang of thugs, who seem to be ubiquitous, appearing wherever a riot, rape, theft or murder takes place—the deeply unsettling folk symbol of the changeling has been transformed into a one-dimensional emblem of "the violence overtaking Britain and the world"[20] and the book itself reduced to a monitory fable of social breakdown and moral decay—a sermon in the guise of a horror story. In short, for all its ingenuity, Lessing's conceit—her use of an ancient folk superstition to make a sociological point—ends up depleting the changeling archetype of its rich, if disquieting, suggestive power.

By contrast, Larry Cohen's cheaply made movie aspires to nothing more than the manufacture of crude, horror-film frissons. The movie concerns another contentedly married couple—Frank Davis and his very pregnant wife, Lenore—who, along with their preadolescent son Chris and pet Siamese cat, inhabit a cozy suburban tract house in southern California. As in Lessing's book, the happy household is wrecked by the arrival of Lenore's newborn—a malevolent mutant who has somehow ended up inside her womb in place of a human baby.

One of the most effective features of Cohen's production was its advertising slogan: "There's only one thing wrong with the Davis baby—It's Alive!" In point of fact, however, there are lots of things wrong with the Davis baby, who possesses all the classic attributes of its kind: a frightening appearance (bulging head, fangs, claws), a bestial growl, a monstrous appetite (he guzzles bottles of milk by the quartful), prodigious strength, and an exceedingly nasty temper. Like little Ben Lovatt, the Davis baby kills the family pet, but—this being a go-for-the-throat gore film instead of a Work of Art—he doesn't stop there, dispatching a bunch of human victims as well, beginning with the entire obstetrical staff of the hospital in which he is delivered. Eventually, he is gunned down by a police fusillade, but at movie's end, a radio report informs us that another of his kind has just been born, thus paving the way for *It Lives Again* and *It's Alive III: Island of the Alive,* the inevitable sequels to Cohen's moneymaking original.

As a piece of filmmaking, *It's Alive* is absolutely rudimentary. But it is precisely its lack of artistic pretension that gives the movie its distinctly folkloric quality. Instead of employing the nightmare symbol of the changeling baby for thematic ends, Cohen is content to do nothing more than conjure it up for the viewer's entertainment. And in doing this with a certain crude narrative skill, he ends up performing—like many exploitation filmmakers—the traditional role of the folk raconteur, whose primary goal is to arouse certain basic, even primitive, emotions (wonder, awe, dread, etc.) in unsophisticated audiences. Moreover, like all folk narratives, Cohen's movie is capable of yielding important insights into contemporary cultural issues, as the writings of various horror-film critics make clear.[21]

In short, for all its crudeness (indeed largely *because* of its crudeness), *It's Alive* possesses a genuine symbolic richness that Lessing's novel—which becomes more narrowly allegorical, even didactic, as it progresses—ultimately fails to achieve. Thus, Cohen's shocker not only exemplifies the folkloric function of contemporary popular art but also embodies one of its greatest strengths. In terms of aesthetic or intellectual content, it can't be said to have much (if any) value. But in a way that isn't always true of more respectable works, it is powerfully and indisputably alive.

Notes

[1]Alan McGlashan, "Daily Paper Pantheon: A New Fantasia of the Unconscious," *The Lancet,* (31 Jan. 1953): 238-239.

[2]For the comments on Speedy Alka-Seltzer, see *Advertising Age.* May 2, 1985, p. 12. Campbell's remarks can be found in *The Power of Myth* (New York: Doubleday, 1988), 144 f. The book is a coffee-table transcript of his televised conversations with Bill Moyers, which originally ran as a six-hour series on PBS.

[3]"Myth and Archetype in Science Fiction," *Parabola* 4 (Fall 1976): 45.

[4]*Ibid.*

[5]*The Secular Scripture* (Cambridge, Massachusetts, and London: Harvard University Press, 1976) 6.

[6]See *Motif-Index of Folk Literature* (Bloomington: Indiana University Press, 1955-1958).

[7]*The Folktale* (New York: Holt, Rinehard and Winston, 1946) 217.

[8]*Caligari's Children* (Oxford and New York: Oxford University Press, 1980) 40.

[9]Collected in *Awake in the Dark,* ed. David Denby (New York: Vintage Books, 1977) 33.

[10]See, for example, Leslie Fiedler, "Giving the Devil His Due," *Journal of Popular Culture,* XII (1979) and Marshall McLuhan, *The Mechanical Bride* (New York: The Vanguard Press, 1951). For an extensive analysis of the folkloric content of contemporary

popular art, see Harold Schechter *The Bosom Serpent: Folklore and Popular Art* (Iowa City: University of Iowa Press, 1988).

[11]*The Folktale,* 5.

[12]See *The Great Cat Massacre and Other Episodes in French Cultural History* (New York: Basic Books, 1984) 3 f.

[13]*The Secular Scripture* 7.

[14]*The Science of Fairy Tales* (London: Walter Scott, 1891; rpt. Detroit: The Singing Tree Press, 1968) 93-94.

[15]*Ibid.,* 110.

[16]*The Fairy Mythology* (London: George Bell and Sons, 1892; rpt. London: Wildwood House, 1981) 355-356.

[17]Doris Lessing, *The Fifth Child* (New York: Alfred A. Knopf, 1988) 18-19. Subsequent references in the text are to this edition.

[18]See *The New York Times Book Review* (22 April 1984): 16.

[19]See Mervyn Rothstein, "The Painful Nurturing of Doris Lessing's Fifth Child," *New York Times* (4 June 1988, Section C): 21.

[20]Michiko Kakutani, "Family Relations, Society and a Monstrous Baby," *New York Times* (30 March 1988, Section C): 23.

[21]See, for example, Robin Wood, "The Return of the Repressed" and Dana B. Polan, "Eros and Syphilization: The Contemporary Horror Film," both collected in *Planks of Reason,* ed. Barry Keith Grant (Metuchen, New Jersey and London: The Scarecrow Press, 1984).

Symbolism's "New Spin"

Richard G. Peterson

"I *looovve* you!" cries Brother Love. He thrusts a grinning face right up to the camera lens then backs away, microphone in hand—a stocky, youngish fellow with slicked-back hair and resplendent in a brilliant white suit. Under the hot lights a sheen of perspiration coats his forehead. "Ah *reallly* do!" Even though there is no doubt that Brother Love's sincerity and Southern-honey drawl are pure carnival hokum, the World Wrestling Federation *likes* Brother Love. His segments are part of their television programming and help to spotlight colorful wrestlers like "Macho Man" Randy Savage and Jake ("The Snake") Roberts. Brother Love simply helps viewers tell the "good" guys from the "bad" in the WWF wrestling community.

Pure caricature, Brother Love uses the measured speaking cadences of the rural tent revivalist and cheerfully calls his interviewees (the wrestlers and their managers) "brother" or "sister." Love's performance succeeds so well because it uses both visual and audible symbols immediately familiar to most of his viewing audience: his oversized "Book of Love" (the quasi-sacred text); his white suit (purity); and his proclamations of *looovve* for all God's creatures (his preacher's message).

Some would say the buffoonish Brother Love isn't really an exaggeration at all. But that is another issue. Instead, let's delve beneath the superficialities of milk-white suits and Deep South accents to examine the use of meaningful religious symbols by today's televangelists (TV preachers). And whether the latter may have contributed anything new to the world of religious symbolism. Of course, when we first think of such symbols, what quickly surfaces from the churchier precincts of memory is a mixture of objects and experiences stemming from our total church-going. For most Christians those memories include sanctuaries, pulpits, sacraments, devotional songs, robed choirs, the cross, the Bible, slender-white candles, stained-glass windows, and so on. And since conservative Protestants dominate the religious airwaves, our attention will be focused mostly upon them.

There be little doubt that some preachers secretly fantasize about joining the exalted ranks of Jerry Falwell, Oral Roberts, Marilyn Hickey, Kenneth and Gloria Copeland, et al. But at those rarified levels, the glare of public scrutiny can become quite hot. And the more markets a televangelist penetrates with his/her broadcasts, the more burdensome (even crushing!) become the costs of television programming. The uncertain or faint-hearted need not apply.

Observers have pointed out that breaking into, *and* staying in, the Kingdom of Television often call for a dash of spectacle and a touch of flash. Helpful, too, are attractive, tasteful sets and telegenic people. And since television is a very competitive arena, one's sermon/message must be highly effective. That is, it should pack a "punch." Surely a good measure of that punch comes from the skillful use of symbols via illustrations, pictures, parables, images. Lavender-and-pink studio sets and glee club-cheery songsters will carry you only so far. Successful televangelists must be sensitive to the importance of verbal and visual religious symbolism.

Ideally, televangelists (indeed, all who preach God's word) use symbols so they may help others to see more clearly the nature and purposes of their Creator. Believers pose that God is ineffable and beyond our puny comprehension; but He will *remain* unknown and unknowable unless something of His nature and purposes can be expressed in familiar terms—in short, in a symbol or image. (You may call God God, but no one is any the wiser. But use a symbol and say "The Lord is my shepherd" and at once understanding is heightened.) So a meaningful symbol helps to give sharpness and form to what beforehand we have known only vaguely and with little comprehension. But we must also note that while strict accuracy in language is of utmost importance to scientists and doctors, in matters theological, such accuracy will not help more than a tiny minority to know the kingdom-power-glory of God any better. What *is* essential is that religious symbols be vibrantly *alive* to us as congregants and TV viewers. Such symbols open our eyes and go on "working" in our minds long after the actual, spoken words have been forgotten.

So if religious symbols are to remain relevant to the continuing experience of humankind, there should be a profoundly important relationship between them and their users. In his book *Time Eternity,* W. T. Stace tells us that a religious symbol evokes an experience, and by doing so, stirs up feelings, moods, and emotions; it must also suggest and inspire. The Reverend F. W. Dillistone, Fellow and Chaplain of Oriel College, Oxford, adds that a true and effective symbol must be flexible, expansive, and directed towards a reality richer and more mysterious than itself. A symbol comes into its own, says Dillistone, when we find ourselves dealing with *mysteries* beyond our immediate understanding. And only through such symbols can the realm of mystery be approached.

Dillistone takes care to differentiate between *symbols* and *signs/signals.* Signs/signals come in various forms: red and green lights on a traffic signal (instead of the police giving signals); paper money; and in the ringing of a telephone bell. Along with animals, we humans are able to emit and respond to signals that bear a single, immediate, and direct connotation. But, says Dillistone, to speak of these as *symbols* is to rob the term of any distinctive meaning of its own. Symbols, in effect, belong on a higher level of meaning. Dillistone concludes,

> It seems to me that much confusion can be avoided if...we use the word symbol for that which points towards, shares in, and in some way conforms to, a reality which cannot be *fully* expressed through any descriptive languages or visual forms already available to us.

Dissecting the term another way, philosophers of language, such as Carnap and Langer, distinguish between "discursive" and "presentational" symbols. In "discursive thought" we arrange word-symbols in a logical sequence. Psychologist Goodwin Watson of the Teachers College, Columbia University, points out that in the religious traditions, discursive symbols are what make up creeds, commandments, and apologetics. But the really rich field for psychological study are the expressive or presentational symbols. Presentational symbols of religion tend to center about the mysteries of birth and death, the relationships among human beings, and the cycles of stars and planetary seasons. For instance, the fish—often seen today affixed to the posteriors of automobiles—was a comprehensive symbol in the Early Christian faith. It meant practically everything: Baptism, Resurrection, Eucharist, and Kingdom. To explain the meanings of such concepts is a lengthy task, yet in a brief moment, the symbol of the fish can inspire believers through the feelings it evokes. As Watson says, "It is the words which fall short, not the experience."

TV ministries use religious symbols in much the same manner as they have been traditionally used by Christian churches. However, says sociologist William Martin of Rice University, because of the mass medium of television, the symbol-concept of *the church* has lost its *local* content almost completely. Televangelists do mention the local church from time to time, but it's not anything they emphasize. Instead, the concept of the Church Universal is stressed. But what other symbols does Pray TV use? Let us turn to a few specifics.

Televangelists on crusade are ever mindful of keeping down the costs of travel and broadcasting. Consequently, they often adopt a "bare bones" stage presentation, *sans* religious pageantry, robed choirs, or sanctuaries. Of course, not all is economics: the affirmation of their Protestant freedom dictates a shunning of alb and stole and other Catholicisms. So whatever symbols they use must be potent ones. For many, a plexiglass lectern, some written notes and a Bible satisfy their needs, with greenery and flowers providing texture and splashes of color.

For a pledge of $500 or more, the Jack Van Impe Ministry (JVI) in Troy, Michigan, will thank you with "a meaningful art piece": a porcelain, white dove on a polished wooden base. The dove symbolizes the power of the Holy Spirit (John 1:32: "I saw the spirit descending from heaven like a dove"). JVI is comprised of the husband-and-wife team of Jack and Rexella Van Impe, and its letterhead uses the logotype of an impressionistic blue dove superimposed over a world globe.

As evangelist Jimmy Swaggart prowls back and forth across his crusade stage—necktie loosened and suit coat flopping open—he invariably clutches a microphone in one hand and holds aloft a large Bible in the other. Preaching before tens and hundreds of thousands of the faithful in huge arenas and amphitheaters, Swaggart needs only that Bible and a music stand as lectern. The symbols on the Swaggart Ministries logotype are bedrock traditional: a golden cross, a white dove.

A much more symbol-rich environment is offered by "The Coral Ridge Hour" television program. That program, originating from the Coral Ridge Presbyterian Church in Fort Lauderdale, Florida, is actually a televised portion of worship services—complete with impressively ornate sanctuary, robed choirs, and thundering pipe organ. Celebrating ten years on the air, the handsome, gray-haired Dr. D. James Kennedy used that occasion to offer loyal TV viewers a 10-year commemorative gift: a symbol of belonging in the form of a golden pin, which depicts the Coral Ridge Church's soaring bell tower. (Psychologist Watson reminds us that the most personally influential religious symbols are those learned in ceremonies in which people participate together—as members of a family, neighborhood, or community. And, I might add, as part of a "video family.") Explained a Coral Ridge spokesperson, "The pin is a symbol of hope, hope in a nation where faith abounds and believers are free to live out their faith."

You can find enduring religious symbols in the most unusual places. *Charisma* magazine ("the magazine about spirit-led living") carried one advertisement promoting "faithful timepieces." Readers could purchase watches with faces containing pictures of doves (Acts 2:4) or fish (Matthew 4:19) or world globes (John 3:16). The latter is quite a popular symbol among TV ministries. Obeying the scriptural dictum to "cover the Earth with His Word," evangelist Marilyn Hickey (Denver, Colorado) uses the logotype of an open Bible suspended over a globe. And when Kenneth and Gloria Copeland (Fort Worth, Texas) preach, their backdrop is always a large, wooden-looking logotype containing the words "JESUS IS LORD," which extend horizontally across an elliptical world map.

For years Beverly LaHaye and her Baptist preacher husband, Tim, hosted a weekly television show and call-in radio talk show. Today, as head of the 600,000-member Concerned Women for America (CWA), Mrs. LaHaye uses the long-stemmed red rose as her logotype/symbol. The rose was chosen, she says, "as the visible symbol of our respect and reverence for human life—for our unwavering dedication to the abolition of the wholesale slaughter of precious, innocent babies by abortion on demand in our beloved America."

The "Rock Alive!" program of Pentecostals John and Anne Gimenez prominently features shots of a granite boulder that rests along one wall of their Rock Church in Virginia Beach, Virginia. They have chosen Matthew 16 to remind viewers of the foundation for their evangelizing ("And I say also unto thee, that thou art Peter, and upon this rock I will build my church; and the gates of hell shall not prevail against it"). On "Rock Alive!" Anne Gimenez often encourages viewers to send in a contribution and receive a rhinestone "JESUS" pin, just like the one she wears. It is common for televangelists to offer such symbols to encourage viewers to join their particular Pray TV "family." (*Sidenote:* My earlier remark about the "crushing" costs of television programming was not a flippant one. The production costs of "Rock Alive!" were finally too much and the Gimenezes, very reluctantly, pulled the program off the air during the last quarter of 1988—after almost ten years of programming. A viewer wrote to them, "We cried when we learned it was our last time to see you on television! Rock Church has been a source of strength for me and my heart breaks to know you will not be coming into my home again. . . ." The Gimenezes are hoping they can appear in front of the cameras again some day.)

Certainly church buildings themselves are potent religious symbols. (Jimmy Swaggart and Jerry Falwell use their own sanctuaries from which to broadcast the Word.) Indeed, a prime example of what Mircea Eliade, that renowned historian of religions, calls "sacred space" may be seen in the Gothic cathedral. That space, detached from the profane, transcends the world and makes possible human communication with what might be called the trans-world realities.

The Gothic cathedral has been described as transparent, diaphanous architecture. No segment of its inner space was allowed to remain in darkness, and the multicolored light pouring through stained-glass windows created an atmosphere of mystical Christianity. As the symbol of the kingdom of God on earth, the cathedral looked down upon the medieval city, transcending all other concerns of life; its sanctuary was considered the very threshold of heaven. Through the ages people have gazed in awe at the lofty grandeur of Chartres, Notre Dame, and Beauvais. And yet a variation of that type of "sacred space" resides on our own West Coast.

In 1955 Robert Schuller, a young seminary graduate of the Reformed Church of America, arrived in southern California with a dream, a second-hand organ, and $500. He began holding worship services in the Orange Drive-in Theater in Garden Grove, proclaiming, "Come as you are in the family car." Evidentally his message of "With God all things are possible" was well received. By 1975, Schuller was unveiling plans for a new sanctuary for his Garden Grove Community Church. That new building, which would become home to Schuller's "Hour of Power" television broadcasts, was dubbed the "Crystal Cathedral." The name stuck. According to Schuller Ministries, it was a concept that had never been tried before in church architecture. The $18-million Cathedral was completed in 1980, and Dr. Schuller proudly called it "God's Landmark."

The "crystal" of the Cathedral is made up of more than 10,000 windows of tempered, silver-colored glass, which gleam in the California sun. The Cathedral draws thousands of visitors each week to marvel at what has been praised as a "spectacular multi-faceted gem" and "timeless piece of architectural art." Among its features are a $1,000,000 organ (13,000 organ pipes) and two 90-foot doors behind the pulpit that can be opened and closed by remote control to reveal a spectacular view of the sky. And running the length of the sanctuary's center aisle are 12 fountains representing the Apostles.

The primary symbolism inherent in the Cathedral is, simply, *light*. With such a transparent structure, natural light floods in—a luxurious bath of heavenly radiance. Biblical references to light and dark are many, from Genesis ("And God said, Let there be light: and there was light") to Revelation (And the city had no need of the sun, neither of the moon, to shine in it: for the glory of God did lighten it, and the Lamb is the light thereof"). The atmosphere of the interior, said a Cathedral spokesperson, should evoke feelings of *closeness* between congregants and God. One might say that, similar to the sacred initiatory hut of certain Algonquin and Sioux tribes, the Cathedral represents the Universe. Symbolically, its lofty roof becomes the celestial canopy and its floor, the Earth. And with the illusion of being so near to the Almighty and the Pearly Gates, worshipers will hopefully be infused with feelings of great joy and inspiration. So many churches are so dark, the spokesperson opined, they almost make you feel sinful.

Robert Schuller

Crystal Cathedral

Inside Crystal Cathedral

Returning to the television studio, we must ask, are there "new" symbols that have been generated/baptized by the Video Vicars? Well, it has been speculated that the television set *itself* may have become a kind of symbol. Some viewers, conceivably, look upon their sets as surrogate altars. When they obey a televangelist's request to lay hands on their sets and pray—such requests *do* occur—those individuals may sincerely feel a connection has been made. And, for a time, their TV set loses its secular character and becomes an instrumental part of a sacred experience. Along those lines, cassettes (both audio and video) have become excellent marketing tools for the messages/sermons of televangelists. When, for example, devotees purchase audiocassettes and listen to them over and over again (the sermon eternal?), these cassettes may become looked upon as personal artifacts of religious value. However, as intriguing as such ruminations may be, it is extremely doubtful that television sets or cassette tapes will ever lose their essentially secular character and become viewed by the masses as religious symbols.

Said another way, we should understand that objects may be constructed and given some religious connotation within a limited context, but that *doesn't* mean they are necessarily religious symbols. The black slab/monolith in Stanley Kubrick's film "2001: A Space Odyssey" (1968) was perceived by at least one moviegoer as a source of infinite knowledge and intelligence. Co-writer of the script was Arthur Clarke, the famous science-fiction novelist. Shortly after the film's release Clarke noted, "We had our first freakout in Los Angeles. A kid went up to the screen and screamed, 'It's God, it's God.' " Fortunately that fellow's choice of symbols did not capture the popular imagination: few people today are worshipping black monoliths—at least not on Pray TV.

We have seen some televangelists attempt to appropriate old symbols or put a new "spin" on those symbols. This "new spin" may present itself in the form of trying to make an association in the minds of the public. For example, says William Martin, in more politically oriented ministries—those of Pat Robertson and Jerry Falwell come to mind—we see a pairing of Old Glory and conservative Protestantism, with the former used for lavish backdrops, on printed materials, and so on. On the distaff side, Beverly LaHaye's Concerned Women for America often uses patriotic themes and symbols in its literature and extensively during CWA's annual conference in Washington, D.C.

One might also point to Heritage, USA, in Fort Mill, South Carolina—the famous ecclesiastical "empire" formerly under the ministrations of Jim and Tammy Bakker. At least one observer (who shall remain anonymous) has voiced the opinion that the Bakkers had altered the symbol of *Church* to *Church as Amusement Park*. Jim Bakker certainly put a definite "spin" on the old-fashioned camp meetings of his youth when he created Heritage, USA. But for some believers, that Christian community had become materialistic and hedonistic; the concept of personal sacrifice had faded into the shadows.

Today, if a televangelist entertains the idea of "introducing" new symbols or of putting new "spins" on time-honored ones, he/she would be wise to proceed carefully. From a pragmatic marketing viewpoint, any act that alienates segments of audience could be crippling. And alienation of large segments, devastating. The dual scandals of Jim Bakker-PTL and of Jimmy Swaggart have horrified the televangelist community. Caution is the watchword. And since competition in the religious television market seems to have escalated in recent years, smaller and smaller slices of the religious audience "pie" are available to each televangelist. That has a chilling effect, one that strongly encourages them to avoid controversy and to do nothing that might "turn off" their video congregations—whether by a misuse of venerable religious symbols or other misstep.

It is risky business to speculate about the future, much less about the future of religious symbols on Pray TV. But while traversing this mushy ground of speculation, we note some relatively firm spots. The Reverend David Cox, author of *Jung and St. Paul,* explains that while symbols are not consciously created, they may be deliberately preserved. Logic and religious history tell us that the preservation of time-honored symbols is an important function of the Christian Church. So rest assured that much of the religious symbology used by modern televangelists will prevail, long after you and I have shed our mortal coils.

But it is also true that, occasionally, religious symbols lose their power or become passé. Cox says it seems likely that in the early Church, the symbol of the fish was possibly considered more powerful than that of the cross. But, again, it seems sensible to assume that certain religious symbols will retain their potency, as long as Christians have any say in the matter. For example, the Church has decreed that the symbolically powerful sacraments of Baptism and Holy Communion are of unending value and importance.

In the evolution of religious symbols, if increasing knowledge brings their reality fully within our comprehension or under our control, those symbols will become just "signs" or "signals." Or if the entity symbolized ceases to be of interest or concern, it will become a kind of museum piece, an indication of past relevance but powerless to evoke any contemporary response.

Quo vadis? There is a kernel of truth to the allegation that our increasingly secular society is moving away from the mystical and the visionary, and that we are becoming, to some degree, symbol deficient. For the sake of argument, even if we do *not* invest our religious symbols with as much meaning and richness as our forbears did, religion is *still* a vital force in the land. And that, says William Martin, "indicates we have a great deal of hunger and thirst for the mystical and spiritual. Both of these strains [secularity and religiosity] are evident in American life. And there's also a strong *un*secular aspect of American society that doesn't seem ready to go away."

American Mobility

Michael Aaron Rockland

A restless temper seems...one of the distinctive traits of this people.

Alexis de Tocqueville[1]

Alexis de Tocqueville wrote this in the 1830s. It is still true. Mobility, perhaps more than any other factor, has formed the American character. While mobility is a concept rather than a symbol, the various artifacts we associate with mobility, most particularly the automobile, are powerful indices to American life. Nowhere else in the world do these symbols of mobility have the same poignancy. Mobility is one of the salient features of American life. It has been central to our experience from the very start and still is today.

The essay which follows will examine the impact of mobility on American life. Our discussion will fall into five areas: the immigrant and frontier experience; the role of the automobile in transforming American life; mobility in American arts and design; the extent to which mobility has suffused our national literature; and the future of mobility in America.

The Immigrant and The Frontier

Among a people who advance their frontiers a hundred leagues each year, set up states in six months, transport themselves from one end of the Union to the other in a matter of hours, and emigrate to Oregon, the feet would naturally enjoy the same esteemed position as the head among those who think and the chest among those who sing.

Domingo Faustino Sarmiento[2]

The United States is a country of people who came here from somewhere else. Except for the Indians, who were already here, and the blacks, who were dragged here against their will, the rest of us became Americans to get away from something or to seek opportunity. We traveled great distances to get to these shores and faced considerable hardships. Thus, from the start, Americans were a mobile people.

The migration of the immigrants was followed by the migration westward of the pioneers. Americans landed on these shores and kept moving. The question is whether we ever stopped. As one scholar has written, "We have been and are still today the most mobile people on the face of the earth."[3] Is movement in our very nature? Is it possibly even in our genes? Are we culturally and biologically a society of adventurers?

John Steinbeck, in his *Travels With Charlie,* wonders the same thing.[4] "Could it be," he asks, "That Americans are a restless people, a mobile people, never satisfied with where they are as a matter of selection?" Is it possible, he continues, that we have "inherited this tendency?"[5]

Natural selection would seem to have been involved in who emigrated to America, who survived and prospered, and who embarked on the trek westward. As Steinbeck writes, "The pioneers, the immigrants who peopled the continent, were the restless ones of Europe. The steady, rooted ones stayed home and are still there."[6] Those who came here were neither established nor rich. They were disenfranchised, persecuted, poor, of low status.

David Potter in his landmark book, *People of Plenty,* sees an intimate relationship between mobility and status.[7] The traditional and feudal societies of Europe were physically, economically, and socially stagnant. Status tended to be assigned. In America, status was up for grabs; it might be earned. But the way it might be earned was important: if one wanted to prosper, one had to move. As Potter points out, the uncertain status of Americans, combined with freedom of movement and a virtually uninhabited continent, inextricably linked prosperity and mobility. Thus from the very beginnings of our history there has been a connection between social mobility and physical mobility.

The existence of almost limitless fertile land played a central role in this connection in the American mind between mobility and prosperity. There was land to be had, but it was, of course, *out there.* If the immigrant was willing to endure further travel, deprivation, and loneliness he might make his fortune. This spirit has continued into contemporary times. It is found among corporation executives whose ascent of the ladder of success is linked to accepting constant transfers.[8] It is found among entrepreneurs willing to risk all on ventures far from home. It is found among young Americans who went to California in the 1950s, Colorado in the 1960s, and Alaska in the 1970s and 1980s.

Daniel Boone is often thought of as the progenitor of this spirit. He is the preeminent example of the courage to pick up roots wherever one is and look for something better. Boone always moved on when he could see the smoke from his neighbor's chimney fire. As was written of him, everytime he settled somewhere,

> His old troubles pursued him; men again began to come near. The crash of falling trees was heard, as the new settlers leveled the forests; huts were seen springing up all around him; other hunters were roaming through the woods, and other dogs than his were barking. This was more than he was willing to bear. Happy as he had made his home, he determined to leave it, and find another in the wilderness, where he could have that wilderness to himself.[9]

Modern Americans imbued with what we might call the Daniel Boone Syndrome, continue to seek a piece of the "wilderness" for themselves; Boone lives on in the suburbs and exurbs of our time.

He also lives on in the continuing craving of Americans to be on the move. As John Steinbeck reported about Americans when he traveled about the country in the early 1960s,

I saw in their eyes something I was to see over and over in every part of the nation—a burning desire to go, to move, to get under way, any place, away from any Here. They spoke quietly of how they wanted to go some day, to move about, free and unanchored, not toward something but away from something. I saw this look and heard this yearning everywhere in every state I visited. Nearly every American hungers to move.[10]

While there is much to celebrate in a country where the freedom to move is axiomatic, there is a negative side as well. Daniel Boone and the people Steinbeck talked to on his travels may have been free, but they were anti-social as well. Does the extraordinary mobility of Americans reveal a flaw in their character: the inability to build a viable community? Americans abandoned European societies which, for whatever reason, did not suit them. Did this also make them less capable of building communities on these shores? Americans are enormously energetic and enterprising people. But can they also live together?

While we justly celebrate the courage of the immigrants and pioneers, there may be negative features to the legacy they have left us. They had good reasons for leaving where they were. But do Americans always move today for good reasons, or is their mobility sometimes escapist? America was for many years Europe's escape valve, and the American West was America's escape valve. As a teacher of mine once joked, "The West was a place where, if you had a problem, you could take it out and shoot it." But there is little free land now in the West, and our problems are too complex to be dispensed with so simply. Is it possible that we inherited an extreme tendency towards mobility from the immigrants and pioneers and now, when it is less appropriate, we cannot stop moving?[11]

America has always prided itself on the unparalleled opportunity it offered the individual. At the same time, in a society where everyone supposedly has a chance to better himself, everyone must strive to succeed. The psychological implications of this are manifest. America is probably the freest society on earth, but it may also be the most stressful. Thus mobility would seem to be a double-edged sword. Inextricably connected to freedom, it may be similarly linked with the anomie and social disintegration we are experiencing today. How much mobility is healthy—where does mobility end and rootlessness begin?—remains a puzzle for Americans.

Automobility in American Life

When America needs/ a better idea/ Ford puts it on wheels.

Ford Motor Company Singing Commercial.

Around the turn of the century, and during its first quarter, two events signalled a change in mobility. In 1892, the historian, Frederick Jackson Turner, read his famous paper, "The Significance of the Frontier in American History."[12] Turner argued that the existence of great expanses of open lands in the West had been the most important factor in the creation of American civilization. Now that the frontier was coming to an end, he supposed, other factors would weigh more heavily.

The other event was the ending of free immigration to the United States during the 1920s. Theretofore, virtually anyone who wanted to was granted entry to the United States. From the 1920s on, quotas would be maintained and immigration drastically curtailed. Thus two key factors in keeping America moving and changing—vast territories of free land and infusions of new people—were no more.

With these changes, one might have expected America to settle down, to become a more traditional society, to find roots. This did not happen. Americans were used to being a people on the move. They did not know how to settle down.

Nor did they need to. If the existence of free land and a continuing influx of immigrants were no more, something else took their place in keeping America a mobile society: the invention of the automobile. As James Flink has written, "Since its introduction in the United States...the motor vehicle has been the most significant force shaping the development of modern American civilization."[13] With the invention of the automobile American mobility became intercontinental. The great migrations of this century have been those of the rural poor into the cities; the middle class to the suburbs; organization men to outposts of their corporations; vast populations to the formerly almost barren Sunbelt States; and the semi-annual migrations of "Snowbird"-retirees. All of these migrations have been dependent—indeed, have derived—from the invention of the automobile.

The United States has remained the most mobile country in the world in the twentieth century. Today, at least one-fifth of all Americans change their home addresses once or more each year. Because of this, Vance Packard suggests in the title of one of his books, we are *A Nation of Strangers*.[14] Packard writes:

> I know a corporate manager who has moved his residence twenty-one times since he got married. I talked with an airline stewardess who said she had been raised on eleven military bases. She added, "When people ask me where I am from, I say 'No where.' "[15]

There is not a single country in the world where people change their residences at even half the rate of Americans.

In many of these countries motor vehicles exist in large numbers. But nowhere have they had the same impact as in the United States. First, we are really a continent in size and in outlook. The nations where there are large numbers of cars, almost all of them in Europe, are small countries, whose boundaries are traditional barriers to free movement. In none of these countries is there a literature and music, a mythology, celebrating movement for its own sake.

Europeans do not share the American fantasy of driving nonstop over vast distances.[16] Such exploits are not associated in the European mind with qualities of endurance, courage, and the ability to endure solitude. There is no equivalent in Europe to the picaresque literature centered on the automobile, Country-Western music with its steady emphasis on "movin' on," and films like "The Last Cowboy," "Smokey and the Bandit," and "Convoy" which celebrate the truck driver. Interchangeability of "trucker" and "cowboy" in these art forms suggests that the automotive vehicle has been substituted for the horse in the American imagination. (In this connection, it does not seem accidental that we calibrate the power of our vehicles in "horse-power"). Two students of mine recently drove from New Jersey to Los Angeles in under 50 hours. "Just to do it," they said. Both of them wore cowboy hats and boots for their trip and said, "We always wanted to see the 'wide open spaces.' "

A comparison of European and American driving folkways is instructive. Europeans have always driven smaller cars, and their machines take up a smaller place in the landscape. This was not originally for fuel economy. Things are smaller and closer together in Europe. Also, Europeans are more gregarious in their motoring, almost never going anywhere without packing their cars with people. Europeans lack the tradition of the solitary hero; they value communality more than Americans do. A friend of mine visiting America from Holland for the first time remarked almost as soon as I picked him up at Kennedy Airport on "how lonely" Americans appear. "Look at all those little heads in those big cars," he said, in reference to the solitary Americans piloting their cars along the expressways. European automobile accidents also tend to differ from American ones. Europeans have many more accidents but far fewer fatal ones. The most common accidents in Europe are sideswipes and rearenders, caused by cars driving too close (gregariously?) to one another.

Another difference in American and European attitudes towards the automobile is found in a survey conducted by the National Traffic Safety Administration on seatbelt utilization in the United States.[17] This survey showed wide disparity in seat belt usage depending on brand of car, with usage in foreign cars far outstripping that in American cars. A high of 44.6% of Volvo owners used their seat belts regularly. Less than 15% of Cadillac owners used them. If purchasers of foreign cars may be thought to subscribe, in part, to European automotive values, the avoidance of seat belts by purchasers of American cars might indicate that, for Americans, the automobile is an extension of their personal freedom. The last thing they want to do in their automobile is to be "roped in."[18]

Another example of differences in attitude towards the automobile in America and in Europe concerns public transportation. The United States has the worst system of public transportation in the developed world. Why should this be? Surely a key reason is that Americans see travel as a private or solitary activity. Public transportation schedules are anathema to a people who feel that they have a God-given right to go where, when, and *how* they wish.

This right is so important to Americans that it has spurred the growth of a giant industry in recreation vehicles which has added to life on the road the capacity to take along all the comforts of home. From the van (or "rolling room" as some call them) thru the truck camper and trailer and on up to the giant motor home larger than a commercial bus, Americans have managed to combine mobility with hearth and home in a manner the world has never seen before. Small wonder that when Samuel Dodsworth, in Sinclair Lewis' novel *Dodsworth,*[19] returns to America after spending several years in Europe and rejecting it as a model for his life, he decides to become a manufacturer of recreation vehicles. What better way for an American to reaffirm his Americanness than to resume his love affair with motorized vehicles?

Today, significant numbers of Americans live on the road year round in trailers and motorhomes. Some winter in the South, summer in the North. Others earn their keep traveling East and West, selling products scarce on the other coast at high mark-ups. There is even a story, possibly apocryphal, about a family in Los Angeles which lives entirely on the freeways in their motorhome.[20] Recreation vehicles carry automobility to its logical extreme.

Mobility in American Art and Design

As he grew accustomed to the great gallery of machines, he began to feel the forty foot dynamo as a moral force, much as the early Christians felt the Cross.

Henry Adams[21]

In his essay, "What's 'American' About America,"[22] John A Kouenhoven argues that certain objects are quintessestially American. "I am aware of generalizing," Kouenhoven writes, "and yet it would be silly...to assert that there are not certain things which are more American than others."[23]

Kouenhoven presents a list of twelve items which he thinks are typically American: the Manhattan skyline; the gridiron town plan; the skyscraper; the Model-T Ford; the Constitution; Mark Twain's writing; Whitman' *Leaves of Grass;* comic strips; soap operas; assembly-line production; chewing gum; Jazz.[24] What in essence, do these disparate items share?

Kouenhoven argues that these objects are process rather than product oriented, that they all involve movement and change. They have an open-ended, unfinished quality and may be added to infinitely. The Manhattan skyline changes each year; the grid-iron town plan stretches endlessly over the landscape; the skyscraper has no natural (height) nor aesthetic limitations (which is not the case, of course, with classic architecture); the Model-T Ford, and the assembly-line which gave birth to it, celebrate infinite movement; the Constitution is an ever growing document; Mark Twain's writing style has a flowing quality, and *Huckleberry Finn,* his most important book, celebrates movement for its own sake; *Leaves of Grass* is, in a sense, one long poem to which Whitman added all his life; comic strips and soap operas are endless serials; chewing gum is movement incarnate.

As for Jazz, it is characterized by innovation—a constant bobbing and weaving, informal beginnings and endings. In short, it moves. What is true of Jazz, often thought of as our most characteristic music, is also true of American music in general as far as content is concerned: mobility seems to be its most characteristic theme. A student of mine recently did a survey of the L. P. albums in her collection and found that "69 of my 72 albums include at least one song that mentions mobility in one form or another."[25] Throughout our musical history, and not just in the case of contemporary composer-performers such as Bruce Springsteen, Billy Joel, and James Taylor, being on the move (or on the lam) has been a central theme.

While Kouenhoven's essay is extremely perceptive, there are many items which might be added to his list. The American film is one. Its very name in English, "motion pictures" or "movies," suggests the manner in which this art form was first perceived by Americans. Further, the content of the American film, reflecting American civilization in general, is mobility oriented. As one critic has written,

> To Europeans, what epitomized American life was movement. Compared to themselves—encrusted with traditions, weighted down by forms, customs, habits, procedures; measured, lugubrious, drained of life—American motion, and therefore American motion pictures, possessed an enchanting, irresistible allure.[26]

It was the action in American films that excited Europeans. This is still true. In the most characteristic American films—cowboy movies, with their horse culture, gangster movies, with their automobile culture, and musicals, with their dynamic choreography—movement is central to impact and meaning.

Modern dance is another item for Kouenhoven's list. Practically an American invention, modern dance is characterized by its free form, informality, and celebration of pure movement. It is in revolt against the classic movements of European ballet.

American painting has a similarly free form quality. What most characterizes it is its "framelessness." In comparison with European painting, American painting is less concerned with formal composition and more concerned with suggesting infinite possibilities beyond its borders. It has a slice of life quality (as, of course, is also true of the American short story). We see this as much in the nineteenth century paintings of the Hudson River School as in Abstract expressionists such as Jackson Pollock. Pollock's painting illustrates our theme from another perspective: in swirls of poured paint, the artist has endeavored to capture the essence of movement itself.

Turning to sculpture, the figure most worthy of our attention is, of course, Alexander Calder. Calder has been called "the most American of American sculptors." This is because he is the originator of the mobile, perhaps the most significant innovation in sculpture since its origins. Calder's notion was that sculpture should never be static. Rather, it should move, changing its form with every breath of air and with each environment in which it is placed. A Calder sculpture, thus, is forever becoming, never being. It is, like the items in Kouenhoven's list, process rather than product oriented.

As for architecture, what is most characteristic of America are not the classic structures found in our older towns and cities but suburbia, strip development, drive-in establishments—i.e., architecture created in response to the automobile. Tom Wolfe argues that Las Vegas, with its elongated, car-oriented strip, is the only truly American city, "the Versailles" of America. "Long after Las Vegas' influence as a gambling heaven has gone," he writes,

> Las Vegas' forms and symbols will be influencing American life. That fantastic skyline! Las Vegas' neon sculpture, its fantastic fifteen-story-high display signs, parabolas, boomerangs, rhomboids, trapezoids and all the rest of it, are already the staple design of the American landscape. They are all over every suburb, every subdivision, every highway...every *hamlet,* as it were, the new crossroads, spiraling Servicenter signs. They are the new landmarks of America, the new guideposts, the new way Americans get their bearings.[27]

What characterizes this architecture, Wolfe writes, is its illusion of free form and of movement. While many Americans may decry it, the philosopher-engineer, Buckminster Fuller, creator of the geodisic dome, celebrates it—perhaps from a perspective other than Wolfe's. Fuller's point is that architecture should be only temporarily placed on the land. Just as our planet travels constantly through the heavens, so architecture, Fuller argues, should have the potential for being moved from place to place.[28]

Whether Fuller is right or not, Americans have excelled at a particular kind of architecture which has movement built into it: the mobile home. These homes on wheels may be towed from place to place, and while they are now being copied in other countries, they are American in origin. Only Americans need to have their cake and eat it too by combining luxury and comfort with movability. In some years as much as one-half of all single family housing starts in the United States have been mobile homes.

Mobility has expressed itself in other, almost exclusively American, architectural forms. One of these is the drive-in movie. Although fading now in the United States due to VCRs and other factors, drive-ins have existed virtually nowhere else in the world. Outside Madrid, Spain, for example, is a bizarre sight: a drive-in movie overgrown with trees and vines, mouldering away. It was built by an American who thought he could make a great deal of money with the only drive-in in Spain. He did not reckon on the fact that for Spaniards, despite a large automotive industry and plentiful cinema, watching a film from an automobile is simply inconceivable.

In addition to the drive-in movie, there are a number of drive-in institutions and architectural forms virtually exclusive to the United States. The drive-in bank is one. So are shopping malls, drive-in day care centers, motels, drive-in fast food emporiums, and even drive-in churches, where services are piped into every car and the collection plate is passed by attendants who walk among the rows of parked cars.[29] Finally, there are now even drive-in funeral parlors, where one may view the deceased, propped up in a window, without leaving one's automobile. Only in America.[30]

The Literature of Mobility

Oh public road... you express me better than I express myself.

Walt Whitman.[31]

As with the arts and design, mobility suffuses American literature. Characteristic of our literature is its celebration of movement for its own sake. Protagonists typically crave to get away from the ensnarements of civilization and move towards some mythical free place, usually in the West. In our literature we remain frontiersmen.

This has been true almost from the beginnings of our literature. In James Fennimore Cooper's Leatherstocking series, Natty Bumpo eschews the values of civilization in favor of nature, preferring the forest, wild animals, and American Indians as companions. Like Daniel Boone, Natty Bumpo seeks solitude rather than community.

Henry David Thoreau similarly celebrates aloneness. This is of course true of his classic *Walden*. Elsewhere in his writings, in the essay "Walking,"[32] Thoreau tells us that freedom and the trappings of civilization are incompatible. As if paraphrasing Janis Joplin's famous line, "Freedom's just another word for nothin' left to lose," Thoreau writes:

> If you are ready to leave father and mother, and brother and sister, and wife and child and friends, and never see them again—if you have paid your debts, and made your will, and settled all your affairs, and are a free man, then you are ready for a walk.[33]

Thoreau's strolls were usually in a particular direction. "Eastward," he informs the reader, "I go only by force; westward I go free."[34] Like the pioneers, Thoreau wishes to escape from the East, which he sees as inextricably linked to Europe's traditional culture. "I must walk toward Oregon, and not toward Europe," he writes, for "that way the nation is moving, and. . . mankind progresses from east to west. We go eastward," he continues, "to realize history and study the works of art and literature. . .; we go westward as into the future, with a spirit of enterprise and adventure."[35] The West, Thoreau seems to be saying, is free because it exists outside of history.

Walt Whitman espouses values similar to Thoreau's. Rejecting civilization, he informs the reader in "Song of the Open Road" that he is

> Done with indoor complaints libraries, querulous criticisms
> Strong and content I travel the open road.[36]

In Whitman it is not important where the traveler is going. What is important is to go. The essential thing about the road is not where it may reach, but its function in providing a vehicle for movement. As suggested earlier, the formlessness of *Leaves of Grass* is a rejection of classic European aesthetic values in favor of informal American ones.

A similar set of attitudes pervades Mark Twain's writing, especially his masterpiece *Huckleberry Finn*.[37] Throughout the novel, Huck is conflicted between the dictates of propriety and nature. At the end of the story, though all seems resolved, he nevertheless is preparing "to light out for the Territory."[38] Equally important is the central image of the novel, the Mississippi River. As John Kouenhoven points out, "the real structure of *Huck Finn* has nothing to do with the traditional form of the novel—with exposition, climax, and resolution. Its structure is like that of the great river itself—without beginning and without end."[39] Huck and Jim are so caught up with the river that they pass Cairo, Illinois, where the Ohio joins the Mississippi, cutting off Jim's chance of escape. That they continue floating South anyway, deeper into slave territory, is illogical and can only be explained by the fact that flowing along with the current, no matter where it may lead, represents a form of freedom and, thus, of psychological escape. The real geographical tension in *Huckleberry Finn* is not so much between North and South as between life on the raft (where Huck and Jim always feel "mighty free and easy and comfortable"[40]) and life on the shore, where civilization, with all its pretense and complications (represented best by the Duke and the Dauphin), constantly intrudes.

In the twentieth century, mobility remains a dominant theme in our literature. "Americans are always moving on" is the opening line of Stephen Vincent Benet's epic poem "Western Star."[41] Another example is found in Robert Penn Warren's *All the King's Men.*[42] In this novel, Jack Burden works for the Governor of Louisiana, one Willie Stark, obviously patterned after Huey Long. One day, Burden, oppressed by the weight of everything his name implies—history, civilization, corruption—decides he cannot take it any more and, like Huck Finn, lights out for the West:

> I. . .went down to the bank and drew out some money and got my car out of the garage and packed a bag and was headed out. I was headed out down a long bone-white road, straight as a string and smooth as glass and glittering and wavering in the heat and humming under the tires like a plucked nerve. I was doing seventy-five but I never seemed to catch up with the pool which seemed to be over the road just this side of the horizon. Then, after a while, the sun was in my eyes, for I was driving west. So I pulled the sun screen down and squinted and put the throttle to the floor. And kept on moving west. For West is where we all plan to go some day. It is where you go when the land gives out and old-field pines encroach. It is where you go when you get the letter saying: *Flee, all is discovered.* It is where you go when you look down at the blade in your hand and see the blood on it. It is where you go when you are told that you are a bubble on the tide of empire. It is where you go when you hear that thar's gold in them-thar hills. It is where you go to spend your old age. Or it is just where you go.[43]

Jack Burden's experience in a 1940s novel is reflected in representative novels of the past three decades as well. Much of the 1950s literature of the celebrated Beat Generation is written around the theme of escaping from the troublesome and complicated East into the boundless freedom of the West. We see this especially in Jack Kerouac's *On the Road,* where the narrator, Sal Paradise, sits on an "old brokendown river pier" in New York City sensing "all that raw land that rolls in one unbelievable bulge over to the West Coast. . .all that road going, all the people dreaming in the immensity of it."[44] The characters in *On the Road* race aimlessly back and forth across the country. The central figure, Dean Moriarity, not a little reminiscent of Huck Finn, "is the perfect guy for the road because he actually was born on the road, when his parents were passing through Salt Lake City in 1926, in a jalopy, on their way to Los Angeles."[45]

In the 1960s, probably Tom Wolfe's *The Electric Kool-Aid Acid Test* best illustrates our theme.[46] Wolfe's documentary novel concerns the travels about the country of Ken Kesey and his Merry Pranksters. Purchasing an old school bus dubbed "Further," which they paint in psychedelic colors and fit out as an ambulatory commune, the Pranksters endeavor to go "with the flow, the whole goddamn flow of America."[47] Neal Cassady, Jack Kerouac's friend and the model for Dean Moriarity, is in Wolfe's book as well, still moving, "flipping a small sledge hammer up in the air over and over, always managing to catch the handle on the way down with his arms and legs kicking out the whole time and his shoulders rolling and his head bobbing, all in a jerky beat," still "chasing, or outrunning" life.[48] In Wolfe's book, as in Kerouac's, movement for its own sake is central.

In the 1970s, two books deserve mention. The first is Robert M. Pirsig's *Zen and the Art of Motorcycle Maintenance*.[49] In *Zen* a man and his son travel by motorcycle between Minneapolis and San Francisco, "more to travel than to arrive anywhere."[50] Pirsig's central and characteristically American point is that there is no necessary conflict between the machine and the garden, that automobility is not in conflict with nature.[51] "The Buddha or Godhead," Pirsig writes, resides quite as comfortably in the circuits of a digital computer or the gears of a cycle transmission as he does at the top of a mountain or in the petals of a flower."[52] Pirsig travels by motorcycle because, "On a cycle...you're completely in contact with it all. You're in the scene."[53]

Even more in the scene is Sissy Hankshaw, Tom Robbins' heroine of *Even Cowgirls Get the Blues*,[54] whose exploits are an indication that mobility may hold the same attractions for the modern American woman as it does for the man. Sissy, who was born with giant thumbs, her "guardian angels,"[55] believes that "the road was freedom, and the freest way to ride the road was hitchhiking."[56] Hitchhiking is Sissy's "way of life, a calling to which she was born."[57] "Please don't think me immodest," she informs a doctor endeavoring to change her ways, " but I'm really the best. When my hands are in shape and my timing is right, I'm the best there is, ever was or ever will be." "In the Age of the Automobile," Sissy continues,

> and nothing has shaped our culture like the motor car—there have been many great drivers but only one great passenger. I have hitched and hiked over every state and half the nations, through blizzards and under rainbows, in deserts and in cities, backward and side-ways...I am the spirit and the heart of hitchhiking...And when I am really moving, so clearly, so delicately that even the sex maniacs and the cops can only blink and let me pass, then I embody the rhythms of the universe, I feel what it is like to *be* the universe, I am in a state of grace.[58]

What Sissy celebrates, what she *is*, is pure movement, movement for the sake of movement.

The Future of American Mobility

> Roots? Roots are not modern. That's a peasant conception, soil and roots.
>
> A character in Saul Bellow's *Mr. Sammler's Planet*.[59]

From what we have seen thus far, it appears that mobility is one of the, if not *the*, most salient features of American life. Two questions remain: Is mobility good for America? Will mobility continue to be so important in the United States into the indefinite future?

A number of commentators feel that while mobility may be central to American life, it is also enormously destructive. They sense that often Americans move for the sake of movement and that the quality of their lives suffers as a result. As Fletcher Knebel has written, "We are all part of the unmentionable conspiracy that sacrifices life to locomotion."[60]

Phillip Slater, in his seminal work *The Pursuit of Loneliness*,[61] argues that mobility, as an extension of American individualism, has created a society devoid of community values. Mobility is the means by which Americans escape from intimacy, living in private, encapsulated worlds.

Mobility, other critics feel, undermines the American home. Americans usually prize two possessions, their home and their vehicle. Emphasis given to one usually conflicts with emphasis given to the other. In a stable, traditional society, more emphasis is given to one's home. In a dynamic, changing society, more emphasis is given to one's vehicle. One commentator, speaking of Los Angeles, often regarded as the center of mobile culture in America, says, " 'People here don't buy houses to live in, they buy them to sell.' "[62] As George W. Pierson asks in *The Moving American,* "Have we lost the gift of home?"[63]

The critics of mobility also feel that it is responsible for a society of superficial relationships, a rootless society. In a personal note which precedes his book *A Nation of Strangers,* Vance Packard bemoans the fact that the society into which he was born no longer exists. "To the best of my knowledge," Packard writes, "all my aunts, uncles, and grandparents spent most of their lives within thirty miles of Troy, Pennsylvania." In contrast, Packard continues,

> Today...several of my cousins, my nieces, my brother, and my sister are scattered in many states. The nearest relative to my home in New Canaan, Connecticut, is a niece who lives about a hundred and ten miles away. My two sons live in Wisconsin and Pennsylvania; my mother-in-law, until her recent death, lived much of the time in Florida. I have no idea where my daughter will be living by the time this is published because her husband has just returned from Vietnam to re-establish himself in civilian life.[64]

Packard's family seems to illustrate the line in Carole King's song "Far Away" which goes, "Doesn't anyone stay in one place any more?"

Packard feels that mobility robs us not only of community but of continuity. "We are in danger," he argues, "of becoming a rootless, nomadic people."[65] He describes mobility in the United States as a "chronic" condition which

> deprives people of emotional satisfactions that can only come with a chance to get to know people well. According to a Harvard psychiatrist, people without roots have a hard time developing four kinds of relationships needed for a sense of well being:
> Having a few close friends they can see frequently:
> Having shared concerns with a number of people they know;
> Having people know them well enough to recognize and appreciate their special competencies;
> Having a few people they can depend on in a pinch.[66]

John Steinbeck, in contrast to Packard, questions whether roots are essential to one's well-being. Like Saul Bellow's character quoted in the epigraph heading this part of the essay, he associates roots with traditional and undynamic civilizations. Steinbeck argues that roots may be a concept relatively recent in human history:

> Only when agriculture came into practice—and that's not very long ago in terms of the whole history—did a place achieve meaning and value and permanence...Roots were in ownership of land, in tangible and immovable possessions. In this view we are a restless species with a very short history of roots...Perhaps we have overrated roots as a psychic

need. Maybe the greater the urge, the deeper and more ancient is the need, the will, the hunger to be somewhere else.[67]

According to Steinbeck, rootlessness is not necessarily a new or even a negative condition.

Steinbeck formed these views while traveling about the country in a truck camper. Recreation vehicles are often thought of as embodying an extreme form of rootlessness. At the same time, most Recreation Vehicle Industry advertising stresses the communitarian aspect of friends and families embarking on trips together in vehicle-homes. Brochures from manufacturers suggest that families who travel together stay together because they face challenges on the road as a unit. Recreation vehicle enthusiasts often travel together in caravan, with titles like "Wagonmaster" and "Scout" assigned to leaders and with constant communication by C. B. radio.

Recreation vehicles may, thus, mirror pioneer wagon trains. We usually think of pioneers in wagon trains as rugged individualists. Yet, because of common hazards faced, frontiersmen may have been, per force, much more communitarian than generally acknowledged. It was on the frontier, after all, where community suppers, quilting bees, and neighbor-assisted barn raisings were common. People who live in mobile home parks (and recreation vehicle owners who belong to clubs or attend rallies) often stress the heightened community feeling they experience and which they lacked in suburban towns and cities. Perhaps it is precisely when people are "on the road" that they tend to work together and build community.

This discussion on the positive and negative aspects of mobility may, of course, prove to be academic. In recent years there have been signs that mobility in America may have passed its high water mark, that we may be on the verge of becoming less mobile, of slowing down. First, of course, there is the energy problem, which could cause Americans to be less mobile whether they choose to or not. With the concern over energy, movement for the sake of movement has lost much of its appeal and now seems almost criminal.

An article in *Time* suggests that some Americans, at least, are becoming less mobile. Titled "Mobile Society Puts Down Roots, Young Executives—and their Families—Resist the Nomadic Life,"[68] the article points out that many executives are refusing to move even when it means passing up advancement. A decade ago no more than 10% of executives ever refused assignments to new locations; now one-third to one-half do. As *Time* argues, the old "onward and upward" ethic doesn't work for many any more.[69] Partly this is because women have a heightened sense of themselves as well as careers of their own, which means that men cannot move their families at will. Children, similarly, are now accorded more rights than heretofore. The *Time* article is accompanied by a cartoon showing a man, his wife, their two children, and their dog carrying signs into a corporate personnel office saying "H-LL No We Won't Go."[70] Even corporations, according to one commentator, are beginning "to appreciate the true financial and emotional cost of relocations."[71]

There are other indications that America may be slowing down, becoming a more traditional society or, as some might put it, becoming an older and more mature civilization. If maturity may be defined as recognizing one's limitations, the Viet Nam War taught Americans that they are not the Paul Bunyans of the world, capable of solving all problems everywhere. The decisions not to build the S.S.T. and to proceed more slowly in space exploration are signals of a similar recognition of limitations. The general questioning of suburbanization and the beginnings of a return to the cities of the middle class may suggest an enhanced respect for the values of community. Americans' image of themselves as Huckleberry Finns flowing with the current may be fading, as the realization grows that a society where cooperation, rather than individual initiative, is paramount may be necessary if the United States is to meet the challenges of an increasingly complex world.

But can the United States make such a radical shift in ideology? And will world conditions necessarily demand it? Perhaps we are just in a lull right now and mobility, based on alternative energy sources, will increase in the near future. However it turns out, the power and hegemony of the United States, if not its very survival—associated as they have always been with mobility, and with that great symbol of American mobility, the automobile—will probably hinge on these questions.

Notes

[1]Quoted in George Pierson, *Tocqueville and Beaumont in America* (New York, 1938) 118.

[2]*Sarmiento's Travels in the United States in 1847,* trans. Michael Aaron Rockland (Princeton, 1970) 149.

[3]George W. Pierson, *The Moving American* (New York, 1973) 4, 5.

[4]New York, 1962.

[5]*Ibid,* 93.

[6]*Ibid.* The late General George Patton carried this theme much further in remarks to American troops about to invade Sicily during World War II. Said Patton: "Many of you have in your veins German and Italian blood, but remember that these ancestors of yours so loved freedom that they gave up home and country to cross the ocean in search of liberty. The ancestors of the people we shall kill lacked the courage to make such a sacrifice and continued as slaves." Quoted in Geoffrey Gorer, *The American People: A Study in National Character* (New York, 1964) 23.

[7]Chicago, 1954.

[8]A letter in the July 3, 1978 *Time* magazine (p. 4) comments: "Those of us who have adapted ourselves and our families to this mobile life-style consider ourselves to be latter-day pioneers.

"The strength of the free enterprise system depends upon the availability of people who are willing to accept challenges and responsibilities—the movers and shakers of a complacent society."

[9]From *The Life of Daniel Boone,* author unknown (Dayton, 1856) 26, 27.

[10]*op. cit.*

[11]Might not the Viet Nam War, for example, as well as our quest to be first on the moon (in both cases avoiding problems at home) be thought of, in part, as a logical extension of American escapist mobility?

[12]Published in *The Frontier in American History* (New York, 1920).

[13]*America Adopts the Automobile 1895-1910* (Cambridge, 1970) 2.

[14]New York: Pocket Book edition, 1974.

[15]"Restless America," *Mainliner*, XXI, 5 (May, 1977) 33.

[16]Nor do Europeans think of their automobiles as surrogate homes or make ready associations between automobiles and sexuality.

[17]See Ernest Holsendolph, "Seat-Belt Use Found Highest in Foreign Cars," *New York Times* (December 9, 1977) 1.

[18]In this connection, a recent issue of *National Lampoon* had a painting of American cowboys lassoing and branding a foreign car. See December, 1977, p. 67.

[19]New York, 1929.

[20]William Bronson, "Home Is a Freeway," *Cry California* (Summer, 1966) 8-13.

[21]*The Education of Henry Adams* (New York: Modern Library Edition, 1931) 380.

[22]*Beer Can By the Highway* (Garden City, 1961) 38-73.

[23]*Ibid. 41.*

[24]*Ibid. 42.*

[25]Margie A. Gallagher, "Mobility as Reflected By The Music of the 1970s" (an unpublished paper) 1.

[26]Robert Sklar, *Movie-Made America* (New York, 1975) 103.

[27]*The Kandy-Kolored Tangerine-Flake Streamline Baby* (New York: Pocket Book edition, 1966) xvi, xvii.

[28]*Buckminister Fuller to Children of Earth,* compiled and photographed by Cam Smith (Garden City, 1972) no page numbers.

[29]See George Vecsey, "Preacher Who Pioneered Drive-In Religion Gains Followers With His Upbeat TV Show," *New York Times* (January 31, 1977) 26.

[30]"Drive-Up Funeral Home Gaining Acceptance," *New York Times* (January 31, 1977) 26.

[31]"Song of the Open Road," *Leaves of Grass* (New York: Modern Library edition, 1950) 120.

[32]*The Works of Thoreau,* ed. Henry Seidel Canby (Boston, 1937) 659-86.

[33]*Ibid.* 660.

[34]*Ibid.* 668.

[35]*Ibid.*

[36]*Op. cit.* 118.

[37]*The Adventures of Huckleberry Finn* (Boston: Houghton Mifflin Riverside edition, 1958).

[38]*Ibid.* 245.

[39]*Op. cit.* 62.

[40]*Huckleberry Finn,* 99.

[41]Quoted in Pierson, *The Moving American,* 5.

[42]New York: Bantam edition, 1951.

[43]*Ibid.* 270.

[44](New York: New American Library edition, 1957) 253.

[45]*Ibid.* 5.

[46]New York:Bantam edition, 1969.

[47]*Ibid.* 75, 76.

[48]*Ibid.* 12, 13.

[49]New York: Bantam edition, 1975.

[50]*Ibid.* 5.

[51]The reference is to Leo Marx's *The Machine in the Garden: Technology and the Pastoral Ideal in America* (New York: 1964).

[52]*Op. cit.* 18.

[53]*Ibid.* 4.

[54]New York: Bantam edition, 1977.

[55]*Ibid.* 170.

[56]*Ibid.* 52.

[57]*Ibid.* 12.

[58]*Ibid.* 53, 54.

[59](Greenwhich, Conn: Fawcett Crest edition, 1970), 224.

[60]"Counting The Cars On The New Jersey Turnpike," *New Jersey Monthly, II,* 1 (November, 1977) 34.

[61]Boston, 1970.

[62]A "New York editor" quoted in John Johns, "Nomad's Land," *Mainliner* XXI, 5 (May, 1977) 38.

[63]*Op. cit.* 108.

[64]*Op. cit.* v, vi.

[65]"Restless America," *op. cit.* 68.

[66]*Ibid.* 35.

[67]*Travels With Charlie,* 94.

[68]June 12, 1978, 73, 74.

[69]*Ibid.* 73.

[70]*Ibid.*

[71]Jonathan Miller, "The Power of Positive Moving," *Mainliner,* XXI 5 (May, 1977): 40.

The Changing Image of Workers in Popular Culture

Tom Juravich

The world of work has long been claimed as the turf of the economists, and to a lesser degree the sociologists, who can provide seemingly endless detail on wages, labor markets and their relationship to the business cycle. Yet no matter how elaborate these statistical analyses, they have never been able to compete with the short stories of Jack London in the early 1900s, the photographs of Walker Evans during the 1930s, or the songs on the country and western charts of the 1950s in their portrayal of the American worker.

But examination of these images in popular culture is more than a recognition of how powerful they have been in expressing the reality of working Americans. For, as the cultural theorists back to Max Weber would remind us, these images have in turn shaped the experience of work and the societal image of workers. Analysis of popular images of workers in the past century shows us not only how the experience of workers has changed, but how our overall conception of workers and work—what they are as symbols—has as well been transformed.

The Emergence of the American Worker

The development of a class of American workers was inextricably bound to the industrial revolution in the first part of the century that allowed for a centralization of production. With this concentration of production came a segmentation and de-skilling of tasks that demanded vast numbers of unskilled workers.

It was in this context that some of the earliest popular images of workers emerged. Many of the early images, especially those in the "polite" press portrayed workers as part of the immigrant hordes. Typical were images like the one expressed by George Baer, president of the Reading Railroad. When asked if he thought the young children working in his mines suffered he responded, "Suffer, why these kids can't even speak English."

But an alternative to this view developed as part of the "muckraking" tradition of Jacob Riis and Lincoln Steffans. Although hardly a mass image, it was an early social realism that anticipated what would become a more universal aesthetic in the 1930s.[1] Upton Sinclair's *The Jungle,* first published in 1905, was among the first popular characterizations of workers in mass industry.

> Trimming beef off the bones by the hundred weight, while standing up from early morning till late at night, with heavy boot on and the floor always damp and full of puddles, liable to be thrown out of work indefinitely because of a slacking in the trade, liable again to be kept overtime in rush seasons, and to be worked till she trembled in every nerve and lost her grip on her slicing knife, and gave herself a poisoned wound.[2]

These early popular images saw workers as victims of a new form of production. But *The Jungle* is not just a sociological expose of working conditions in the meatpacking industry. Much of the novel focuses on how the production system reverberated throughout the rest of society, as the main character Jurgis is not only exploited by his bosses but by the landlords, the house swindlers and the furniture salesmen. Although the term "socialist realism" is often narrowly used to refer to a later state controlled Soviet art, many of these early accounts of workers were clearly in the American socialist tradition, which as a political movement was flourishing during this time.[3]

Jack London, a contemporary of Sinclair, best known for his nature and adventure stories like "Call of the Wild" and "To Build a Fire," was even more overtly political. In the preface to his 1905 *War of the Classes,* a series of essays about contemporary social problems including his autobiographical "How I Became a Socialist" London suggested that "...it is the hope of the writer that the socialist studies in this volume may in some slight degree enlighten a few capitalist minds."[4] *The Iron Heel* (1907) a novel set in the future, in many ways prophesied the rise of fascism, but it is *The Valley of the Moon* (1913) that best represented this early socialist image of workers.

Not unlike Jurgis in *The Jungle,* Billy in *Valley of the Moon* is the naive worker exploited by bosses, co-workers and landlords alike. Yet like London himself, through a dogged regimen of self study he discovers the socialism that sets him free. Although faced with trials and tribulations along the way, he and his mate Saxon arrive at their worker's paradise, "the valley of the moon"—a pastoral garden.

This image of workers confronting early capitalism was not just expressed by literary figures like London and Sinclair, but by the major workers' organization that emerged during this period, the Industrial Workers of the World (IWW). Although rooted in the socialist and anarchist movements, the Wobblies, as they were known, represented an independent and uniquely American radicalism.

Unlike the craft unionism of the American Federation of Labor (AFL) founded earlier in 1881, the IWW sought no working contract with the employers, but rather advocated abolishing the wage system through direct action by workers. This was a simple class ideology which lent itself well to popular images. Perhaps more than any other labor organization in American history, the IWW was extremely successful in expressing its ideology in popular forms through cartoons, posters and songs.[5]

Reminiscent of Nast's depiction of Boss Tweed, the IWW's capitalist was portrayed as a rotund, cigar smoking, top-hatted exploiter often crushing workers or feasting on their blood. But the images also pictured the power of workers when organized into what the IWW called the "one big union." Although considerably harsher, they had much in common with the images in *The New Masses,* a well known magazine of the left at the time.[6]

The starkness of the Wobblies ideology found expression in their songs, which often consisted of new words written to the popular songs of the day. "Solidarity Forever," written by Ralph Chaplin to the tune of "The Battle Hymn of the Republic", is still considered the anthem of the labor movement. It originally contained verses like,

Is there aught we hold in common
With the greedy parasites?
That would lash us into serfdom
And would crush us with their might?
Is there anything left for us
But to organize and fight?
For the union makes us strong.

The IWW reached its pinnacle in 1912 after winning a strike in Lawrence, Massachusetts. It then lost a bitter struggle in Patterson, although an interesting footnote of the strike was the massive workers' pageants of songs and theater that were held to build public support and raise money. But with a growing nationalism and in part because of the IWW's opposition to WWI, the IWW came under strong government intervention in 1917 and 1918. The organization was ultimately dismantled by the ransacking of offices, the jailing of some officials and the deportation of others.

In many ways the destruction of the IWW marked the end of an era and the end of this early socialist view of the worker, an image that still exists in many European countries. Just as leaders of the IWW were deported, the worker in this political context was deported too—given over to the Soviets as a symbol, never again to return to American culture.

Rediscovering the Forgotten Worker

The 1920s was not an era of workers as dominant symbols. In fact, workers almost disappeared altogether from popular view in this era of flappers and high rollers. As F. Scott Fitzgerald discovered, it was the rich and not the poor that captured the imagination of the decade. Yet it was hardly an era of prosperity and once the stock market crashed, the poor could be ignored no longer.

Perhaps more than any other single period in American history, the 1930s produced an aesthetic unity with the development of what has been termed "social realism." As Shapiro argues, "So strong was its lure [social realism], so true to the realities of life did it seem, that its assumptions influenced an entire generation of artists."[7]

But it was not just a period of aesthetic unity but it was a time in which art, literature and music, in part because of this unity, flourished. It was also in large measure due to government support of the arts through the Federal Writers Project, the Farm Security Administration and numerous other New Deal projects. Murals were painted in Post Offices and other public building, thousands of older Americans were interviewed, many thousands of photographs were taken and scores of posters were designed and printed.

It is difficult to appreciate the wealth of cultural materials that were produced during this period, many of them still uncataloged to date. But in keeping with the central tenants of social realism, it was not just art about the masses, but for the masses and there were great efforts to make this work accessible to everyday Americans.

One could envision a variety of "social realisms" that could have developed as a consequence of hard times, but a constellation of social and political forces came together to forge a form of realism in art, music and literature we now associate with the 1930s. As in the socialist realism of the first part of the century, there was no shortage of victims in the popular culture of the 1930s. The dust bowl ballads of Woody Guthrie and the photographs of Dorthea Lange, for example, chronicled these victims in the tenements, in the jungle camps or on the road. As the popular song by Harburg and Gorney suggested,

> Once I built a railroad, I made it run,
> I made it run against time.
> Once I built a railroad, now its done,
> Brother can you spare a dime.

But no matter how stark the images, how horrific the circumstances, there was a fundamental dignity and optimism in these images. Discussing the documentary photographers of the 1930s, Peeler suggests, "What they discovered was that Americans bore their trials with apparent dignity and courage, which to the photographers seemed reassuring evidence of an emotional stability somewhere beneath the decade's confusion."[8]

Although there was also a certain kind of optimism in the songs and cartoons of the IWW, the optimism of this era had a quite different genesis. The hope of the 1930s was less the overthrow of capitalism reflected in the early socialist realism, but in many ways the rationalization of capitalism. "Despite the real suffering that Americans endured because of the Great Depression, the belief grew than an energetic and expanding government could work for the individual and the local community to alleviate misery, restore political faith, and improve the very structure of society."[9]

Roosevelt's New Deal saw a number of pieces like "The Chislers's Sorrow," celebrating this new sense of fairness,

> We've counted on Franklin to give us a break.
> Our lives and our money was all at stake.
> Come all you good people and stand up like men,
> And over these chislers a victory will win.[10]

The 1930s were clearly not an apolitical time, but in a certain sense it was a time of political unity. Even the Communist Party, during what is referred to as the popular front, fell in step with the social reformers and the business unionists who they had long opposed.

Workers played a fundamental role in this vision of rebuilding and are a dominant symbol throughout much of the 1930s. The image here is less that of the worker as the militant socialist, but more as the responsible citizen, who is loyal, hard working and energetic in exchange for fair treatment. In this context one can't help but recall the arrival of the Joad family in Steinbeck's *The Grapes of Wrath* at the government supervised camp. Although hardly the "valley of the moon," this was the 1930s version of a worker's paradise.

Trade unionism in the 1930s adopted a similar rhetoric quite distinct from the IWW. The Congress of Industrial Organizations (CIO), formed in the 1930s in opposition to the business unionism of the AFL, inherited much from the IWW. Like the IWW it was interested in organizing the unskilled workers in the mass industries, for example.

Nevertheless, the CIO grew in a very different social and political context. During the era of the IWW, unions were not only unacceptable but illegal. The CIO, however, matured during a time when, due to the passage of the National Recovery Acts and similar legislation, trade unionism was not only legal but encouraged. FDR himself was quoted as saying that if he were a working man that he would join a union.

This hardly meant that trade unionism was accepted throughout the business community without a struggle. Indeed some of the most bitter battles between labor and management were waged during this period, some of them finely recorded by the photographers, songwriters and journalists of the 1930s.

Although this was at times a militant trade unionism, its goal was not the abolition of the wage system, but collective bargaining.

> Collective Bargaining in our shops, C-I-C-I-O.
> And in our shops it makes us strong, C-I-C-I-O.[11]

With its new found ally of the U.S. government, both in law and in spirit, a modus operandi between labor and management was for the first time possible, if not always probable. In this sense not only was the image of workers changing, but even workers' organizations were becoming palatable in the American scene, beginning the process that would continue in the next decades of the normalization of the American worker.

The Normalization of the American Worker

The populism of the 1930s was in part reinforced by the War years, both through the experience of the soldier and with austerity measures on the home front. But the populism of poverty soon became the populism of prosperity, at least as portrayed by the films, photographs and the new form of popular culture, the television.

Through the war experience, we had become a world industrial power, and the worker was seen no longer downtrodden and alienated but as an integral part of this new industrial order. In the popular image the government supervised labor camp had become the tract house bought under the G.I. bill. We were an industrial society, one that depended on the industrial worker.

Although there were intense labor-management battles immediately after the War, the labor movement too had become mainstreamed as part of the War experience. The CIO's acceptance of a no-strike pledge and participation in the War Relations Board brought in huge numbers of new members, but also had the effect of discouraging rank and file militancy and shoring up labors' institutional partnership with business and government. As Kim Moody suggests, "...the major features of labor-capital relations as they were to be practiced for the next three and a half decades were well into place by the end of World War Two..."[12]

The growing tide of McCarthyism purged any remaining vestiges of socialist influence and further softened the rhetoric of the CIO, allowing for the merger of the AFL and CIO, once arch enemies. Although union membership increased and labor continued to be successful in securing improved contracts for its members, the image of the labor movement had become less an advocate for workers' rights and social change and more of a traditional social institution. This began the process by which labor was ultimately characterized as "just another special interest group" during the 1984 Presidential election.

This transformation was apparent in the decline of labor culture within the trade union movement. The labor songs and theater which had flourished during the 1930s were gone as a bureaucratic institutional unionism prevailed.

What is particularly interesting about this period however is that work became so normalized and so routine that it played a very minor role in popular culture. For example, although Ralph Crandon in "The Honeymooners" or Anne Southern in "Private Secretary" were workers, it is surprising how little their work was involved in their character. Although "The Honeymooners" depicted working class life, it did not address their worklife. Ralph would occasionally bring home some aggravation from the job, but it was so minor that he could have had another job or no job at all.

To a large extent this was the beginning of what Harvey Swados called "the Myth of the Happy Worker,"[13] of which Ralph Crandon may be the best example. Here was the worker portrayed as not too smart, and often simple minded, who overall was pretty happy about the world he lived in, or at least he was not smart enough to realize that it might not be great. So the worker as citizen of the new deal became the "Joe six-pack" of the 1950s and 60s.

This became even more heightened in the 1960s when the worker and unions who had only a generation ago had been such a major force in generating change were now perceived, especially by the youth, as part of the establishment. Thus the image of the "Hard-hat" and Archie Bunker became the dominant image of the worker.

Work and people at work, however, were not entirely absent from popular culture. In fact, throughout the century workers and work itself have often been used to provide drama in a variety of cultural forms. But in earlier times this drama was often connected to some political struggle as in *The Jungle* or *The Grapes of Wrath*.

The 1950s saw the emergence of the rough and tumble "working man" unconnected to larger issues. Often portrayed as the loner or the marginal man, his work was often dangerous. Tom Joad had been replaced by Marlin Brando who single-handedly was going to clean up the waterfront. Or as Tennessee Ernie Ford sang in "16 Tons"

> If you see me coming you'd better step aside,
> Another man didn't and another man died.

You load 16 tons and what do you get,
Another day older and deeper in debt.

It was still a song about the struggles of workers, but gone were the "greedy parasites" or the power of the union or the contract, replaced by a single struggling hero, who continues to be a mainstay of country music to the present.[14]

Wither the Worker in Popular Culture?

As we have seen, the images of worker and workers' organizations have changed dramatically through the century. Through the New Deal, workers became integral to American society and labor unions became a permanent institution in American life.

But our economy has changed significantly in the past two decades, with an increasing concentration of capital by multinational corporations, rising imports and new areas of employment. Millions of American workers are employed in relatively low paid jobs with little chance of advancement in the service sector, and millions of Americans continue to work in basic industry not unlike a generation ago.

Yet they are very much ignored in contemporary popular culture which focuses on executive work, computers and high technology, when it focuses on work at all. The workers and unions which became normalized in the post war era, have in a sense almost become trivialized as we approach the 1990s. If the 1930s and 40s were a era of labor, the 1980s clearly became an era of business. Workers, manual work and unions are seen only in their relationship to the past and are clearly not part of the fast track in the pursuit of excellence.

A culture of clerical and service work has been developing in a struggling labor movement, and a few muckrakers have been writing about the difficulties of the work in the 1990s. But to a large extent we have come full circle in terms of our image of workers and workers' organizations. As in the first part of the century or the 1920s, workers are strikingly absent from our contemporary popular culture. Only history will tell how much of the cycle we are destined to repeat.

Notes

[1]For the most comprehensive anthology of the period see, Upton Sinclair (ed), *The Cry of Justice* (New York: The John C. Winstin Company, 1915).

[2]Upton Sinclair, *The Jungle* (New York: Grosset & Dunlap, 1905) 41.

[3]James Weinstein. *The Decline of Socialism in America* (New York: Monthly Review Press, 1967).

[4]Jack London. *The War of the Classes* (New York: The Regent Press, 1905).

[5]Joyce Kornbluh, *Rebel Voices: An I.W.W. Anthology* (Ann Arbor: The University of Michigan Press, 1964).

[6]Rebecca Zurier, *Art for the Masses: A Radical Magazine and Its Graphics, 1911-1917* (Philadelphia: Temple University Press, 1988).

[7]David Shapiro, *Social Realism: Art as a Weapon* (New York: Frederick Unger, 1973) p. 4.

[8]David P. Peeler. *Hope Among Us Yet: Social Criticism and Social Solace in Depression America* (Athens: The University of Georgia Press, 1987) 59-60.

[9]Marlene Park and Gerald E. Markowitz, *Democratic Vistas: Post Offices and Public Art in the New Deal* (Philadelphia: Temple University Press, 1984) 3.

[10]"The Chislers Sorrow," *Hard Hitting Song For Hard Hit People* ed. Lomax, Gurthrie and Seeger (New York: Oak Publication, 1967) 188.

[11]"Collective Bargaining Our Shops," *Hard Hitting Song For Hard Hit People* ed. Lomax, Gurthrie and Seeger (New York: Oak Publication, 1967) 248.

[12]Kim Moody, *An Injury To All: The Decline of American Unionism* (London: Verso, 1988) 248.

[13]Harvey Swados, "The Myth of the Happy Worker," *The Nation,* (Vol 185, 1957): 65-69.

[14]Tom Juravich, "Workers and Unions in Country Music," *Labor Studies Journal* (Vol 13, summer 1988): 51-60.

Symbols of Ethnicity and Popular Culture

John G. Cawelti

Throughout the nineteenth and twentieth centuries American popular culture has been deeply and continuously involved with issues of ethnicity and race to a far greater degree than what has become known as classic American literature. Indeed, one could almost say that the more popular the medium or genre, the more intense the involvement. While the nineteenth century novel tends to ignore ethnic groups and racial minorities except as picturesque background to the trials and triumphs of white protestant heroes and heroines, the theater, vaudeville, the minstrel show and popular humor are intricately expressive of the presence of ethnic and racial groups in American culture. Not only does the content of these popular forms manifest much more of the diversity of cultural groups in America than the more respectable artistic traditions of American culture, it is in the popular arts that members of ethnic and racial minorities have found access to audiences, the opportunity to display their talents and the chance to become rich and famous.[1]

The richness and the importance of the contribution of ethnic and racial minorities to American popular culture is unique. Here, more than in any other area of American life, much more so than in the realms of business and social life, the ideal of the melting pot came closest to reality. It is in popular theater and similar areas that we find the first relatively sympathetic and complex characterizations of ethnic and racial groups, while some of the first instances of ethnic and racial integration can be found in the world of the popular performer in drama, the mass media, music and sports. Many ethnic Americans have found in the world of popular culture a route to the success denied them in other spheres of American culture.

This is the positive side. American popular culture has also been instrumental in the persistence of negative stereotypes of racial and ethnic subcultures. Though it is difficult to assess the degree to which the drunken Irishmen, grasping Jews and childish Afro-Americans portrayed in popular media are a symptom or a cause of prejudice, they are nonetheless there in full measure. In addition, though popular culture has exploited ethnic materials and assimilated immigrant performers and producers, its primary symbolism of American life until after World War II was a homogeneous picture of WASP supremacy with the ethic and racial characters presented largely as intruders. This seems now to be changing quite drastically, but until recently this aspect of popular culture was symbolized by the fascination of Louis B. Mayer, Jewish movie tycoon, with the Andy Hardy pictures and their idealization of small town protestant life in America.

There is, then, a paradox at the root of the relationship between popular culture and race and ethnicity in America. On the one hand, popular culture seems more open both to the representation of ethnic experience and to members of ethnic and racial groups than the official culture, but, on the other hand, it has preserved some of the most negative aspects of American culture's response to its minority groups. In this paper, I will explore some of the factors involved in this paradox, first by discussing some of the special characteristics of American popular culture which shaped ethnic involvement, then by discussing some of the different functions which ethnic representations played in the popular arts, and finally, by commenting on some of the significant changes of recent years in the treatment of race and ethnicity in popular culture.

I

Two related structural characteristics of American popular culture are its high degree of commercialization and its broad accessibility. Though popular culture everywhere tends toward commercialism, several features of the American situation intensified the importance of profitability in the production and distribution of popular culture. For one thing, the relative ambiguity of the class structure in the United States, particularly when it came to matters of taste, encouraged cultural entrepreneurs to direct their products to the widest and most diverse audience possible, rather than, as in other countries, concentrating their attention on particular classes or segments of the public. In nineteenth century England, for example, distinctions in entertainment were drawn along class lines to a degree that never appeared in America. Of course, many respectable nineteenth century Americans rarely attended the theater, but this was more a matter of religious and moral taboos than of class prejudice. Since class ideologies and tastes were less significant in the development of the popular arts in America, profitability became a dominant concern. The greatest profit lay in attracting the largest and most diverse audiences, and cultural entrepreneurs quickly learned how to tailor their product for an audience of many different cultural and class backgrounds. By the 1870s, the ethnic diversity of major urban centers, particularly New York City, had made ethnic groups a significant part of the audience for popular theatricals. The great success of ethnic performers like Harrigan and Hart indicated that ethnic materials could draw a large and diverse audience to the theater. Even earlier than this, the popularity of minstrel shows, Tom shows and stereotypical ethnic characters in comic theater had already paved the way for the extensive use of such materials in later nineteenth century theater and vaudeville.

Regional stereotypes in earlier American popular culture may well have been a precedent for the later development of ethnic characters. As early as 1787 in Royall Tyler's play *The Contrast* the figure of the stage Yankee had been introduced. Throughout the first half of the nineteenth century, a procession of Yankee peddlers, Southern rapscallions, and Western hell-raisers made their way across America through the pages of numerous periodicals.[2] Characters like Sam Slick, Jack Downing, Simon Suggs, Sut Lovingood, Davy Crockett, and Mike Fink, embodied what were thought to be the distinctive characteristics of different regional subcultures. They presented to the American public the image of diverse cultural styles. In addition, these regional stereotypes often displayed an ambivalent mixture of positive and negative characteristics not unlike those later ascribed to such ethnic stereotypes as the brawling Irishman, the Jewish mother, and the Italian gangster.

The commercialism of American popular culture also emphasized the development of new media and methods of distribution. The use of new methods gave a certain advantage to cultural entrepreneurs and creators who were not bound by traditional modes of cultural production. In addition, because the popular arts were considered morally and religiously suspect by many members of the established cultural elite, members of these groups did not commonly seek a career in the production of the popular arts. Therefore, members of ethnic groups had a freer access to popular culture than to other kinds of careers. Bright and inventive entrepreneurs from ethnic backgrounds would have been effectively barred from successful careers in such traditionally respectable enterprises like banking or manufacturing, but found the popular arts more open. First the Irish and then Eastern European Jews moved into popular culture on a large scale so that while the popular New York theater in the later nineteenth century was dominated by Irishmen like Bouccicault and Harrigan, the early twentieth century movies quickly became a fiefdom of Eastern European Jews like Selznick, Mayer, Goldwyn and Lasky.

Because of the imperatives of mass distribution, popular culture became increasingly centralized and urban-oriented. Even in the mid-nineteenth century, when America was still both demographically and ideologically centered in the small town and rural areas, the major media of popular culture—travelling theater troupes, story and sporting periodicals, minstrel shows—were organized and dispatched from the cities into the hinterlands. Because the larger cities had more concentrated ethnic populations, there was, first of all, a greater likelihood for members of these groups to drift into the theatrical and other popular cultural professions, a trend intensified by the prejudice against ethnic Americans in so many other areas. Moreover, since most popular productions were first put on in major cities, the presence of a potential audience made the introduction of ethnic materials a profitable thing. Both of these factors were evident in the later nineteenth century development of popular theater and made the increasing importance of Irish performers and producers a notable feature of popular culture. From the 1870s on, men like Dion Bouccicault, Edward Harrigan and George M. Cohan introduced Irish themes, settings, songs and characters. Their success was mirrored in other areas such as newspaper humor culminating in the great success of Finley Peter Dunne's "Mr. Dooley." Large cities were also centers of constant tension between ethnic groups, and this, too found expression in the interplay and rivalry between ethnic stereotypes in popular theater and vaudeville.

II

Another important factor in the relationship between ethnic groups and American popular culture was the impact on the immigrants themselves of the cultural uprooting which accompanied the journey from Europe to America. While most immigrants tried to bring their customs, traditions, and institutions along with them, the arrival in America created wholly new cultural situations for most of them.[3] People who had been rural peasants in the old country found themselves becoming urban factory laborers in the New World. Men who had been farmers became businessmen; laborers became clerks. People accustomed to the isolated homogeneous life of a small village were suddenly thrust into the midst of chaotic cultural diversity. The force of culture shock must have been great and the strength of traditional cultural institutions like the church, the extended family, or the village community inevitably weakened, particularly as the second generation sought greater assimilation into the new country. The decline of traditional institutions and the rebellion of young people against the attempt to impose traditional customs created a particularly tense situation in difficult areas like courtship. Rejecting the rigidity of Old World codes regulating relations between the sexes, younger members of ethnic groups found a different and more flexible mode of encounter and courtship in conjunction with popular amusements like the theater and the new amusement parks. John Kasson insightfully describes the way in which Coney Island offered a new kind of courtship institution for ethnic young people:

> Though traces of class and ethnic backgrounds still clung to Coney Island's amusement seekers, in arriving at the resort they crossed a critical threshold, entering a world apart from ordinary life, prevailing social structures and positions...Sidewalks, public parks, dance halls and amusement parks offered opportunities to meet and enjoy the company of the opposite sex away from familial scrutiny. At Coney Island in particular, unattached young men and women easily struck up acquaintanceships for the day or evening. According to Coney Island folklore, some couples even married on the spot. The freedom of anonymity together with the holiday atmosphere of the resort encouraged intimacy and an easing of inhibitions and permitted couples to display their affection in public. (41-42)

In this way, popular culture was a very important educational and ideological influence on American ethnic groups. The increasingly large scale spectator entertainments, sports and places of amusement brought members from different ethnic groups into more or less peaceful contact with each other;[4] they also inculcated a new ethic of personal enjoyment and fun which could be shared by people of diverse religious and social backgrounds. This new ethic not only permitted, but encouraged and rewarded the pursuit of individual pleasures and the delights of consumption. It stressed the more immediate and ephemeral gratification of needs for relaxation and escape as opposed to self-denial, saving to carry out future responsibilities and the long-term pursuit of religious salvation.

III

The amusement park, the dance hall, the circus, the Wild West show and other forms of late nineteenth and early twentieth century mass entertainment offered to ethnic Americans not only a temporary release from cares, but the chance to try on new roles and aspirations. For these entertainments created worlds of fantasy and encouraged various modes of participation in these worlds ranging from the vicarious enjoyment of the Wild West to direct involvement in the artifice of luxury, glamor and eroticism generated by the amusement park and the dance hall. Because these palaces of mass entertainment were places of fantasy different from the burdensome realities of urban world, they became modes of transition between ethnic tradition and newer styles of behavior and morality. The amusement park created a frame in which experimentation with looser and more playful modes of action, with more open expressions of sexuality and affection, and with impulsive spending and various forms of gambling became possible. In such environments associations between people of different social levels and backgrounds could take place without completely subverting or overturning the religious and social traditions of different ethnic groups. In frequenting the institutions of popular culture, younger persons from immigrant backgrounds learned how to live in different worlds, to play a variety of roles, and to try out new forms of belief and behavior.

The new ethic of pleasure and consumption fostered by the popular amusements which grew so rapidly in the late nineteenth century was in some ways as strongly subversive of traditional American Protestant values as it was of the customs of immigrant groups. Because it stressed spending rather than saving, pleasure rather than self-discipline, and release and relaxation rather than the pursuit of salvation, the new ethic of popular culture encouraged young Protestants into a similar cultural rebellion against the mores and tastes of an older generation. Thus, through the medium of popular culture, the phenomenon of generational conflict, so characteristic of twentieth century American culture was both created and expressed. The bonds of common experience and attitude which participation in popular amusements gradually began to forge between native Protestant and immigrant young people, did not, of course, immediately eclipse the deep feelings of ethnic hostility and prejudice felt by most Americans. Yet, insofar as participation in the institutions of mass amusement encouraged younger Americans to leave their ethnic identities behind and try out new patterns of casual association with members of other groups, popular culture functioned to create new forms of self-reference, particularly in identifying with a distinctive age-group.

Twentieth century popular culture has continued to intensify the phenomenon of age-grouping, especially in the area of popular music. Three trends were involved in this development. The first was the development of technologies of broadcasting and recording which made possible the mass national distribution of popular music. Gradually, the recorded performance of a particular song replaced the local group of musicians as the primary method of transmission of popular music. This led to a second phenomenon, the rapid and regular changing of fashions and fads for particular songs, musical styles and performers. These two trends came together with the generational phenomenon in twentieth century American culture, because of the particularly intense relationship between individual and popular music during the years of courtship, a pattern probably related to the central role that institutions like the dance hall and the amusement park had come to play as a frame for the development of erotic relationships between young people. From the 1930s on, the development of broadcasting and recording imprinted each successive generation with its own repertoire of song, styles, and performers, creating a linkage between members of a particular generation which has increasingly transcended the boundaries of class, ethnic group and, in recent years, even that of race. The tremendous generational impact of performers like Frank Sinatra, Elvis Presley, the Beatles, and the Rolling

Stones, and the way in which dedication to such performers and their style of music became a rallying point and focus of identification for a generation illustrates popular culture's ability to subvert traditional social patterns and to foster the development of new cultural groupings and attitudes.

Another popular cultural institution, mass spectator sports, was also very important in diffusing traditional ethnic identities and creating new patterns of association. An afternoon at the ball park was, like a visit to an amusement park, an entrance into a different world where traditional identities and current anxieties could be momentarily left behind while the individual blended into the larger mass of spectators. At highly climactic moments, the individual self could be absorbed into the collective concern for the fortunes of the home team. During a baseball game or a horse race, the individual is partly swallowed up onto the mass, his or her single voice absorbed into the hum and roar of the crowd and the individual gesture of excitement swept up into a mass ballet of motion. In such situations, the individual member of an ethnic group could sense a new kind of belonging, a participation in collective entities which transcended the limits of neighborhood and subculture. In addition, the powerful loyalty which so many sports fans gave to their favorite teams indoctrinated immigrants in the idea of new centers of loyalty and identification. To become a Yankee, a Giant, or a Dodger fan, a status available to anyone willing to attend an occasional game or even to follow the team through newspaper reporting and later, through radio and television, offered ethnic Americans a sense of participation in the mainstream of American culture. This sense of belonging was further intensified when members of ethnic groups or minorities became leading sports heroes. Generally, mass spectator sports played a role for members of ethnic communities similar to that ascribed by Albert F. McLean to American vaudeville:

> Vaudeville took over a function of the historical church: through its inculcation of the people with some sense of common humanity, a feeling for community which transcended the boundaries created by ethnic origins, specialization and the impersonalism of urban life. (217)

Popular culture, then, was a positive factor in the process of adjustment and adaptation to American culture which confronted immigrant groups. The entertainment and sports organizations of popular culture were more open to talented members of immigrant groups than many other social and economic institutions, providing access to wealth, status, and celebrity for particularly gifted (and lucky) members of minority groups. Popular theater and vaudeville provided a kind of education and indoctrination in American values and attitudes for immigrant publics, while popular places of entertainment, such as dance halls and amusement parks, introduced ethnic Americans to new life styles and ethical ideas, helped create new patterns of courtship and association among the young, and, to some extent, took the place of traditional institutions and customs which were not readily adaptable to the new social circumstances. Other forms of popular culture, in particular the increasingly important mass spectator sports generated new objects of personal and group loyalty and helped create new patterns of community within the large urban centers. Finally, many forms of popular culture stimulated new kinds of self-identification and awareness, most significantly in the creation of generational identities and conflicts which crossed subcultural lines. Whether one judges the end result of these various processes to be good or bad, they all worked in the direction of easing the immigrant's adjustment to a new way of life.

IV

However, like most other areas of American culture, popular entertainment's relation to ethnic and racial minorities was deeply divided and ambiguous. What it offered with one hand, it took away with the other. While more open to ethnic and racial groups than most areas, the same patterns of prejudice and segregation characteristic of the culture as a whole also dominated popular amusements.

In spite of the fact that the minstrel show was one of the primary genres of nineteenth century entertainment, this form not only perpetuated negative stereotypes of black American characters, but offered few opportunities for black performers. Even the Tom shows, which derived from Mrs. Stowe's powerful indictment of the oppression of black people in America, were more often than not performed by white actors in blackface. Irish music and comic stereotypes had long been a staple of American popular entertainment, but it was not until the 1880s that Irish performers and cultural entrepreneurs began to break into the popular theater in large numbers. Yiddish theater was a thriving ethnic tradition in New York City throughout most of the later nineteenth and early twentieth centuries.[5] However, Jewish entrepreneurs moved into powerful positions in popular culture only in the twentieth century with the new technologies of film, radio and television. Only in the 1930s were Jewish performers widely accepted in media like radio and the movies. The difficulties faced by black producers, directors, and performers as they struggled to make their way in the film industry has been carefully documented by Thomas Cripps in his excellent chronicle, *Slow Fade to Black*. It was not until after World War II that talented performers and entrepreneurs from the whole range of American minorities and ethnic groups found access to positions of power and importance in popular culture increasingly open.

Perhaps the most destructive aspect of popular culture's relation to ethnicity was its tendency to develop and perpetuate negative stereotypes of racial and ethnic minorities. These stereotypes reflected attitudes toward such groups, but also helped to shape prejudices on the part of many people whose awareness of ethnic groups was largely mediated through the images of popular culture. Negative stereotypes such as the shiftless Negro, the drunken Irishman, the greedy Jew and the sinister Oriental maintained and justified the cultural ascendancy of the white Protestant majority by characterizing other groups as morally, psychologically and culturally inferior. These images not only supported the majority's self-esteem they also intensified minority group member's sense of insecurity and inferiority. Philip Roth's Alexander Portnoy speaks bitterly of his childhood fascination with the white Protestant children he constantly encountered on the radio, in comic books and in movies:

The kids whose neighbors aren't the Silversteins and the Landaus, but Fibber McGee and Molly and Ozzie and Harriet, and Ethel and Albert and Lorenzo Jones and his wife Belle, and Jack Armstrong! Jack Armstrong, the All-American Guy!—and Jack as in John, not Jack as in Jake, like my father—Look, we ate our meals with that radio blaring away right through to the dessert, the glow of the yellow station band is the last light I see each night before sleep—so don't tell me we're just as good as anybody else, don't tell me we're Americans just like they are. No, no, these blond-haired Christians are the legitimate residents and owners of this place, and they can pump any song they want into the streets and no one is going to stop them either. (16)[6]

Many stereotypical images of ethic and racial character not only asserted the inferiority of minority groups, but, in addition, served as projective fantasies for modes of behavior Protestant mores condemned, but which many individuals yearned to indulge in. By projecting this behavior onto ethnic or racial stereotypes, it was possible to give a vicarious expression to forbidden impulses and, at the same time, to dissociate oneself from them. This is probably one reason why the minstrel show enjoyed such a long term popularity not only as professional but as amateur entertainment. Manic exuberance, comic eccentricity, and clownish larking were expressions of the carnival spirit deeply needed in a country as religions and serious in its surface mores as Protestant America. Thus, in the minstrel show, the desire for the liminal experience of carnival was projected onto stereotypical black characters. Burnt cork came to symbolize a kind of license.[7] The power of this symbolism is evident not only in the wide popularity of the minstrel show and of its various Irish analogues such as Harrigan's Mulligan Guards series, but also in the impact of blackface on individual performers. Donning the black persona released a powerful energy in the performances of white entertainers, and, ironically, sometimes had a similar effect on black performers. Robert Toll points out that:

Blackface—a comic mask that minstrel endmen wore even when the rest of the companies shunned it—liberated Bert Williams the (black) comedian, as it had many others, both black and white. "Then I began to find myself," he recalled of the first time he blacked up. "It was not until I was able to see myself as another person that my sense of humor developed." As "clown white" did for some performers, the black mask allowed Williams to act differently than he otherwise could have. But Williams was not just another clown. He was a black man wearing a black mask, a mask that had come to symbolize the stereotyped, simpleminded black fool, a symbol of racial inferiority in race-conscious America. The mask liberated Williams as an entertainer, but it stifled him as a man. (123)[8]

The complex mixture of fascination and repulsion embodied in such projective stereotypes has been a dominant element in the portrayal of such groups as Afro-Americans, the Irish, Jews, and Native Americans in popular culture. Such uses of stereotypes reinforced the fear and hostility which so often characterized relationships between white Protestants and ethnic and racial minorities.

V

In spite of these destructive stereotypes, which have persisted in many ways, the basic tendency of popular culture, particularly in recent years, has been toward a more positive and sympathetic treatment of ethnic and minority subcultures, as well as an increasingly broader acceptance of performers and producers from these groups. This has included, as well, a growing appreciation of the actual subcultural styles created by these groups, as opposed to the earlier popularity of more artificial, white-mediated popular genres like the minstrel show. Several different trends of the last two decades are part of this general pattern.

First, throughout much of the nineteenth century, the artistic styles created by ethnic and minority groups were not taken over and transformed by white performers. That is, not only were black and ethnic performers discriminated against, but the original styles of their creations were altered to conform to the expectations of white audiences. This is most obvious in the area of popular music. Jazz was primarily the creation of black performers, but it did not gain wide popularity with the white public until it was taken up by white bands like Gene Goldkette and Paul Whiteman in the 1920s. Throughout the 1930s and 1940s it was the big bands, largely directed by white leaders like Benny Goodman, Glenn Miller, Harry James, Tommy Dorsey, and Artie Shaw, that were most popular among white audiences. Though these bandleaders were, on the whole, much less racially prejudiced than their fans, and inclined to use black talent, like the great arranger Fletcher Henderson, in unobtrusive ways, the great white and black jazz musicians rarely played together in public until the famous Carnegie Hall concert of 1938 which brought together members of the Benny Goodman and Count Basie bands. During this period a few great black swing bands, most notably those of Count Basie and Duke Ellington, began to be successful with white audiences.[9] By the 1950s, the intermixing of white and black musicians in both swing and jazz was increasingly accepted.

However, the transformation of jazz and the blues into white-styled swing left many talented black musicians and enthusiastic black audiences out in the cold and there developed among these largely black circles a new musical style, "Rhythm and Blues," which had a distinctively different style from traditional jazz and swing. R and B was entirely created by black musicians and was recorded on so-called "race" labels, sold largely in black areas of the major cities. Again, as in the case of jazz, R and B was gradually discovered by more adventurous white musicians and audiences and eventually transformed, primarily through the impact of Elvis Presley and other white musicians, into Rock and Roll. But this time, the transformation was far closer to the spirit of the black original and as Rock and Roll developed, there was more and more interplay between black and white musicians and audiences. The broad success of Motown records, a label which specialized in developing black performers like Diana Ross and the Supremes along stylistic lines that would be successful with both black and white audiences, became increasingly the wave of the future. Today, the complex spectrum of popular music manifests a continual interplay between white and black performers, and new stylistic ideas are likely to be picked up developed by both black and white performers, regardless of the ideas' origins. Good examples of this can be seen in the rapid spread of the rap style of music, which emerged from a black tradition, but which was very quickly picked up by white performers of all sorts. Not only in music, but in dance, the same pattern increasingly obtains as with the black style of break-and dirty-dancing, quickly adapted by white dancers and then recreated by other black dancers.

A similar development has taken place in the area of comedy. For a considerable period, the more profane and "dozens"-centered style of black comedy featured by such traditional black performers as Redd Foxx and Moms Mabley, was known to white audiences only through a few rebellious white comics, most notably Lenny Bruce. In recent years, however, Redd Foxx has developed a large white following through his more sanitized work in the television series *Sanford and Son,* where, even though the more overt profanity of Foxx's nightclub performances has been cleaned up, the funky rascality of his comic persona still shines through. Moreover, younger black comedians, like the tremendously popular Eddie Murphy have made the public accept and even cherish some of the roughest aspects of the black comic tradition, while Bill Cosby has become one of the most successful (and wealthy) performers of our time by his adaptation of essentially white traditions of situation comedy and family to a black setting.

The second trend also seems to relate to a more positive attitude toward ethnic and minority groups. This is the development of more positive stereotypes and even of attempts to present for the mass public more complex and realistic portrayals of the life and histories of racial and ethnic minorities. Positive stereotypes like the heroic black detective, the warmhearted Jewish mother, and the witty and irreverent Irishman have flourished in recent films and televisions series. The culture of the Cheyenne Indians was treated with considerable depth and sympathy in Arthur Berger's *Little Big Man* and the film adaptation by Arthur Penn. Mario Puzo's *The Godfather* along with the enormously successful Coppola films based on it, have, in spite of perpetuating a stereotypical association between Italian-Americans and organized crime, offered a very positive and striking picture of some aspects of Italian-American culture. Michael Cimino's film of *The Deerhunter* made the members of a working-class ethnic community into a moving symbol of the perplexities of America in the Vietnam Era. And Alex Haley's television mini-series *Roots* showed that black families had histories and a heritage as strong and significant as that of whites.

These novels, films, and television series are one expression of a broader trend in recent American culture toward a reaffirmation of cultural pluralism, of ethnic identity and distinctiveness, a tendency that has been evident in such diverse phenomena of the Black Power and Black Aesthetic movements of the 1960s and in what Michael Novak has characterized as "the rise of the unmeltable ethnics."[10] These new ideologies of ethnic and racial separatism and identity seem, on the surface, to be a final repudiation of the "melting pot" ideal of assimilation of minorities. Indeed, recent sociological and historical studies have shown that despite changing levels of income and status, many members of minority groups have tried very hard to hold to traditional subcultural patterns. But the new more positive ideologies of ethnic separatism may be, in the American context, more subversive of ethnic traditions than one might expect. It is typical of American life that when one group claims to have a special quality of its own, other groups will hasten to imitate and adopt some portion of that groups' values and cultural patterns. In the nineteenth century, it was the dominant white Protestant majority that claimed to have the mission of defining what was most valuable in American life. But, in recent years, representatives of ethnic and racial subcultures have become increasingly important in popular culture and the arts, and as spokespersons for American values. If this trend continues, we may well see an increasing decline in the cultural authority of non-ethnic Americans as the American middle class becomes fascinated by ethnicity and seeks to adopt some of the patterns and attitudes characteristic of ethnic and racial minorities.[11]

This third trend is already apparent in the area of food and entertainment with more and more Americans experimenting with different culinary traditions, and attending "heritage weekends" and other festivals and ceremonies which spring from ethnic traditions. The complex relationship of ethnicity and American popular culture may well be entering a new phase in which the distinctive identities of ethnic communities become an object of emulation and a source of positive values. If this happens, the paradoxical result may be a further attenuation of the very cultural distinctiveness on which an ethnic or racial identity is based.

On March 17 of every year, rain or shine, sun or sleet, the city of Chicago holds its annual St. Patrick's Day Parade. On this day, the Chicago river, already a bilious olive drab, is dyed a bright Kelly green. Some say this is by the application of an orange dye, but I cannot vouch for that. The St. Patrick's Day Parade was once an assertion of the ethnic pride of Irish-Americans, and it was a major Chicago event both because of the city's large Irish-American population, and because, since the end of the nineteenth century, its politics was dominated by Irish-American leaders. However, in recent years, the parade has become a celebration of all ethnic and racial groups in the city. One will see blacks dressed as leprechauns, and Polish-Americans wearing T-shirts stenciled "Kiss me, I'm Irish!" There are likely to be floats representing in some way the heritage of nearly all the city's numerous ethnic groups, Jews, Poles, Lithuanians, Ukrainians, Serbians, Mexicans, Germans, and Italians as well as the Irish. It has become a sort of United Nations parade, a symbolic testament to cultural pluralism. To me, this parade is deeply representative of the contemporary relationship between ethnicity and American popular culture, but whether it foreshadows a renewed affirmation of ethnic subcultures or an attenuation of ethnicity as a force in American life, only the future can reveal.

Notes

[1]A few examples will demonstrate the point. While William Dean Howells did write one novel about an octoroon, race is otherwise largely absent from his work and ethnicity appears only in such portraits as that of Dryfoos and Lindau in *A Hazard of New Fortunes*. Race is completely absent from Henry James and ethnicity is present only in his ominous fulminations about the decline of the lower East Side in *The American Scene*. Melville did do a brilliant parable of racism in *Benito Cereno* and there are men of different races aboard the Pequod, but this is his only treatment of the issue; Hawthorne has almost nothing to say about race or ethnicity. Cooper creates some comical black stereotypes, but has no significant Irish, Jewish, or German characters. The stock comical Irishman appears as an incompetent servant in Brackenridge's *Modern Chivalry*, but there is certainly no treatment of Irish-American culture. Even in the early part of the twentieth century, only Southern literature has much to say about race. Though F. Scott Fitzgerald was an Irish-American, there is nothing about ethnicity except perhaps implicitly in the

unfinished *The Last Tycoon.* Race appears only in the silly apocalyptic racism of Tom Buchanan in *The Great Gatsby.*

[2]These developments are chronicled in Rourke, *American Humor,* Blair, *Native American Humor,* and Blair and Hill, *America's Humor.*

[3]It is interesting to compare the situation of nineteenth century Eastern European immigrants with that of the 1980s, which have brought large numbers of Asian and South and Central American immigrants to the United States. Indications are, however, that the culture shock of America is, ironically, much less for Asian immigrants, partly because American popular culture has had such a world-wide influence that immigrants are already somewhat familiar with some of its basic patterns.

[4]This was much less the case with racial encounters in places of popular entertainment, where forms of segregation continued to be the case until a much later period.

[5]See Irving Howe's superb evocation of New York's Yiddish culture in *World of Our Fathers.*

[6]From Philip Roth, *Portnoy's Complaint* (1969).

[7]Mikhail Bakhtin's *Rabelais and His World* (1965) discusses the significance of carnival as an aspect of life and literature. On liminality and carnival see the work of Victor Turner, especially *Dramas, Fields and Metaphors* (1974).

[8]Robert Toll, *On With the Show* (1976). Apparently white audiences would not allow black performers in minstrel shows to appear without blackface for a considerable period of time.

[9]For example, a recording survives from 1940 when Duke Ellington played a concert in Fargo, ND, for a very enthusiastic and largely white audience. Basie and Ellington both toured extensively in the 1940s playing for increasingly mixed, though still predominantly white audiences.

[10]Michael Novak, *The Rise of the Unmeltable Ethnics* (1972). For black power and the black aesthetic see, Robert Lee Scott, The Rhetoric of Black Power (1969) and Addison Gayle, The Black Aesthetic (1971). Werner Sollors, *Beyond Ethnicity* (1986) is a very interesting treatment of the whole issue of ethnicity in American culture.

[11]Cr. Norman Mailer's famous conception of the "white negro."

Works Cited

Bakhtin, Mikhail. *Rabelais and His World.* Cambridge, MA: M.I.T. Press, 1968.

Blair, Walter, and Hamlin Hill. *America's Humor.* New York: Oxford University Press, 1978.

Blair, Walter. *Native American Humor.* San Francisco: Chandler, 1960.

Cripps, Thomas. *Slow Fade to Black: The Negro in American Film, 1900-1942.* New York: Oxford University Press, 1977.

Gayle, Addison. *The Black Aesthetic.* Garden City, NY: Doubleday, 1971.

Howe, Irving. *World of Our Fathers.* New York: Simon and Schuster, 1976.

Kasson, John. *Amusing the Millions: Coney Island at the Turn of the Century.* New York: Hill and Wang, 1978.

McLean, Albert F. *American Vaudeville as Ritual.* Lexington, KY: University of Kentucky Press, 1965.

Novak, Michael. *The Rise of the Unmeltable Ethnics.*

Roth, Philip. *Portnoy's Complaint.* New York: Random House, 1969.

Rourke, Constance. *American Humor: A Study of the National Character.* Tallahassee: Florida State University Press, 1986.

Scott, Robert Lee. *The Rhetoric of Black Power.* New York: Harper and Row, 1969.

Sollors, Werner. *Beyond Ethnicity: Consent and Descent in American Culture.* New York: Oxford University Press, 1976.

Toll, Robert. *On With the Show: The First Century of Show Business in America.* New York: Oxford University Press, 1976.

Turner, Victor. *The Forest of Symbols: Aspects of Ndembu Ritual.* Ithica, NY: Cornell University Press, 1967.

Turner, Victor. *Dramas, Fields and Metaphors: Symbolic Action in Human Society.* Ithaca, NY: Cornell University Press, 1974.

Regionalism and Popular Culture: From Social Force to Symbolism

John G. Cawelti[1]

Before there was a United States of America, there were thirteen more or less independent colonies whose squabbling was bitter enough that it was something of a miracle that they were ever able to unite. Only mutual animosity toward the British and the way in which groups of colonies were linked by common religious attitudes, cultural patterns, economic interests and eventually dialects and lifestyles made the development of a union finally possible. This linkage was regionalism, and the ties between colonies of common attitudes and interests eventually developed into the three major regional cultures of New England, the middle colonies, and the South, to which was soon added that hopelessly vague and ever shifting region known as the West, from the beginning, perhaps, more symbol than geographical place. In time, the West itself became regionalized to a certain extent as areas like the Midwest, the old and new Southwests, the Great Plains, the Pacific Northwest, and California began to develop somewhat distinctive cultures. In addition, the older regions had many subregional cultures with distinctive qualities of their own. Professor J. A. Bryant, Jr. tells me that once "Kentucky alone had four or five [subregions]; Tennessee, at least three; North Carolina, three also; Virginia, more than any of these and so on."

Of course, these American regional characteristics never approached the differences between the countries and regions of Europe, Africa and Asia which were embodied in differences of language, religion, history and culture. There are still regional cultures in such larger nations as the Soviet Union, China, India, and in certain smaller ones such as Nigeria, Zaire, and Yugoslavia that exhibit far greater differences than were ever the case in America. Though some New Englanders once tried to secede from the Union, it was only part of the South that ever seriously tried to break its ties to the rest of the country. There were too many centralizing and nationalizing tendencies in the United States for any region to become permanently established as a distinctive culture.

Interestingly, some of the most effective concepts of region in America have emerged not from the people's awareness of their own cultures but from the hindsight of folklorists, historians, social engineers, and politicians. The concept of Appalachia, for instance, would probably have been meaningless to nineteenth century Americans, at the very time when the distinctive culture of that region was at its strongest. Appalachia was really the creation of twentieth century scholars and social engineers, particularly those associated with the New Deal, who sought not only to preserve dying traditions, but to break up what was left of the "solid South" as a regional political bloc. The Tennessee Valley Authority may well have had more to do with the emergence of Appalachia as a regional culture than the common interests and traditions of certain residents of Pennsylvania, Virginia, West Virginia, Kentucky, Tennessee, and Georgia. But in the twentieth century Appalachia has become a great success, with a flowering of crafts, literature, and music developed through folkloric research and fostered by a variety of interests who hope to develop tourism and the sale of arts and crafts as a stimulus to the desperately precarious economy of the region.[2] The fact that Appalachia has so widely "caught on" as an American regional culture is an indication of the importance of regionalism as a symbol, if not an actual social and political force, in twentieth century American popular culture.[3] That is essentially the subject of these reflections.

Another dynamic of American life has always existed in a complex dialectic with geographic regionalism. Ethnicity and race have also been significantly productive of distinctive subcultures in the United States. Sometimes these subcultures have reinforced regionalism, as in the case of the black slave subculture in the South or the Jewish subculture in New York City, but more often ethnic and racial subcultures have tended to displace the distinctiveness of regional subcultures by providing a different ground for cultural differentiation. One might even argue that, in certain ways, race and ethnicity have become the most important contemporary source of cultural distinctions in America. Certainly if one looks to the scholarship in history and sociology, studies in race, ethnicity and gender presently far outnumber studies in regional history and culture, a nation totally different from the late nineteenth and early twentieth centuries when, under the influence of Frederick Jackson Turner, regional and frontier studies were the dominant school of American historical research.[4]

Paradoxically, the increasing importance of ethnicity and race was, in part, a result of the nationalizing of the American consciousness. The muting of regional differences and antipathies in the later nineteenth century depended on a new kind of Americanism. This new American "nativism" was a response to the fear that the black demand for equality after the Civil War and the concurrent influx of non-English speaking non-Protestant immigrants would corrupt American civilization. This fear was common among those whose families had originated in the British Isles of Western Europe and who now came to think of themselves as "Native Americans," a phrase which came to have a drastically different meaning in the mid-twentieth century. This new kind of Native Americanism began in the 1880s and reached its climax in the 1920s and 1930s with immigration restriction, prohibition, the perpetuation of Jim Crowism in the South, the renaissance of the Ku Klux Klan as a national movement and the rise of the isolationist "America First" movement.[5]

These widely popular movements had their somewhat more benign counterparts in intellectual circles in such movements as Southern agrarianism or in the highly popular regional histories of American literature to which Van Wyck Brooks and others turned in the same period.[6] Actually, these trends foreshadowed the end of regionalism as a significant factor in American culture by insisting more on race and ethnicity as the decisive factors. In a sense, the judgment of the Ku Klux Klan was ratified by the revisionist historians who began, in the 1950s, to attack the dominance of Turner's frontier theory. After two world wars in which men and women from every part of the United States found themselves thrown together in war and in war production, it seemed clear that, by the 1950s, regionalism was ceasing to be a major force in American life.

Another development affecting this situation was the enormous transformation wrought by technology in the twentieth century and particularly after World War II. Technology not only increased the mobility of Americans, thereby breaking down any remaining geographical barriers, it also led to a growing standardization of the American landscape, and through mass communications, to an increasing homogenization of the American mind. Even more significantly, technology made it possible for Americans to recreate essentially the same life styles anywhere in the country, whatever the local climate, topography or flora and fauna. Air conditioning and refrigeration bit deeply into whatever remained of a distinctive architecture, cuisine and pattern of living in areas like the deep South and the Southwest. The creation of homes and places of business with artificial climates no longer made the long hot summer of these areas restrict where people could live and what they could do. In the form of the housing development, the North Central Standard lifestyle has become the rule from Maine to California and from Florida to California.

Yet, the decline of regionalism as a social and cultural influence has certainly not ended the significance of regions in the imaginations and symbolic networks of Americans. Instead, a complex form of regional symbolism, derived from patterns of culture and qualities of character and attitude once associated with the different regions, has become a major source of myths, images, and symbols in American popular culture. Once actual geographical places and subculture, the great American regions have become part of a landscape of the imagination. Here, their characteristics have become more fixed and standardized since they are no longer expressions of the interplay of living subcultures. Though, as we shall see, these patterns of regional symbolism still manifest a considerable hold over the American imagination, attempts to revitalize regional traditions through the process we shall describe as reregionalizing, are probably doomed in the long run to failure. Though these parks and historical reconstructions are a highly desirable variation in the increasingly standardized American landscape, they can only exist as artificial enclaves against the disintegration and levelling of cultures all across the genuine mosaic that America used to be.[7]

II

American regional symbolism is most fundamentally structured around the tripartite division of North, South and West, though there are some contexts in which the bipartite divisions of East and West, North and South and city and country are also significant. Though the ascribed geographical boundaries of these regions have shifted considerably since the first beginnings of regional symbolism in the colonial period, the basic characteristics supposed to be embodied in the major regions have remained remarkably constant.[8] Within these major divisions, there have been subdivisions which have frequently shifted both in boundaries and in ascribed characteristics: in the North we have New England vs. the middle colonies and later the Midwest; the South is sometimes divided into areas such as the Deep South or Dixie, the middle South, the Old Dominion, and, more recently Appalachia; the West has such geographical divisions as the Great Plains, the Southwest, the Rocky Mountains and California, as well as a shifting series of historical places indicated by such terms as "The Old West," "The Wild West" and "The Frontier." Once, for example, anything a few miles from the Atlantic coast was the West. Now, in some contexts, the West begins only at the Rocky Mountains, or occasionally, at the California border.

Regional symbolism is articulated and expressed in a number of different ways. There are styles of dress and architecture, characteristic activities and tastes in food and drink associated with the different regions. Drinking a mint julep on a pillared porch while watching the cotton grow has never, to my knowledge, been associated with New England. The eating of roast turkey to celebrate Thanksgiving is done all over the country, but it is particularly associated with New England as the Pilgrim costumes and decorations associated with the turkey would indicate. But the most important expression of regional symbolism is through a cast of archetypal figures connected with each region. This symbolic cast seems to have evolved first through the emergence of a representative figure like the Pilgrim for New England or the Cavalier for the South. Frequently, this usually positive figure seems to have evolved in tandem with or to have in some way evoked a negative antitype, standing for the less desirable qualities associated with the region. Thus, the heroic Pilgrim, figure of the persecuted minority seeking freedom and asylum in the New World, relates to an antitype, the repressive Puritan who seeks to control everybody's morals and to make others into the gloomy and frustrated character he symbolizes. In addition, all three major regions seem to have become connected with archetypal characters who are outsiders. The nature of the alienation represented by these outsiders is a key factor in defining the symbolic significance of each region. The North, for example, is symbolized by the Pilgrim (positive) and the Puritan (negative); the good housewife (positive) and the bluestocking (negative). The most significant outsider figure in this symbology seems to be the witch. For the South, the archetypal cast consists of the Cavalier or Southern gentleman (positive) and the lazy poor white rogue (negative), the benevolent plantation mistress (positive) and the flirtatious belle (negative). The black slave is, of course, the outsider in this system. In the West we find the pioneer frontiersman (positive) and the outlaw (negative), the schoolmarm (positive) and the dance-hall girl (negative), with the Native American and the Mexican being the outsiders.

The relationships and transformations between these figures can become quite complex. One of the best ways to create a highly popular fictional character is to link positive and negative archetypes together creating a tension that generates excitement and interest. In *Gone With the Wind,* that great anthology of Southern regional symbolism, Margaret Mitchell linked the Southern gentleman and the rogue to create the irresistible figure of Rhett Butler. She also very effectively transformed the negative image of the flirtatious belle into the heroine of her novel, Scarlett O'Hara. The modern Western hero frequently links the opposed figures of the pioneer and the outlaw. Other sorts of transformation can also be effective. One can shift insiders with outsiders, as in stories of Indian captivity from the seventeenth century down to Thomas Berger's *Little Big Man.* One can even join different regional archetypes to generate a new figure as Owen Wister did with the Southern gentleman and the Western outlaw to create the very popular protagonist of *The Virginian.*

These archetypal casts of regional characters exemplify the qualities, themes, and significances symbolically associated with the major regions. The North embodies such traits as solidity, respectability, success and, to some extent, rectitude; the South is particularly associated with warmth, sensuality, and the interesting combination of down-home goodness and country values with a certain decadence and corruption.[9] The West is particularly characterized by simplicity, honesty, originality and adventure. There is a wide variety of specific characteristics that can from time to time be associated with any particular region, but anything that strays too far from the accepted, relatively fixed complex of regional themes risks losing the symbolic power of a regional identification. This becomes particularly significant when someone is trying to sell a product or to elect a candidate.

III

The persistence of regional symbolism is hardly surprising since it has a high recognition value and is connected to strong emotional attachments to childhood or to the feeling of nostalgia still associated by many Americans with the places and patterns of culture symbolic of the traditional regions. Because of this potency, regional symbolism can and has been exploited for a variety of purposes. To look at these various functions seems to be the best way to understand the contemporary significance of symbolic regionalism in American popular culture.

The commercial use of regional symbols was perhaps the earliest and most pervasive to develop. Its use in creating recognizable and attractive brand names for advertising is the simplest and most basic level on which regional symbolism has operated. In general, the archetypal casts or regional characters discussed above are used in brand names and images to signal the good and positive qualities supposedly possessed by a product. The range of positive qualities connected with the symbolic figures belonging to different regions are evoked by typical names and images. One can see from the products involved something about the range of qualities commonly associated with different regions. New England is most often associated with tradition and high-minded idealism, though there is also a set of symbols relating to rural wit and cracker-barrel philosophizing of the Yankee variety. A good example of New England symbolism is an advertisement I saw recently for a new housing development called The Bradford Colony. Whoever named this group of condominiums and townhouses was clearly trying to send the potential buyer a message that by buying a Bradford condo one was getting a form of housing so solid and traditional that it could be associated with the Pilgrims. The South is connected more frequently with sensuous pleasures, with warmth, affection and down-home goodness. Foodstuffs are the commodity most often connected with Southern regional archetypes—Aunt Jemima pancakes, Col. Sanders Kentucky Fried Chicken, Dixie Donuts. The West represents adventure, potency and good health. One of the longstanding connections is that between the American Indian and medicinal remedies, which at one time included tobacco. Because of his closeness to nature and his mysterious tribal wisdom, the Indian became the symbolic guarantor of the potency and healing power of innumerable patent medicines, and, as cigar store Indian, of the flavor and goodness of tobacco products. This tradition has come down to the present in the icon of the Marlboro man who connects the qualities of the West and cigarette smoking. This dweller in "God's country" associates cigarettes with daring and adventure, but also, ironically, with good health and clean living.

There are many such ironies in the commercial exploitation of regional symbolism, most notably in the way a fast food chain like Kentucky Fried Chicken dresses itself in regional symbolism, but actually has been a force in the standardization of the American diet and the elimination of regional differences in food. As early as the beginning of the twentieth century, a gifted observer like Stephen Crane noticed how regional symbolism was being thoroughly commercialized and then returned to the region as items of food and dress, just as, today, western ranch-hands like to model themselves on the cowboys they see in the movies:

> A man in a maroon coloured flannel shirt, which had been produced for purposes of decoration and made principally by some Jewish women on the East Side of New York, rounded a corner and walked into the middle of the main street of Yellow Sky....And his boots had red tops with gilded imprints, of the kind beloved in winter by little sledding boys on the hillsides of New England.[10]

The political exploitation of regional symbolism has also been extremely important in American history. The most important pattern of political symbolism is that of the Western hero storming the bastions of Eastern moral corruption and political incompetence. This pattern of symbolism was adumbrated at the very beginning of two party American politics by Thomas Jefferson in his Republican campaign against Federalist John Adams. Its first major triumph was the election of Andrew Jackson. Soon, however, the same pattern was turned against the Democrats by the Whigs in the campaign of 1840. Possibly inspired by Davy Crockett's Whiggish use of the role of Western hero, William Henry Harrison and his advisers created the first modern political campaign complete with pervasive media usage and a totally artificial symbolism: the aristocratic Harrison was dramatized as a simple log-cabin and hard-cider Western hero opposed to the supposedly aristocratic (though actually plebeian) Easterner Martin Van Buren.[11]

From 1840 to the present, the political symbolism of the Man of the West has been a recurrent feature of presidential campaigns. Lincoln used it quite brilliantly in 1860 as the railsplitter candidate, taking some of his symbolism directly from the log cabin campaign of 1840. Theodore Roosevelt, an archetypal Eastern patrician, so effectively made himself over into a Western hero through his western ranch and hunting trips, writings, such as *The Winning of the West,* and his rough rider regiment in the Spanish-American War that Mark Hanna is supposed to remarked after the assassination of William McKinley, "My God! Now that damned cowboy will be president."

William Jennings Bryan tried unsuccessfully to exploit his actual Great Plains heritage, but he may have misunderstood the significance of Western symbolism by making himself more a symbol of farmers and laborers than a cowboy hero.[12] Others in the twentieth century, including Truman, Eisenhower, and Reagan have all enacted versions of the corrupt East- honest West symbolism. Reagan has somehow managed the symbolic miracle of remaining the simple, honest, Western outsider in corrupt Washington, in spite of his Illinois birth, his involvement in the movie industry and his many years in Washington.

Other regional symbols have been important in politics such as New England rectitude (Calvin Coolidge), middle colony affability and sophistication (Grover Cleveland, Franklin Delano Roosevelt) and Southern geniality, but these are more difficult political roles and fewer have mastered them successfully on the national level. The Man of the West paradigm continues to be the dominant political symbolism and even such a complete New Englander as John Fitzgerald Kennedy found it effective to adopt an updated version of the rhetoric of the frontier.

IV

A third important use of regional symbolism in American popular culture is in Mass Entertainment, which has always needed effective, easily recognizable stereotypes and formulas. Regional symbolism has been an important source of such patterns. First of all, there are major popular genres associated with the major regions: the Western and its many variants; the nostalgic historical romance particularly connected with the South; the Our Town story which tends to use either New England or the Middle West as setting; and the various sagas of the city ranging from such sensational and minatory fictions as George Lippard's *The Quaker City or the Monks of Monk's Hall* to modern day gangster sagas.

In the eighteenth and nineteenth centuries when regional cultures were still developing, regional symbolism was a vital element in many areas of American literature and popular culture ranging from fiction and the drama to popular humor. Indeed, it was in humor particularly that such distinctive regional characters as the New England Yankee, the Western frontiersman and the Southern rogue and gambler peopled the pages of popular "sporting" papers like the *Spirit of the Times*.[13] In drama and in fiction, heroic counterparts to these essentially comic figures developed such as the Western pioneer and the Southern cavalier.[14] Later in the nineteenth century as Americans began to feel that regional subcultures were being eroded, a kind of story known as "local color" became very popular, but the rise of local color was already an indication of the declining significance of regional traditions, since most of these stories treated regional dialects and cultural traditions with a nostalgic regret as phenomena that were already threatened by social and cultural changes.

In the twentieth century, one major sign of the decline of regional cultures was the rise of ethnic and racial stereotypes as primary sources of American humor. By the 1920s, ethnicity and race were much more important aspects of American humor than regional characters and traditions.[15] Since humor is both the most immediate and the most volatile form of cultural expression, the increasing dominance of racial and ethnic themes in comedy seems another indication of the decline of regional traditions as major shaping influences on twentieth century American culture.

However, regional symbolism continued to be a vital part of mass entertainment, particularly in the more historically oriented and "serious" forms of popular drama, fiction, and music such as the Western, the historical romance, country and Western music, and the story of the quest for "roots." The complex symbolism associated with the West, for example, remained a major source of material for popular literature, movies and television series down to the 1980s. The history and structure of the literary and cinematic genre known as the "Western" has been sufficiently studied that there is no need to go into it in detail here.[16] However, in addition to the traditional Western with its opposition of pioneers and Indians or outlaws, its heroic figure divided between oncoming civilization and the wilderness, and its landscape of adventure, a number of additional genres have made effective use of the basic Western symbolism. One of these is the story which reverses the usual movement from East to West by having a Westerner come to the East and employ his special moral qualities and his willingness to go beyond the law against the more sophisticated villains of the urban East. We have already commented on the political rhetoric which exploits this symbolism. Many novels and films use this political pattern, the most famous being Frank Capra's *Mr. Smith Goes to Washington.* In addition, a successful genre has developed around the situation of the Western lawman coming to the Eastern city. Clint Eastwood's *Coogan's Bluff* was an early example and it inspired a television series, *McCloud* which ran for several years.[17] In addition to its tremendous importance in twentieth century popular culture, the position of East and West has been important in mainstream fiction as well. *The Great Gatsby* developed a brilliantly complex and ironic treatment of the myth of the West which Fitzgerald worked into an expression of the tragic failure of the American dream.

In the 1970s and 1980s there was a significant shift in the use of the symbolism of the West away from the idea of the West as a region or a space to the West as symbolizing racial and sexual conflict. In a novel such as Thomas Berger's *Little Big Man,* which was made into a successful film by Arthur Penn, the clash between Native American and white cultures became far more important than the idea of the West as a moral space or region. In still other novels and films, the portrayal of the West as a flawed macho culture, or as an anachronism in the modern world, has become more typical. These trends suggest that the traditional symbolism of the West no longer has the hold on the American public that it once had, and that new symbolic structures are needed to take the place once occupied by the West.[18]

The symbolism of the South has also inspired a number of different popular literary genres, to say nothing of the complex area of country-and-Western music which, despite its somewhat misleading name, is dominated by Southern associations both in style and in content. The two most important literary genres employing Southern symbolism have, in fact, developed out of the two major Southern symbolic characters: the dashing cavalier and the poor white rogue. Two of the greatest literary successes of the century, Margaret Mitchell's *Gone With the Wind* and Erskine Caldwell's *Tobacco Road* exemplify these basic genres. The historical romance of the Civil War and Reconstruction developed in the later nineteenth century out of the nostalgic ante-bellum romances of writers like Thomas Nelson Page and of William Faulkner's great-grandfather whose *The White Rose of Memphis* was a considerable success. But the genre first became tremendously popular around the turn of the century in works like Thomas Dixon's *The Clansman* (number 4 best seller in 1905) and its film adaptation by D. W. Griffith, *The Birth of A Nation* (1914). Presumably the heroic romance's popularity had something to do with the way in which the First World War made Americans look back on their own Civil War, but it is significant, and probably an ironic tribute to the strength of racism in America that the South was largely able to co-opt the heroism and romance of the Civil War and Reconstruction. The continued success of this genre during the 1920s inspired Margaret Mitchell to embark on her great success which helped to fix the symbolism of the South in the minds of more than one generation.

Tobacco Road exemplified the comedy and decadence which was the negative counterpart to the heroism and romance of the cavalier South. Perhaps because of the South's peculiar status in the regional hierarchy, it was possible to portray on a popular level the neurotic decadence and salacious sleaze which were, on the symbolic level, the dark side of Southern aristocracy and down-home warmth. Even before Caldwell's great success with *Tobacco Road* (1932) and *God's Little Acre* (1933) William Faulkner thought that the way to write a best-selling novel about the South was to stress the violence, perversion, and decadence with which he laced his intended pot-boiler, *Sanctuary* (written in 1929). As Jack Kirby points out in *Media-Made Dixie,* This decadent image of the South persisted into the 1950s and 1960s:

> By the late fifties the typical southern film was a Hollywood version of stories or plays by Faulkner, Caldwell, or Tennessee Williams. Most of these movies were very good box office and critical successes. Blacks again had few roles, either as individuals or as preoccupations of whites. Whites appear as bigger-than-life characters preoccupied with each other. They are frequently perverse, but usually in ways somehow to be envied by movie goers. The South was so *interesting;* it became chic. Except for the Irish and the Jews, perhaps, other white minorities were hopelessly bland in comparison with these silver-screen rustics, parvenus, decadent gentry, nymphomaniacs, neurotics and psychopaths. Passion flourishes in the same steamy earth as tobacco and cotton. (p. 106)

Though a very important influence of popular fiction in the nineteenth century, New England has not been as important in twentieth century popular culture as the South and the West. In fact, the successful television series associated with New England have depended heavily on the outsider figure of the witch and its counterparts, the ghost and the vampire.[19] Perhaps this was because of the image of rectitude and decency and its negative counterpart of Puritanical repression which tended to generate a certain blandness, as Kirby suggests. In many ways, the Middle West inherited the symbolic patterns associated with New England, adding one very important additional element.[20] While the setting of the Midwestern symbolic tradition was the decent, god-fearing small town or village, the Midwestern story almost always added an additional element of a quest for escape. This was already evident in the later nineteenth century in such varied works as Twain's *Huckleberry Finn,* where the hoped for escape was into the "territory," in the Horatio Alger series, whose protagonist left the country to seek success in the city, and in Baum's *The Wizard of Oz* in which the heroine fled repressive Kansas for an imaginary land of fantasy. The symbolic connection of the Middle West with New England is also illustrated in the Oz books by the importance of witches.

From the village exiles of Sherwood Anderson and Sinclair Lewis to the Iowans and Oklahomans fleeing to California in West's *The Day of the Locust* and Steinbeck's *The Grapes of Wrath* the quest for escape from a seemingly decent but actually repressive small town remained the most vital element in the novels, movies, and plays based on the symbolic patterns associated with the Middle West. However, after World War II, a strange development took place. In the 1950s with the explosive growth of television, the Our Town story was transplanted from the Middle West to California. This transformation was foreshadowed in the 1930s and 1940s by radio programs and movies like *One Man's Family* and the Andy Hardy series, but this development reached its peak in the family situation comedies of the 1950s and 1960s such as *Father Knows Best, My Three Sons, Leave it to Beaver,* and the *Ozzie and Harriet Show*. Since, as Nathaniel West pointed out, California was the end of the line, the escape theme could no longer be used as it had been to add an element of conflict and excitement to the bland repressiveness of Our Town. Instead, many of the most successful family comedies began to treat themes of gender conflict, either directly as in *I Love Lucy,* or more indirectly in such one-parent families as that in *My Three Sons*. This, however, was already a sign of the attenuation of regional symbolism as a factor in this genre. It was clear in the new breed of situation comedies of the 1960s, such as *All in the Family, The Jeffersons,* and *The Cosby Show* that conflicts between parents and children, husbands and wives and ethnic groups were now much more important than regional symbolism.

Though its significance as a source of popular fictional, film, and television genres seems to be on the decline, regional symbolism has been very important in many other areas of popular entertainment. Country-and-Western music has been one of the twentieth century's major areas of popular music. The role of regional symbolism in tourism is another significant development. Many states have depended heavily on their supposed regional traditions in publicizing and even creating interesting places for tourists to visit. Closely connected to tourism, the tremendous flourishing since World War II of the regionally symbolic theme park is another sign of the times, but these developments take us into another area of the role of regional symbolism in twentieth century American popular culture.

V

The fourth and last area where regional symbolism is still important to American popular culture is at once very obvious and yet intangible and difficult to define. I refer to the use of artifacts, styles, dress, foods and other patterns symbolically connected with the traditional regions to establish some sense of identity and continuity in a culture which seems increasingly to lack these qualities. It is certainly no secret that Americans feel very anxious about their identities and about their relation to historical traditions, as the increasing interest in "roots" and "heritage" indicates. The two major studies of the American character after World War II—David Riesman et. al. *The Lonely Crowd* (1950) and Robert Bellah et. al. *Habits of the Heart* (1985) both emphasized the public's increasing dissatisfaction with traditional American individualism. Riesman stressed the transition for the traditionally individualistic "inner-directed" character to a more anxiously search "other-directed" character. Bellah stressed an increasing dissatisfaction with the isolated individual and the search for an increasing commitment to traditions of community and locality. Both studies make it clear that since the Second World War, Americans have increasingly tried to identify themselves with historical traditions. Since regional traditions are among our most obvious historical symbols, the power of regional traditions for the imagination has increased in proportion to their decline in social and political significance.

The most obvious examples of this use of regional symbolism are such fashions as those for Western clothing and boots in the urban East. The spectacle of Wall Street lawyers and investment brokers dressing up in cowboy boots and hats in order to go to expensive night clubs where they can ride machines simulating the bucking of rodeo bronchos reminds one of the fascination with cowboys and Indians once so characteristic of American boys, but such actions must also serve some significant purpose for adults. Indeed, when we notice that America's largest investment firm, Merrill Lynch has created an advertising icon by imaging the long dead metaphor of Wall Street "bulls" as a herd of rampaging Western steers, it seems clear that the quest for traditional regional associations is more than a passing fad.

The adoption of regionally symbolic clothing and foods is a simpler and more obvious form of the more complex tendency toward reregionalization which I have already mentioned. Reregionalizing is a use of the techniques and the technology of modern American popular culture to establish artificial enclaves which represent traditional regional cultures. By entering these enclaves one can imagine oneself stepping back into the past and becoming momentarily a seventeenth century Southern colonial, an eighteenth century New England townsman, or a nineteenth century Westerner. In such places trained "interpreters" who have learned traditional crafts such as soap-making, candle-dipping or broom-making not only replicate these crafts, but explain them as if the past had become a "text" to be read and interpreted. If the visitor wishes, he or she can even purchase the products created by these scholar-craftpersons, thus bringing a symbol of a traditional culture into modern urban life.[21]

In addition to the increasing availability of regionally symbolic products for sale, an important new trend in journalism is the regional or local magazine such as *Southern Living* or *Sunset* or *Arizona Highways* which offers not only postcard views of regional scenery—this was the original format of *Arizona Highways*, one of the very earliest of the regional magazines—but instruction in the preparation of regional foods and the niceties of other regional traditions. Many of these magazines have collaborated with tourist bureaus and travel agencies to develop heritage tours of monuments, museum, theme parks and such buildings and places as still have some traditional regional aura about them. Frequently these tours, like the reregionalized theme parks, offer "interpreters" trained to help us learn how to read the past and to feel that we are thereby reestablishing our links with regional traditions.

Reregionalized spaces, the contemporary production of traditional crafts, and the new regional journalism and tourism are extensions of the interest in American regional antiques which is itself of relatively recent origin. In the nineteenth century people inherited furniture and other artifacts from their families and used them if they could not afford newer products. Insofar as there was a collector's interest in antiques, it focused on English, European and other non-American antiques. So little interest was there in American antiques at the beginning of the twentieth century that there were many instances of prescient individuals acquiring priceless collections of, e.g. Shaker furniture, for almost nothing. However, since the 1930s, interest in American antiques has grown to the point where good quality nineteenth century American furniture has become prohibitively expensive and largely unavailable, except in the form of reregionalized reproductions. As the actual artifacts as regional cultures become increasingly unavailable, a partially artificial regional symbolism takes its place.

A fascinating aspect of the American quest for identity and tradition through the incorporation into individual "lifestyles" of regional symbolism is that people are no longer limited by geography, but can create many different combinations of regional symbolism. Thus we find Cape Cod houses in steamy Florida and Southern plantation mansions in cold New England. Kentucky Fried Chicken is not only available all over the United States, but in Europe and the Far East as well. Western suits, hats and boots can be purchased from Maine to California, as can New England clam chowder. One hardly blinks to see an Ohio farmer driving his pickup truck with a Confederate flag stenciled on the cab, while listening to Country and Western music on his Japanese made car stereo,

As this freewheeling incorporation of many different regional symbols goes on, the authenticity of regional traditions comes increasingly into question. Many of the best young writers associated with particular regions have made the exploration of the shallowness and inauthenticity of contemporary regional cultures a central theme. In her story "Shiloh" (1982) the Kentucky writer Bobbie Ann Mason tells about Leroy Moffitt, a truckdriver so badly injured in an accident that he cannot any longer drive his truck. He finds that being in motion all the time has kept him from thinking much about his life. Now that he is forced to be still, Leroy begins to feel the need for roots and for deeper connections with his family and community. But he finds that nothing is there anymore. His wife, Norma Jean, is more interested in bodybuilding and computers; she would like to transform herself into the image of the successful modern woman she sees on television. First, Leroy tries to reestablish connections with his heritage by thinking about building a log cabin with his own hands. When that comes to nothing he tries to revitalize his rapidly disintegrating marriage by taking Norma Jean on a trip to Shiloh, not only a major turning point in the Civil War, but also the place where Norma Jean was conceived during her parents honeymoon at the battlefield. But Shiloh is meaningless for them and the trip only hardens Norma Jean's decision to go ahead with her plans for a divorce. In the end, Leroy can only realize that "he is leaving out the insides of history. History was always just names and dates to him. It occurs to him that building a house out of logs is similarly empty—too simple. And the real inner workings of marriage like most of history have escaped him. Now he sees that building a log house is the dumbest idea he could have had."[22] This may, in the end, prove to be the fate of most American regional traditions, but for the moment, the symbols of American regionalism are still a significant part of popular culture.

Acknowledgment

I would like to dedicate this essay to Professor J.A., Bryant, Jr. who has so generously shared his wonderful insights into Southern literature and culture with me over many years. No one could be better qualified to "tell about the South."

Notes

[1]My colleagues J. A. Bryant, Jr., Gurney Norman, and Thomas Blues read a draft of this paper and I am very grateful to them for their many helpful suggestions.

[2]This recent development of the concept of Appalachia does not mean that it is either false or ineffective. In fact, it has been the most large-scale example of the trend toward "reregionalizing" which I discuss more fully in parts IV and V of this essay. Whether there are any other large areas of the country which can be reregionalized in this way, I do not know.

Some indication of the newness of the concept of Appalachia can be seen in the dates of the books published on the subject. In the University of Kentucky Library which has a special Appalachian collection, the first book entries are in the 1930s and there are only two books from that decade. The remaining entries by time period are as follows:

1940-1950: 1
1950-1960: 4
1960-1970: 31
1970-1980: 140

[3]Another good example of the emergence of a transformed modern regional symbolism is the changing symbolic significance of the South described so delightfully by Jack Temple Kirby in *Media-Made Dixie* (1978).

[4]The history and cultural significance of ethnicity and race in America are treated brilliantly by Werner Sollors in *Beyond Ethnicity: Consent and Descent in American Culture* (1986). For some idea of the large scale of studies in ethnicity see Stephan Thernstrom, Ann Orlov and Oscar Handlin, eds. *Harvard Encyclopedia of American Ethnic Groups* (1980).

[5]Among the many works which treat these developments I have particularly depended on John Higham, *Strangers in the Land* (1967) and *Send these to Me: Jews and Other Immigrants in Urban America* (1975), Sam Girgus, *The New Covenant* (1984), C. Vann Woodward, *The Strange Career of Jim Crow*, Joseph R. Gusfield, *Symbolic Crusade: Status Politics and the American Temperance Movement* (1963), Andrew Sinclair, *Prohibition: Era of Excess* (1962) David M. Chalmers, *Hooded Americanism: Ku Klux Klan, 1865-1965* (1965). A recent book which gives an interesting account of the rise of a new national consciousness in America is Wilbur Zelinsky's *Nation Into State: The Shifting Symbolic Foundations of American Nationalism* (1988).

[6]Alfred Kazin *On Native Grounds* (1942) discusses the emergence of a twentieth century American fascination with the national and regional past, particularly in chapter 15.

[7]I have adopted this phrase from a comment by Professor Bryant that seemed particularly eloquent to me. In his note to me, Bryant goes on to remark that he was particularly depressed by a recent visit to New Orleans' famed Bourbon Street, "now hardly more authentic than the new French Quarter out on Richmond Road" (in Lexington, Kentucky).

[8]Many of the basic regional archetypes appear in some of the earliest documents of American literature such as Bradford's account of Plymouth Plantation, Byrd's *History of the Dividing Line* or Crevecoeur's *Letters from an American Farmer.* Important studies of nineteenth century regional archetypes in American literature and popular culture are Taylor, *Cavalier and Yankee,* Rourke, *American Humor,* and Blair, *Native American Humor.*

[9]Even though they may be increasingly attenuated, it's amazing how some of these archetypes hang on. The connection between down-home values and corruption and decadence in the South was amusingly exploited in the recent series of films *Porky's, Porky's: The Next Day,* and *Porky's Revenge.*

[10]Stephen Crane in "The Bride Comes to Yellow Sky."

[11]This campaign and its symbolism is covered in Robert Gunderson, *The Log Cabin Campaign.*

[12]The same sort of mistake seems to have bedevilled the State of North Dakota in its twentieth century attempts to create an attractive image for itself to win tourists and new residents to the region. At first, North Dakota tried to portray itself as a great Garden of Eden under the rubric of the Peace Garden State. This evidently fooled neither tourists nor possible residents so North Dakota turned to the symbolism of the Wild West and, exploiting a connection with Theodore Roosevelt, now calls itself "The Rough Rider State." Just recently it was reported that some prominent North Dakotans have proposed to call the state simply "Dakota" presumably to eliminate the unfortunate associations of the word North with snow and cold. Thus, the vicissitudes of a state that doesn't fit conveniently into the established tripartite symbolism.

[13]For discussion of regional figures in American humor cf. Constance Rourke, *American Humor;* Walter Blair, *Native American Humor; Blair and Hamlin Hill, America's Humor;* and Blair and Raven McDavid, *The Birth of a Nation.*

[14]For the Southern cavalier see particular William R. Taylor, *Cavalier and Yankee.* For the heroic Westerner, Henry Nash Smith's *Virgin Land* supplemented by such recent studies as Richard Slotkin's *Regeneration Through Violence* and *The Fatal Environment* are indicative.

[15]Cf. Stephen J. Whitfield, *Voices of Jacob, Hands of Esau* for a treatment of the dominant role of Jews in mass entertainment, particularly in humor. Robert Toll, *On With the Show* treats the rise of racial and ethnic humor in American popular theater.

[16]John G. Cawelti, *The Six-Gun Mystique* (1984) provides a structural and historical analysis of the Western along with an extensive bibliography and filmography.

[17]Eastwood later developed the basic character of Coogan into his tremendously popular Dirty Harry series, but significantly the regional symbolism associated with the vigilante hero has almost completely disappeared, remaining perhaps only in Harry's great skill with his Western-style revolver, the famous Magnum .357.

[18]The earlier films of Sam Peckinpah such as *Ride the High Country* and *The Wild Bunch* were brilliant evocations of nostalgia for a bygone heroic era. Significantly, Peckinpah moved away from the Western to the crime thriller and the spy story in search of new material. Clint Eastwood also moved away from the Western, though he has periodically tried to return to the genre. However, it is doubtless significant that in his last attempt at the genre *Pale Rider,* the Western hero is probably a ghost.

[19]Examples of this would be the series *Bewitched* and *Dark Shadows.* In addition, many of Stephen King's horror novels and the movies based on them exploit this symbolism: cf. *Salem's Lot.*

[20]An indication of the basic continuity between New England and the Middle West as symbolic moral landscapes is Thornton Wilder's highly successful play *Our Town,* which was actually set in New England, but so resembled the popular image of the middle western town that it might as well have been set in Iowa. *Our Town* could never have been set in the South or the West.

[21]The reregionalizing phenomenon has assumed major proportions in the years since World War II after a tentative beginning with Colonial Williamsburg and Henry Ford's Dearborn Village in the 1930s. Now there are regional theme parks and living museums in nearly every part of the country, including such as Old Tucson, Six Flags Over Texas, Harold Warp's Pioneer Village, Mystic Seaport, Old Sturbridge Village, Shakertown at Pleasant Hill, Fort Boonesborough, Grand Old Opryland and many, many more. The highly successful Disneylands have also created many attractions based on regional symbolism. One of the newest and most striking of the reregionalizing theme parks is Dollywood in Tennessee created to celebrate the Appalachian culture, which, as we have already noted, was itself an example of reregionalizing on a major scale.

[22]Bobbie Ann Mason, "Shiloh" from *Shiloh and Other Stories* (1982), quoted from Perkins, et. al. *The American Tradition in Literature* vol. 2, pp. 1925-35.

Works Cited

Bellah, Robert et. al. *Habits of the Heart: Individualism and Commitment in American Life.* Berkeley: University of California Press, 1985.

Blair, Walter, *Native American Humor.* San Francisco: Chandler Pub. 1960. Orig. Pub. 1937.

Blair, Walter and Hamlin Hill. *America's Humor.* New York: Oxford University Press, 1983.

Cawelti, John G. *The Six-Gun Mystique.* Bowling Green, OH: Bowling Green Popular Press, 1984.

Chalmers, David M. *Hooded Americanism: Ku Klux Klan, 1865-1965.* Chicago: Quadrangle Books, 1968.

Girgus, Sam. *The New Covenant: Jewish Writers and the American Idea.* Chapel Hill: University of North Carolina Press, 1984.

Gunderson, Robert G. *The Log Cabin Campaign.* Lexington: University of Kentucky Press, 1957.

Gusfield, Joseph R. *Symbolic Crusade: Status Politics and the American Temperance Movement.* Urbana:University of Illinois Press, 1963.

Higham, John. *Send These to Me: Jews and Other Immigrants in Urban America.* New York: Atheneum, 1975.

——. *Strangers in the Land.* Brunswick, NJ: Rutgers University Press, 1988.

Hobson, Fred. *Tell About the South: The Southern Rage to Explain.* Baton Rouge: Louisiana State University Press, 1983.

Kazin, Alfred. *On Native Grounds: An Interpretation of Modern American Prose Literature.* Garden City, NY: Doubleday, 1956. Orig. pub. 1942.

Kirby, Jack Temple. *Media-Made Dixie: The South in the American Imagination.* Baton Rouge: Louisiana State University Press, 1978.

Klein, Marcus. *Foreigners: The Making of American Literature, 1900-1940.* Chicago: University of Chicago Press, 1981.

Bobbie Ann Mason, "Shiloh" from *Shiloh and Other Stories* (1982) reprinted in George Perkins, et. al. *The American Tradition in Literature.* Sixth Edition. Vol. 2. New York: Random House, 1985.

Riesman, David et. al. *The Lonely Crowd.* New Haven: Yale University Press, 1950.

Rourke, Constance. *American Humor: A Study of the National Character.* Tallahassee: Florida State University Press, 1986. Orig. pub. 1931.

Sinclair, Andrew. *Prohibition: Era of Excess.* Boston: Little, Brown: 1962.

Slotkin, Richard. *The Fatal Environment: The Myth of the Frontier in the Age of Industrialization, 1800-1890.* New York: Atheneum, 1985.

_____. *Regeneration Through Violence: The Mythology of the American Frontier, 1600-1860.* Middletown, CN: Wesleyan University Press, 1973.

Smith, Henry Nash. *Virgin Land: The American West as Symbol and Myth.* Cambridge, MA: Harvard University Press, 1950.

Sollors, Werner. *Beyond Ethnicity: Consent and Descent in American Culture.* New York: Oxford University Press, 1986.

Taylor, William R. *Cavalier and Yankee: The Old South and American National Character.* Cambridge: Harvard University Press, 1979. Orig. Pub. 1961.

Thernstrom, Stephan with Ann Orlov and Oscar Hendlin, eds. *Harvard Encyclopedia of American Ethnic Groups.* Cambridge, Mass. and London: Harvard University Press, 1980.

Toll, Robert. *On With the Show: The First Century of Show Business in America.* New York: Oxford University Press, 1976.

Whitfield, Stephen J. *Voices of Jacob, Hands of Esau: Jews in American Life and Thought.* Hamden, CT: Archon Press, 1984.

Woodward, C. Vann. *The Strange Career of Jim Crow.* New York: Oxford University Press, 1974.

Zelinsky, Wilbur. *Nation into State: The Shifting Symbolic Foundations of American Nationalism.* Chapel Hill: University of North Carolina Press, 1988.

Pornography and Popular Culture

John G. Cawelti
and
Mary C. Flannery

The hardest part of writing about pornography lies in deciding what it is. If, for example, one were to compare the works of art and literature included under the term by a civil libertarian and a fundamentalist Christian, we would no doubt find some overlap, but, on the whole, the two catalogs would be totally different. The term itself, as everybody knows, is derived from two Greek words, *porne* meaning prostitute, and *grapho* meaning to write. However, though the Greeks certainly had the idea of corrupt literature (Socrates in Plato's *Republic* even suggests at one point that all poetry may be corrupt) they did not have a word for pornography. Instead, the term seems to be a nineteenth century coinage, possibly by the Germans.[1] The first *Oxford English Dictionary* reference to pornography is from 1857 in Dunglison's *Medical Dictionary* where it evidently does mean literally writing about prostitutes: "Pornography—a description of prostitutes or of prostitution as a matter of public hygiene." The word's first appearance in the American *Webster* was in the 1864 edition where it meant "licentious painting employed to decorate the walls of rooms sacred to Bacchanalian orgies, examples of which exist in Pompeii."

These and other entries recorded by the *OED* suggest that the term came into existence initially either to describe the medical and sociological study of prostitution, or to designate certain of the more overtly sexual statues, paintings and writings of the ancient world. By 1880, however, the term had been extended to that modern literature, most notably French, which tried to treat sexuality more frankly: "They call themselves naturalists—but they are in fact only pornographers, and immature, inexperienced, conceited love-mad youngsters." (*Literary World (US)* May 1, 1880). As this quotation indicates, the word soon lost whatever objective signification it may have once had, and became pejorative and value-laden, especially when applied to contemporaneous works of art and literature. In general, pornography now means literature and art which is obscene and therefore should not be publicly presented or distributed.[2]

Clearly the concept of pornography and its connection with obscenity arose out of the surge of Victorian moral reform, which, if certain present-day scholars are correct, was a reaction to the emergence of a new concept of sexuality. Michel Foucault makes the point in his *History of Sexuality* that sometime in the mid-nineteenth century "we. . .arrived at the point where we expect our intelligibility to come from what was for many centuries thought of as madness; the plenitude of our body from what was long considered its stigma and likened to a wound; our identity from what was perceived as an obscure and nameless urge [sexuality]—Hence the fact that over the centuries it has become more important than our soul." (155-56)[3] One major response to this new conception of sexuality was an anxious attempt to tame and control it. Thus, in both New England and America there was a great surge of censorship, obscenity prosecutions, anti-prostitution campaigns and other kinds of "moral" reform. The evolution of the concept of pornography to something resembling our present-day notion was apparently one aspect of this later nineteenth century trend.

Today, pornography is, among other things, a complex intersection of legal, political, literary, psychological, moral and technological issues. In law, there is the problem of definition and its application particularly with regard to censorship. There are several political dimensions of pornography, most significantly the use of government commissions to amass information and make recommendations concerning the treatment of pornography and the interplay of political pressure groups who support or are opposed to censorship. In the sphere of literature and the arts, the crucial questions is that of defining the point or boundary at which the literary or artistic treatment of sexuality becomes inartistic and is therefore no longer covered by the concept of "redeeming social or artistic value,"[4] if, indeed, such a point can be defined. Morally and psychologically, pornography raises the problem of effects and impact and the degree to which potentially bad effects on children or women morally oblige us to censor pornography. Finally, the results of technological development, particularly related to the widespread use of videotape, have vastly increased the availability and the acceptability of pornography, bypassing the more visible and vulnerable adult bookstores and theaters and creating a more invisible mode of distribution through hundreds of videotape rental establishments.

A thorough treatment of the relationship between pornography and American popular culture would require a careful consideration of all these issues and their interconnections, but that is far beyond the scope of a short essay. Here, we will narrow the field by defining pornography not as the presentation of sexuality *per se,* but as the representation of modes of sexuality considered forbidden or taboo, morally or legally, by the American public. Though a common practice in both literary criticism and the law, such a definition is uncomfortably vague and is particularly fuzzy at the edges or boundaries. There may, however, be a way to clear up at least some of the haze. Let us consider two modes of sexuality which would certainly fall into most definitions of the forbidden: incest and the sexual abuse of children. What are we to do about, for instance, Sophocles' *Oedipus,* chapter two of Ralph Ellison's *Invisible Man,* or Faulkner's "The Bear" from *Go Down, Moses?* Or what about the novel or film of Vladimir Nabokov's *Lolita,* which represents the sexual abuse of children. While a fervent fundamentalist would probably consider all of these to be pornographic, few others would. The question is why not.[5] The reason would seem to be that we make a practical distinction between what might be called erotic realism and pornography.[6] Pornography is the presentation of the forbidden *for its own sake* and therefore in a positive and tantalizing fashion, while erotic realism deals with such themes as incest, rape, pedophilia, bestiality, without concealing or glossing over the reasons for their being forbidden, namely, their harmfulness to vulnerable human beings.

In addition to its representation of the forbidden, pornography has also typically depended on the development of certain fantasies, presumably masculine, which relate to the erotic significance of the forbidden. These fantasies are not exactly taboo per se, but their ultimate implications almost inevitably cross over the boundary into the forbidden areas of rape, sexual abuse and incest. The most important of these fantasies are, first, the nearly infinite rigidity and potency of the male genitals, second, the potential sexual accessibility of all women, and finally, the idea that women basically desire to be sexually dominated.[7]

Two double examples may help indicate how it is possible to make a distinction between pornography, as we have defined it, and erotic realism, even though the distinction will always be tentative. The first is the contrast between Yeats' poem "Leda and the Swan" and a typical pornographic scene of intercourse between a woman and a dog, a feature of thousands of pornographic novels, and also probably a realm of male fantasy.[8]

The typical pattern of a pornographic scene of bestiality involves bestial intercourse initially forced upon a woman, but which she comes to enjoy for its pure animalistic lust. Nancy Friday speculates that the attraction of this scene involves a male fantasy of total domination and sexual power, an image, in other words, of the most brutal sort of rape. This aspect of the scene, however, is covered over by the supposed revelation that the woman's own sexual powers have been concealed and that they are, in fact, unleashed to her great pleasure by this attack.

In Yeats' poem, however, the full horror of the great swan's attack and Leda's helplessness is indicated from the very beginning. At no point is there any suggestion that, in any way, she enjoyed the episode. Moreover, the result of the bestial rape is not an erotic revelation or fulfillment to Leda, but the gestation of a terrible catastrophe for humankind:

> A shudder in the loins engenders there
> The broken wall, the burning roof and tower
> And Agamemnon dead.[9]

Our second example is less clear, yet the same distinction applies. In Hubert Selby's collection of stories, *Last Exit to Brooklyn,* there is, in the final story, a horrifying scene of gang rape. The same sort of scene is another set piece of pornography and as an example we would cite the obscure novel *Soldier's Girl.* There are two major points of difference. First, as in Leda and the Swan, Selby's rape victim does not invite in any way nor does she enjoy the rape. In fact, Selby's protagonist is a prostitute for whom sex is not a fulfillment but an occupation. The only difference between her average day and the gang rape is the greater brutality of the rape and the fact that she receives no pay for it. In addition, the rapists are the regular crowd of the bar where the attack begins and the rape is portrayed as a kind of horrifying frenzy in which even decent men are caught up and encouraged to perform terribly brutal and inhuman acts, which the story portrays in a nastily clear fashion.[10] In the end, the victim has been turned into nothing but a bleeding hunk of meat. It is butchery and sexual hatred rather than erotic arousal that is the subject of Selby's story.[11]

In *Soldier's Girl,* however, several factors make the scene of gang rape a fantasy of the forbidden. In the first place, the rapists are exotic orientals. The rape is directed by a Vietnamese Montagnard general whose great wish in life has been to humiliate a white woman. Moreover the rape is directed and photographed by the general, bringing in the element of voyeurism as well as the degradation of the white female. Finally, the protagonist survives the brutal rape undamaged and is quite able to go on, in the final scene of the novel, to have a passionate sexual episode with a legless Vietnam veteran. Clearly, this victim suffers no lasting ill effects from her mistreatment. Indeed, the episode is treated by the author as a sort of justified punishment which turns into an occasion of sexual excitement for one and all.

It seems that such examples indicate that one can make a fairly clear distinction between the exploitation of "forbidden" fantasies for their own sake, and a representation of sexually taboo actions that is realistic and artistic. Many works lie somewhere between these categories—soft-core pornography is an important example that will be discussed later. In addition, we must recognize that what is forbidden is not universal and that it changes as culture changes. Therefore, we must also be ready to acknowledge that what is pornographic at one time may not be so at another. We have no doubt that a glamorized representation of a naked female, such as the famous calendar painting "September Morn" was considered highly pornographic in the later nineteenth century, while such an image is hardly forbidden at the present time. In fact, it is difficult for aspiring contemporary pornographers to discover ways in which the unclothed female can be made pornographic.[12] Historically changing conceptions of the forbidden can also work backwards, so to speak. Works from the past which clearly exploited the forbidden can easily be redefined as works of art once they achieve a patina of antiquity. Examples are the erotic art of ancient Rome, such as that found in Pompeii or even that eighteenth century masterpiece *Fanny Hill,* recently freed from censorship by the U.S. Supreme Court because of its historical and artistic significance.

Our treatment of the use of pornographic symbols in popular culture, then, will depend on the distinction between art as a treatment of human life and pornography as a relishing of forbidden fantasies. That we can define certain works as pornographic does not mean that we are in favor of censorship, but there are too many complexities in that issue to discuss it here.[13]

II

Pornography and popular culture intersect in four different ways: 1) pornography as a social institution is itself an important part of the structure of popular culture; 2) pornographic symbolism frequently appears in a disguised or latent fashion in many different popular genres such as advertising, romance, horror stories, etc.; 3) since the later nineteenth century there has been a gradual spreading of what would once have been considered hard-core pornographic symbolism into non-pornographic areas of popular culture; this is what we like to call the "seepage" effect; 4) finally, since pornography, apart from its sexual content is extremely derivative, there is a continual flow of influence into pornography from other popular genres; thus, we have pornographic westerns, detective stories, horror stories, spy stories, etc. Any highly successful film or television series is likely to inspire a pornographic counterpart such as *Wet Dream on Elm Street, Rise of the Roman Empress, Saint X-Where, Black Dynasty,* or *Barbara the Barbarian.* Sometimes these porno tributes are clever sexual versions or burlesques of the originals. More often, the connection is limited largely to the titles.

After a few words on pornography as a social institution, we will concentrate our attention on the two related ways in which pornographic symbolism is imported into other popular genres, through disguise and through "seepage." These two aspects of symbolic interplay are quite closely connected and sometimes hard to distinguish from each other, but, as we will see, the distinction is a useful one in understanding how pornography and the rest of popular culture interact.

Since its beginning in the later eighteenth or early nineteenth centuries until the 1960s, pornography was largely an underground male-dominated social institution, limited, with the exception of certain seepages and disguises in the popular press, largely to male members of the middle and upper classes. Though certain pornographic genres like the stag film and the eight-page pornographic comic book probably reached some members of the working class during their heyday in the 1920s and 1930s, the character of traditional pornography made it accessible almost entirely to males, and its cost kept it from reaching a mass public. It is difficult to say to what extent it was morality and to what extent economics that kept the availability of pornography very limited, but as late as the studies carried out by the President's Commission on Obscenity and Pornography in the later 1960s the typical customer of adult bookstores and movie theaters was apparently a middle-class male in his early middle age.[14]

This situation changed drastically in the 1970s. The use of new technology for the distribution of pornography, most notably videotape and the telephone, made pornography more widely and easily accessible. The customer who wanted to purchase or rent a pornographic videotape no longer had to go to a seamy adult bookstore in a rundown part of town or to a smelly unhygienic and decaying theater. He/she could walk into any one of thousands of video rental stores, where pornographic films as well as family comedies and other kinds of videotapes were all available. The exploitation of new technologies of distribution was made possible by a changed moral and legal climate created by the more sexually permissible attitudes of the 1960s and by a series of Supreme Court decisions, which, though not exactly bringing about "the end of obscenity" that one libertarian lawyer announced, certainly made the prosecution of pornography more difficult.

One consequence of these changes was that the production of pornographic movies became a quasi-respectable enterprise and the pornographic film "industry" became increasingly visible and assumed the form of a parody of the Hollywood motion picture establishment. Certain pornographic performers claimed something like the dignity and cult following of real movie stars, directors started to consider themselves artistes or auteurs, and an annual pornographic academy awards ceremony began handing out sexual Oscars. The impact of AIDS seems to have brought about a halt in the increasingly bumptious visibility of the pornographic film "community," but it is not yet clear whether this development is temporary or permanent.

Another uncertain aspect of the new accessibility of pornography is the question of whether its new social and cultural position is leading to any significant changes in the nature of pornography, particularly with regard to its portrayal of and use by women. Feminist critics like Kate Millett, Andrea Dworkin, and Susan Griffin have become some of the most powerful and effective opponents of pornography by defining it as inherently sexist and exploitative of women. This view has generated a new conception of pornographic censorship based on the idea that the erotic exploitation and demeaning of women by pornographic works is an assault on equal rights. Several municipalities have attempted to pass ordinances embodying this new feminist definition of pornography, but it is as yet too early to tell whether these movements will lead to the revitalization of censorship in this area.

Others, including a few women who have become successful directors of pornographic films, argue, in effect, that pornography's increasing accessibility to couples and women may stimulate the development of new kinds of pornography. They speak of the evolution of a new erotic realism in which the explicit portrayal of sexual acts becomes a celebration of heterosexual sexuality rather than the prurient exploitation of the forbidden. Or they suggest that there are forms of pornography that could be truly enjoyable and even liberating to women, by exploring and presumably combatting such restrictive aspects of female sexuality as culturally generated difficulty in acknowledging women's full sexual needs or the ideology that women need to associate sex with romance.[15]

Though a few pornographic films have been produced that might be interpreted as tentative gestures in this direction,[16] the vast majority of pornographic works and artifacts continue to be produced along traditional lines, emphasizing male potency and associating it with the performance of forbidden sexual acts.[17] There are as yet no convincing signs that the new technology and the new social and cultural significance of pornography has changed its basic symbolic structures. To these we now turn.

III

At this point, we need to define more fully the structure of pornographic symbolism, which, as we have seen, has traditionally consisted of fantasies of male potency and total female accessibility in connection with sexual acts which are, in some way, considered forbidden. There is a great variety of forbidden acts, but before we discuss some of them, we must clarify further what we mean by "forbidden." Indeed, some "forbidden" sexual acts, such as oral and anal sex, are very widely practiced; others, such as bestiality, are probably more widely performed by men, though it is female bestiality that is a primary motif of pornography, and that according to sexual researchers, is relatively rare except in disguised form. "Forbidden" means rather that there remains some aura of shame, of danger, of possible disapproval, or secrecy, about the sexual behavior in question. Oral sex, for example, is a widely practiced and enjoyed form of sexual behavior highly recommended by most sexual counselors and manuals; yet there are still laws against sodomy on the books in many states. It would be possible to be sent to jail for oral sex, though highly unlikely. This seems to be one sort of forbiddenness that the most frequently represented pornographic acts possess. There are also, of course, much more forbidden acts, such as rape, bondage or other forms of sexual cause. Thus there appears to be a continuum of forbidden acts ranging from the widely tolerated though traditionally tabooed to the truly illegal and criminal. This continuum is matched to some degree by a range of pornographic genres from those dealing primarily with straightforward heterosexual sex to those of a heavily sadomasochistic content. Just as pornographic symbolism seeps into other popular genres, so the most forbidden sexual symbolism continually seeps into the tamer forms of pornographic representation.[18]

The connection between these acts and various fantasies of male potency seems to be the idea that to make a woman perform a "forbidden" sexual act is an assertion of male potency, even if the woman appears to perform the act willingly enough. In addition, male control of the sexual act, a central feature of current pornography, is an assertion of emotional distance and control—the men in pornographic films being notoriously unlikely to show any strong feeling or involvement in the sexual acts they are performing. This combination of distance and control reaches its climax in the so-called pull-out shot which is the single most distinctive form of erotic symbolism in modern cinematic pornography. By removing his penis at the moment of orgasm, the male becomes the focus of a "wet shot" which seems to make a number of assertions: first, that the erect male penis in ejaculation is the central pornographic icon; second, that the man in question has actually been brought to orgasmic climax;[19] third, that the man has distanced himself from the act of intercourse and presumably from its possible consequences such as conception; and finally, that the symbolic male rod or scepter of authority has become an object of adoration by an admiring female. In other words, the sight of the ejaculating cock is shown to be more important to the female partner than the experience of her own orgasm, an event that is rarely even faked in pornographic films.

Forbidden acts seem to be of three main kinds. There are forms of sexual activity which are considered forbidden such as sodomy; there is sexual intercourse with forbidden partners such as incest, pedophilia, homosexuality, lesbianism, bestiality and various forms of miscegenation or sex with members of forbidden racial or ethnic groups; finally, there are those types of action in which sexuality is distorted into the exercise of power and the administering or feeling of pain and physical injury, such as rape, bondage, sado-masochism, etc. These are the major activities portrayed in pornographic works and, while ordinary genital sexual intercourse is also commonly portrayed, it is far outnumbered by the representation of "forbidden" acts. In fact, heterosexual genital intercourse as well as other forms are transformed in the context of pornography into a forbidden realm by virtue of the voyeuristic context of the reader or viewer who witnesses and enjoys these basic and profound human acts without being implicated or responsible in any way for them. Thus, the basic context of pornography involves a kind of distancing which is reinforced by many other aspects of the genre such as the unemotional performances and generally primitive literary styles through which the forbidden acts are represented.

One major way in which non-pornographic popular genres make use of pornographic symbolism is through disguise or transformation. Advertising is one of the major areas in which we can see such disguising in its most simplified fashion. One of the most strikingly successful ads of recent years was sponsored by the Coppertone company which makes a suntan lotion. This ad portrayed a rather curvaceous and sunburned young female child whose panties were being pulled off by a dog to reveal a small portion of the little girl's untanned buttocks. The practical message of this ad seems a little unclear when one thinks about it. Is the idea that the panties which kept the little girls buttocks from becoming sunburned are analogous to Coppertone, which supposedly protects the skin like an item of clothing? It's a bit hard to tell just what the point is, and that is, of course, the point. It's the disguised presentation of the symbols of pedophilia and bestiality that rivets the eye to the advertisement and makes it take in the same glance, the name of Coppertone.

Ads are so full of disguised pornographic symbolism that it would take a book simply to catalog the variety of such images. One remarkable example was the long-running series of ads for Maidenform Bras which presented numerous variations on the theme of "I dreamed I went shopping in my Maidenform Bra" showing an attractive young woman fully and appropriately dressed for the occasion in question except that her upper torso is wearing nothing but a brassiere. The implicit motifs of control, humiliation and voyeurism in this ad make one wonder why it was so successful as it apparently was with women. Perhaps the answer is that women have traditionally been socialized into a male-dominated culture and therefore have absorbed some of the same pornographic feelings as men. In any case, to leaf through copies of almost any fashion of women's magazine such as *Vogue* or *Confidential* is to discover a treasure trove of disguised pornographic symbolism. In this context the most important symbolism relates to a woman being forced to expose herself or strip before a male or group of males, a symbolism which disguises the forbidden act of rape under the tamer aegis of voyeurism. In addition the implicit suggestion of male control and distance seems to be an important part of the language of fashion with its pattern of male photographers and female models.[20] This complex of symbolism is also clear in the Maidenform Bra ads.

In addition to advertising, many popular genres have made extensive use of disguised or latent pornographic symbolism to intensify their effects. We might take the typical romance, for example. The romance genre seems on the surface to be the very antithesis of pornography, being dedicated much more to romantic love than to sex. However, romance and pornography not only have an inverted structural relationship, they share a number of basic motifs. One of the most important is that of the alien seducer, the character who appears to be racially, socially or culturally beyond the pale, but who poses a basic threat to the heroine's romantic vulnerability. Historical romances are full of lustful turks, rajahs and sheiks who lust after the heroine, periodically threatening to reduce them to a fate worse than death. The mustachioed villain of traditional melodrama is another example of this motif. In romances, at least until very recently, these alien seducers were usually foiled by the escape of the heroine or the timely intervention of the hero. Thus, the nonperformance of the forbidden acts became their disguised representation. In one subgenre of the romance, very popular in the 1920s and 1930s, the threatening sheik appeared, against all taboos, to have won the heroine's heart and body, but fortunately turned out to be an acceptable English gentleman after all. The immensely popular Tarzan, aka Lord Greystoke, was another version of this kind of disguise, and the fantasy of bestiality was clearly latent throughout that saga.

More recently in the bodice-ripping historical romances of such writers as Rosemary Rogers, the representation of the heroine's rape becomes a central narrative element. In works like Rogers' *Sweet, Savage Love* the heroine is not only raped by the hero before she recognizes her love for him, but is raped or nearly raped by several other men before finally being reunited with her true love. Even in the most innocent of romances, those by writers like Barbara Cartland, or the Harlequin industry, a disguised presentation of incest frequently plays a central role with the hero presented symbolically as a father-surrogate. Where the hero is not explicitly the heroine's guardian or protector, he is invariable older and more experienced, with the worldly knowledge and aura of mature sexuality associated with father figures.[21]

Many other popular genres make use of disguised pornographic symbolism. One of the most striking is that of the horror film, which is a virtual repository of transformed images of pornographic acts. The contemporary "slasher" movie such as the omnipresent *Friday the 13th* series, or the *Halloween* films, or the now "classic" *Texas Chain-Saw Massacre* are so nearly explicit in their uses of pornographic symbolism that they could also be treated as instances of "seepage." However, the element of disguise persists in these films, not only in the fact that most of the "slasher" heroes are either masked or so badly deformed as to be unrecognizable, but in the substitution of a phallic weapon for an erect penis, and of murder for rape. The intimate relationship between violence and sex is almost always emphasized by representing the "slasher's" violence as being evoked by the sexuality of his victims. Another way in which the latent sexuality of the relationship between murderer and victim is typically symbolized is by having these films, after a bloodbath involving both sexes, come to a climax in a duel between an attractive and nubile young woman and the "slasher" protagonist. The formula here seems to call for the young woman to be apparently victorious over the "slasher" only to become the first victim in the next film of the series.

Rape and the phallic weapon are by no means the only latent pornographic symbols characteristic of these films. Incest is a very common theme, as in Hitchcock's *Psycho* where Norman Bates assumes a transvestite disguise as his mother in order to carry out his "rapes." In *Friday the 13th,* it is Jason's mother who is the original slasher motivated by a desire for revenge against the camp counselors who let her son drown while engaging in sexual activity. When the mother is destroyed at the end of the first film in the series, Jason returns from the dead to become united with his mother, whose severed head he keeps as an icon of worship. Bestiality is latent in another subgenre of horror films beginning with the vampire and the werewolf and continuing into such contemporary works as Stephen King's *Cujo,* where a large rabid dog becomes the slasher, or *The Howling* and *Wolfen,* contemporary werewolf films. Needless to say, homosexuality, lesbianism, fetishism, transvestism, child rape, are all frequent latent symbols in the horror tradition.

Another important genre involving disguised pornographic symbols is the spy story. Here, the theme of voyeurism is a primary element in that most spy stories are about the uncovering and exploitation of secret acts. However, voyeurism is far from the only pornographic symbolism latent in spy stories. That successful spying somehow enables the hero to become an incredibly potent stud with a limitless accessibility to beautiful women is, of course, a staple of such spy stories as the James Bond series. Bondage and sado-masochism frequently lurk in the scenes of interrogation and torture so much a part of the espionage formula. Frequently the villain is implicitly portrayed as a forbidden partner because of his race. His gestures toward rape of the heroine, usually staved off, are another important element of the genre, where the symbolism of sexual abuse and bondage become disguised as pursuit and capture. Less obvious, but still clearly present in many spy stories, are themes of homosexuality and lesbianism. Ian Fleming clearly recognized this aspect of the genre and he delighted in playing games with it. In *Goldfinger,* for example, the marvelously named Pussy Galore is the lesbian leader of an elite corps of women pilots, who is, of course, converted to heterosexuality when she is raped by James Bond. Bond, himself, gets it back in spades, when, in *Casino Royale,* he is captured and beaten about the genitals by the villain, or when Doctor No stands over his drugged body with the most blatant sort of homosexual interest:

> The man spent longer beside Bond's bed. He scrutinized every line, every shadow on the dark, rather cruel face that lay...on the pillow...[When] he had pulled down the sheet, he did the same with the area round the heart...For another minute the tall figure stood over the sleeping man, then it swished softly away and out into the corridor and the door closed with a click. (*Doctor No* 122-232)[22]

Similar observations could easily be made about such related popular genres as the detective story or the western, but we will only mention one more important area of popular culture which has been traditionally pervaded by latent symbolism of the forbidden: tabloid newspapers such as *The National Enquirer* the widely circulated form of popular culture which can be purchased almost universally, not only at newspaper and magazine stores, but in the checkout lines at grocery stores. Obviously the gossip and scandal which are the major contents of these papers are largely of a sexual nature and imply both the fascination and the shame of celebrity access to forbidden sexual delights. Recently, for example, the violent marriage between Mike Tyson, the boxer, and Robin Givens, the television actress, was given space in these papers week after week. Clearly the element of rape and sexual abuse in this marriage was one reason for its importance, but even beneath this there lay the latent theme of bestiality and the forbidden relationship between Beauty and the Beast, which also played a central role in one of the few recently successful new television series. In fact, forbidden partners seems to be the central theme of the tabloids, ranging from cases of incest, to marriages between children and octogenarians, to sexual relationships between human beings and animals, demons, and aliens.[23]

Clearly pornographic symbolism in its disguised or latent form is pervasive in many genres of popular culture and has been for a long time, perhaps from the very beginnings of folklore and literature. The presence of these latent images of the forbidden and their relationship to the many contours of human sexuality have, however, become more evident with the development of a widely circulated and increasingly accessible, and explicit pornographic literature and art. The influence of this development can be considered in terms of the conception of "seepage."

IV

Seepage, as we indicated earlier, is our term for the spread of increasingly explicit forms of pornographic symbolism into other areas of popular culture, as opposed to the use of disguised or latent images of the forbidden. The latter process has existed for a long time and has certainly been an aspect of Western civilization, if not from the beginnings, at least from the beginning of the Christian era with its general prohibition of the explicit representation of sexuality and its tendency to emphasize the forbiddeness of all sexual activity except that involved in procreation. Seepage, however, is a more recent phenomenon growing out of the increasing acceptability of explicit sexual imagery in the later nineteenth and earlier twentieth century. This phenomenon is clearly a counterpart to the increasing openness of pornography itself, yet it is not the same thing.

To indicate the difference between the acceptance of explicit pornography and the seepage effect, let us look at the cultural phenomenon known as the pin-up girl, or cheesecake. While the female nude has been an artistic subject since prehistoric times, and there must always have been some sexual content in these images, most pre-nineteenth century representations of naked women were associated with religion, or with ideals of aesthetic beauty. Early prehistoric images of women with large genitals and many breasts were presumably more concerned with fertility magic than with sexual arousal, just as the beautiful female nudes of the ancient Greeks were images of the divine. While explicit sexual imagery can be found on certain Greek vases or in Roman paintings such as those at Pompeii, such images were prohibited with the emergence of Christianity and portrayal of the female nude did not really surface again until the Renaissance, where, again, its associations were probably more religious and aesthetic than sexual. Botticelli's famous painting of the Birth of Venus, for example, is clearly a highly idealized artistic image of the goddess who, for at least some of the ancient Greeks, was the veritable symbol of rampant eroticism. We doubt that anyone with the slightest degree of visual or artistic sophistication has ever perceived Botticelli's Venus as a pin-up girl. She is far too aristocratic, too removed, too much an expression of the aura of her own divinity.

What, then, is the difference? We think it lies in our recognizing the successful pin-up girl not only as sexually attractive but as inviting, vulnerable and willingly obedient. The pin-up girl, then, is an image of submissive sexuality, just as the female portrayed in pornography has been, at least until very recently, a representation of female sexuality dominated by male potency and forced thereby into forbidden acts. In this sense, one of the forbidden acts involved in the pin-up tradition is that of the woman revealing her secret sexuality.

If this interpretation is correct, then it seems clear that the pin-up version of the unclothed or partially clothed female derives from the late eighteenth and early nineteenth centuries, which, as we have seen, was approximately the period in which modern pornography, the modern idea of sexuality, and the first organized movements of sexual censorship and obscenity prosecution emerged. To modern eyes, there are a number of eighteenth century French paintings of women, such as those of Francois Boucher, which have a decidedly pin-up air about them, but that is debatable. We would say that the first female nude we are aware of that is unmistakably a pin-up was the tremendously popular statue of the "Greek Slave" by the American sculptor Hiram Powers, which dates from around 1850. Though this is an idealized female nude with its genitals delicately concealed (by the sculptural equivalent of airbrushing) the pose of the statue, its demurely prurient combination of innocence, sexiness and vulnerability, is decidedly in the realm of cheesecake. In addition, the statue is in chains showing her to be at the mercy of some lustful Turk, who is not present in marble, but certainly in the aura of the figure. The implication is that this nubile young virgin is being displayed in a Turkish slave market where she will be purchased, deflowered, and turned into a willing concubine for some forbidden dark-skinned partner.

The fact that this statue was widely popular and accepted in spite of these implications (the statue was displayed openly at the Crystal Palace exhibition in London and widely circulated in both copies and illustration) indicates one important aspect of pin-up art which was true up through the cheesecake of World War II and still has some importance in this area of popular culture. It must be possible to interpret the pin-up girl as both innocent and virginal, as sexually inviting and potentially lustful and sexually dependent. This was clearly important as an aspect of the wide acceptability of the bathing suit pin-ups of World War II, such as those of Betty Grable. These pin-ups concentrated on legs, rather than on breasts or genitals, and they generally had the sort of wholesome innocence about them which apparently made many people think that the young men who painted these images on their planes or hung them on their barracks, were seeing them as much in a brotherly as in a lustful way and that, therefore, to display such images was not immoral or obscene.

Perhaps the most interesting case of World War II pin-ups was the most popular one of all which portrayed the actress Rita Hayworth in a negligee. Actually, very little of Ms. Hayworth's body was explicitly revealed in this photograph, but the suggestiveness of her bedtime attire and its tantalizing translucency combined with Ms. Hayworth's more sultry and sexually suggestive expression to make this pin-up a masterpiece of its kind. Yet, in spite of its more explicitly sexual content, the photograph was widely accepted and even printed in magazines like *Life* which aspired to a family audience. The secret of this was, we think, revealed a year or so later, when Ms. Hayworth appeared in an enormously successful film called *Gilda,* in which she played a singer who appeared at first to be little more than a prostitute, but who was later revealed to be playing this role in order to help support her true love. This was what later critics called the "good-bad" or more accurately perhaps, the "bad-good" girl in whose story apparent sexual availability was eventually revealed as a form of morality and purity.

Between Powers' "Greek Slave" and the Rita Hayworth pin-up there was a gradually increasing representation of explicit sexual availability which involved such symbolic elements as pose, the associations of clothing and setting, the explicitness of the portrayal of the pin-up's sexual parts such as nipples, etc. In this respect, the famous painting "September Morn" might be seen as a transition between the "Greek Slave" and the Hollywood pin-ups and the Petty and Vargas drawings of the 1930s and 1940s. Thus, a gradual seepage seems to be operating here, which became intensified after World War II.

In the pin-up genre, the next major step was the evolution of the Playboy girl in the late 1940s and early 1950s. The Playboy girl was first of all a more explicit physical image particularly with respect to the portrayal of sexual features. Though pubic hair and pudenda were either concealed or airbrushed, the breasts were increasingly exposed with nipples and areolae made sharper and clearer. Two other features of *Playboy* were important indications of a stronger flow of seepage. *Playboy,* first of all, insisted on its image as a respectable magazine, not just another *Girls on Parade* or nudist magazine with limited distribution. *Playboy* was to be a general magazine of culture, the arts, and good taste in all areas of life, and within a few years it was also becoming philosophical and educational about all things connected with the world of sexuality. It was, in other words, to become the "pioneer" of a new and freer "lifestyle" and thus could lay claim to be in the great American tradition of moral and cultural reform. Secondly, *Playboy* turned increasingly to amateur, or supposedly non-professional, models for its naked imagery. Here, instead of the Betty Grable pin-up which tried to make a bit of flesh respectable by its sisterly or girl-next-door wholesomeness, the *Playboy* playmate was the girl next door corrupted and made to reveal all her secrets. Thus, the pornographic image of the woman forced into sexual exposure and vulnerability seeped into the world of the glossy general magazine.

Once *Playboy* had shown the way and succeeded in resisting the powerful reaction against the new pin-up, others were quick to follow and, indeed, to take over leadership in the field, at least insofar as increasing pornographic seepage became the trend. *Penthouse* followed *Playboy* with still more explicit representation of female genitals and pubic hair, along with explicit motifs of bondage and lesbianism in its pictorals. *Hustler* went still further, with an exploitation of images of rape, flagellation and fetishism, until virtually the only sexual secret that remained to hard-core pornography was the portrayal of heterosexual genital penetration and the erect male penis in orgasm. It is, indeed, an interesting indication of the theme of male dominance and distance, that the last sexual image short of outright perversion to be found in generally circulated magazines was that of the erect male penis. Amusingly, what might be called R-rated magazines and movies had come to feature full frontal female nudity, then side and rear views of men, and finally contact between men and women but only if the man's penis was not erect. *Playgirl,* which was supposedly intended to be the equivalent of *Playboy* for women, had naked male centerfolds of both famous people like Burt Reynolds and of the man next door, but for many years was not able to show these males in full erection. Yet, utter limpness was apparently not desirable either, for *Playgirl* pioneered an amazing series of portraits of the male penis in semi-erect state, a pose that must have been extraordinarily difficult for the models to hold.

Such is basically the story of pornographic seepage and it could be illustrated with many other media and genres. The r-rated or softcore film, for example, developed techniques for representing sexual intercourse with increasing explicitness, though always holding back from the closeup revelation of genital contact and of male ejaculation. Instead, r-rated films exploited fetishism, as in the mammoth mammary mediations of Russ Meyer, or in the increasingly explicit portrayals of rape and bondage in horror films. In addition, the somewhat idealized representation of sexual intercourse once characteristic of the r-rated softcore film has increasingly seeped into area of PG-13 ratings. Other forbidden images have become increasingly explicit in certain styles of art: the pop artist Mel Ramos has had considerable success with a nearly explicit representation of bestiality while others have moved into fetishism with representations of enormous breasts. The same process was clearly underway with the popular novel where explicit portrayals of lesbian and homosexual relationships, of bondage and rape, are becoming increasingly hard to differentiate from similar episodes in hardcore pornography. The main difference in these cases is that these explicit portrayals of the forbidden are embedded in much more elaborate and complex narratives of plot and character. Both literary and cinematic pornography largely remain dedicated to those minimal skeletons of plot and character necessary to get from one explicit sexual scene to another. When, if ever, we will have reached the limits of the seepage of explicitly pornographic symbolism remains to be seen.

V

While it is difficult to predict either what will happen to pornography as a cultural institution, or how far the process of pornographic seepage will go, we would like to offer a few tentative speculations about what might happen. To begin with, it seems clear that one aspect of pornographic symbolism, the use of latent or disguised forbidden images to, as it were, spice up other popular cultural genres like the romance, the spy story, or the western has long been a feature of western civilization, if not of human culture in general. In fact, the forbidden has long been a primary theme of folklore and of most types of literature, and will probably continue to be.

However, there may well be some changes in the nature of latent symbols of the forbidden if the deeply sexist patterns of western culture continue to be challenged and transformed. As we have seen, the disguised pornographic symbology in popular culture has traditionally been dominated by images of female subservience, abuse, and degradation. If modern American culture should seriously attempt to continue the trend toward democratization and equalization in sexual roles, we can probably expect to find this misogynistic aspect of pornographic symbolism much less acceptable in popular culture. On the other hand, feminist agitation and challenge to male hegemony may result in an increasing emphasis on anti-female symbolism since one function of the disguised expression of the forbidden seems to be the latent expression of hostilities between different social groups.

If the presence of latent pornographic symbolism is a more or less constant feature of popular culture, the phenomenon we have entitled seepage is much more subject to variation. Of course, a total seepage would make the distinction between hard-core pornography and popular culture irrelevant, but this seems unlikely. Instead, there seem to be limits to the degree to which explicit pornographic imagery can permeate non-pornographic genres, as well as cycles of greater or lesser amounts of seepage. While, in the course of the twentieth century, there has been a gradually increasing spread of explicit erotic images throughout the culture, there have also been periods of reaction when large segments of the public have sought to limit the expression of the forbidden. Such movements as the attack on the erotic content of motion pictures in the 1930s, on comic books in the 1950s, and the recent resurgence of prosecutions of the distributors of pornographic films and magazines, have worked to slow down the spread of pornographic movies. Where once almost every city in America had its complement of adult cinemas and bookstores, such businesses are becoming far less common. This is, of course, partly the result of the great success of pornographic videotapes, but the current situation also reflects increasing legal pressure based on a series of recent court decisions and the report of the second presidential commission on pornography which was far more critical than the commission on pornography and obscenity of the Johnson era.

It is possible, then, that we may have reached a kind of limit to the American public's willingness to accept the increasingly open and explicit expression of pornographic symbolism. However, if, as Peter Michelson suggests, pornography is a way of knowing something about human life that cannot be known in any other way, the current move toward the restriction of pornographic seepage may be only a temporary halt in an irresistible cultural trend. If this proves to be the case, it will mean that pornography in ceasing to be the secretive expression of the forbidden, will become something else altogether. That possibility is clearly the subject of another essay.

Notes

[1]The *OED*'s earliest listing of a cognate is from 1850 in an English translation of C. O. Muller's *Ancient Art*. The word is pornographer and the phrase is "the pornographers of later times."

[2]Of course, that doesn't help much, since obscenity is equally empty of specific signification, and has proved, in modern jurisprudence to be equally impossible to define. The latest tactic of the U.S. Supreme Court has been to turn the whole problem over to local option. Despite its vagueness, the concept of obscenity is clearly older than that of pornography with examples in the OED dating back to the sixteenth century. This dating suggests that the idea of obscenity may have begun to split off from the more religiously oriented concepts of blasphemy and heresy as a consequence of the Protestant reformation and the rise of Puritanism which laid particular stress on the prohibition of public performances which might corrupt the spectators. Thus, the first major assault on obscenity was probably the Puritan closing of the theaters in the 17th century.

[3]See also on this point, Arnold Davidson, "Sex and the Emergence of Sexuality." Peter Gay in *The Education of the Senses* also treats convincingly of the nineteenth's centuries realization of an fascination with sexuality.

[4]Roger Thompson, *Unfit for Modest Ears* (1975) and Felice Flanery Lewis, *Literature, Obscenity and Law* (1976) give some idea of the history of obscenity as a literary and legal category. Charles Rembar, defense counsel in the *Tropic of Cancer* and *Fanny Hill* cases announced *The End of Obscenity* in 1968. In light of recent court decisions, however, that seems unduly optimistic.

[5]Nabokov has an interesting argument about this in his defense of *Lolita.* He argues that the artistic style of the book is what makes it non-pornographic. A pornographer, he argues, would use the simplest possible style, since it is the content his audience is most interested in. As Nabokov puts it: "in modern times the term 'pornography' connotes mediocrity, commercialism, and certain strict rules of narration. Obscenity must be mated with banality because every kind of aesthetic enjoyment has to be entirely replaced by simple sexual stimulation which demands the traditional word for direct action upon the patient...Thus, in pornographic novels action has to be limited to the copulation of cliches. Style, structure, imagery should never distract the reader from his tepid lust." (Nabokov 1970, 315)

[6]This distinction was first most clearly articulated by Phyllis and Eberhard Kronhausen in their *Pornography and the Law* (1959). Though successive critics and scholars of pornography have pointed out the flaws and problems with this distinction, they still tend to fall back on it when some sort of definition of pornography becomes necessary. Michelson, for example, wants to argue that pornography is "like any literature" a legitimate "way of knowing" which "has revealed a new and larger being, *homo sexualis.*" In other words, "pornography creates an image of human sexuality which not only inspires erotic gratification but also suggests the anthropological dimensions of sexual libido." This leads him to the view that pornography is capable of undergoing an "evolving psychic and artistic complexity" which will increasingly legitimate it as an artistic genre. But what is this other than pornography becoming erotic realism? Michelson, *The Aesthetics of Pornography:* pp. 4-11.

[7]These fantasies are treated by Steven Marcus under the general heading of "pornotopia" in *The Other Victorians.* Michelson also deals with these fantasies as basic to pornography in *The Aesthetics of Pornography:* "[pornography] has two images, the erect phallus and the carnal woman." (p.4)

[8]Nancy Friday relates several such fantasies in her study of masculine sexual fantasy *Men in Love.* Fantasies of bestiality are clearly not as important in Friday's studies of female sexual fantasies.

[9]Quoted from *The Collected Poems of W. B. Yeats,* 241.

[10]A somewhat similar though less brutal treatment of gang rape appeared in the recent film *The Accused,* which was in turn based upon an actual case in New Bedford, MA, where a woman had been gang-raped in a bar while other people looked on.

[11]In fact, Judge Woolsey's famous comment that *Ulysses* was more emetic than erotic, while perhaps inaccurate with respect to Joyce's work, would certainly apply to *Last Exit to Brooklyn.* The *Ulysses* example illustrates, we think that the traditional connection between pornography and erotic arousal or prurience is a complete red herring. Works like *Ulysses* and *Lady Chatterly's Lover* are erotically arousing and they were probably intended to be by their authors. But the kind of sexuality they describe is not really forbidden in modern society. There are no laws against masturbation, except in public, and while there may be residual statutes and even significant moral reasons against adultery and fornication, there are few serious attempts to enforce them. Even in the nineteenth century Hawthorne's *The Scarlet Letter* was not considered pornographic except by a few fanatics. Of course, Hawthorne's novel was about the moral and psychological results of adultery and not the act itself.

[12]The most successful efforts along these lines are probably those in *Penthouse* and *Hustler* with their use of the symbology of sadism. Another approach is that of fetishism, particularly with the representation of extraordinarily large-breasted women, which is probably a concealed fantasy of incest. This brings up another aspect of the subject which there is no space to treat in the present paper: the extent to which one condition of

pornography is the displacement and concealing of the forbidden act that is being represented.

[13]In general, our approach to this problem is similar to that taken by the Kronhausens in their sensible *Pornography and the Law*. The Kronhausens draw a distinction between erotic art and pornography, mainly on aesthetic grounds, but, while such a distinction might become a rationale for censorship, they deplore censorship and hope that it will never prove necessary or politically expedient to restore the kind of censorship that prevailed until the 1950s, in part because important works of art are more likely than pornography to be hurt by censorship. Morse Peckham in his traditional role of Peck's Bad Boy of cultural criticism takes an even more complex approach to the question of censorship, because he believes that pornography with its cultivation of the forbidden has been the greatest force for innovation of the modern era. The question of censorship is not whether pornography is obscene and therefore immoral, but whether we can stand any more innovation: "what should be done about pornography is extremely complex. Ideally, the New Left should be subjected to the policing both of sexual behavior and access to pornography in order to lock in free energy; the still stable Old Left, a very small group, to be sure, and the Center should be encouraged by free access to pornography to increase their tolerance for innovation; and the Right should be managed by increasing their tolerance for sexual behavior, and by subjecting them not only to a much easier access to pornography but even a deliberately undertaken exposure to it." *Art and Pornography,* 301. We have also depended considerably on the Kronhausen's treatment of the element of the forbidden in pornography, though our approach to this is not identical to theirs.

[14]CF the report of the Traffic and Distribution Panel the New York Times edition of *The Report of the Commission of Obscenity and Pornography* (1970), pp. 83-168.

[15]A number of feminist scholars such as Mary Jane Sherfey have presented considerable evidence suggesting the greater sexual desires and interests of women. Other indications of female interest in sexuality per se include Nancy Friday's studies of female sexual fantasies, Shere Hite's surveys of female sexual activity and Erika Jong's fantasy of the "zipless fuck" which runs counter to the ideology that women necessarily associate love and romance.

[16]A recent pornographic film about the G spot starring veteran porno star Annette Haven made the fullest attempt of any film we are familiar with to represent female orgasm. That this film is unique in our experience suggests the extent to which pornographic films are still dominated by sexist ideologies.

[17]Any catalog of sexual publications, films, videotapes and other appliances, such as that of the company that calls itself (misleadingly) *Adam and Eve,* indicates the extent to which pornographic production continues to cater primarily to male interests and attitudes. Even if one assumes that vibrators and other kinds of dildos have some interest for women, publications and articles catering mainly to male sexual fantasies are still vastly in the majority. And this is obviously a questionable assumption since dildos might be equally attractive to homosexuals, to men worried about their sexual potency, or to sadists who would use them for some forms of sexual torture.

[18]A good example of this was a recent pornographic film which began with a brutal scene of a rape in which a young woman was raped by a gang wearing ski masks. However, as the film proceeded it was revealed that the young woman had paid the gang to rape her since only through the acting-out of rape could the woman truly feel the greatest sexual arousal.

[19]Evidently the economies of filming have required the development of many techniques to fake male orgasm. One book reports that Tame Creme Rinse is a perfectly undetectable substitute for semen.

[20]Michelangelo Antonioni's film *Blow-up* exposed this symbolism quite powerfully through its story of a fashion photographer and his sexual power over female models.

[21]Several striking historical parallels between romance and pornography indicate that the presence of latent pornographic symbolism in romance is of long standing. Just as the romance originated in the late eighteenth century with the novels of Samuel Richardson, so the first modern pornographic work, *Fanny Hill,* was written in the same period and reads in many ways like an inverted *Pamela.* The gothic romances of the early nineteenth century such as those of Ann Radcliffe and Monk Lewis developed the motif of the alien seducer which was a staple in such works of hard-core pornography as *The Lustful Turk* (1828?). The favorite Victorian romance theme of the agnostic male converted to evangelical Christianity by the purity and spirituality of a young girl had its pornographic counterpart in *A Man and A Maid,* where a free-thinking young man entraps a prudish young woman in a secret room and by the tactics of bondage and rape converts her to the delights of lust. One problem with these parallels is that it is a little hard to determine which comes first, the romance motif or its pornographic counterpart. Thus, our formulation of the romance-pornography relationship in terms of the transformation of pornographic symbolism into latent motifs in romance may be too reductive and that the actual process consists of a very complex dialectic between pornography and other popular genres. To trace this dialectic, however, would be too lengthy and complex an analysis for this essay. Steven Marcus has made a considerable contribution to the discussion of this issue in his *The Other Victorians* (1966).

[22]For a more detailed analysis of various sexual themes in Ian Fleming and other spy writer see John Cawelti and Bruce Rosenberg, *The Spy Story* (1987).

[23]We have no idea why the tabloids seem so obsessed with forbidden partners, but it is certainly an interesting phenomenon about which to speculate. Could it be that people in unhappy sexual relationships or in no sexual relationships at all feel some comfort in thinking that it might be worse, or is it simply the inescapable lure of the forbidden? As a sample of this type of tabloid theme, the front pate of the *Sun* for Feb. 7, 1989 has ten headline stories of which one, "Man Shot Dead by Champagne Cork," does not seem to relate in any significant way to our theme. Of the remaining nine, two are questionable, but the other seven are clearly disguised examples of forbidden partners: "Girl Raised by Wolves:Now She's Queen of the Forest;" "Cheating Father Meets Daughter Working in Brothel;" (Shades of Pirandello) "Wife's Strange Story; I Fell in Love With a Vampire and Married Him;" "Brothers Share the Same Wife for 6 Years;" "UFO Aliens Talk to Woman Through Old TV Programs;" "Giant Man-Eating Mermaid Attacks Scuba Diver;" and "Beautiful Gals Who Are the Toughest Wrestlers in U.S."

Works Cited

Braun, Rex. *Soldiers' Girl.* North Hollywood, CA: American Art Enterprises, 1984.

Cawelti, John and Bruce Rosenberg. *The Spy Story.* Chicago: University of Chicago Press, 1987.

Davidson, Arnold. "Sex and the Emergence of Sexuality." *Critical Inquiry.* Vol. 14, no. 1 (Autumn 1987) pp. 16-48.

Foucault, Michel. *The History of Sexuality.* Quoted in Calvin Bedient. *He Do the Police in Different Voices.* Chicago: University of Chicago Press, 1987, (pp 24-25).

Friday, Nancy. *Men in Love: Men's Sexual Fantasies: The Triumph of Love over Rage.* New York: Delacorte Press, 1980.

Gay, Peter. *The Bourgeois Experience: Victoria to Freud. Vol. I: Education of the Senses.* New York: Oxford University Press, 1984.

Kronhausen, Eberhard and Phyllis. *Pornography and the Law: The Psychology of Erotic Realism and Pornography.* New York: Ballantine Books, 1959.

Lewis, Felice Flanery. *Literature, Obscenity and Law.* Carbondale, IL: Southern Illinois University Press, 1976.

Marcus, Steven. *The Other Victorians: A Study of Sexuality and Pornography in Mid-Nineteenth-Century England.* New York: Basic Books, 1966.

Michelson, Peter. *The Aesthetics of Pornography.* New York: Herder and Herder, 1971.

Nabokov, Vladimir. *The Annotated Lolita.* (ed. Alfred Appel, Jr.) New York: McGraw-Hill, 1970.

Peckham, Morse. *Art and Pornography: An Experiment in Explanation.* New York: Basic Books, 1969.

Rembar, Charles. *The End of Obscenity.* New York: Random House, 1968.

Selby, Hubert. *Last Exit to Brooklyn.* New York: Grove Press, 1964.

The New York Times. *The Report of the Commission on Obscenity and Pornography.* New York: Bantam Books, 1970.

Thompson, Roger. *Unfit for Modest Ears.* Totowa, NJ: Rowman and Littlefield, 1979.

Yeats, W. B. *The Collected Poems of W. B. Yeats.* London: Macmillan, 1950.

Wilderness: Ambiguous Symbol of the American Past

Philip G. Terrie

Americans have seldom been certain what the wilderness means to them. Because their response to wilderness has always been a function of a complex cultural situation making ambiguous and sometimes contradictory demands of the American relationship with all of nature, Americans have had a hard time deciding what the wilderness is and what to do with it. But through much of our history, the wilderness has constituted an obvious, significant reality, and Americans have expressed their responses to wilderness—often confused, nearly always ambivalent—in a constant stream of popular forms, beginning with the histories and other narratives of the Puritans, running through the travel literature, fiction, and paintings of the nineteenth century, and culminating (for the present, at least) in the films, nature writing, and other popular literature of the twentieth. Early Anglo-Americans condemned wilderness as the dwelling place of Satan, the physical obstacle to the divinely ordained American mission to civilize the New World. More recently, some Americans have turned this hostility on its head, valuing the wilderness as a treasured remnant of our frontier past or investing it with its own divinity and insisting that the redemption of the modern soul depends on our efforts to preserve and respect what remains of the once vast wilderness.

The individual's response to wilderness reflects his or her cultural situation, the combination of values, assumptions, and preconceptions that organize and indeed determine the way one perceives and interacts with both the natural and social world. A person perceives nature through the needs of his or her culture. An agricultural society inevitably invests the rural landscape with special meaning; likewise, the meaning of wilderness for any individual is largely the product of that person's culture and how that culture has expressed its environmental, social, economic, and spiritual needs. Thoreau knew this well. After trekking and canoeing through the Maine wilderness in the middle of the nineteenth century, he observed, "Generally speaking, a howling wilderness does not howl: it is the imagination of the traveller that does the howling."[1] In a visual metaphor that particularly suits our purposes here, the anthropologists Clyde Kluckhohn and Henry A. Murray have put this a different way: "Culture directs and often distorts man's perceptions of the external world.... Culture acts as a set of blinders, or a series of lenses, through which men view their environments."[2]

Attitudes toward wilderness, moreover, suggest a culture's sense of itself. The wilderness acts as a great mirror, reflecting back upon a culture its hopes, fears, values, and conceptions of nature and its place in nature. Each age has its dominant "metaphors for environmental change," as the historian William Cronon has characterized this phenomenon, and in them we discover clues to both what a culture thinks of nature and what it (perhaps unconsciously) thinks of itself.[3] Thus the seventeenth-century Puritans looked around at the incredible vastness of the New England wilderness and saw temptation, seduction, and endless opportunities for humankind's innate depravity to manifest itself. According to Richard Slotkin, in the wilderness "the Puritans saw a darkened and inverted mirror image of their own culture, their own mind.... The wilderness was seen as a Calvinist universe in microcosm and also as an analogy of the human mind. Both were dark, with hidden possibilities for good and evil."[4]

Before the Puritans arrived, the first Americans peacefully inhabited an environment they treated well and which in turn supported them well. As historians of native American attitudes and values have shown, the Indians lived comfortably in a landscape they altered to suit their needs but whose capacity to support them was not disturbed. Although it is crudely reductive to speak of Indian culture, when in fact there were hundreds of different cultures, it is safe to generalize about nature, which, for virtually all native Americans, was something familiar, benign, and close; indeed, most Indians saw themselves as part of nature, as no more or less significant than the forests they lived in or the animals they hunted. The important point is the notion of a culture's perceiving itself to be *in* nature, related to it, deeply involved in both physical and spiritual ways. This is the profound implication of native American stories—creation myths, for example—wherein animals like beaver or wolves are referred to in anthropomorphic terms and as the Indians' brothers and sisters.[5] The value of understanding the Indian relationship with nature is that its example lay dormant in the white subconscious, unrecognized and often scorned, to be rediscovered in the late twentieth century.

The attitudes of the early Europeans in the Northeast differed radically from those of the Indians they quickly displaced. When William Bradford, the first governor of Plymouth Plantation, described the initial reaction of his fellow Pilgrims and himself to the Massachusetts wilderness, he could do so only in negative terms, responding exclusively to those features of the wilderness that were the opposite of civilization and of what he hoped to find in the New World:

> Being thus passed the vast ocean...they now had no friends to welcome them nor inns to entertain or refresh their weatherbeaten bodies; no houses or much less town to repair to, to seek for succour.... Besides, what could they see but a hideous and desolate wilderness, full of wild beasts and wild men...which way soever they turned their eyes (save upward to the heavens) they could find little solace or content in respect of any outward objects.[6]

The Pilgrims, like the other Englishmen who followed them, came to establish a new civilization; the wilderness was the palpable and all too obvious barrier in the way of this mission. Like other Calvinists, moreover, the Pilgrims believed that the physical manifestations of this world, the material realm of trees, rocks, water, etc., were merely shadows of the truly significant next world (in viewing the Cape Cod landscape, the Pilgrims found "little solace" in "outward objects" except when they turned their eyes "upward to the heavens"). In its most extreme form, as carried to the New World by the Pilgrims and their Puritan brethren, this doctrine interpreted all earthly things as sensual, dangerous seductions from proper pursuits—worshipping God and contemplating the next world. Thus the wilderness, in addition to appearing "hideous and desolate," was but one more illusion, a shadow, an entity not to be taken seriously, and certainly not to be vested with inherent value. Bradford, moreover, was invoking an image of the wilderness familiar to his Bible-reading comrades: in this tradition wilderness represented a stopping place—often hostile and brutal—for the faithful on the way to a better, holier domain. The Bible, the most popular book of the first English-speaking Americans, thus provided the first set of popular images for the vast American wilderness.[7]

Many of the themes first invoked by Bradford were repeated and elaborated in the first indigenous popular literature to emerge in the English-speaking colonies; this was the genre of the captivity narrative, tales written by English men and women who had been captured by Indians, were forced to live in the wilderness for a while, and after escape or ransom returned to civilization. One of the best of these was written by Mary Rowlandson and first published in Boston in 1682. It was enormously popular and remained in print for a century and a half.[8] In Rowlandson's account "the vast and howling wilderness" is described as the terrestrial manifestation of hell itself and the Indians as so many vicious devils.[9] As Richard Slotkin writes, "For the captive, the wilderness is the physical type of metaphysical hell. For the reader, the wilderness is a vivid analogue of the condition of his own inner being—a paradigm of his mind and soul in which his sins, hidden under hopes and rationalizations, are suddenly made manifest."[10]

The Puritan distrust of and hostility toward wilderness persisted throughout the sixteenth and seventeenth centuries (with exceptions of course). By the eighteenth century, however, as more and more Americans lived in settled areas away from the reality of the wilderness, the attitudes of some Americans began to change. So long as the wilderness was just beyond the fence and so long as it was actually inhabited by people thought to be the living manifestation of Satan's hatred for Christian civilization, it was natural to despise the wilderness. But as soon as the wilderness no longer seemed threatening, a slow process of mythologization and nostalgia began.[11] For Americans living in towns or in agricultural areas away from the frontier, the wilderness began to take on historical significance; it was the place where one's grandparents had performed the heroic deeds of first settlement—clearing the land, fighting off the hostile Indians.

Nostalgic faith in the dramatic quality of the wilderness experience was further encouraged by popular romanticism, a set of beliefs permeating American culture by the third or fourth decade of the nineteenth century. In nature, believed most romantics, modern man, beset by the horrors endemic to a culture rapidly becoming urban and industrial, could find moral, spiritual, and physical regeneration. As Ralph Waldo Emerson declared in his important first book, *Nature,* "In the Wilderness I find something more dear or connate [meaningful] than in streets and villages."[12] Although the Concord sage's actual experience with what we would call wilderness was minimal, his assertion of this characteristically romantic article of faith illustrates the tendency of the age to see value in wild nature and to deprecate life in the city. And although Emerson is often associated with the heady atmosphere of intellectual New England, he was declaring here a widely shared American conviction.[13]

Joel T. Headley expressed similar sentiments in an 1849 narrative about camping and hunting in the Adirondacks. This book was reprinted, plagiarized, and pirated in numerous editions over the next twenty-five years and reflected the commonly held tenets of popular romanticism.[14] Musing one evening about the rigors and benefits of camp life, Headley concluded,

> I love the freedom of the wilderness and the absence of conventional forms there. I love the long stretch through the forest on foot, and the thrilling, glorious prospect from some hoary mountain top. I love it, and I know it is better for me than the thronged city, aye, better for soul and body both.... A single tree standing alone, and waving all day its green crown in the summer wind, is to me fuller of meaning and instruction than the crowded mart or gorgeously built town.[15]

Like other romantics, Headley expressed an inchoate suspicion that the road to industrial, urban progress might not be the best choice for American culture. Antimodernism ran deep in popular American romanticism, but it was seldom articulated explicitly. For it was also the age of manifest destiny and faith in the ultimate goodness of the obvious mission of American civilization to settle the continent and extend its improvements from coast to coast. The antimodernism of Headley and his ilk promoted wilderness camping trips and hackneyed encomia to the virtues of life away from the bustling city; behind it was an apprehension that American culture, by committing itself to the exigencies of the smokestack and the marketplace, was abandoning truths found only in the wilderness.[16]

But although the romantic consciousness was sensitive to the Wordsworthian doctrine of the virtue of all of nature, Americans, especially those equally attuned to popular values, also believed in the inevitable disappearance of the wilderness and the superior merits of a landscape where human impact, especially in the form of agricultural improvements, predominated. Consequently, romantics often responded to wilderness with an implicit suspicion that wilderness was a violation of God's mandate to make the earth fruitful and productive. The chief characteristic of the popular romantic response to wilderness was ambivalence.

Headley, in a book ostensibly devoted to singing the glories of the wilderness, overtly declared his preference for the bucolic over the wild; musing on the appeal of various types of scenery, he observes, "The gloomy gorge and savage precipice, or the sudden storm, seem to excite the surface only of one's feelings, while the sweet vale, with its cottages and herds and evening bells, blends itself with our very thoughts and emotions, forming a part of our after existence."[17] The wilderness, he suggests, supplies a temporarily interesting stimulation, but like most Americans of his day he believed in the inherently greater importance to his culture of a continent where the wilderness had been subjected to human will and turned to the production of useful goods. This vestigial reluctance to embrace the wilderness fully has never been absent from American culture.

But an interest in wilderness, however qualified, was still a step away from earlier hostility. Combined with the peculiarly American idea that the wilderness of the new world could be the subject of a national literature, as in the novels of James Fenimore Cooper, or a national art, as in the paintings of the Hudson River School and the luminists, romantic assumptions about the wilderness eventually led to the conclusion that at least parts of the wilderness were worth saving.[18] Shortly after the Civil War, when Americans were looking in every conceivable direction for ways to reassert their culture's sense of direction and stability, the idea of setting aside for posterity the most startling and spectacular of the continent's scenery seemed increasingly appealing.

In 1872, after considerable debate, the United States Congress established Yellowstone National Park. But the move to protect the Yellowstone did not reflect a popular wish to preserve the wilderness as such; it was inspired by public awareness of the monumentality of the scenery and an urge to protect for tourism such oddities as Old Faithful, various hot springs, and other natural "curiosities." In order to combat public misgivings over removing any part of the nation's real estate from the domain of progress and improvement, the sponsors of the bill to set aside the Yellowstone had to assure one and all that the region was too high and too cold to be cultivated or otherwise turned to useful purposes.[19] In the popular consciousness, wilderness remained a sort of place that might contain items of interest, but it was not of inherent value. The modern cliché that the American character, with all the attendant notions of individualism, ruggedness, and inventiveness, was forged in the wilderness remained short of the popular authority that it later enjoyed.

But in 1893, when Frederick Jackson Turner delivered his now famous address on "The Significance of the Frontier in American History" to an audience of academics, he tapped an idea that had been stirring in the American mind throughout the nineteenth century. In a contemporary but somewhat different exposition of a similar idea, the young Theodore Roosevelt also appealed to this popular conceit in a series of books and essays on western history. To Roosevelt, the wilderness was the locus of events of great individual heroism, and it was the arena where American culture worked out its destiny, hunting wild animals, killing Indians, and generally developing those talents—self-reliance and initiative—he thought so important to the nation as it confronted a complex modern world.[20] As the country became steadily more urban in the twentieth century and as more and more Americans were removed geographically from the realities of actual wilderness, this idea of the historical importance of wilderness became increasingly powerful.

The popular fascination with wilderness in the early twentieth century is nowhere better illustrated than in the story of Joseph Knowles, a middle-aged, sedentary Bostonian who in 1913 electrified the nation by abandoning civilization (even to point of shedding all his clothes) and heading off into the Maine woods, alone and unequipped, for a two-month experiment in self-reliance. Newspapers across the country picked up Knowles's escapades and relayed his adventure—which he passed along to reporters via messages inscribed on birchbark with charcoal—to a public eager to hear how a civilized, modern man could survive in the wilderness. That Knowles turned out later to have been ruminating snugly in a remote cabin does not diminish the public enthusiasm for what it thought he was doing.[21] Americans felt an intense need to connect themselves with their past, even if that past was a mythologized invention. The idea that American strengths and values had been nurtured through the contact between rugged individualists like Kit Carson or Jim Bridger with the wilderness became a fundamental conviction of American popular culture.

Wilderness advocates in the twentieth century took full advantage of this public association of the wilderness with American history and used it in their efforts to advance the cause of wilderness preservation. Robert Marshall and Aldo Leopold, both scientists educated at prestigious universities and both effective popularizers of the growing preservation movement, pushed the historical significance of wilderness. Writing about his explorations in the Central Brooks Range of Alaska in the 1930s, Marshall explained that his "ideology" of wilderness was "formed on a Lewis and Clark pattern" and consistently emphasized the adventure and opportunities for recreating the frontier experience.[22] To Marshall, though he was trained as a biologist, the chief appeal of the wilderness was that it was there he demonstrated his woodcraft and his physical strength. The word "frontier" pops up repeatedly in Marshall's narrative, as he associates the wilderness with such traditional frontier virtues as self-reliance, ruggedness, and stamina. The wilderness was a proving ground, and Marshall loved it because he tested himself against its imperatives and prevailed.

Aldo Leopold did not go quite so far in suggesting that the value of wilderness lay chiefly in its capacity to supply an arena for acting out the adventures of the pioneers; he was sensitive to aesthetic and other values, such as the need for preserving habitats for wildlife. But in his classic *Sand County Almanac* he outlined a list of reasons for protecting wilderness and included under the rubric "Wilderness for Recreation" the following:

> Physical combat for the means of subsistence was, for unnumbered centuries, an economic fact. When it disappeared as such, a sound instinct led us to preserve it in the form of athletic sports and games. Physical combat between men and beasts was, in like manner, an economic fact, now preserved as hunting and fishing for sport. Public wilderness areas are, first of all, a means of perpetuating, in sport form, the more virile and primitive skills in [sic] pioneering travel and subsistence.[23]

Throughout this century wilderness has continued to appeal to many Americans because of its association with a frontier thought of in traditionally masculine terms. A characteristic expression of this is the 1972 film *Jeremiah Johnson* which mythologized the exploits of an actual frontier personality (played by Robert Redford) and paid particular attention to a detailed treatment of Johnson's developing hunting, fishing, and other skills required for survival in the wilderness. To many Americans the image of the solitary man, living and even prospering amid the grandeur of the Rocky Mountain wilderness, carries archetypal significance.

In its more extreme form this association has led to the obsessive fascination with wilderness and wilderness skills evinced by the current fad of survivalism. The followers of this movement are curiously drawn to both modern technology (in the shape of generators, communications gear, etc., and an endless array of firearms) and the wilderness. Inspired by an antimodernist fear that civilization is on the brink of imminent disintegration, either through nuclear war or collapse of the world economy, survivalists fantasize in their magazines and books about retreating to the wilderness. *American Survival Guide* and *Shooter's Survival Guide,* for example, two of the primary journals in the survivalist subculture, routinely publish articles like "Backcountry Survival Tips," "Digging In: Winter Shelters," "Alpine Adventure: Mountain Trekking," "Edible Ferns," "Wilderness Medicine," and "Building an Indian Wickiup."[24]

A popular novel with survivalist overtones hit the best-seller lists in 1987 and illustrated perfectly this aspect of the continuing public interest in the wilderness. Louis L'Amour's *Last of the Breed* tells a mostly incredible yarn about a captain in the American Air Force who is kidnapped by Russian intelligence, spirited away to Siberia, and subjected to a brutal interrogation. The officer, who, significantly, is half Indian, quickly escapes, and most of the novel relates his adventures in the wilderness of Siberia, as he survives two winters despite horrible cold and deprivation and gradually makes his way to the Pacific coast, where he steals a small boat and heads for North America, approximately via the same route his Asian ancestors had used thousands of years earlier.

In the context of a simplistic cold-war contempt for Russian communism and an equally simplistic faith in American self-reliance, the chief activity of the novel involves a precise narrative of how the American recovers his heritage—a combination of Indian and frontier-white woodcraft—and comes up with one ingenious scheme after another for surviving in the wilderness. He improvises shelters and weapons, navigates by the stars, and clothes and feeds himself. Retreating ever further into his racial memory, the hero absorbs energy and encouragement from the earth itself, as the tale becomes a *macho* parable chanting the need of Americans to recover their own wilderness past if they are to survive in a hostile world.[25]

An interest in an ostensibly Indian ethos accounts for another facet of the contemporary cult of wilderness, also profoundly antimodernist, but staking out a less right-wing position than that of the survivalists. As modern industrial civilization makes increasingly devastating conquests of the world's natural environment and as people feel more and more alienated from each other and from nature, many radical environmentalists look to the example of native Americans for a model of a way of life and of living in harmony with nature. The chief feature of this modern version of romantic primitivism is the belief that hunter-gatherers, people living close to nature, existed in a state of pervasive spirituality, nourished by the primal forces of the earth itself.[26]

To this way of thinking, the wilderness itself becomes divine, suffused with ultimate meaning. Modern man has lost touch with this source of meaning but can recover it through intimacy with its base in the wilderness. Dick Cook, who abandoned a career as a real-estate appraiser in Ohio to find spirituality and meaning in the wildest of solitudes in the Alaskan bush, told writer John McPhee, "I feel a part of what is here. The bush is so far beyond what anybody has been taught. The religious power here is beyond what anybody has been taught. The religious power here is beyond all training. There are forces here that a lot of people don't know exist. They can't be articulated. You're out of the realm of words. You are close to the land here, to nature, to what the Indians call Mother and I call Momma."[27]

These two threads, the association of wilderness with our frontier past and the conviction that wilderness is the locus of spiritual meaning, converge (along with a scientific interest in preserving ecosystems and natural habitats) in the modern wilderness preservation movement. In 1964 Congress passed the National Wilderness Act, reflecting the American desire to see some of the remaining wilderness preserved in perpetuity.[28] Since then the acreage of designated wilderness has grown, and the wilderness has acquired a powerful lobby in Washington. Our Puritan ancestors would be utterly astonished. But their hostility to wilderness has not disappeared. Where the Puritans feared wilderness in religious terms, the modern objection to wilderness is couched in the language of progress and commerce. Wilderness, as it did to the exponents of manifest destiny in the nineteenth century, continues to represent to some Americans an obstacle to progress, a failure of civilization to take efficient advantage of natural resources. William Tucker, outspoken foe of designated wilderness, writes scornfully, " 'Wilderness,' in the hands of environmentalists, has become an all-purpose tool for stopping economic activity."[29]

Wilderness remains as ambiguous a subject in American culture as it has ever been. Some of us love it, finding the only genuine meaning for our lives in the idea of a landscape undefiled by human refinements. Some of us retreat to the wilderness in an effort to recreate the putative intense experiences of the pioneers, convinced that the strengths and skills of the American character developed in the wilderness and can be recovered only through a renewed immersion in the wilderness environment that nurtured Daniel Boone and Jeremiah Johnson. Others of us continue to see the wilderness as our enemy, an affront to the American pursuit of progress, modernity, and prosperity. As Richard Slotkin observed of the Puritans, what a culture thinks about the wilderness is an index of what it thinks of itself. Our modern attitudes toward wilderness show us to be a complex, occasionally confused culture, with an often profound ambivalence about who we are, what nature is, and what our life in and with nature ought to be.

Notes

[1]Henry David Thoreau, *The Maine Woods* (Princeton: Princeton University Press, 1972) 219.

[2]Clyde Kluckhohn and Henry A. Murray, *Personality in Nature, Society, and Culture* (New York: Alfred A. Knopf, 1948) 45.

[3]William Cronon, *Changes in the Land: Indians, Colonists, and the Ecology of New England* (New York: Hill and Wang, 1983) 5.

[4]Richard Slotkin, *Regeneration Through Violence: The Mythology of the American Frontier, 1600-1860* (Middletown, CT: Wesleyan University Press, 1973) 57, 77.

[5]See, among others, Neal Salisbury, *Manitou and Providence: Indians, Europeans, and the Making of New England, 1500-1643* (New York: Oxford University Press, 1982); Calvin Martin, *Keepers of the Game: Indian-Animal Relationships and the Fur Trade* (Berkeley: University of California Press, 1978); Frederick Turner, *Beyond Geography: The Western Spirit Against the Wilderness* (New York: Viking, 1980). Cronon, *Changes in the Land,* argues for a more materialistic interpretation of the Indian relationship with the natural environment, suggesting that it was an inherent understanding of efficient modes of production that led to the harmonious, unexploitative use of nature that characterized New England before white contact.

[6]William Bradford, *Of Plymouth Plantation* (New York: Random House, Modern Library, 1981) 69-79.

[7]Cecelia Tichi, *New World, New Earth: Environmental Reform in American Literature from the Puritans through Whitman* (New Haven: Yale University Press, 1979) 23-24.

[8]Slotkin, *Regeneration Through Violence* 95-96.

[9]Mary Rowlandson, *The Sovereignty and Goodness of God, Together with the Faithfulness of His Promises Displayed: Being a Narrative of the Captivity and Restauration of Mrs. Mary Rowlandson* (Cambridge, MA: Samuel Green, 1682).

[10]Slotkin, *Regeneration Through Violence* 109.

[11]Roderick Nash, *Wilderness and the American Mind.* 3rd ed., (New Haven: Yale University Press, 1982) 44-83.

[12]Ralph Waldo Emerson, *The Complete Works of Ralph Waldo Emerson* (Boston: Houghton, Mifflin, 1903-04) 1: 10.

[13]For further discussion of Emerson's attitudes toward wilderness, see Philip G. Terrie, *Forever Wild: Environmental Aesthetics and the Adirondack Forest Preserve* (Philadelphia: Temple University Press, 1985) 59-64.

[14]For more on Headley and the popularity of his book see Philip G. Terrie, "Introduction" in Joel T. Headley, *The Adirondack; Or, Life in the Woods* (Harrison, NY: Harbor Hill, 1982).

[15]Headley, *The Adirondack* 167-68.

[16]On antimodernism in American culture, see Peter J. Schmidt, *Back to Nature: The Arcadian Myth in Urban America* (New York: Oxford University Press, 1969), and T. J. Jackson Lears, *No Place of Grace: Antimodernism and the Transformation of American Culture, 1880-1920* (New York: Pantheon, 1981).

[17]Headley, *The Adirondack* 182.

[18]See Barbara Novak, *Nature and Culture: American Landscape and Painting, 1825-1875* (New York: Oxford University Press, 1980).

[19]Alfred Runte, *National Parks: The American Experience* (Lincoln: University of Nebraska Press, 1979) 33-47; Nash, *Wilderness and the American Mind,* 108-16.

[20]Richard Slotkin, "Nostalgia and Progress: Theodore Roosevelt's Myth of the Frontier," *American Quarterly* 33 (Winter 1981): 608-637.

[21]The Knowles story is retold in Nash, *Wilderness and the American Mind* 141-43.

[22]Robert Marshall, *Alaska Wilderness: Exploring the Central Brooks Range* (Berkeley: University of California Press, 1956) 1; on Marshall see James M. Glover, *A Wilderness Original: The Life of Robert Marshall* (Seattle: The Mountaineers Books, 1986).

[23]Aldo Leopold, *A Sand County Almanac* (New York: Oxford University Press, 1949) 192; on Leopold see Susan Flader, *Thinking Like a Mountain: Aldo Leopold and the Evolution of an Ecological Attitude toward Deer, Wolves, and Forests* (Lincoln: University of Nebraska Press, 1974).

[24]*Shooters Survival Guide,* no vol. (October 1981): 28-31, 75-76; *American Survival Guide,* 6 (December 1983): 76-87; 7 (July 1985): 76-78; 7 (December 1985): 54-55, 74-75; 10 (September 1988): 44-47, 63; 10 (October 1988): 72-74; see also Ragnar Benson, *The Survival Retreat: A Total Plan for Retreat Defense* (Boulder, CO: Paladin Press, 1983).

[25]Louis L'Amour, *Last of the Breed* (New York: Bantam, 1987).

[26]See Bill Devall and George Sessions, *Deep Ecology: Living as If Nature Mattered* (Layton, Utah: Gibbs Smith, 1985).

[27]John McPhee, *Coming Into the Country* (New York: Bantam, 1979) 255.

[28]Nash, *Wilderness and the American Mind* 200-226.

[29]William Tucker, "Is Nature Too Good For Us?", *Harper's,* 264 (March 1982): 27-35.

The Tamed Wild: Symbolic Bears in American Culture

Elizabeth A. Lawrence

Virtually every animal with which people interact has in addition to its own physical being a symbolic identity which may or may not accurately reflect the animal's nature but which arises out of individual and cultural perceptions of that species. Study of the symbolic aspects of animals can shed light on the deeper dimensions of human-animal relationships and help to explain why certain species have occupied such an important role in human life and culture. Bears, for example, have been a source of fascination in many societies for countless ages. As large, spectacular creatures, bears have often commanded awe, respect, and admiration, as well as evoking fear and antagonism.

Since the dawn of human consciousness, wherever bears have been encountered they have been special objects of attention that often figured prominently in the mental and spiritual life of the people. Bears may well have inspired humankind's first mystical feelings and concepts, for according to Joseph Campbell "the earliest evidence anywhere on earth of veneration of a divine being is in the Alpine bear-skull sanctuaries of Neanderthal man." Through studying such areas, archaeologists have found indications that during paleolithic times the remains of the now-extinct cave bear were used in worshipful rites and ceremonies (1983: 147, 54-56). Ancient peoples identified huge bear images in the night sky and named two great constellations, Ursa Major and Ursa Minor, in honor of the awesome creatures. These configurations—the big and little bear—are two of the oldest star groupings known, and were recognized long ago by such divergent peoples as the North American Indians, the Basques, and the early Chaldeans (White 1942:7).

In numerous non-industrial societies of the world, extending into the present, attitudes of esteem and reverence for bears have been recorded as important cultural elements. Bear ceremonialism was once widespread among certain peoples of North America, Asia, and Europe (Hallowell 1926), and has persisted into modern times (Speck 1977; Nelson 1983; DeMallie 1984). Bears were admired for strength, courage, and the special wisdom that allows them to live all winter in hibernation without eating (Hallowell 1926: 148-49). Though bears were hunted and eaten, special rites were performed to insure respect and proper treatment for the slain animals. Contemporary Koyukon Indians of Alaska still retain a cultural tradition of deep reverence for bears, regarding them "near the apex of power among the spirits of the natural world" (Nelson 1983: 173).

Belief in and admiration for the supernatural power of bears and desire to obtain these powers resulted in formation of bear cults among Plains Indian tribes in the nineteenth century. The Ute Indians performed an annual sacred bear dance, paying tribute to "the bear as the wisest of all animals" who possess magic and medicinal power. Dancers were able to send messages to the dead and sometimes could obtain curative abilities through the agency of the bears (Reed 1896). Bears have often been associated with healing. The Cheyenne held that a bear can cure itself and other bears (Grinnell 1923, 2:105). The Lakota "believed that their knowledge of healing wounds had been taught by the grizzly bear," and in a healing ceremony the medicine man and his helpers dressed and acted like bears in order to cure the sick (DeMallie 1984:178-80). Among certain Gypsies as well, bears have magic power for curing and alleviating suffering (Vukanovic 1959:12-23). Even today, especially in Asia, certain bear products such as bile from the gall bladder are believed to have medicinal value (see Lawrence 1986b:18).

In some nonindustrial cultures, actual kinship between bears and people is recognized. The Utes, for example, acknowledge bears as their ancestors. Northwest Coast mythology includes intermarriage between human beings and bears, with offspring having the characteristics of both species. There is a belief among gypsies that the bear came into existence through birth to a virgin girl and thus has a close association with humankind (Reed 1896; Wood 1982:48-52; Vukanovic 1959). Virtually all people who live in contact with bears recognize the animals' similarities with human beings. Bears walk upright, appear tailless, are omnivorous, exhibit facial and bodily expressions similar to people's, may whine and shed tears in distress, are devoted mothers to their playful and dependent young, and seem to behave with conscious intelligence. Even objective scientists attribute conceptual abilities to bears, and grizzlies have been described as the only animals to understand that their tracks reveal their movements and to take pains to conceal them (McNamee 1982:69; Mills 1919:9, 18).

The Anglo-Europeans who came to explore and later to conquer and settle in the New World wilderness, however, brought with them an entirely different ethos; bears were generally seen as antagonists. They were formidable predators, an intrinsic part of the obstacles that had to be overcome in the untamed new land. Known for their courage and ferocity, bears came to represent the challenge of a harsh life that brought the pioneers into daily contact with the wild elements that they sought to tame. Not just a matter of survival, killing a bear became a ritual of manhood, a traditional way for frontiersmen to prove their strength and virility—and to assert human supremacy over nature. Bears were perceived as enemies who threatened the progress of civilization, the working out of Manifest Destiny on the American continent.

It is not coincidental that a change in attitude toward bears began to be apparent at around the time of the turn of the century. In 1890, the American frontier of settlement had been declared officially closed. In 1893, historian Frederick Jackson Turner put forth his now-famous frontier thesis, *The Significance of the Frontier in American History*. Turner asserted that the frontier had been the most important factor in shaping American character and history. From the wild and rugged land itself, he argued, had come the main stimulus for the development of the strength, self-reliance, and individualism that characterize Americans and formed the basis for the growth of American democracy (Turner 1894). Once the American empire extended to the Pacific and the domination of nature on the continent was generally established, the wilderness gradually came to be viewed as a value to be cherished rather than merely a resource to be exploited. Though attitudes toward wild animals were still characterized by ambivalence, they began to be viewed somewhat more benignly, and even the ferocious bear could be seen, at least by some Americans, with an appreciative eye.

Probably no person represents that newly emerging dual view of the wild in which the urge to conquer was counterbalanced by a simultaneous admiration that held back a course of total destruction than Theodore Roosevelt. Though the twenty-sixth President of the United States (1901-1909) was an enthusiastic big game hunter whose countless trophies attested to his prowess in killing animals, he was at the same time a dedicated conservationist who accomplished a great deal in preserving American wilderness and wildlife. Interestingly, Roosevelt expressed agreement with Turner's thesis about the significance of the American frontier; he wrote to the historian "I think you have struck some first class ideas." Roosevelt had in fact anticipated some of Turner's concepts in his own book, *The Winning of the West,* published in 1889. As a champion of the strenuous outdoor life and of pioneer virtues, Roosevelt was alarmed by the realization that the frontier had vanished, fearing the detrimental effect this loss would have upon the vigor, virility, and greatness of the nation (Nash 1982:149).

An incident that occurred during one of his hunting exploits forever links Theodore Roosevelt with American bears and created one of the most powerful and enduring symbols in American culture. In 1902, the president went on a bear hunt near Smedes, Mississippi. Sources differ as to the official reason for his presence in that area, citing it as either "a touchy political situation involving racial equality" or a boundary dispute between Mississippi and Louisiana. After several days of unsuccessful hunting, a bedraggled black bear was run down by the dogs, hit on the head with a rifle, and then roped and tied to a tree. The president was called upon to kill the bear, but he refused to shoot the animal under such unsportsmanlike conditions. He reportedly told the guide to put the animal out of its misery, and the bear was dispatched with a knife.

The next day, the story of the president's refusal to shoot the captive quarry was reported in the newspapers, and several cartoons appeared depicting the bear first as a full-grown animal and soon afterward as a small cub. Clifford Berryman of the *Washington Post* immortalized the incident in consecutively published cartoons entitled "Drawing the Line in Mississippi"—the caption referring both to Roosevelt's distinction between good sportsmanship and bad and his involvement with the "color line" of the racial issue or the state boundary line (Mullins 1987:32-40; Schullery 1983:10).

Most significantly, when examined carefully the bears of the two cartoons are quite different. In the earlier depiction, the realistic-looking adult bear is large in proportion to its captor, and defiantly tugs against the rope that is tied around his neck. In the subsequent version, the bear has been transformed into an appealing little cub, its eyes wide with fright. The young animal, unresisting, is pulled much closer to the man who holds the rope (see Mullins 1987:32-33).

Drawing inspiration from Berryman's cartoons, Morris Michtom, operator of a Brooklyn toy and candy store, created a stuffed bear for the Christmas season. Allegedly, he requested and received permission from the president to call his product "Teddy's Bear," a name which soon became teddy bear. Sales were so good during the first year that Michtom formed a new larger company, the Ideal Toy Company (Schuller 1983:10-11). In 1903, the Steiff family, German toy manufacturers, also produced stuffed bears which were first marketed in New York, and which contributed to the widespread popularity of teddy bears.

The bear soon became Roosevelt's mascot and a symbol of his presidency. A series of cartoons featuring the adventures of two bears known as *The Roosevelt Bears* appeared in twenty newspapers, including the *New York Times,* and were later published in book form. Almost all cartoons depicting the president included the bear, generally a small cub, as a character. During his presidential campaign, teddy bears were featured in special pins, buttons, and posters advocating his election.

Soon after their creation, teddy bears gained immense popularity that never diminished, and they have always occupied a very special niche in the lives of countless numbers of people. In our society, these symbolic bears often represent an infant's first introduction to non-human creatures and serve as many children's earliest and closest companions. Although teddy bears are popular with youngsters, they also possess considerable appeal for adolescents, adults, and the elderly. Recently, teddy bears have been successfully employed in many age groups for stress reduction and for various therapeutic purposes. During the last decade or so there has been a remarkable surge of interest in and appreciation for teddy bears. Collecting and restoring old teddy bears has become an absorbing adult hobby, and prices of antique bears have soared (Bohlin 1986:108). A 1920 bear brought $86,350 at a 1989 auction (Seavor 1989:E2). Numerous books, as well as periodicals, on the subject of teddy bears have appeared. Stores entirely devoted to teddy bears have been established throughout the country. Special teddy bear sales, rallies, contests, jamborees, clinics, and exhibitions are often held, and clubs for devotees (known as arctophiles) are active.

Currently, the concept of the teddy bear as companion animal is truly a remarkable American social phenomenon. Particularly in childhood, but also during other life stages, the toy carries extremely potent symbolic value. Teddy bears are increasingly recognized for their extraordinary functional powers to bring consolation and comfort to people, and are utilized to counteract anxieties ranging from mild routine daily stress to extreme trauma and crisis.

Recently I was asked to give a children's sermon in church on the theme of teddy bears. I undertook this assignment with reluctance, since comparison of the comforting role of the teddy bear with that of the church was the obvious implication, and I felt the parishioners would construe this association as sacreligious. Such fears, however, were groundless. My message concerning the history and significance of teddy bears was extremely well received. Each child was given a small teddy bear before proceeding to Sunday School. And on the way out of church adults were offered teddy bears as well, though it was not expected that many would actually take them. As it turned out, not one person refused a bear. Men and women alike took special pains, some even aggressively, to claim their bears, and even asked to take extras for relatives and friends. Not one seemed embarrassed or thought the idea foolish; not one believed teddy bears were just for children. I observed that every parishioner exhibited a broad smile upon receiving a bear, and immediately held it tightly to his/her body. One elderly woman expressed special joy; she told me this was her first teddy bear.

The minister revealed that "ordinarily people scatter after church; only ten percent shake hands with me on the way out. Today, every person went through the line to get a bear." A man who usually goes out the side door to avoid shaking hands even jumped the line to insure getting a bear. One woman who had never greeted the minister after the service before told him "That's the best service I've ever attended!" She hugged her teddy bear and hugged and kissed the minister as well. "The woman acted giddy, like a child, as though she'd had a drink or two," the minister noted. After the service, the janitor asked for and received a bear, then set it down while he began tidying the church. A few minutes later, visibly upset, he frantically sought the minister to request another. "They stole my teddy bear!" he exclaimed.

In the following weeks, many comments from church attendees attested to the value placed upon the bears. I learned that one person took the animal to bed each night, one gave it to a sister in a nursing home, who adored it, several carried it everywhere in pocket or purse, or displayed it on the dashboard of the car. The administrator of a large hospital kept his bear on his desk, next to his wife's photograph. "It's there when I need it," he said. "I need hugs, too. I only wish I'd had several teddy bears to help me during the difficult time of the merger a few years ago."

The tension-easing effect of teddy bears was recently utilized by a Rhode Island bus company to combat what it termed "busphobia," the irrational fear of riding buses. This fear, felt to be the reason that more people did not use buses, was said to be composed of three main elements: anxiety that "the bus would not go where the rider wants; that the rider will have to sit next to an undesirable character; and that the rider might be embarrassed to be seen riding the bus" (R. I. Uses Teddy Bears 1987). A bus company official told me that many citizens had negative perceptions of people who ride buses, believing that passengers are "automatically of a low class, poor, and without much education. The teddy bear campaign was undertaken to stop busphobia and make people proud of their transit system. For six months, we gave teddy bears free to anyone who rode the bus and wanted one. The program was successful; the ridership was increased by one percent. The teddy bear is different—it's cute, cuddly, and not offensive; it's a positive thing in people's lives."

The same positive effect has helped in overcoming "dental phobia," a phenomenon that, according to the findings of the Dental Fears Research Clinic at the University of Washington, is present to some degree in two-thirds of the population. "Bring a teddy bear" is one suggestion made to those who find it difficult to "face the chair" at the dentist's office (Tooth Care 1986:4D). Teddy bears are also utilized by hospitals to "introduce children to what goes on in an emergency room in hopes that if they have to come during a real emergency, they won't be as frightened." During the annual "Teddy Bear Clinic Day" at Rhode Island Hospital, for example, youngsters bring teddy bears in for checkups or surgery. On display are x-rays of teddy bears, bears with oxygen masks, i. v. tubes, and casts on their legs, and bears in wheel chairs. The bears' "parents" are allowed to give shots to the patients. Staff members sew up injured teddy bears, replace parts, and prescribe "lots of hugs." As one "grandparent" explained, her child had "been hesitant to go to the doctor's, so we thought this was a good idea to come here in a non-threatening situation" (Emery 1986:A1, A2). At some pediatric hospitals, a teddy bear with the same "ailment" as the child is used to reduce fear—for example, just before treatment is begun a bear with an eye patch is given to a youngster with an affected eye.

Many charitable organizations throughout the country raise money to provide teddy bears to pediatric wards and children's hospitals for distribution to sick children to aid in easing the young patients' pain and loneliness. Dr. Paul Horton told me of a National Cancer Institute program in which forty-five countries were involved in providing bears for children dying of cancer. In New York state, the teddy bear campaign is held to commemorate Theodore Roosevelt's birthday, and is sponsored by the National Park Service's Manhattan sites (including Roosevelt's birthplace) and the Theodore Roosevelt Association. During the second annual Theodore Roosevelt Drive in 1987, 10,000 bears were obtained for presentation to hospitalized children at Christmas and Chanuka.

Teddy bears can fill the physical, as well as the emotional needs of some adult patients. At one Florida hospital, all convalescents from open-heart surgery are given a unique bear called "Sir Koff-a-lot." Surgeons explain that following the operation it is very important for patients to cough up phlegm from their lungs, but that doing so causes a lot of discomfort due to the newly sutured wounds. When the patient hugs the large specially contoured stuffed bear to his/her chest while coughing, however, the pain is eased. The teddy bear also has been found to "divert the patient's attention from the trauma of surgery to the excitement of recovery"...and to provide patients with "the warmth and tenderness they so badly need after heart surgery." Teddy bears have made "a real difference in attitude during recovery," being "not just physically therapeutic but a mental tonic." A nurse noted that "everybody loves teddy bears. Even the most macho male patients come around to hugging their bears in the end. It definitely eases their post-op pain." Patients are extremely enthusiastic about the curative effects of their bears, who wear T-shirts with the message:

> A cough for your lungs
> A hug for your heart
> I'll help you bear it
> By doing my part.
> (Nature's Clinic 1987:13)

Teddy bears have recently found another area in which to do their part—as "recruits" in the police force of many American cities. Officers who are now using teddy bears in their daily work report "a teddy bear is quite a tool; it's almost as important as my pin and gun. It has worked miracles." The idea of policemen armed with bears as well as bearing arms began several years ago, and its astounding success has caused teddy bear programs to spread to many areas of the United States. Requests for help in starting similar projects have come from Australia, England, Scotland, and Germany. The program involves police officers giving bears to people undergoing stress and trauma. The teddy bears are generally supplied to the police through fund drives carried out with the help of the local media in which individuals or large companies donate bears or money to buy them. The bears are permanent gifts, and are most frequently given to children, but they are also used for adults.

Teddy bears have proven to be beneficial in any traumatic situation, especially for traffic accident victims, runaways, confused, frightened, and lost people, abused and sexually assaulted individuals, for youngsters who witness a killing or whose parents are arrested, and for children who must testify in court. Policemen say that whenever people are scared, hugging a teddy bear soothes and calms them so that they can communicate with those who have come to help. As one officer expressed it, "in my twenty-seven-year career, I've never seen anything work better. The teddy bear is our emissary, calming the situation down. People may be frightened of policemen, but the bear builds a bridge between the officer and the person, so it helps us to help people." Policemen say that "giving a bear to a stressed individual to hold, love, name, and keep works better than anything else. The bear breaks down the language barrier by speaking a common language that says 'here's a friend.' " Police call the bear a "security blanket," and an "ice breaker." They say "it helps make a child understand he is not alone, that the police officer cares." The director of one city's "Best Buddy" program told me "at first, no macho cop wanted to carry a teddy bear, but once they discovered what the bear does, they won't go anywhere without it. Officers get very possessive of their bears. The bear program has caught on like wildfire."

One police official revealed that "even hard-core, street-wise kids with colored hair are intrigued that police have teddy bears. They come up to the patrol cars and look in to see if the bear is really there. They use any excuse to interact with the bear. There's positive interaction between the police and these kids. Also, it's amazing that hardened criminals picked up in a police car say they want to sit in the back seat with the bear. Criminals claim 'I won't hurt it!' The bears create good feelings. One motorcycle cop carries a bear on the back of his bike. Though he doesn't distribute bears, when he gives out a ticket, he still gets a smile, even from the person getting the ticket."

Countless cases demonstrate the beneficial effects of teddy bears. Following an auto accident, a mother was badly hurt and unconscious. Her child, only mildly injured, clung to her hysterically and was totally incoherent. Police were able to "replace mom with a bear," so that the panic-stricken child grabbed the bear, quieted down, and allowed the paramedics to aid the mother. Officers tell of an adult accident victim who was pinned in her car. She was given a bear to comfort her while a crew worked to extricate her. She took the bear into surgery and still has it in her bedroom. She calls frequently to thank the policemen.

Confronted with a badly injured mentally retarded child who would not communicate with the ambulance attendant, police worked through the teddy bear. The child told the bear where he was hurt and this information was relayed to the paramedics. As an officer explained, "it's easier to tell your problems to a friendly, fuzzy face." In this case, as in others, officials showed the child what they were going to do by first doing it to the bear. The teddy bear given to one frightened child while in the ambulance became an advocate when police told him "the bear will stay with you and help you, and will make sure the doctor takes good care of you." Teddy bears are allowed to accompany children when they need x-rays and tests, and they still hold on to the bear when they go home.

Abused children, unresponsive to human contact, react positively to teddy bears. One policeman tells of being called to investigate the case of a four-year-old child who had been severely beaten. "He was terrified and refused to speak. When given a teddy bear, his face lit up like a Christmas tree. It broke the barrier and the child communicated. As a result, we were able to put together a good case for court." Many months later, at the trial, the officer observed the child still clutching the teddy bear he had been given at the time of the crisis. "The bear was misshapen, where the kid had taken out his aggressions on the poor bear by squeezing and punching it, but he still had it," the officer told me. Policemen often find that rape and incest victims, both children and adults, will talk to the bear but not to a person. An investigator revealed that "one twenty-year-old was completely incoherent after a sexual attack, but was calmed down enough by the bear to enable us to get crucial information quickly to help us get the perpetrator."

As a police officer explained the use of bears as fear-fighters for assault victims, "This is where the positive meaning of the program starts to work. You watch tears and sobbing turn into little glistening sparkles in their eyes. They grab the bear and hold on for dear life. The uniformed officer is no longer merely the policeman who is going to help. He just took away some of the pain and hurt, and probably made a friend for life. ... Many questions that are sensitive to the victim can be addressed through the bear. The bear acts as the extension of the child. The child starts talking to the bear and in most cases will answer the questions." Bears also provide a source of comfort for a child who has to be taken from his parents and sent to a foster home, and give strength to youngsters who must testify in court. "Even when lost kids can't speak English," officers say, "we usually make friends with them through the bear while we make arrangements to help."

Upon entering a home to serve a narcotics warrant, an officer found the suspect's toddler sitting precariously on an outside third-storey window ledge. The child was coaxed inside by the officer's promise of a teddy bear. Quick thinking and use of the "Best Buddy" averted a possible tragedy. At the other end of the age scale, an unidentified old woman wandered from a nursing home and would not communicate with police who found her. "We were getting nowhere," the officer says. "But when we gave her a teddy bear, it was like turning on a key. We got the information necessary to get her back into her facility."

A police official told me about the janitor in the police barracks who lost his wife of fifty years. "He was distraught, and unable to sleep. We gave the man one of the patrol bears to take home. He talked to the bear and slept with it. Next day he came to work more cheerful and said that last night he had been able to sleep for the first time since his wife took ill and passed away. He was greatly comforted by reaching out to touch the bear. It was there for him, friendly and warm. This is an example of our exciting and wonderful bear program."

Those who participate in the program are enthusiastic about its success. "Teddy bears are an old tradition," one policeman explained. "Everyone had a teddy bear sometime in their life as a friend to hug, love, cry and laugh with. They're soft and cuddly, with arms long enough to hug back. They're not like a plastic doll. They're warm and loving, not harmful or threatening." An officer with a long career in the police force revealed "Everybody's perception of teddy bears is good. They're important to me. As a child I saw one in a store, begged my parents for it and they bought it for me. It was my companion in childhood, adolescence and on up. I still have it packed in a case in the attic. It's a sign of love, affection, and warmth. I told that bear every one of my secrets. It's a good thing the teddy bear can't talk."

An officer who heads the "Best Buddy" project in a large city found that in addition to making trauma for the victim "more bear-able," the program "removes some of the stress a police officer faces every day. Men are proud of their teddy bears because they made someone happy and they could stop some of the hurt. There have even been reports of the police officers giving the teddy bear a squeeze when under stress." An officer who is dubbed "Officer Teddy" because he often uses the bears says "Kids love teddy bears. I always did. I still do. I really believe in them." An official of one city's crime prevention program notes that "Americans are slow to touch each other and police hope bears will bring people together more. We are less outwardly affectionate than Europeans. You often see them walking arm-in-arm, but you don't see it here."

City police point out that crime against children is on the rise in this country, so the program is more important than ever. The teddy bear's good image enhances the usefulness of the police force, for it is recognized that police are often at a disadvantage in giving comfort because they are viewed as authoritarian figures. A uniformed officer with a gun is a source of fear, but bears are able to break down the barrier between child and officer. In one city, an officer who gives out a bear also provides two junior police badges—one for the child and one for the bear. The badges enhance the positive association between the youngster and the police officer as a caring friend. By destroying negative stereotypes, bears are credited with "helping to instill confidence in law enforcement in a whole new generation."

Teddy bears can have a comforting effect in the lives of senior citizens as well. Some charitable agencies have distributed them to nursing home patients and found that they are received joyfully. At the final stage of life, too, bears sometimes fill an important role. Several funeral directors have told me of their experiences with teddy bears. One funeral home keeps a teddy bear handy for visitors. The director explained "we bought it for children to play with, but we found that adults like it too. They often pick it up and handle it and then hand it on to someone else." Another funeral director revealed that "sometimes as much as twenty years ahead we've had people make arrangements with us to be buried with their teddy bear in the casket." I was also informed by a funeral home operator that "some children are buried with teddy bears, but more frequently older people are involved. These people have a fixation on the teddy bear and feel strongly about it. They tell someone else of their request or notify us directly. It's always an old teddy bear that has been in their possession a long time. These people identify with that bear and want it with them in death. It's their friend."

To understand the remarkably potent role of the teddy bear as a lifelong friend and comforter in death, one must begin with the stuffed bear's origin. There is now definite evidence from a newly-discovered photograph that the bear which Theodore Roosevelt refused to shoot was in fact full-grown, according to the executive director of the Theodore Roosevelt Association (personal communication 1988). Why, then, did the cartoonist immediately transform the bear to a cub? This action can be explained by the inherent power of juvenile forms (both animal and human) to elicit a positive emotional response from people. The phenomenon is well known, and was identified and analyzed by ethologist Konrad Lorenz. Lorenz's studies showed that the configuration of traits such as big head in relation to the body, high prominent forehead, large eyes, chubby cheeks, small mouth, and short rounded limbs—all characteristics of young children or animals—evoke a nurturing, protective response from adults, who perceive such an object as lovable (Lorenz 1981:165). Toy manufacturers successfully exploit and exaggerate this "infant schema" to make their products cute, cuddly, and appealing (Eibl-Eibesfeldt 1972:21-23). Figures such as "Bambi" and "Snoopy" have been depicted in the same way, and Stephen Jay Gould has traced the progressive juvenilization of Walt Disney's Mickey Mouse over the years as he became more and more popular (1980:95-107). In the domestication of animals, human beings exerted selection toward neoteny, which refers to the retention of infantile or juvenile traits in the adult form (see Lawrence 1986a). Results of this process (which can involve behavioral as well as physical traits) are particularly visible in dogs such as pekingese and Boston terriers, but are also present in other breeds and in almost all domesticated species (see Clutton-Brock 1981).

Cartoonist Berryman, consciously or unconsciously, employed this same juvenilizing process in making Roosevelt's bear into an immature, frightened cub with a whimsical expression. The young bear in later cartoons is small, defenseless, and docile, and evokes a sympathetic response. The animal is rendered powerless, subservient to its human captor. Thus the cartoonist set the stage for the creation of the immensely appealing stuffed teddy bear who little resembled its wild antecedent and does so even less after 86 years of unflagging popularity. Teddy bears themselves have shown an overall tendency toward increased neoteny over the years since their inception (though with some intermittent exceptions). Older bears generally tend to have more pronounced noses, longer limbs, and more realistic proportions, as compared to later editions which often have larger heads, flatter faces, and shorter, thicker limbs. Whereas older teddy bears were apt to be firmly stuffed, a recent variety is constructed with an extremely soft and yielding body to allow more for more effective huggability. As one contemporary observer noted, trends are "moving away from the proud, stiff classical bear toward those that are easier to snuggle, with fluffier fur and bodies. Traditional bears don't mush" (Hirsh 1988:C17).

Whenever teddy bear companions are discussed, it is difficult to keep in mind that they are inanimate objects, so powerful are their symbolic attributes. It is commonly stated by owners that each has its own personality, and all manner of thoughts, emotions, and actions are attributed to the bears. This strange, pervasive phenomenon is complex, with deep-lying roots. Teddy bears have diverged greatly from their origins. Although wild cubs are extraordinarily appealing, live bears generally make very unsatisfactory pets, and are trained to do human bidding only by drastic and usually barbarous methods. "Lady Washington," the favorite captive bear of Grizzly Adams by his own admission had been chained to a tree and brutally beaten into submission (Hittell 1967:102-103). At best, the wild bear is no "buddy," even to its staunchest admirers. Rather, it is a species that requires for its very existence a habitat undisturbed by humankind and its presence is said to be a "barometer" of the status of the primeval ecology. Bears signify the wilderness and as one grizzly bear researcher noted, are "the ultimate symbol of nature uncontrolled by people" (Enos 1983:11).

Differing so greatly from its antecedent, the teddy bear seems to be the actual bear's counterpart of oppositions, a sort of contrary alter ego to the real bear. Whereas living bears are unpredictable wild creatures whose "hugs" may be injurious or fatal, and who are aloof, ferocious hunters, teddy bears are completely tame, dependent and dependable, caring friends whose hugs combat anxiety and are even curative. To please us, they wear clothes, go to school, read, cook, or ski, wait endless hours for our return, and sleep and eat with us. Real bears are never subservient. Just as members of the animal kingdom are so like us and yet so different, thereby giving us an image by which to measure our humanity, so the teddy bear, modelled after the living bear yet so different, gives us a way to reflect upon what has been lost in the transformation. Missing qualities are autonomy, risk, and the wild spirit that cannot be controlled. Teddy bears are neutered, civilized, humanized, and sanitized. Through the process of creating this version of a bear, it seems we have taken their former strength unto ourselves. This power usurped from the animal quiets our anxieties perhaps because it establishes us as total masters. There is no more to fear, for we have reached the limit of conquest. Our charming teddy bears, still not quite dolls, embody the ultimate taming, the extreme polarity in the wild-to-tame transition, the conversion of nature to culture. Dr. Paul C. Horton explains the effects of this wild-tame dichotomy in psychological terms, suggesting that the child achieves a soothing illusion of conflict resolution by controlling the symbolic wild animal. The choice of a representation of a dangerous animal as a soother, he believes, "marks the beginning of the child's ability to seek out and integrate the paradoxical and contradictory" (1981:107, 115).

Living bears are mighty and ferocious, the archetypal predator. It is possible that human beings still carry a vestigial inborn fear of predators, as a survival mechanism inherited from our ancestors who were physically defenseless as compared to the bear, and whose offspring were so vulnerable to predation. By totally subjugating the bear to make it an effigy to cuddle, we have allayed our collective fears, and soothed all manner of anxieties.

And yet, there is our characteristic ambivalence. We admire wild nature, even as we fear it and seek to control and destroy it. I believe that the ever-popular teddy bear represents a gigantic collective wish-fulfillment of humankind's ancient dream of unity with the animal world. A deep desire to befriend our fellow creatures is attested to by the fact that some members of almost every known society are motivated to keep and cherish pets. Human beings reach out for camaraderie with wild creatures, but are often disappointed by the lack of reciprocity. The teddy bear, however, will not let us down. He mitigates our failure to connect with the animal world at the same time as he softens our hurt and disillusionment with our own kind. He assuages the grief that results from dual alienation from both human and animal society. The strength and intelligence drawn from the real bear and its strikingly human characteristics, with all the antagonistic traits removed in the teddy bear, make it a useful bridge between animal and human spheres. Teddy bears are animals that nearly, but not quite, became people, and serve as buffers from the pains of the human condition.

Appreciation of the qualities that preindustrial peoples admired in bears may still lie deep in the human unconscious, giving the teddy bear some of the magical virtues that exploitative eyes often overlook. Teddy bears remain symbolic healers of great intelligence and wisdom. They are idealized beings adapted solely to specific human needs, possessing the innocence that comes from their animal roots and the ability to counter loneliness through a projected social perfection. With our teddy bears, whose sinlessness and solicitude sustains us, at least temporarily, we can make our world safer.

Horton, a psychiatrist, has shed light on the teddy bear phenomenon through his studies of transitional relatedness, which is defined as the person's unique experience of an object (called the transitional object) which provides soothing comfort symbolic of the maternal presence. The transitional object, which in our society is commonly a teddy bear, represents a "spill-over" of attachment to the mother; it is the infant's "first not-me possession" and becomes a vehicle for solace (Horton 1981: 18, 35; Horton, Gewirtz and Kreutter 1988: 323). Horton's research has shown that forty percent of children choose stuffed animals as their first solacer, and of these, sixty percent are teddy bears. Thus he asserts that one child in four derives its first extra-maternal solace from teddy bears. At five to six years of age, sixty-three percent of children use stuffed animals, with sixty percent of these being bears. After that, Horton found that attachment to teddy bears drops off. Then there is a burst of re-attachment in the late teens. According to his studies, eighty percent of female and forty percent of male college freshmen have teddy bears (personal communication 1988).

Psychiatrists have found that use of transitional objects is nearly universal and necessary to healthy human development. Horton believes that the achievement of a state of solace is a prerequisite to a person's capacity for positive emotions such as joy and love (1988). He points out that the existence of transitional relatedness shows that a child is already working to master the anxiety that accompanies separation from the mother. One nine year-old whose parents were divorced described how her stuffed animals helped her deal with being alone after school now that her mother had a job outside their home: "They keep me company. Like when I'm watching TV downstairs, and no one's at home, they watch TV with me. And when it's a funny part, I think they're laughing" (Horton 1981:160; Horton, Gewirtz, and Kreutter 1988:260).

Ever since Theodore Roosevelt's refusal to shoot a captive bear was perceived as a gracious gesture toward the natural world, the gentler image of America's most formidable predator has been personified in an immensely appealing and popular toy. The fearsome wild animal, once held to be invulnerable, is now tamed as a teddy bear—a trusted friend, confidante, and protector for vulnerable human beings. For young and old, teddy bears have come to represent trust, love, and reassurance. When hurt and disillusioned by people, the symbolic meaning with which the stuffed bears have been endowed allows them to afford comfort and to personify goodness and kindliness. Their dependability makes them always there when needed, especially in warding off human fears that come with the darkness of night. Teddy bears are nurturers, even as they are nurtured.

As one of society's most cherished shared symbols, the teddy bear denotes the spirit of caring and unconditional affection. Peculiarly adapted to combat the fears and anxieties resulting from the alienation prevalent in modern society, the bear not only provides companionship and solace, but also amusement. It adds gentle humor and fun to many lives. As one adult arctophile who participated in the "All America Teddy Bears' Picnic" noted, "It must sound insane—adults, even grown men with their Teddies in the competition—but we had such a wonderful time" (Utterback 1988:3). It is not surprising that the protective attributes of teddy bears are utilized in advertisements. Celestial Seasoning's TV commercial for "Sleepy Time Tea," for example, features a bear that, like its product, provides peace and serenity at bedtime. And a recent ad for Kodacolor film that promises to "show your true colors" depicts an apprehensive child clutching a teddy bear during his first visit to the barber shop, with the caption reading "True Courage." The image of the teddy bear in contemporary society has become universally positive. During the 1988 presidential campaign, officials who planned Michael Dukakis' strategy for the second debate with George Bush reportedly raised the question "Should Dukakis come out fighting, Duke as Rambo? Or should he accentuate the positive, Duke as teddy bear?" (Stengel 1988:56). As events in modern life come more and more to reflect the spirit of Rambo, the teddy bear—epitome of the wild that has been tamed—becomes an even more powerful symbol of the beneficence people seek.

References

Bohlin, Virginia. 1986 The Bear Fact of the Matter: Teddy's Not For Just the Young. *Boston Globe,* June 1:108.

Campbell, Joseph. 1983 *The Way of the Animal Powers.* San Francisco: Harper & Row.

Clutton-Brock, Juliet. 1981 Domesticated Animals from Early Times. Austin: University of Texas Press.

DeMallie, Raymond J. 1984 *The Sixth Grandfather: Black Elk's Teachings Given to John Neihardt.* Lincoln: University of Nebraska Press.

Eibl-Eibesfeldt, Irenäus. 1972 *Love and Hate: The Natural History of Behavior Patterns.* New York: Holt, Rinehart and Winston.

Emery, C. Eugene, Jr. 1986 Teddies Show Tots A Hospital's Heart. *Providence Journal,* September 22: A1, A2.

Enos, Amos. 1983 Symbol of Wild America. *Audubon Action,* vol. 1, no. 2 (February): 11.

Gould, Stephen Jay. 1980 *The Panda's Thumb.* New York: W. W. Norton & Company.

Grinnell, George Bird. 1923 *The Cheyenne Indians: Their History and Ways of Life.* 2 vols. New Haven: Yale University Press.

Hallowell, Irving. 1926 Bear Ceremonialism in the Northern Hemisphere. *American Anthropologist,* n. s., 28, 1:1-175.

Hirsch, James. 1988 Teddy Bears' Work Is Never Done. *New York Times*. September 28: C1, C2.

Hittell, Theodore. 1967 "Lady Washington." in *The Grizzly Bear*. Bessie Doak Haynes and Edgar Haynes, eds. pp. 91-106. Norman: University of Oklahoma Press.

Horton, Paul C. 1981 *Solace: The Missing Dimension in Psychiatry*. Chicago: University of Chicago Press.

——— 1988 Positive Emotions and the Right Parietal Cortex. *Psychiatric Clinics of North America,* vol. 2, no. 3 (September): 461-74.

Horton, Paul C., Herbert Gewirtz, and Karole J. Kreutter, eds. 1988 *The Solace Paradigm: An Eclectic Search for Psychological Immunity*. Madison, Connecticut: International Universities Press.

Lawrence, Elizabeth A. 1986a Neoteny in American Perceptions of Animals. *Journal of Psychoanalytic Anthropology,* vol. 9, no. 1 (Winter): 41-54.

——— 1986b Relationships With Animals: The Impact of Human Culture. *National Forum,* vol. 66, no. 1 (Winter): 14-18.

Lorenz, Konrad Z. 1982 *The Foundations of Ethology*. New York: Simon and Schuster.

McNamee, Tom. 1982 Breath-holding in Grizzly Country. *Audubon,* 84, 6: 69-83.

Menten, Ted. 1985 *The Teddy Bear Lovers Catalog*. Philadelphia: Courage Books.

Mills, Enos. 1919 *The Grizzly: Our Greatest Wild Animal*. Boston: Houghton Mifflin.

Mullins, Linda. 1986 *Teddy Bears Past & Present*. Cumberland, Maryland: Hobby House Press.

——— 1987 *The Teddy Bear Men: Theodore Roosevelt & Clifford Berryman*. Cumberland, Maryland: Hobby House Press.

Nash, Roderick. 1982 *Wilderness and the American Mind*. New Haven: Yale University Press.

Nature's Clinic: Care Bears Speed Healing. 1987 *Woman's World,* vol. 8, no. 15 (April): 13.

Nelson, Richard K. 1983 *Make Prayers to the Raven: A Koyukon View of the Northern Forest*. Chicago: University of Chicago Press.

R. I. Uses Teddy Bears for Security on Buses. 1987 *Boston Globe,* September 13.

Reed, Verner. 1896 The Ute Bear Dance. *American Anthropologist,* 9, 7: 237-48.

Schullery, Paul, ed. 1983 *American Bears: Selections from the Writings of Theodore Roosevelt*. Boulder, Colorado: Colorado Associated University Press.

Seavor, Jim. 1989 Most Expensive Teddy. *Providence Journal-Bulletin,* October 4: E2.

Speck, Frank. 1977 Naskapi: The Savage Hunters of the Labrador Peninsula. Norman: University of Oklahoma Press.

Stengel, Richard. 1988 The Election: Nine Key Moments. *Time,* vol. 132, no. 21 (November 21): 48-56.

Tooth Care Doesn't Have to be A Pain. 1986 *USA Today,* September 24: 4D.

Turner, Frederick J. 1894 *The Significance of the Frontier in American History*. Annual Report of the American Historical Association 1893. Washington: Government Printing Office.

Utterback, Shirley. 1987 Bristol Women Win 'Teddy' Event. *Providence Journal-Bulletin,* July 30:3.

Vukanovic, T. P. 1959 Gypsy Bear Leaders in the Balkan Peninsula. *Journal of the Gypsy Lore Society,* 38, 3-4: 106-27.

White, W. B. 1942 *Seeing Stars*. n.p.: Rand McNally & Company.

Wood, Marion. 1982 *Spirits, Heroes & Hunters from North American Indian Mythology*. New York: Schocken Books.

Recreational Architecture as Popular Culture: The Symbolic Design of the American Movie Theater

Gary Edgerton

Recreational architecture has been the most consistent and stable genre of structural design through the ages. There are certainly disparities in arrangement and ornamentation between the original Greek theaters, the Renaissance Roman theaters, the establishments built across Europe in the 17th, 18th, and 19th centuries for opera, drama, and ballet, and a thrust or arena stage of today. Even an inspection of the contemporary American landscape will provide a seemingly eclectic array of theatrical options, such as the Guthrie Theatre in Minneapolis, the Grand Old Opry in Nashville, the Mark Taper Forum in Los Angeles, and Radio City Music Hall in downtown Manhattan, all exhibiting slightly altered symbologies that reflect variations in region, social class, subculture, and function.

The basic similarities in the composition and construction of most theaters, auditoriums, and even sporting arenas, however, far outweigh any surface and textural differences. Performance spaces highlight a prominent area where some combination of art, entertainment, and illusion can be enacted; in turn, audience participation is relatively passive, as edificial priorities tend to emphasize comfort, and the ability to hear and see well. The point is not to downplay the wealth, beauty, and plurality of superstructures that have been conceived for recreational purposes through antiquity; this kind of architecture has simply been more uniform in its broadest outlines and appearance, than what has subsequently appeared in the domestic, religious, governmental, educational, and commercial spheres.

Specific meanings can, nevertheless, be revealed by examining the existing repertoire of theatrical designs. Any type of public performance rarely requires housing in permanent installations until this general activity has begun to assume the characteristics and qualities of a ritual for its culture. The creation of support facilities usually happens concurrently with the process of institutionalizing a dramatic pursuit, an amusement, or a sport; and operates as a pivotal signal that a society is embuing the conventions of this performance or rite with its myths, metaphors, and values.

Researchers in art, architecture, American studies, and popular culture, have long understood this process, and focused on the signs, symbols, and allusions that are evident in a style of building, its decor, color scheme, and adornments.

This unit of analysis is uncommon in film studies, though, since primary concern in reception theory has typically concentrated on the relationship between the traditions of aesthetics, content, economics, social impact, and audience effects. Movies, together with the rest of mass communication in the United States, do, in fact, compose a singular institution whose influence is presently comparable to the older and more venerable varieties in America. The biases and predilections of domestic culture are just as recognizable in the environmental strategies of film exhibition, as they are in our respective halls of government, houses of worship, or fashions in family homes nationwide.

Motion picture theater design has actually changed along with what the moviegoing experience has meant to Americans throughout the 20th century. The nickelodeon, the movie palace, the studio chain theater, and the multiplex have dominated domestic exhibition during their respective eras. Each phase has defined customer, product, and architectural contingencies, such as who constitutes the moviegoing public, what film content eventually receives national exposure, and how theater design contributes to the overall meaning of attending the movies. Most times these questions are left unasked, as the answers lie hidden in the socio-cultural subtext of the film viewing experience. The place where the ritual of moviegoing in America is held, however, symbolizes both the business ethos that motivates the exhibition arm of the industry and some of the cultural inclinations of contemporary Americans and how these tendencies have evolved over the last century.

American film forged the beginnings of an identity between 1896 and 1912, struggling for a visibility beyond the automata or lower billings in vaudeville. As early as the late 1890s, make-shift storefront theaters holding little more than seats, a screen, and a projector began appearing. These initial operations were significant since they were the first establishments designed specifically for presenting movies, as film form evolved from mere reproduction to a storyline, and soon gained added narrative sophistication. As movie producers were stumbling through the trial and error process of developing film art, early exhibitors were correspondingly learning how best to exploit this new means of public entertainment. Exhibitor strategies would actually develop slower than motion picture aesthetics, primarily because priorities in retailing are characteristically subject to changes in product quality and output.

The age of the nickelodean had arrived by 1905 as the number of storefront theaters nationwide exceeded 1000 for the first time.[1] This figure would multiply more than ten times by 1913, as movies were becoming big business complete with antitrust litigations, numerous state and municipal censorship laws, and the genesis of multi-reel storytelling. Occurring concurrently with these developments, the era of the movie palace was also beginning with the opening of the Regent in New York in 1913, and later this period of film exhibition came to full fruition during the decade following the end of World War I in 1918.[2]

The story of the age of the movie palace, approximately 1913 to 1931, was initially described by Ben M. Hall in *The Best Remaining Seats,* written three decades after the era's demise in 1961.[3] These movie houses were substantially more than just theaters; these symbolic structures were decorated with the most expensive rugs, furniture, and fixtures available. These "dream palaces," as they were nicknamed, were both part of the show and indices of a more general aspiration for achieving the "good life" which millions of Americans paid money week after week to share collectively. As Hall recalled,

> The United States in the twenties was dotted with a thousand Xanadus. Decreed by some local (or chain-owning) Kubla Khan, these pleasure domes gave expression to the most secret and polychrome dreams of a whole group of architects who might have otherwise gone through life doomed to turning out churches, hotels, banks and high schools. The architecture of the movie palace was a triumph of suppressed desire and its practitioners ranged in style from the purely classic to a widely abandoned eclectic.[4]

The widespread proliferation of these movie palaces throughout the teens and the 1920s demonstrates that these "most secret and polychrome dreams" must have struck a responsive chord with America's moviegoing public during the Jazz Age. As has never before or since been the case with motion picture exhibition, the architectural designs and furnishings of America's motion picture theaters were blatantly alive with the nation's materialistic ethos, leaving the movie palaces to function as a new cultural form expressing an older, mythic content of how Americans felt about their country and themselves.

It was almost as if the dream spilled off the screen and embellished the walls, the statues, the domed ceilings, and the army of attendants. The entire moviegoing experience had become an opportunity to enter a new and exciting cultural phenomenon, ripe with mythic messages in which the environment itself signaled loudly that it was time to dream, even before the lights went out. Movie palaces were also an indication of a culture running blindly into a realization of its own excesses. The stock market crash would make society stop and think in 1929; in turn, movie exhibitors found dream palace upkeep and overhead an expensive burden as the motion picture industry in the United States began to feel the backlash of the great Depression in 1932.

The next phase in American film exhibition started in 1932 and ended in 1948 with the Paramount Decision.[5] The most successful theater type during this era was the studio chain theater, corporative and operating en bloc in order to corner as large a portion of the marketplace as possible.[6] The economic realities of the Depression changed the tendency in domestic film exhibition from house extravagance, to methods of booking, bookkeeping, and promotion conducted more in line with the rationality of a company policy.

A crucial development was the theater owner's changing attitude toward his or her role as a retailer. With the substantial drop in movie attendance in the early 1930s, "the 'double feature'. . . games, cash prizes and other inducements were. . . added by exhibitors to the regular movie program in an attempt to prop up sagging box office receipts."[7] Added to these promotional gimmicks, concessions were also introduced into the film viewing experience for the first time. Initially candy, and then ice cream were provided as convenience items, and also as a means of attracting additional revenues by increasing the number of admissions. Concessions would become money-making ends unto themselves by 1948, as the exhibition arm of the film industry entered its mature phase at the outset of the 1950s.

In the mature state of an industry, businessmen maximize profits rather than volume. Specifically, prices increase faster than unit volume, new product development slows, and competitive industries capture market share at the older industry's expense.[8]

Exhibition did not spring right into a mature phase in 1950; industrial maturation is an incremental and deliberate process. Phillip Lowe, president of the National Association of Concessionaires during the late 1970s and early 1980s, recounted that this change in the theater business was, nevertheless, identifiable after the Paramount Decision.

What happened was that really, when television came in, that was in the early fifties, that was the beginning of the mature phase...in fact that was when film production started going down. So for historical precedent probably the fifties, but it really didn't impact until the seventies.[9]

In the 15 years following the Paramount case, the major distributors curtailed their total number of releases by more than one-half, 448 to 223, as both a reaction against dwindling admissions and as a method of keeping demand high which, in turn, allowed them to maintain their oligopolistic control over the domestic marketplace.[10] Competition from television also entered into the equation that lowered supply by cutting movie attendance even further. Consequently, major product for the movie retailer diminished substantially leaving exhibitors with few alternatives as a result. Domestic theater owners had to either compromise their role as showmen to a greater degree by devising new means of generating capital, or leave the business of exhibiting films altogether.

Whether by force or choice, the latter alternative had more takers than expected. Over 20% of the domestic four-wall theaters closed by 1953.[11] On the other hand, the total amount of drive-ins nationwide increased from 820 in 1948 to a peak of 4,063 in 1958, as a more convenient method of adapting to the needs of America's growing number of suburban families and the widespread baby boom.[12] Concession sales for outdoor theaters also grew, along with menu size.

Hard-top exhibitors followed suit as they too became increasingly conscious of concessions in the early 1950s. "In 1948, concession sales accounted for 7.8 percent of all receipts, in 1954 for 20.8 percent, in 1958 for 16 percent, and in 1963 for 15 percent."[13] From 1954 through 1972, "monies per customer" spent on concessions grew from 12.8 cents to 26.3 cents for four-wall and drive-in theaters combined.[14] By 1977, this figure would double again breaking "the magical 50 cents per person barrier," a highwater mark that Phillip Lowe called "the four minute mile for concessionaires" in 1979.[15]

During the past four decades, selling concessions has become a much more sophisticated business evolving its own unique retail strategies. Since 1948, as the major distributors have come to demand a higher share of box-office revenues from exhibitors, the emphasis in exhibition has switched from projecting films to selling concessions; moreover, theater owners have simultaneously passed on as much of this cost as possible to their merchandising of secondary products.[16] In the last 15 years, the squeeze from the distributor's split of box-office revenues has risen to such an alarming proportion, in fact, that exhibitors have responded by retailing concessions at a 60% profit margin.[17] Industry estimates gauge that increased pricing has alienated moviegoers to a point where only one in six now buys concessions.[18] Phillip Lowe suggested that high pricing is really more beneficial to theater owners than the option of lowering prices in the hopes of attracting a few more customers.

> The concept of how to sell refreshments to a captive audience is an interesting one because in that point in time they are locked in for all intents and purposes. Now the question then is, for call it one hundred people in your theater, will more, depending on whether you have high pricing or low pricing, if you have low pricing will that many more on an incremental analysis basis buy? We're talking about will refreshment price merchandising to a captive audience increase with unit elasticity? The answer is no. What that means is if you sell a candy bar for fifty cents or a dollar...you will not sell twice as many at fifty cents as you will at a dollar, and therefore, you might as well extract the highest possible price that you can from people in that type of captive environment.[19]

The above quotation actually has wider implications for the American motion picture industry at large. Customers are being treated by exhibitors in much the same way that exhibitors are being concurrently manipulated by the major distributors. Within the oligopolistic market structure that exists, domestic exhibitors are the distributor's captive audience; in turn, the major distributors "extract the highest possible price" from the exhibition arm of the industry.

Phillip Lowe also elaborated on other ways that the theater owner/moviegoer relationship has changed over the last two decades.

> Theater owners are constantly looking at other ways of maximizing income. One of the things that they're doing is they're putting pinball machines and electronic game machines in their lobbies...it's become an accepted national strategy...Prints, artwork, T-shirts, all kinds of stuff. This is quite successful...no it doesn't alienate customers, quite the opposite. It's voluntary so it can't alienate customers. It's a way of offering them a total entertainment experience, or stated another way, it's a way of maximizing a theater owner's revenue.[20]

In the mature phase of motion picture exhibition, the most important development is the changing concern from movies to secondary products. Industrial concensus across the board agrees that if a theater owner is to make money and stay in business, his profits must come from concessions and other ancillary merchandise. Exhibitors presently generate only 1.5% profit on box-office revenues, and this figure would allow inflation alone to sound the death knell for domestic motion picture theaters if movies were their only source of income.[21]

This shift in emphasis from merchandising feature films to selling concessions also shows up in contemporary motion picture theater design. The message implicit in the decor and surroundings of the modern theater is no longer "to dream." Its function, color, and design communicate to the moviegoer an entirely different signal. Today, the most progressive type of theater, and the most characteristic of its era, the multiplex, tells its occupants it is time "to buy."[22]

CHART 1

U.S. MOTION PICTURE THEATERS
(end of year)

	1939 (Census)	1948 (Census)
Indoor	n.a.	17,811
Drive-In	n.a.	820
Total	15,115	18,631

	1954 (Census)	1958 (Census)	1963 (Census)	1967 (Census)
Indoor	14,716	12,291	9,150	8,803
Drive-In	3,775	4,063	3,502	3,384
Total	18,491	16,354	12,652	12,187

	1972 (Census)	1972 Est. Screens	1974 (Census)	1974 Est. Screens
Indoor	9,209	10,694	9,645	11,612
Drive-In	3,490	3,734	3,519	3,772
Total	12,699	14,428	13,164	15,384

	1975 (Census)	1975 Est. Screens	1979 (Census)	1979 Est. Screens
Indoor	9,857	12,168	9,021	13,331
Drive-In	3,535	3,801	3,197	3,570
Total	13,392	15,969	12,218	16,901

	1988 (as of May 1) Screens
Indoor	15,768
Drive-In	549
Screen Total	16,317
Site Total	4,583

Sources: U.S. Department of Commerce, Bureau of Census; MPAA Statistics; and Jim Robbins, "Survey: Exhibition Worldwide/U.S. & Canada Theater Circuits Ranked by Size," *Variety*, May 11, 1988, p. 91.

The first multiplex in the United States was built in Kansas City by the American Multi-Cinema Corporation in 1963. Multiplexing has since proven to be a major stimulant, enabling a handful of chains to grow gradually at the start, then meteorically over the last three decades.[23] Chart 1 suggests the industry-wide increase in multiplexing during the past 25 years. Drew Eberson, whose family has been in the business of constructing domestic theaters since the 1920s, accurately forecasted the future of movie theater design at the 1963 national Theatre Owners of America (TOA) Convention in a speech entitled, "A Look Ahead at Theatre Trends."

> During the 1920s the boom was on. We were designing and opening at least one theater a month. The seating capacities were between 2,000 and 5,000 seats. The "golden age" of the motion picture palace was with us. Cost budgets were not too important—get it done—have it bigger, grander, more ornate and more palacelike...
>
> Then came the depression and from then on there were peaks and valleys in theater construction. During the 30s and 40s...the watchword was economy. High cost and certain types of labor ruled out ornamental plaster, iron work and bronze. We then created a theater by using extremely simple lines and a great deal of color splashes-so-called "modernistic"...
>
> And now the boom is on again! But what a different theater! The modern design of course has eliminated the heavy ornamentation, the rising orchestra pit and the elaborate playrooms of the past. The theaters of the 30s with their loud, crass, vulgar colors are gone...
>
> My theme is the theater of tomorrow, an auditorium functional in design, a comfortable seat with plenty of leg room and sufficient lighting to prevent groping and tripping; a lobby and foyer with attractive eye appeal, colors harmoniously blended to soothe and yet be admired and a sales area with a head-on shot and equipment which blends with the architectural design and with no unsightly bulges...[24]

This ability to "blend with the architectural design...with no unsightly bulges" is exactly what sets the multiplex apart from older theater models and makes it the characteristic movie-house of today. Theater architect, Robert W. Kahn, put it another way in 1965 when he explained the appeal of the shopping center theater. "In recent decades motion picture theaters have gone from wild rococo to dullest soap box. Today good design calls for a practical, economical theater that is comfortable and pleasurable to attend, and that will stay attractive beyond the life of any fad or current style."[25] In other words, Kahn has alluded to the fact that in being "beyond...any fad," theater design is presently either a style for all seasons, or no fashion at all depending on one's perspective.

The atomism of the 1920s which set the Roxy in New York City apart from the Midland in Kansas City, or Radio City Music Hall, has given way to an unprecedented move toward homogeneity where an AMC theater in Missouri looks much the same as one does in New York; in addition, an AMC multiplex anywhere strikingly resembles a respective United Artists Theater Circuit or General Cinema complex, which together conjure up hints of recognition when comparing design, format, and color scheme to the neighborhood mall stores and fast food outlets.

The entrepreneurial spirit which enlivened the movie palaces of yesterday, and was reflected in the individuality and audacity of their designs, has now been replaced by the efficiency and corporate rationality that invigorates the decor of the multiplex. The dream palace way of doing business has today been grounded in the dollars and cents realities of streamlining and increasing profitability to equity invested. Put another way, the exhibitor as merchant has won out over those psycho-social regions of the mind that are usually exercised by the exhibitor as shaman or showman.

The contemporary theater is no longer an exclusive showcase for dreams, but a combination projector-screen and retail outlet. An exhibitor's role at present has about as much to do with promoting movies as art, or popular art, as a manager at McDonald's concerns himself or herself with nutrition and dietetics. The decor for each of these establishments reflects their common intent of transmitting a simple, yet effective message to the prospective consumer. The evolving language of American commercialese communicates: bright colors, vinyl and laminated covered furnishings, plastic panel art, sloping wall and ceiling design with glaring lights highlighting a centrally located concession area; and an imitation brick linoleum walkway leading to air conditioned auditoriums I, II, III, and IV.

Services that immediately gratify are the modes of making money today, and motion picture exhibition is no different than any other sector of the American marketplace. Let the consumer relax, make him or her both responsive and compliant, and above all manipulate the environment so it will be easy to spend money. After all, a comfortable consumer is an uncritical buyer, a message implicit in Phillip Lowe's explanation of the advantages of a circular, centrally located concession area as opposed to the traditional backbar, freestanding counter.

> They have the capacity of having more people. If you look at the circumference of that circle versus the front space at a counter, you can just get more people around that circle, and they all think they're going to be next. If you're the third person in line, or the third row of persons waiting to be served, it takes a lot more patience. So we can get more people around a circular stand than you could three or four deep in a back-bar stand.[26]

The evolution of theater design from movie palace to multiplex is a switch in emphasis from consumer dreaming to buying. No longer is the imagination meant to be titillated, as much as the senses soothed. Robert L. Beacher, president of the Forest Bay Construction Company, commented in 1976 on these strategies.

> The primary objective of the designer is to create an innovative lobby effect by removing the standee wall and enclosing the inner lobby for a friendly living room atmosphere...the secret in effective redesign and twinning of existing theaters depends upon the utilization and retention of a portion of the "old look" to allow the more conservative film-goer a sense of both newness and familiarity. At the same time a mood of comfort and warmth is created.[27]

The relationship between the theatrical environment and the moviegoer has always been a vital supplement to the more obvious dynamic between the audience and the filmmakers in determining what the moviegoing experience means to those who attend films. Movie theater architects are presently concerned with establishing "a mood of comfort and warmth." Contemporary motion picture theater design both maintains and reflects this ever growing stress on tactile concerns, quite unlike the movie palace's emphasis on the imagination. The highest priority in the structuring of theaters today is placed on creating a calming ambience and a sense of convenience, while always ensuring cleanliness and an upbeat milieu.

This changeover in theatrical architecture is consistent with the developments in the movie business that now make it essential that exhibitors increasingly earn their livelihoods from the sale of goods in their concession areas, rather than from box-office receipts. American theater owners must exert maximum effort in order to corner the captive movie audience before it retreats into the darkened auditorium. These exhibitors hope to soothe, mollify, and placate the senses of as many compliant customers as possible. After all, that is what their retail and environmental stratagems are designed to accomplish.

Over the last 100 years, the form, shape, and decor of domestic movie theaters have adapted to subtle developments in society, adjustments in audience preferences, and the workings of the film business. Before the advent of motion pictures in the final decades of the 19th century, first-hand acquaintance with theatrical entertainment was actually beyond the experience of nearly four out of every five Americans. By 1913, the mass audience was flocking to the cinema by the tens of millions, as both the language of film and places of exhibition began to more decisively reflect a compelling, though exaggerated version of popular sentiments, aspirations, and concerns. No longer would the symbolic design of theaters in the United States express only the hopes and beliefs of the few and the privileged; movie palaces would now encase and embody the goals of the American Dream in a way that was responsive to almost everybody.

These so-called, "cathedrals of the cinema," also created the illusory environment and encouraged the suspension of disbelief that has consistently been a part of dramatic art and entertainment since the Greeks. This tradition continues unabated today in the altered fashion and landscape of the multiplex. All theaters, irrespective of their purposes, or whether they are hosts to "live" or recorded performances, are always designed as public sites where audiences can indulge themselves in wishful fantasies and flights of imagination; at the same time, their surface textures continue to be timebound, mirroring a social context and a specific era. The dynamic jumble of rites, symbols, and setting that constitute the theatrical experience still persists, even as architectural conventions become outmoded, and styles from an earlier period are lost within the inevitable currents of creative enterprise and cultural change.

Notes

[1]Kenneth MacGowan, *Behind the Screen: The History and Techniques of the Motion Picture* (New York: Dell, 1965) 129.

[2]Ben M. Hall, *The Best Remaining Seats* (New York: Bramhall, 1961) 30.

[3]Hall.

[4]Hall, 93.

[5]In 1948, the Supreme Court upheld a lower court's decision that the eight Paramount defendants had violated antitrust laws according to the Sherman Act. According to the Paramount Decision, Paramount, MGM/Lowe's, RKO, Twentieth Century-Fox, and Warner Brothers were considered "majors" because of their size and the fact that they owned theaters. Three smaller yet dominant companies, Universal, United Artists, and Columbia, were also implicated in the litigation. The "majors" were eventually forced to divest themselves of their theater holdings.

[6]The theater chains linked to the five major studios were: United Paramount Theaters, Twentieth Century-Fox Theaters, Warner Brothers Theaters, Loew's, Inc., and the RKO Corporation. Actually during the 1930s and early 1940s, these five major companies, along with Universal, United Artists, and Columbia, all formulated preferential deals with the remaining large-sized independent theater chains nationwide. Consequently, theater circuits solely owned by the five major studios, or owned by compliant large-sized independent theater chains had cornered the motion picture marketplace in virtually every important American region, state, or municipality.

[7]*U.S. Department of Commerce, Social and Economic Statistics Administration, Bureau of Economic Analysis* (Survey of Current Business) lists U.S. Motion Picture Box-Office Receipts 1931 - 719; 1932 - 527; 1933 - 482; 1934 - 518; and 1935 - 556; and Robert H. Stanley, *The Celluloid Empire: A History of the American Movie Industry* (New York: Hastings House, 1978) 84-85.

[8]Phillip M. Lowe, "The Beginning of the End," in the National Association of Theatre Owners, *Encyclopedia of Exhibition,* 1979; 18.

[9]Interview with Phillip M. Lowe, July 30, 1980.

[10]National Association of Theatre Owners, *Encyclopedia of Exhibition,* 1979; 58.

[11]*Problems of Independent Motion Picture Exhibitors Relating to Distribution Trade Practices,* hearings before a subcommittee of the Select Committee on Small Business, U.S. Senate, 83rd Congress, 1st Session (Washington, D.C.: Government Printing Office, 1953) 947.

[12]U.S. Department of Commerce, Bureau of Census, in the National Association of Theatre Owners, *Encyclopedia of Exhibition,* 1979; 42.

[13]Robert D. Lamson, "Motion Picture Exhibition: An Economic Analysis of Quality, Output and Productivity," Unpublished Ph.D. dissertation, University of Washington, 1968, p. 56.

[14]These figures are computed from data that are found in the U.S. Department of Commerce, *1972 Census of Selected Service Industries,* Motion Picture Industry, pp. 3-4; and Motion Picture Association of American (MPAA) statistics.

[15]Phillip M. Lowe, "Don't Bite the Hand That Feeds You," in the National Association of Theatre Owners, *Encyclopedia of Exhibition,* 1979; 120.

[16]The estimated split of the domestic box-office dollar earned by America's film distributors has averaged more than 40% during the 1980s.

[17]John Larmett, Elias Savada, and Frederick Schwartz, Jr., *Analysis and Conclusions of the Washington Task Force of the Motion Picture Industry* (Washington, D.C.: 1978) 16.

[18]Lowe, "The Beginning of the End," 21.

[19]Interview with Phillip M. Lowe, July 30, 1980.

[20]Interview with Phillip M. Lowe, July 30, 1980.

[21]Larmett et al., *Analysis and Conclusions of the Washington Task Force of the Motion Picture Industry,* p. 14.

[22]Multiplexing is the practice of housing two or more screens under one roof, thus

maximizing audience size while essentially paying building and management overhead costs, employee's salaries, etc., for only one structure.

[23]Jim Robbins,"Survey: Exhibition Worldwide/U.S. & Canada Theater Circuits Ranked by Size," *Variety,* May 11, 1988, p. 85, 91. By May 1, 1988, the four top theater circuits in North America boasted 6817 screens (United Artists Theater Circuit with 2264; Cineplex Odeon with 1667; American Multi-Cinema with 1528; and General Cinema with 1358), or a concentration of 41.7% of the domestic total. Over the past three decades, these four chains did substantial multiplexing, which along with a willingness to diversify into other business pursuits; a corporate plan for persistent growth and centralization; a de-emphasizing of the drive-in theater; and an exploitation of the suburban market, were the major policy positions that separated the successful motion picture theater circuits from the also-rans.

[24]Drew Eberson, excerpts from the speech, "A Look Ahead at Theater Trends," *1963 Theatre Owners of American Convention Program,* Speech 13.

[25]Robert W. Kahn, "What's Playing at the Shopping Center?" *1965 Theatre Owners of American Convention Program,* 41.

[26]Interview with Phillip M. Lowe, July 30, 1980.

[27]Robert L. Beacher, "A New Look in Twin Theatre Design," in the National Association of Theatre Owners, *Encyclopedia of Exhibition,* 1976; 110.

Discourse of the Deal: The Car Salesman as Symbol

Marc Baldwin

As any member of Frederic Jameson's Dukedom will tell you, America is in its late stages of capitalism. Whether a subscriber to this Marxist theory or not, one would be hard pressed to declare capitalism ethically healthy with the Ivan Boeskys, Ed Meeses, Ed Mechams, and dozens of other Reagan Revolutionaries recently indicted for crimes of the wallet. It's a question of who can you trust and how do you know if you can trust him or not.

The arena of big business, though far removed from the dealings of the average man, shares with us a common discourse of the deal. In one way or another, we are all salesmen. Just as Boesky, Meese, and Mecham convinced others that their deals were good, we also seek to sell our own products, ideas, pleas, and protestations to others on a daily basis. And not all of us always tell the truth. As salesmen, we occasionally bend, delete, alter, and cover-up the truth the better to get our way, make the sale, and otherwise earn profit for ourselves. The salesman in society is a reflection, a symbol of the salesman in all of us.

To understand who that salesman is inside us all, I offer as a model perhaps the "best" salesmen—"best" meaning most effective, not the most ethical—in the business world: a legion of deal cutters and glad handers known collectively as car salesmen.

Car salesmen are masters of a discourse in which two sides duel in opposition over terms, over numbers and words, over signs and signifiers. In his negotiation for a car, the customer attempts to pin down, to define certain terms which the salesman attempts to obfuscate. Since the salesman earns a percentage of the profit, the more the customer pays for the car, the more money the salesman makes. The system, the ideology, the discourse of car sales stresses and stretches profit at any cost. Its very mode of production—commissioned sales—sanctions this war of deceit. The salesman's words are his weapons; his pitch, his living. He'll say anything to define the terms profitably. As Michael Foucault notes, the truth of a discourse is a rhetorical imposition.

During my five years on car lots, whenever people asked me what I did for a living I would always say: "I sell cars, but I'm not a car salesman." It was my way of suspending the displacement of my values and the effacement of my self. Which is what happens to men who sell cars. They trade their honesty for deals. When they first set foot on a car lot, they don a mask and their face grows to fit it. It may take a few days, it may take a few years, but eventually a man who sells cars reifies into a car salesman. He can't help it. Car salesmanship is inscribed into the discourse he employs. As Foucault notes: "Discourse is not the majestically unfolding manifestation of a thinking, knowing subject, but on the contrary, a totality in which the dispersion of the subject, and his discontinuity with himself may be determined" (Foucault, *The Archaeology of Knowledge*, 1969, trans. 1972).

Though I tried to deny it, I'd become a car salesman all right. I entered the symbolic state in which the discourse of the deal, the ideology of the car lot became my mirror, the looking glass in which I saw my imaginary unified self.

The reification of a man into a car salesman is, in fact, a classic case of Jacques Lacan's version of Freud's Oedipal rite. When a "new man"—and that's what they are called on the car lot, those rookies: new men—when the "new man" is hired he is generally graced with a training session run by a sales manager. A hardened, fully inscribed inner party member, the sales manager acts as the "old man" to the "new man", a father to the male child. The new man enters life on the showroom floor as a mere infant, in an "imaginary state" with no awareness of what he will become as a car salesman. He has yet to learn how the business will subject him in his role as a salesman whose sole object is to write up, to sell, to subject the customer. The sales manager as father instructs the new man in the ideology of the car lot and the terms of his existence as a salesman. Once the new man has been constructed in training, he's thrust headlong onto the lot where his new and radically split personality must—to mix a metaphor—step "up" to bat and deliver his pitch.

"Who's up?" That question is shouted out in the showroom regularly. "Who's up?" "Up" is the object position of the salesman whose turn it is to "work" the next customer. Always already "up" or soon-to-be "up" again, the salesman is forever bounced back into an imaginary state as the object of the unknown customer's uncertain arrival. Only that arrival can allow the salesman to leave the object position. When the next customer drives onto the lot, he becomes the salesman's "up". The salesman can say "There's my up," thus shifting the object position to the customer. By identifying customers as objects or "others", the salesman can then sell them with a clear conscience, once again secure in the mythical unification of his selfhood. Mythical because, to paraphrase Louis Althusser, the subject—in our case, the salesman—is himself a subjected being who submits to the authority of the social formation. On the showroom floor, the man is dead and the salesman must author his own discourse of deals.

If he's a "good" salesman—"good" meaning he's effective at earning high commissions, not necessarily maintaining the highest ethical standards—one of his standard lines is: "I'll give you a good deal." Yet, even as the salesman says it, the man inside him knows he's lying. He's not going to give the customer a good deal because if he does he won't make a big commission. A good deal for the customer is not a good deal for the salesman. Thus, a splitting, or what Lacan calls "Spaltung", occurs between the man and the salesman. He has "mediated himself in his discourse, in effect destroying the immediate relation of self to self. By constructing himself in language" he has self-destructed (quoted by Anika LeMaire, *Jacques Lacan,* pp. 64).

One of the best salesmen I've ever known has a favorite line he uses over and over again with every customer: "Trust me, folks," he says. "Trust what I'm telling you." All his deals are good deals—for himself, not for the customer. He says "Trust me" and they do, and he screws them good.

And that's the way they term it on the car lot. After the customer leaves with his new car and the salesmen gather in a corner of the showroom floor, they all want to know what kind of a deal their fellow man made. If he made a large commission, he calls it a "good deal" and brags to the other salesmen: "Yeah, I screwed 'em good." This sub-culture of car salesmen regularly communicates in sexual metaphors. As salesmen, they must prove their manhood with every sale. The sales force is a male society where the phallus is king. The rare woman on the force must prove, as the men say, that she at least "has balls." Among car salesmen, the phallus is the privileged signifier.

As evidence of the phallic reign over the salesman's daily lives, I offer this brief representative conversation the likes of which I have heard and participated in many times on car lots. The scene: the showroom. Two salesmen in a corner away from other ears. One salesman has just bid farewell to a customer he successfully closed.

"Did you sell that broad?"

"Yeah, I really stuck it to her."

"Laid her away, huh?"

"Yup. Shoved it so far up she'll never walk straight."

"You got brass balls, buddy boy. You really know how to dicker."

"Hey, whatever it takes, I give. There's an ass for every seat, right?"

"You should talk to the new man. Give him some tips. He's got his hands in his pockets."

"Hey, you can't shoot a scared stick or the people will stroke you over up and down."

And on and on, ad infinitum, ad nauseam.

A salesman often brags in just such sexual metaphors when the customer has bought his definition of the deal's terms. He represents his perceived victory as a misogynistic sexual conquest. The climax of his deal wasn't an honest coming together, but rather a misrepresentation of terms: he simply told her what she wanted to hear, whether it was true or not.

Blinded by his desire for a deal, the salesman sees the customer as an object to control and possess at any cost. His objective, sales, can be best obtained subjectively, with himself and his company's profit in mind. Thus, objectivity exists, if at all, not in the truthful dissemination of his product's relative merits, but in his propensity to objectify the customer. The salesman must, and can only, perceive the object of his subjective discourse as an other, a profit-directed object, a sale.

"I made a sale," says the salesman. He sold an object to an other. Another deal done.

"I closed a deal today, too," replies his fellow salesman. They made, they closed. Subjected men creating objects called sales out of people called customers. For a salesman, the sign of the cross, his faith and face, is a signature, the sign of his object, on a deal. Customers signify sales, the object of the man of sales' desire.

Since desire creates its own sense of truth where it resides within discourse, when the salesman's desire for a sale meets the object at hand, the salesman and his words become signifiers of a discourse always already arranged prior to their meeting. Truth is, and can only be, deranged by the unstable identity of its dictators. The salesman and the customer are unable, incapable of creating a reliable union of signifier and signified. Truth cannot be exchanged between profit-minded adversaries, because each side of the discourse subjects itself to its object of defining the terms in its own fashion. Desire, thus, corrupts communication.

What both the salesman and the customer desire, the contract which they lack, the principle term upon which the sexual encounter, the car deal, any deal hinges upon is the price. When a customer first asks a salesman "What's the price on this car?" the salesman immediately shifts into his split discourse, determining to slide that signifier, "price", as far as he can until the customer is written up on paper and commits to "a price", any price from which to negotiate a mutually agreeable signified. To arrive at the best price for himself, the salesman displaces the signifier, "price", with other unstable signifiers. As they say on the car lot, "sell the sizzle, not the steak." The salesman attempts to sell desire, not price, by projecting his own desire for a deal into his discourse with lines such as: "You deserve a new car," and "Just think how nice it would be to drive home in this car today." Pontiac sells excitement: "Feel the thunder!" Chevy claims to be America's heartbeat. That's catchy. So George Bush claimed the same and was elected. The product any good salesman objectifies is not a car but its subjective correlative: the customer's own desire.

When the customer agrees to the deal and buys her new car, she might be satisfied but, for the salesman, no matter how successful he is, satisfaction is short-lived; desire is incessant. The father/sales manager, the creator of the salesman's split self, demands performance on a daily basis. Statements such as "I sold 3 cars yesterday," or "I sold 20 cars last month," mean nothing on the car lot because the man, not the subject of his enunciation, must perform again today. The salesman is always thrust back into the object position, always "up" again, having to authorize his way out of the object position. A similar situation befalls all of us each time we again perceive another object of our desire.

Salesmen, thus, symbolize not merely American business or the capitalist system, but man's own subjected soul. Many who labor under the spell of buy and sell have bought the ideology and sold their words, their signifiers, the very definition of themselves, for the perceived profit of a favorable position at the end of a deal. For a price, salesman and customer, buyer and seller alike, often sell their words short or long, whatever the market will bear. The question becomes: at what cost profit? Upon the grounds of untruthful terms lies the severed head of man's integrity.

Symbolism in Humor

Sam G. Riley

If technology is, as Max Frisch wrote, the knack of so arranging the world that you don't have to experience it, then humor arranges the world in such a way that you don't have to put up with it. Humor allows us to "manage reality," to simplify the things we experience and to look at them not merely as they are, but as we would prefer to have them.

A religious symbol—the Cross or the Star of David—is a device for simplifying that which is anything but simple, a shorthand device for dealing with unattainable complexity. A corporate symbol (trade names and trade characters such as COKE, IBM, or the Jolly Green Giant) has much the same function, as does another form of business symbology, the corporate slogan.

The highly complex world of humor may be viewed as having its own symbols, as well, though they cannot be quite so neatly isolated as a corporate logo, which may be cut from a printed page and pasted up for easy examination. Many of the important symbols in humor are the kinds of persons (the President, the glutton, the bumpkin), places (Philadelphia, Hoboken), or things (bedpans, pratfalls, custard pies in the face) that frequently signal or invite mirth. Some of these symbolic shorthand devices that alert us, "Here comes something funny" appear to be fairly constant from century to century and across cultures at any given time; others are more time-and culture-specific.

At the fundamental, immutable level, the cute gabble and facial expressions of a baby, or the first wobbly steps of a puppy, or the mock ferocity of a tiny kitten have humor value for virtually anyone, anywhere. Also practically universal in comic suggestiveness are the various devices of slapstick comedy—the frantic chase, the pie in the face, the pratfall.

Other forms of humor are less firmly anchored. A person from a culture in which the elderly are highly venerated would find little humor value in a movie scene in which Dick Van Dyke, dressed and made up as a man in his nineties, maunders absurdly and trips over his own cane. Old Stepinfetchit routines are not only unfunny but actively insulting to today's black. Goldie Hawn's airhead comedy, Marilyn Monroe's exaggerated suggestiveness, or even Margaret Rutherford's portrayal of the mumbling, fuddled Englishwoman are anathema to many women's rights activists. What is funny to an Israeli might well be entirely unfunny to a member of the PLO, and vice versa.

There is a decided generation gap in what's funny. The clever word play of S. J. Perelman or Robert Benchley, or the brilliant lyrics of Flanders and Swan, so hilarious to the middle-aged instructor, are almost altogether lost on the 20-year-old university student reared in the visual world of television and movies and weaned on the notion that comedy consists of Eddie Murphy, Whoopie Goldberg, or any number of other younger comics who so often depend for their laughs on frequent repetition of the word "motherfucker." By like token, tv's "Saturday Night Live" comedy show is not a big favorite in retirement communities. The point is that many humor symbols differ depending on one's age, nationality, sex, race, religion, etc.

It also appears that the sense of humor is a highly individualized thing. Some persons have a hyperactive, or at least highly developed sense of humor and can find mirth in almost anything. At the other end of the humor spectrum are those individuals who appear to have no sense of humor at all, or if they ever did possess one, lost it at birth. For these and other reasons it is dangerous to generalize about humor. Trying to explain why something is funny is rather like trying to grab hold of a plateful of jello.

One way to deal with the symbolism of humor is to discuss it in the context of the more important theories that help account for why we laugh. The two theories of importance are superiority theory and incongruity theory. Within each, prominent humor symbols will be identified and discussed. First, however, a few comments regarding terminology are in order. For purposes of this discussion, the term *archetype* is useless. The original model, or mold for anything connected with what we laugh at is hopelessly lost in antiquity. For our purposes the term *symbol* will be more or less interchangeable with the term *stereotype,* as so much that we find funny appears stereotypical to one degree or another. To meet space requirements, this enumeration of humor symbols will be limited to human types, or stereotypes if you will, that frequently are used to elicit laughter.

Superiority Theory

Basic to much that we find funny is our need, conscious or otherwise, to stay in control. It has been said that all human society is a two-sided coin: on one side envy, on the other, disdain. Because of this peculiar defect in human nature, we exercise our need to remain superior to our surroundings in two directions. We laugh at those we perceive as being lower on life's rungs than ourselves, as when we guffaw at someone who has slipped on a banana peel (They fell; we didn't.), and we also achieve some degree of rationalized or fantasized control over anything or anyone in authority *over* us, as when we poke fun at a powerful politician whose actions will affect us all.

Consider one of the most elemental manifestations of superiority theory, the fall. Comedians adept at the pratfall have always been able to get a laugh: Charlie Chaplin, Buster Keyton, the Three Stooges, Abbott and Costello, Jerry Lewis, Dick Van Dyke, Carol Burnett, Chevy Chase and many others. More fascinating still are people's reactions to *unintended* falls suffered not by comedians, but by ordinary members of the general public. If your elderly aunt falls and breaks her hip, this is not funny in the least. Should a tourist fall and be killed or badly hurt while descending a trail into the Grand Canyon, no one in his right mind would laugh. But ah, those lesser falls. They can make you laugh longer and harder than a roomful of comedians, and superiority theory explains it.

I myself have been witness to several falls that to this day make me laugh when I think of them. One of the best occurred when I was an Army lieutenant serving in West Germany in the early 1960s. Other bachelor officers and I had just moved into a beautiful U.S.-owned three-story mansion outside Frankfurt. One of our group was dignified beyond his years, a young man who never left the house without wearing a coat and tie. One morning I looked out my window and saw this very proper lieutenant trying to take a snapshot of our house. Unable to get the entire structure from his position in the yard, he decided to cross the road to get a longer shot, but he failed to notice the surveyor's line that had been stretched along the edge of the street. As he jumped the drainage ditch, his toe caught the line, and he was sent sprawling face down onto the pavement, his camera smashing to pieces beside him. I didn't laugh immediately, fearing he might really be hurt. Then I saw him get up and brush himself off. His suit was torn in several places, and he was bleeding, though only slightly. I began to chuckle and watched as he, fearing a loss of his own superiority, looked furtively around to see if anyone had witnessed this humbling experience. I laughed harder. Then, just in case he had been observed, he brushed the pathetic remnants of his camera into a pile of spare parts, scooped them up in his hands, and pretended to take a picture with them. I laughed off and on for hours.

For the same reason that I laughed at the fallen lieutenant, most of us are moved to a *downward-directed* brand of mirth at other figures to whom we feel superior, if only subconsciously or temporarily. Common varieties of these figures are identified below as humor symbols.

1. The Fat Man (or Woman)

During the years during which actress Elizabeth Taylor's weight had gotten out of hand, skinny comedienne Joan Rivers got big laughs with the one-liner, "If you stuck Liz Taylor with a pin, gravy would come out." Playing upon the same symbolic stereotype was Jackie Gleason's exclamation, "M...BOY, you're FAT!", made all the funnier because of his own ponderous bulk. They were fat; we weren't. An offshoot of the fat person as a comic symbol is the glutton.

2. The Little Man

In our society, at least, small is not good where the male ego is concerned. In our heart or hearts, most of us would like to be physically able to give Hulk Hogan a run for his money if he picked a fight with us. Though many of us are better constructed for writing than for fighting, in our fantasies we would like to be a burly macho man. This wistful desire for prowess—of physical might, or of wealth, of learning, of fashion—makes us receptive to those of lesser stature as an invitation to mirth. We see the little man attempting to cope with a big, cruel world; we laugh. Charlie Chaplin's Little Tramp, Woody Allen as the little man in the big city, Tim Conway, and Arte Johnson have capitalized nicely on this humor symbol. A variant is Rodney (I don't get no respect around here) Dangerfield, large of body but still sore beset by the world.

3. The Immigrant

At the bottom of any nation's socio-economic structure is the immigrant, who by the standards of his or her new country talks funny, dresses funny, and doesn't quite know how to cope. The long-running show Saturday Night Live has made much of this symbol. John Belushi's excellent "Samuri Delicatessen" routine is an example, as is the show's restaurant skit in which no matter what a patron orders, the waiter, who speaks little English, calls in a hamburger and a Pepsi. Gilda Radnor's character Rosanne Rosanadana, a Hispanic of unknown origin, and the Czechoslovakian Swingers skit so beautifully performed by Steve Martin and Dan Ackroyd also target the unsophisticated immigrant. Earlier examples of note are Finley Peter Dunne's Mr. Dooley in his Irish-American neighborhood, and the Marx Brothers with their Italian-American routines (Groucho: "Eureka!" Zeppo: "You don'a smella so good yo'self.")

4. The Bumpkin

Also lacking sophistication is the bumpkin, or country cousin, long a target of abuse from city dwellers. In the early 1800s a Baltimore wit writing for that city's humor magazine *The Red Book,* poked fun in verse at city people's tendency to write off country people as simple rubes:

> A Book-Worm rear'd in rural shades
> Emerging lately from his glens and glades,
> Came hither to complete his education,
> To learn a modish air
> And study with some care
> What we town-folks acquire without a set probation.
> Our hero was not void of common sense,
> Although he had, we own, some small book-knowledge;
> Could parse a Greek verb through each mood and tense,
> And was an honour-man at Princeton college.
> Our well bred gentlemen may smile to hear
> That he, with all this learning, was no bear;
> Had master'd logic with no wish to prose,
> And bowing, seldom trod on ladies' toes.

More recently, the comedy of Andy Griffith and Jim Neighbors have made use of this symbolic theme.

5. The Minority

Dangerous as it is in terms of touching raw nerves, humor that pokes fun at minorities is still widespread. Minstrel shows are extinct, of course, and one no longer sees the thick-lipped, rolling-eyed cartoon portrayals of blacks so popular in U.S. magazines in the late 1800s and early 1900s. Gone, too, is the now offensive dialect humor of the crackerbarrel school of humor writers, the gravel-voiced Rochester on the Jack Benny Show, Amos and Andy, and the like. Still heard, however, are innumerable jokes made at the expense of America's black minority (Interviewer to Jesse Jackson: "Rev. Jackson, what do you think about Beirut?" Jackson: "Oh, he hit the ball pretty good for a white boy.")

Now long past the great era of European immigration, we no longer find funny the Irish dialect stories of Dunne, the way Italians butchered English on radio's Little Luigi Show, or the German-language copy of Carl Pretzel. Consider, though, the continuing popularity of Jewish princess jokes, Polish jokes, and the way the Archie Bunker Show allowed us to laugh at his cracks about "Pollacks," but still feel good about ourselves knowing that the show's real intent was to satirize prejudice itself. Racial and ethnic humor can still be done and remains popular, but is best performed by a member of the minority being targeted. Allen Sherman could not have done his clever songs had he not been a Jew. Flip Wilson, Red Foxx, and Eddie Murphy could not get away with their performances were they not black.

6. The Homosexual

Superiority theory is also the best explanation for the symbolic humor value of the gay individual. In a more reticent era, American comics tiptoed around this subject, but as gays began to come out of the closet and become more visible and vocal, gay jokes and comedy routines proliferated. (Q: How do you separate the men from the boys in San Francisco? A: With a crowbar.) Actors well known for their spoofs or portrayals of gays are Billy Crystal, Harvey Korman, Robin Williams, and John Ritter. Some of the best use of this humor symbol has been made by the English Monty Python troupe, whose portrayal of a platoon of gay soldiers on parade is a classic.

Superiority theory also operates upwardly. Anyone in authority over us automatically invites the efforts of the cartoonist, comedian and humor writer, who exploit the tension and hostility we feel toward those we perceive as being in a higher or more influential position than ourselves. We have a need to deflate the pompous, to bring the lofty back to earth. After all, we Americans began as underdog colonials subject to the authority of the powerful English. The catharsis of deflating the powerful has always pleased us and reaffirmed our egalitarian beliefs. The Authority Figure, then, is a major American humor symbol. Several of the most important sub-categories of the Authority Figure are presented below.

1. The Politician

The more powerful a political figure becomes, the more frequently he or she will become the target of the humorist. When a new U.S. president takes office, he already bears the scars of many a campaign joke. Regardless how wonderful or how awful the newly elected "leader of the free world" might be, this individual will be lampooned without mercy, and without even the "honeymoon period" usually accorded a new president by the more somber-minded journalistic pundits and commentators.

Every president has traits and features useful to comedy and humor. Johnson's thick, syrupy Texas drawl ("Mah feller 'Muricans,' " he would address us) and general lack of polish (It was said that Lyndon Johnson at least gained in sophistication while in the White House. After his first year in office, he always insisted on *white* catsup being served with the fish course.); Nixon's ski-jump nose and shifty expression (Would you buy a used car from this man?); Carter's teeth (Like Ted Kennedy, his teeth looked perfectly capable of chewing down small trees), his sing-song voice and the way he pronounced 'nu-ceah waw,' 'I-talian,' and 'I-ran'; Ford's alleged clumsiness; and Reagan's shoe-polish black hair, let-them-eat-cake attitude toward the poor, lack of attention to detail, and apparent unconcern over the record number of crooks and blatant opportunists in his administration—all drew humor like a magnet.

For generating humor, the greatest of all our recent presidents was Jimmy Carter. At the beginning of his time in office, the cartoonists made his teeth his primary sub-symbol. As time went by and public appreciation for his policies declined, the Jimmy Carter drawn by the cartoonist actually declined in physical size. He was reduced in the end to being pictured as a small, bewildered child.

Like the president, and in proportion to their own power and prominence, other politicians are similarly brought down a few notches by the machinery of humor. The powerful figure still retains his power, or most of it, after being lampooned and mimicked, the actual effect of the humorous treatment being more symbolic than real. Specifically, the effect is to make us, the peasants in our huts, feel better about this person's dominance over us. Going back to the 1800s for an earlier example, few cartoonists have managed to capture the essence of how we feel about politicians as well as did America's first great political cartoonist, Thomas Nast.

[206] April 15, 1876

The Political Problem.

The law-maker and law-breaker—one and inseparable.

2. The Military Man

In countries not ruled by military strongmen, the military man has been quite a durable humor symbol. The ideal fighting man, one assumes, would be someone answering Mike Tyson's physical description, but how do cartoonists picture our protectors? Fat, or skinny, or diminutive and ineffective.

3. The Lawyer/Judge

Just as durable a target for mirth are lawyers and judges, who are poked fun at even more than are the police. While policemen are often viewed with some sympathy and appreciation due to their dangerous job and low pay, the popular conception of the legal profession is that it frequently does more harm than good. Lawyer jokes abound. (Q: What's the difference between a lawyer and a possum, both run over in the highway? A: There *might* be skid marks in front of the possum.)

4. The Wife/Husband

No authority is quite so immediate as that of one's spouse, and even the happiest marriage contains a certain amount of tension. In marriage, considerations of money and sex come together in a mixture that can be highly volatile. A spouse represents a unique kind of authority over us, restricting our selfish freedom of choice and, especially for men, fostering lingering fears of sexual inadequacy. Readers may recall how this theme was played upon on the television program Three's Company and later on its spinoff The Ropers by Norman Fell (the flacid husband) and Audra Lindley (the blowsy, lusty wife). Matrimonial stress was just as neatly captured in the 1700s by cartoonist Gillray.

5. The Snob

Peering down their noses at us along life's way are a variety of snobs, all of whom invite the barbs of the humorist. Three frequently encountered sub-categories of this humor symbol are the social snob, the fashion snob, and the art snob.

Whether because of his long pedigree or his current superfluity of cash, the social snob fairly begs to have his ego deflated. From the old *Life* magazine (1888) comes an apt cartoon depicting this human failing.

Lacking impressive family background or serious wealth, one can instead follow the dictates of fashion more closely than one's fellows and become a fashion snob. The woman for whom dress and show are all attracts the satirist, as does the dandy.

Among the most irrating of all snobs is the art "expert," who pretends to see things in art, especially abstract art, that are hidden to the rest of us. In 1964 a group of Swedish journalists gave art supplies to a chimpanzee, who produced several "art works." The pictures, attributed to "Pierre Brassau," were hung in a gallery and received rave reviews from the critics, who soon discovered that they themselves had been made monkeys of. The humor-rich delights of abstract art are also satirized in this German cartoon of the late 1800s.

· LIFE ·

CURIOUS EFFECT PRODUCED BY A FEW WORDS WITH A BOSTONIAN.

Incongruity Theory

Much of what we deem funny contains elements of incongruity. This is the case because so many of the persons and events we encounter in everyday life behave in a more or less predictable manner. We expect the minister to be quiet and dignified, and he usually is (unless, of course, he is a television evangelist). Professional wrestlers and football players are expected to be louder, more macho. Most are, but hulking ex-footballer Rosie Greer likes to knit, which he has milked for many dollars via humorous tv commercials. Our minds are set to expect the expected, and when something or someone doesn't turn out the way we thought, the incongruity of the situation can produce a laugh.

At the level of language itself, the pun depends in large part upon the incongruous contrast of words that sound alike yet have different meanings (going to the Olympics in Korea to get Seoul food). Even funnier due to its extra dose of incongruity is the *accidental* pun (the state transportation department that tried to encourage the wearing of seat belts with the slogan "Have you belted your kids today?"), or the unintentionally curdled cliche (The movie was so awful it would make your flesh stand on end).

Humorous incongruity may be more a physical matter, as in the case of the juggler who begins his act by juggling several balls of normal, expected size, then without warning throws in a bowling ball, a ping pong ball, and a chain saw. Steve Martin's celebrated "cat juggling" routine also depends on the element of incongruity.

Many successful comedy teams have appealed to us in part because of the incongruous contrast between the partners. Fat-thin duos such as Laurel and Hardy or Abbott and Costello, the tall-short Mutt and Jeff of the comics page, the smart-stupid routines of Burns and Allen or Rowan and Martin, the suave ladies' man-gangling nerd combination of Dean Martin and Jerry Lewis—all drew on incongruity.

In caricature the artist seizes upon his subject's most prominent feature and draws it even bigger than life: Jimmy Carter's teeth and full lips, Gerald Ford's prominent jaw, Richard Nixon's ski-jump nose, Reagan's jet-black hair. The feature then stands out with incongruous starkness, producing a humorous effect.

Several types of individuals have by their ability to attract laughter through incongruity become humor symbols.

1. The Small Child (or Animal)

To look at a baby, or a puppy, or a kitten is to laugh, at least for those persons who are inclined to laugh at all. They intrude into our full-sized adult world in their ingenuous way and strike us as funny partly because of the contrast between them and us. The person who subscribes to the theory that all laughter comes at the expense of someone else has overlooked the joyous, hurtless laughter we get from looking at the solemn, Churchill-like face of a tiny baby or watching a puppy chase its tail.

2. The Clown

Outrageously incongruous in dress, behavior and painted-on features, the clown transports us from the everyday. Whatever mirth a mime can inspire can also be explained in the same way.

3. The Human as Animal (or the Animal as Human)

The animal pictured as dressed in men's clothing and standing erect has long provided mirthful entertainment, as we see in this page from a German humor magazine of the 1800s:

The delightful incongruity of this symbolic theme was beautifully used by artist Charles Dana Gibson (creator of the Gibson Girl) in this 1888 *Life* cartoon lampooning the anti-smut efforts of the fanatic preacher-reformer Anthony Comstock.

Nowhere has the animal-as-human technique been more heavily used than in movie cartoons, where humans (Elmer Fudd) and animals (Donald Duck, Mickey Mouse) interact as equals. Similarly, Snoopy the dog flies his Sopwith Camel and kisses the hands of "French lasses" in the Peanuts comic strip. Far Side artist Gary Larson, in his "animal nerd" cartoons, gives animals human characteristics that only his zany mindset could produce.

Beiträge zur Lösung der Seelenwanderungsfrage.

1.

2.

5. 6.

1. Der Pudel (Canis domestico-servilis).
Der Pudel ist ein folgsam Thier,
Ihm fehlt nur das Schreiben und Lesen,
Vor seiner Seelenwanderung schier
Ist er Bedienter gewesen.

2. Der Spitz (Canis polizi-spionicus).
Des Spitzes Geruch ist wunderbar,
Auch hat er gar feine Ohren,
Man sollte glauben, daß er war
Als Mensch zum „Spitzel" geboren.

5. Der Jagdhund (Canis Knuto-barbaricus).
Die Hunde, die geschickt dressirt
Das edle Wild zu packen,
Leicht möglich, daß sie einst servirt
In Polen als Kosacken.

6. Das Pintscherl (Canis aristocratico-familiaris).
Das Seidenpintscherl lebt sehr fein,
Es fährt spazieren gar,
Vielleicht, daß es vor Zeiten ein
Theaterschooßkind war.

4. The Sidekick

Thrown into adventure movies and television programs for comic relief is the character known as the "sidekick." Usually shorter, fatter, older, more awkward, or less sophisticated than the lead he or she plays opposite, the sidekick as a symbolic stereotype offers humorous incongruity. Roy Rogers had Gabby Hayes, the Cisco Kid his Pancho, Robin Hood his waddling Friar Tuck, and Sherlock Holmes his bumbling Dr. Watson, played by many actors, but never better for comic effect than by the portly Nigel Bruce, who acted opposite Basil Rathbone.

5. The Man as Woman (or the Woman as Man)

Readers may recall having seen Milton Berle in drag, Harvey Korman's masterful portrayal of a Jewish mother, Lucille Ball decked out in men's clothing and sporting a mustache, Jonathan Winters as "Ma Frickett," Flip Wilson as "Josephine." Again, the humor comes largely from incongruity, what we see having been ripped away from humdrum reality.

Other humor theories not developed here in terms of their symbolism because of lack of space are surprise theory (The punch line of a joke, to be funny, must contain a surprise.), release theory (laughter as a needed outlet for tension), configuration theory (laughter when we suddenly see how disparate pieces of

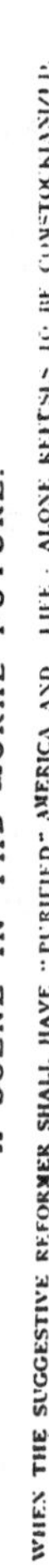

A SCENE IN THE MORAL FUTURE.

WHEN THE SUGGESTIVE REFORMER SHALL HAVE "PURIFIED" AMERICA AND LIFE ALONE REFUSES TO BE COMSTOCKIANIZED.

information fall into place and fit together), and psychoanalytical theory (a look at the therapeutic value of regressing to an essentially childlike mindset to act out aggressive feelings).

References

Helitzer, Melvin. *Comedy Writing Secrets* (Cincinnati: Writer's Digest Books, 1986).

Leacock, Stephen. *Humor: Theory and Technique* (New York: Dodd, Mead, 1935).

Mindess, Harvey and Joy Turek, Eds. *The Study of Humor* (Venice, CA: Antioch University Press, 1982).

Raskin, Victor. *Semantic Mechanisms of Humor* (Boston: D. Reidel Publishing, 1984).

Saks, Sol. *The Craft of Comedy Writing* (Cincinnati: Writer's Digest Books, 1985).

Ziv, Avner. *Personality and Sense of Humor* (New York: Springer, 1984).

Political Cartoon Symbols and the Divergence of Popular and Traditional Cultures in the United States

Roger A. Fischer

Although popular culture is nearly as old as civilization itself, its clear divergence from elite, folk and other traditional categories of culture is a relatively recent phenomenon, occurring on both sides of the Atlantic in the wake of the Industrial Revolution. Thus Shakespeare wrote for the pit as well as the boxes, as did Mozart and other masters who wove so many folk and popular airs into their compositions and like the Bard of Avon commonly exploited the great stories of folk tradition, the classics, and the Bible so familiar to the unlettered as well as the literati. Two great icons of popular culture in the United States during the generation preceding the Civil War were Charles Dickens, whose writings blended fine literature with splendid story-telling, and "Swedish Nightingale" Jenny Lind, who became a pop superstar performing music that would be considered decidedly "longhair" today. Indeed, the Germania Orchestra founders who brought symphonic music to this country would have neither understood nor appreciated the Jekyll-Hyde relationship between the Boston Symphony and the Boston Pops, with the same musicians doing Stravinsky one night under Erich Leinsdorf and "I Saw Mommy Kissing Santa Claus" the next afternoon under Arthur Fiedler.

While exceptions can be noted, it nevertheless remains essentially true that before the cannon sounded at Sumter no hard-and-fast dichotomy existed between popular and traditional culture in the United States and that this divergence was rather slow to develop after Appomattox. A distinctive popular culture did evolve apace with the Industrial Revolution, concomitant population growth in our towns and cities, a proliferation of leisure time and disposable income among urbanites, and an influx of European immigrants alien to the adage "idle hands are the Devil's workshop." For the most part, however, into the new century American highbrows, middlebrows, and literate lowbrows continued to share in common a rather traditional cultural heritage that counted among its components Scripture, the mythology of Homer, the fables of Aesop and *Arabian Nights,* the artistic and historical heritage of the ancients and the Renaissance, the writings of Shakespeare and John Bunyan, and the adventures of Gulliver, Don Quixote, and Oliver Twist.

That this common cultural matrix has waned to the point of extinction during the past century can be demonstrated in many ways. One of the best that I can suggest is by comparing the political cartoon art produced in the United States during the last two decades with that created a century before. By its very nature and purpose, political cartoon art in a democratic society is one of the purest artifacts of popular culture, attempting to influence public opinion through its use of widely and instantly understood symbols, slogans, referents, and allusions. As Don Wright, editorial cartoonist for the Miami *News,* has noted, "Immediate impact is what makes a cartoon good, and in order to have impact, I'm not sure that you should be all that subtle. The best cartoons hit you squarely between the eyes."[1] To do so, the political cartoonist must utilize conventions in fundamental harmony with the mass culture of his or her public or risk almost certain failure, for obscurity and snob wit are fatal to the medium. Thus the symbols, allusions, and referents that make for a truly successful political cartoon can tell us much about the popular culture of its day.

One thing a survey of recent political cartoons reveals is that the lamentations of Allan Bloom and William Bennett over cultural illiteracy have some basis in fact. Apart from an occasional cartoon set in a Roman arena or such infrequent gems [fig. 1] as a 1984 Steve Sack effort drawing "new ideas" candidate Gary Hart as Rodin's "The Thinker" with an empty thought bubble or a 1986 Jeff MacNelly cartoon portraying as "The Trojan Chicken" the Gramm-Rudman deficit bill, the legacy of the classics has been virtually abandoned by cartoonists. The fables of Aesop and *Arabian Nights* have given way to those of Walt Disney or to *The Princess and the Pea* and other fairy tales given new life as animated TV cartoons. The superb mythic creations of Hesiod, Homer, and Virgil no longer conjure visions of heroics or horror, for Hercules, Odysseus, and Aeneas have been supplanted by Rambo and Superman, while Cyclopes, hydras, and the Minotaur have been doomed to extinction by the likes of Godzilla, King Kong, and Darth Vader.

Equally vanquished as cartoon allusions have been Bunyan's ogre and, despite some extraordinary inspiration in recent political high crimes and misdemeanors, Dante's "Inferno." Shakespeare hasn't fared much better, with such compelling cartoon possibilities as Hamlet and the witches of *Macbeth* utilized rarely and Falstaff and Shylock not at all. Virtually alone among the giants of contemporary cartooning with an affinity for the Bard is the Los Angeles *Time's* Paul Conrad, whose magnificent 1973 portrayals of a beleaguered Richard Nixon as Hamlet casting aside the skulls of his fallen lieutenants and as King Richard II pondering his fallen state [fig. 2] rank among the finest political cartoons ever produced in the United States. The sole survivor in recent cartoon art among so many memorable Dickens characters is Ebenezer Scrooge, much in vogue during the 1985 holiday season in the wake of a callous denial that hunger posed a problem in America by Reaganite Ed Meese. Don Quixote also puts in occasional appearances, undoubtedly due less to the literary legacy of Cervantes than to the recent popularity of the musical extravaganza *Man of La Mancha.* Culturally literate political cartoon art is probably faring no better in Canada than here in the United States, although Ed Uluschak's fine 1974 Edmonton *Journal* "Portrait of Dorian Nixon" provides one notable exception.[2]

Figure 1. Rare examples of contemporary political cartoons inspired by classical culture are this 1984 Steve Sack Minneapolis *Star & Tribune* spoof on Rodin's *The Thinker* and Jeff MacNelly's 1986 Chicago *Tribune* portrayal of Gramm-Rudman as "The Trojan Chicken." Reprinted with permission of the artists.

**O that I were as great as is my grief, or lesser than my name!
Or that I could forget what I have been,
Or not remember what I must be now!**

King Richard II, Act III, Scene III

"Alas, poor Agnew, Mitchell, Stans, Ehrlichman, Haldeman, Dean, Kalmbach, LaRue, Mardian, Strachan, McCord, Liddy, Chapin, Hunt, Colson, Krogh, Magruder, Young—I knew them . . . ."

Figure 2. Unusual among current cartoonists for his affinity for Shakespearean allusions is Paul Conrad of the Los Angeles *Times,* winner of three Pulitzers for such fine work as these 1973 cartoons conveying the pathos of Richard Nixon's fall from grace. Reprinted with the permission of the artist.

Also exploited minimally in modern political cartooning has been the legacy of the Bible, with hundreds of characters and themes rich in potential ignored altogether. For the most part, scriptural allusions are limited to personages and situations permitting immediate recognition by theological illiterates—Adam and Eve naked in Eden, Eve and the serpent, Moses with the commandments or parted sea, Jesus walking on water. During Nixon's Watergate difficulties cartoonists exploited his self-serving sanctimony by depicting him walking on mud or the heads of his abandoned subordinates. Mike Peters portrayed him brilliantly as a latter-day Moses with edited tablets deleting three of the ten commandments. Another fine Peters Watergate effort, prompted by the Supreme Court ruling that Nixon must relinquish the tapes, featured the first couple as a naked Adam and Eve, with Nixon pitching the tapes under the accusing finger of God. Nixon's welfare cuts during the 1971 Christmas season inspired a deadly Nativity cartoon by Peters and his 1979 attempt to buy into a Manhattan cooperative provided the same allusion for Doug Marlette, who has often used religious imagery to attack the Moral Majority, PTL Club, and other televangelical insults to his Baptist heritage and flinty liberalism. On a few occasions Pat Oliphant cast born-again James Watt as a bald, maniacal Jesus walking on water or orchestrating the Second Coming during Watt's stormy stint at Interior.[3]

For the most part, though, the venerable characters of Scripture, classical mythology, Shakespeare, and the like have given way to the more familiar, instantly recognized icons of contemporary television, Tinseltown, the top forty, the comic strips, and other manifestations of popular culture. In 1972 Peters satirized the Nixon peace initiatives as "Cracker Jack Negotiations" (with a "Four More Years" button as a prize) and symbolized the disparity between the campaign organizations of Nixon and George McGovern by drawing the latter as a small gumball machine and the former as a huge slot machine dispensing Cabinet posts and ambassadorships for contributions. A decade later in "Watt Man" Conrad portrayed Watt as an enormous Pac-Man gobbling up the United States and in a pair of Minneapolis *Tribune* cartoons Steve Sack lampooned Watt's environmental agenda and Ronald Reagan's arms buildup by reducing them to bumperstickers ("I Brake for Developers," "Have You Hugged your Warhead Today?").[4]

Many recent political cartoons have exploited the lyrics of popular songs. To lampoon Nixon's Watergate woes, Conrad portrayed him at the piano late at night belting out "Don't Blame Me" and in a San Francisco *Examiner* cartoon Ken Alexander drew him with banjo crooning mournfully, "Those Jury Calls are Breaking Up that O-o-o-ld Gang of Mine." Don Wright satirized Reagan's insensitivity to blacks with a cartoon depicting him treating the NAACP to a rendition of "Ol' Man River." A pair of fine 1980 Marlette *Wizard of Oz* cartoons [fig. 3] featured Tin Man Reagan singing "If I Only Had a Heart" and Cowardly Lion Jimmy Carter belting out "If I Only Had the Nerve." In 1982 parodies on the musical comedy *Annie* satirizing Reagan's rosy fiscal predictions, Marlette and Jack Ohman both portrayed a frizzle-haired "Ronnie" singing the upbeat "Tomorrow, Tomorrow" in a rainstorm. The Farm Aid concert crusade of Willie Nelson inspired MacNelly in 1985 to draw Reagan as Nelson doing "In the Red Again" at a "Deficit Aid" gala and Peters in 1986 to feature Reagan with guitar performing at a concert for "Contra Aid."[5]

Figure 3. Ranking with the best 1980 campaign satire are these Doug Marlette Charlotte *Observer* parodies on *The Wizard of Oz* lampooning Ronald Reagan's compassion and Jimmy Carter's courage in command. Reprinted with the permission of the artist.

Given the pervasive influence of television of contemporary American popular culture, it is inevitable that cartoonists draw heavily upon it to convey their messages. Among artists utilizing TV commercials has been Dennis Renault, whose outstanding 1973 "I'm Ronnie—Fly Me" series in the Sacramento *Bee* parodied some blatantly sexist and very popular National Airline TV ads to make mock of Reagan's neglect of gubernatorial duties to position himself for a presidential bid. In their efforts to satirize Reaganomics, Herb Block parodied a popular E. F. Hutton commercial in 1981 and Marlette two years later did likewise with a DeBeer's diamond ad in "Deficits are Forever." A 1973 Peters cartoon featured a hunkered-down Nixon being carried from the set of the popular TV game show *To Tell the Truth.* In 1983 Sack critiqued superbly the Reagan invasion of tiny Grenada by portraying it as an episode on the TV series *Fantasy Island* and enjoyed success in 1987 presenting Reagan, Oliver North, John Poindexter, and other "Iranscam" miscreants as the cast of the TV soap opera *The Young and the Witless.*[6]

Comic books and animated cartoons have also evolved into a useful source for inspiration [fig. 4]. To lampoon the Machiavellian strategies and massive ego of Henry Kissinger, Marlette drew a series in comic strip format entitled "The Professor and his Pals." Among the many parodies on Superman and kindred caped superheroes have been Marlette's 1973 presentation of Nixon as "Law-and-Order-Man" clad in the cloak of executive privilege and a 1981 Hugh Haynie effort portraying "Superreagan" catching his comeuppance from the cane of a "Geriatric Juggernaut" after proposed cuts in Social Security entitlements. As might be expected, the legacy of Walt Disney is too pervasive to have been ignored by political cartoonists. In 1973 Peters caricatured Nixon as Mickey Mouse with tape-reel ears and as a pure and virginal Snow White unsullied by the Watergate mischief being committed around him by subordinates cast as the Seven Dwarfs. Given Nixon's tendency to avoid the unvarnished truth whenever possible, the analogy between him and Disney's Pinocchio proved too tempting to pass up, at least for Haynie and New York *Post* cartoonist Joe Pierotti, both of whom portrayed Nixon as Pinocchio with a growing "Watergate" nose. Among the more memorable Watt cartoons was a superb Peters effort featuring him terrorizing two little children with a bedtime story of the execution of Bambi and Thumper![7]

Of all varieties of contemporary popular culture, the movies have provided cartoonists with the most numerous and on the whole the most creative allusions for political commentary. Nixon was cast in many Hollywood roles, most memorably as *Casablanca's* Bogie in MacNelly's 1972 "Play It Again, Sam" and as King Kong astride the Capitol in a droll 1974 Jules Feiffer critique of the idea that impeachment could ruin the republic. In 1972 Bob Beckett portrayed Nixon's "Phase IV" economic controls as Frankenstein's monster, a referent used adroitly by Marlette to caricature Gerald Ford in his outstanding "Return of Frankenstein." Equally creative was Marlette's presentation of Henry Kissinger's self-serving memoirs as a poster for the film "Apackolies Now." Also skillfully drawn was Haynie's 1982 portrayal of persistent unemployment defying "The Exorci$t." The characters of *Star Wars* and its two sequels have been utilized extensively by cartoonists, the sinister Darth Vader in particular. In his 1983 "Return of the Jimmy," MacNelly drew the 1984 Democratic contenders as *Star*

". . . The whole truth and nothing but the . . ."

Figure 4. Among 1973 cartoons satirizing Nixon's Watergate difficulties were these efforts starring him as Hugh Haynie's Pinocchio, Doug Marlette's "Law and Order Man," and Mike Peters' Snow White and Mickey Mouse. Reprinted with the permission of the artists.

Wars characters. Enhancing this parallel have been the dubbing of the Reagan anti-missile defense "Star Wars" and Reagan's characterization of the Soviet Union as the "evil empire." Thus his "crack team of advisors" appear as Darth, robots Artoo-Deetoo and C-threepio, and E.T. and in 1985 efforts Andrei Gromyko was cast as Darth Vader by Peters and the Soviet military as the loathsome Jabba the Hutt by Bill Mauldin.[8]

The accession to the presidency of Reagan of Warner Brothers and *Death Valley Days* rather predictably inspired a copious array of political cartoons based upon Hollywood themes, most of them at first predicated mainly on the incongruity of an actor (or cowboy) in the Oval Office and, as a result, predictably mediocre as political satire. But as his presidency unfolded, the more creative cartoonists discovered ample opportunities to draw upon Hollywood in lampooning Reagan and his agenda. A splendid 1981 Peters cartoon presented him with an Academy Award as "best actor in a supporting role" to the El Salvador junta. Reagan's deficit difficulties inspired Sack, a cartoonist uncommonly fond of Hollywood allusions [fig. 5], to draw him in 1982 as "E. P. the Extra-Prezestrial" alone, lost, and "146,000,000 dollars from a balanced budget" and his alleged "gender gap" problems prompted Sack in 1983 to portray Reagan as Rhett Butler romancing a Women's Vote Scarlett only to be told, "Frankly, my dear, this time *I* don't give a damn." Robert Redford's performance as an elderly baseball rookie in *The Natural* prompted Minnesota *Daily* cartoonist Kevin Siers to caricature Reagan in baseball pinstripes with a huge "Commie Basher" bat. Reagan's hawkish foreign policy and the Sylvester Stallone epic *Rambo* provided cartoonists with a parallel too tempting to resist, and soon cartoons by Wright and Sack portrayed "Ronbo" Reagan zapping Soviet missiles in outer space and venting his wrath against the Nicaraguan Sandinistas. Even more biting were Sack's 1987 "Iran-scam" parodies of the films *Platoon* and *The Untouchables*, the former [fig. 11] portraying Reagan shooting himself in the foot as star of *Buffoon* and the latter featuring Oliver North and cohorts as *The Uncontrollables* and introducing Reagan as "The Amnesiac." Sack's affinity for Hollywood allusions was again exhibited in a 1988 *Who Killed Roger Rabbit?* spoof presenting George Bush as "Bushy Bunny."[9]

Without such sources of inspiration as Hollywood, television, and the like, the leading cartoonists of a century ago relied upon a more traditional and decidedly more elite pool of cultural referents and allusions in crafting their graphic commentaries. Thomas Nast, whose 1861-1886 work in *Harper's Weekly* has been credited with nearly singlehandedly ushering in the modern genre of political cartoon art, eschewed almost altogether the artifacts of contemporary popular culture. Indeed, Nast was so partial to the trappings of antiquity that it is difficult to deduce from the corpus of his art whether the toga or the business suit served as the typical dress of his day or whether the men who wore them dwelt in columned temples or in brownstones! A wicked 1879 Joseph Keppler *Puck* burlesque of his rival's style featured Nast's most overworked cartoon cliche, a stern female figure of Liberty in classical dress "with a Roman sword in her hand, a Grecian cornice on her head and an expression of mingled agony, enthusiasm, and nausea in her face."[10]

Some of Nast's first true cartoons cast the hated Andrew Johnson as a cruel Roman emperor, although his most sinister portrayal of the beleaguered Tennessean was as a menacing Medusa in his 1867 "Southern Justice." Another

Figure 5. Among the many Steve Sack cartoons drawing on Hollywood blockbusters to lampoon Reagan's shortcomings are these Minneapolis *Star & Tribune* efforts portraying Reagan as E.T., Rambo, and the star of "Buffoon." Reprinted with the permission of the artist.

"TIME WORKS WONDERS."

Figure 6. Examples of Thomas Nast's bent toward Shakespearean themes are these portrayals of Horatio Seymour as Lady Macbeth, Jefferson Davis as Iago, Boss Tweed as Caesar, and James B. Weaver as Oberon's hoax upon Titania in *Harper's Weekly* cartoons of September 19, 1868, April 9, 1870, January 27, 1872, and July 3, 1880 respectively.

successful play on Greek mythology was his "Pan-ic in Session," an 1881 indictment of congressional budgetary chaos that featured half-man, half-goat Pan astride the Capitol. Nast made use of Diogenes and his lamp to impugn the integrity of the anti-Ulysses Grant press corps, Horace Greeley, and Boss Tweed of Tammany. After New York voters ousted the Tweed cabal in 1871, Nast drew him as a dejected, porcine Nero sitting amidst the ruins of the Tammany temple. Cartoons portraying the travails of Tweed, Johnson, and the apostate 1872 Liberal Republicans as Ides of March scenes from *Julius Caesar* combined Nast's fondness for antiquity with an equal affinity [fig. 6] for Shakespearean themes and allusions. In parodies on *Othello* Nast cast as Iago Johnson, New York *Tribune* editor Whitelaw Reid, and Jefferson Davis. He drew 1868 Democratic nominee Horatio Seymour as Lady MacBeth trying to wash away bloodstains of the New York draft riots, Britain's John Bull as a bloated Sir John Bull Falstaff, Democratic party treasurer August Belmont as Shylock, and 1880 Greenback nominee James B. Weaver as the *Midsummer Night's Dream* weaver transformed by Oberon into a jackass to punish Fairy Queen Titania.[11]

Nast borrowed from Austrian folklore in 1872 to cartoon our dispute with Britain over the Civil War "Alabama claims" as William Tell John Bull shooting an apple off the head of son Uncle Sam and in 1874 borrowed from *Arabian Nights* in depicting political gadfly Ben Butler as a menacing genie loosed from his bottle. Less fond of allusions from modern literature, Nast did endow a cartoon mocking the 1872 insurgent Liberal Republicans with the Dickensian title "Great Expectations," exploited Daniel Defoe's *Robinson Crusoe* and Jonathan Swift's *Gulliver's Travels* in cartooning Grant and Charles Sumner, and twice portrayed 1880 Democratic nominee Winfield Scott Hancock in the title role of Jonathan Swift's *Gulliver's Travels.* He rarely drew upon allusions from Scripture, but did utilize the temptation of Christ to cartoon Greeley and feminist Victoria Claflin Woodhull and on one occasion dramatized discrimination in Dixie by depicting a black Samson being shorn of hair and power by a Southern Democracy Delilah. One of his memorable anti-Catholic cartoons, his 1869 "Pilgrim's Progress in the 19th Century," featured Pius IX as John Bunyan's decrepit ogre grinning helplessly at passing Christian pilgrims from a cave strewn with the bones of victims of his prime.[12]

The beginnings of a clear divergence between traditional and popular culture in political cartooning is much more easily discernible in the lithographed color cover and centerfold art published during this period in *Puck* and *The Judge,* the two giants of the genre of illustrated dime humor weeklies that dominated political cartoon art in the United States during the late nineteenth century. Begun in 1876 as a German-language venture by artist Joseph Keppler and publisher Adolph Schwartzmann, *Puck* made its English-language debut a year later and soon established Keppler's style of blithe and immensely colorful graphic satire as the dominant force in American political cartoon art. Popularity begat imitators aplenty, the most noteworthy being *Puck's* Republican rival *The Judge,* begun in 1881 by Keppler protege James A. Wales and brought to the front rank by an epochal cartoon war with *Puck* during the 1884 campaign and by the 1885 acquisitions of publisher William J. Arkell and chief artist Bernhard Gillam, lured away from *Puck* after a superb 1884 series savaging James G. Blaine as the tattooed man. Faced with the task of producing three color cartoons a week with a minimum of trite banality, *Puck* and *Judge* artists found inspiration in a much more varied reservoir of sources than did Nast, including a diverse array of cultural allusions and referents, both elite and popular, traditional and contemporary.

Unlike Nast, the artists of *Puck* and *Judge* exploited to advantage the potential of an aborning popular culture to lampoon the foibles of their political foils. If Nast found in the epic figures and contexts of antiquity and the classics an ideal vehicle for his strident moralism and stark black and white style, Keppler and his lieutenants and imitators found in the exuberant banality of contemporary popular culture inspirations galore for the lighter satire and gaudy color of their fare [figs. 7-8]. Athletics had provided a natural metaphor for political competition since crude, cluttered cartoons of Jacksonians and Whigs as runners and pugilists[14] and in an era obsessed with spectator and participatory sports *Puck* and *Judge* covers and centerfolds often portrayed political contests as boxing and tennis matches, baseball and football games, or as races with bicycles, sailboats, sleds, and toboggans.[15] Other forms of competition exploited were horse and dog shows, and produce exhibits at country fairs, cartoons likely to feature Ben Butler, Roscoe Conkling, and other favorite targets for droll caricature as prize Clydesdales, whippets, or pumpkins. High fashion competition provided another tempting vehicle for cartoonists to lampoon the vanity and vacuity of leading public figures by drawing them as sissified fops, as Frederick Opper portrayed Conkling and Chester Arthur in his 1883 *Puck* front cover "The Original Political Dude Out-Duded," or even better yet, as outlandish society matrons in drag, as F. Victor Gillam savaged Grover Cleveland and David Hill in his 1888 *Judge* front cover cartoon "Easter Bonnets." Keppler seized upon the same schtick and the essential absurdity of beauty pageants to draw two dozen possible presidential contenders as hideous female impersonators in his 1884 *Puck* centerfold "The Contest of Beauty."[16]

Other popular culture innovations of the era exploited by *Puck* and *Judge* artists for political satire included amusement park rides and beach activity, July Fourth fireworks displays, games and puzzles, and shows and theatrical productions of every stripe. Frank Beard debunked Cleveland's 1884 hopes by drawing him on a merry-go-round with six losing Democratic predecessors and C. J. Taylor in 1888 lampooned French political instability by presenting rival leaders as riders on a Ferris-wheel. A favored ploy was the portrayal of leaders looking absurd in swimwear with a zany array of flotation devices splashing in the surf at Coney Island or beach resorts. Predictable Independence Day cartoons featured public men as figural skyrockets fizzled or dead or blazing skyward, April Fool's issues often depicted political wiles as schoolboy pranks, and nary a post-election December passed without cartoons of hopefuls hanging stockings for choice posts in the new regime. Inspired by popular puzzles of the era were Wales' 1880 *Puck* back cover "15—14—13—The Great Presidential Puzzle," featuring Conkling stymied by the figural tiles of contenders in a "15-puzzle" variant, and Grant Hamilton's 1889 *Judge* cartoon "The Democratic 'Pigs in the Clover' Puzzle," with Louisville editor Henry Watterson trying roll balls representing 1892 Democratic hopefuls into a model White House. The urban black cakewalk tradition provided artists with opportunities to draw their foils competing for the cake of political primacy in blackface, often with exaggerated African features.[17]

Figures 7 and 8. Inspired by contemporary vogues in American popular culture was this 1887-1889 *Judge* selection lampooning Grover Cleveland as a highwire daredevil, fashionable matron, circus elephant, baseball player, and blackfaced minstrel and mourner in the cast of *Uncle Tom's Cabin*.

The popularity of minstrelry provided the *Puck* and *Judge* artists with additional opportunities to mix political commentary with white supremacist chic, although virtually no variety of show, exhibition, or theatrical presentation popular during the period was neglected by cartoonists. Comic opera in the Gilbert and Sullivan tradition was a natural for the opportunities it provided to dress characters in outlandish costumes and to lampoon them in satiric librettos. The stage production of *Uncle Tom's Cabin,* the most ubiquitous melodrama of the era, was exploited by Bernhard Gillam to draw Ben Butler as Topsy and the Democratic party as Miss Ophelia in his 1883 *Puck* cartoon "Incorrigible" and to portray the demise of the Cleveland administration as the play's tear-jerking finale in his 1889 *Judge* centerfold "The Last Scene in Uncle Grover's Cabin." Utilizing other vogues in popular entertainment, Gillam savaged the morally flexible Blaine as a carnival quick-change virtuoso in his 1884 *Puck* effort "A Lightning-Change Artist" and Cleveland as an improbable tightrope daredevil trying to cross over Niagara Falls on a frayed rope balancing cumbersome allies and issues in his 1888 *Judge* centerfold "Cleveland Will Have a Walk-Over." Punch and Judy puppetry provided an ideal vehicle for depicting political manipulation, with such figures as plutocrat Jay Gould and party bosses Tom Platt and Tammany's "Honest John" Kelly manipulating their marionette minions at will.[18]

Given the extraordinary influence in American popular culture of P. T. Barnum and the potential his attractions provided for creative caricature and satire, it was natural that cartoonists exploited frequently the circus, carnival, and freak show as context for political commentary. A recurring theme in Gillam's *Judge* cartoons during the 1888 campaign was the portrayal of Cleveland's re-election effort as a traveling circus and menagerie, with the corpulent president almost predestined by nature for the role of Jumbo, "Sacred Civil Service Reform White Elephant." *Puck* artists countered with circus cartoons satirizing Republican inconsistency on the liquor issue and patronage squabbles between Blaine and Benjamin Harrison. Both humor weeklies utilized the carnival sideshow metaphor to poke fun at the splinter-party candidacies of Ben Butler and feminist Belva Lockwood, Bernhard Gillam in 1884 with his *Puck* piece "The Busted Side Show" and brother Victor in 1888 with his *Judge* centerfold "The Neglected Side Shows." The advertising show saw use as a referent; more commonly were ideologies and candidacies cartooned as presentations of itinerant vendors of patent medicine. The freak show provided inspiration for what developed into the premier cartoon creation of the generation, portrayal of Blaine as the tattooed man. In his April 16, 1884 *Puck* centerfold "The National Dime Museum," in league with Conkling as a bearded lady and other notables as sundry oddities of nature, Bernhard Gillam drew Blaine tattooed head to toe with scandals and other compromises of probity, initiating a series so devastating that Blaniacs spoke of lawsuits and censorship legislation and finally exacted revenge by enticing Gillam from Keppler to draw Republican cartoons for *Judge!*[19]

While these artists were creatively exploiting the conventions of contemporary popular culture, they made good use of more traditional resources as well. Keppler and Bernhard Gillam were fond of historical referents, useful to Keppler in portraying Rutherford B. Hayes as Sir Walter Raleigh, lampooning arch-protectionist Samuel Randall as Canute trying to hold back the waves of tariff reform, and savaging commodity manipulators by depicting the crude but effective medieval remedy of nailing them by the ear to the door of a public building. The better Gillam cartoons of this genre include "The True Meaning of Republican harmony," an 1883 comparison of GOP tariff consensus to Rome's House of Tarquin trying to parlay a human sacrifice into a return to power, and "The Last Days of the Democratic Pompeii," an 1887 warning to the Democrats of the consequences of ignoring the labor vote. In other cartoons Gillam drew Cleveland as a reformist Cardinal Richelieu defying the Democratic royal court over civil service, Brutus slaying a civil service Julius Caesar, and Henry VIII courting a spoils system Anne Boleyn. Other historical immortals put to effective use to lampoon the politicos of the day were Christopher Columbus, Napoleon Bonaparte, Louis XIV, and Lady Godiva.[20]

Folklore and fables were also put to creative use. Gambrinus, a mythical Flemish ruler alleged to have invented beer, served Keppler, Taylor, Grant Hamilton as a model for cartoons savaging Charles Dana, labor boycotts, Republican pension fraud, and John Bull respectively. The fables of folklore, Aesop, and *Arabian Nights* found new life in a host of cartoons, with rum shop genies loosed from license law reform bottles, Democratic and Henry George donkeys starving between equally tempting piles of hay symbolizing difficult political options, camels representing British free trade and cattle barons driving from their respective tents American labor and reservation Plains Indians, and a puffed-up Butler greenback bullfrog squished by a "Solid Money" ox. In an especially clever Wales reprise of an Aesop fable, stork Roscoe Conkling invited bulldog John Kelly of Tammany to share the spoils of collaboration, contained in an urn with a long slender neck suited only to the crafty stork.[21]

In sharp contrast to Nast and to his own strong bent toward secular humanism, Keppler was inordinately fond of scriptural referents. His third English-edition centerfold immodestly featured young Puck as the political fulfillment of the prophecy of *Isaiah* 6:11 "and a little child shall lead them: in "The Millenium at Last." In 1880 he spoofed Ulysses Grant's third-term boom as "The Worship of Golden Calf," John Kelly of Tammany as Goliath routed by Samuel Tilden's reform Democrats at the Cincinnati convention and as Jonah tossed overboard by New York Democrats, and Democratic nominee Winfield Scott Hancock as baby Moses and then Samson, first performing mighty feats and then in defeat being shorn of hair and power by a Republican Delilah. When Sarah Bernhardt was denounced during an American tour by censorious evangelists for having a bastard son, Keppler portrayed her as a "Modern Rizpah, Protecting Her Son From the Clerical Vultures" [fig. 9], alluding to the story in *Samuel II* (21:8-11) of the heroic mother who rescued her sons strung up to die by the Gibeonites. As the fatally wounded James A. Garfield lay dying in August, 1881, Keppler acidly drew Republican opportunists including Grant, Conkling, and Arthur as Roman soldiers casting lots for his robes in "A Humiliating Spectacle." This effort was less unusual for its unbridled venom than for its reliance upon a New Testament allusion, although during the decade Bernhard Gillam depicted Cleveland as the Good Samaritan and apostate Republican George W. Curtis as the Prodigal Son, Hamilton portrayed Curtis and other reform renegades as "The Republican Pharisees," and Beard drew the Democratic party as Lazarus barred from a Republican patronage feast.[22]

Figure 9. Inspired by attacks by DeWitt Talmage (caricatured here as a figural vulture) and other holier-than-thou American evangelists on actress Sarah Bernhardt for bearing and raising an illegitimate son was this Joseph Keppler *Puck* cartoon depicting her as "The Modern Rizpah," who in Scripture had saved her sons condemned by the Gibeonites.

Figure 10. Parodies on the Pharoah's daughter finding baby Moses in the bulrushes included this 1880 *Puck* cartoon of Democratic leaders discovering nominee Winfield Scott Hancock and this 1888 *Judge* cartoon of Britain's John Bull discovering free-trade lackey Grover Cleveland.

Much more prevalent were allusions to the epic figures and tales of the Old Testament. The struggles between Cain and Abel and David and Goliath, Noah's Ark and the Flood, the saga of Samson and Delilah, and the temptation of Eve in the Garden of Eden all provided uncommon opportunity for political metaphor, as did the destruction of Sodom and Gomorrah for political corruption and the Tower of Babel for confusion or conflicting ideologies within a party or movement. To brand Cleveland a base hypocrite, Hamilton featured him in his 1888 "Cleveland's Coat of Many Colors" as Joseph parading in a patchwork cloak of contradictory positions. Mosaic analogies were especially ubiquitous [fig. 10]. Appearing as baby Moses in the bulrushes were Cleveland, Hancock, and Hill and in the heroic role of Moses leading the exodus to the Promised Land appeared Butler leading the Democratic Israelites to Washington and Uncle Sam, in a Victor Gillam cartoon leading pauper workers from bondage under pharaoh John Bull to high wages in protectionist America and in a Keppler centerfold with exaggerated semitic features leading eastern European Jews through parted seas of bigotry to safe haven in the United States. Among the more imaginative biblical cartoons utilizing rather obscure scriptural referents were Keppler's 1882 *Puck* centerfold "The Moloch of Arctic Discovery," drawing New York *Herald* publisher James Gordon Bennett as the early Hebrew god infamous for decreeing the sacrifice of children (for Bennett's endowment of a polar expedition that sent several explorers to icy deaths), and the 1884 *Judge* centerfold "The Worship of Ananias," a bitter post-mortem featuring "mugwump" defectors from Blaine kneeling in homage to the champion liar struck dead for his dishonesty in *Acts* (5:1-5).[23]

Exploited nearly as often and with even more creativity was the secular tradition of antiquity [fig. 11-12], especially the heroes and wonderfully gruesome monsters of Homeric legend. In 1882 Bernhard Gillam drew anti-Chinese bigotry as the dog Cerberus, guardian of the infernal regions, with the three heads of a hooligan, a demagogue, and an Irishman and in 1885 portrayed the tariff as a Minotaur "Protection Monster of Pennsylvania" being fed maidens symbolizing the other states in its labyrinth by congressmen William D. "Pig Iron" Kelley and Samuel Randall. Keppler in 1888 depicted trusts and the tariff as "A Hydra That Must Be Crushed," with each head a protected monopoly, and in 1895 Louis Dalrymple drew a "Free Silver Craze" hydra with the heads of eight silverite senators. Wall Street was portrayed as a poisonous Upas tree by Keppler and as the temptress Circe by *Puck* artist Friedrich Graetz, who in "Between Scylla and Charybdis" drew as the Strait of Messina rock and whirlpool personified in mythology as deadly female monsters Cleveland's patronage pests and future mother-in-law. Cleveland himself starred as a muscular Hercules in a pair of 1885 *Puck* cartoons and as a corpulent Apollo playing a free trade lyre for the creatures of the forest in an 1888 *Judge* centerfold.[24]

In other cartoons Harrison appeared as Ajax, Bennett and Gould as rival Neptunes lobbing maritime mud upon each other, and Conkling as Diogenes. Blaine starred as a tattooed Narcissus "mashed" on his own reflection, an Apollo of corruption, the Phoenix rising from the ashes of 1890 party misfortune, and in Keppler's "Tantalus" chained to a rock and taunted by visions of an inaugural gala forever beyond his reach. Although in Greek mythology Tantalus had been condemned by his father Zeus for revealing the secrets of Olympus to stand

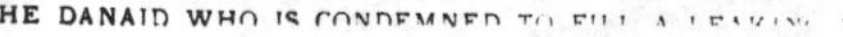
HE DANAID WHO IS CONDEMNED TO FILL A LEAKING VESSEL

THE OLYMPUS OF CORRUPTION.—"APOLLO STRIKES THE LYRE AND CHARMS THE GODS."

VIII.-No. 198 DECEMBER 1, 1880

"What fools these Mortals be!"

MIDSUMMER NIGHTS DREAM

Puck

PUBLISHED BY ... ER & SCHWARZMANN. NEW YORK OFFICE No 21 - 23 WARREN ST

TRADE MARK REGISTERED 1878

"ENTERED AT THE POST OFFICE AT NEW YORK, AND ADMITTED FOR TRANSMISSION THROUGH THE MAILS AT SECOND CLASS RATES"

McMANES

NEW YORK

PHILADELPHIA

THE THREE "DIS-GRACES."

VOL. XVI - No. 306

"What fools these Mortals be!"

MIDSUMMER NIGHTS DREAM

Puck

PUBLISHED BY KEPPLER & SCHWARZMANN NEW YORK OFFICE No

TRADE MARK REGISTERED

ENTERED AT THE POST OFFICE AT NEW YORK AND ADMITTED FOR TRANSMISSION THROUGH THE MAILS AT SECOND CLASS RATES

PRESIDENTIAL CAKE

TANTALUS.

Figures 11 and 12. Among the many themes of classical antiquity in *Puck* and *Judge* cartoons were these portrayals of Chester Arthur as a Danaid, anti-Chinese prejudice as the three-headed watchdog of Hades Cerberus, the Republicans as the "Olympus of Corruption" gods, James G. Blaine as Tantalus and Narcissus, and Irish machine kingpins Kelly, McLaughlin and McManes as the Graces Aglaia, Euphrosyne and Thalia.

starving in water under a ripe fruit tree, Keppler substituted the rock to symbolize the Little Rock & Fort Smith Railroad bonds Blaine had purportedly promoted as Speaker of the House. Keppler portrayed Susan B. Anthony, Lucy Stone, Elizabeth Cady Stanton and other noted feminists as geese waddling to save Rome, a referent utilized by Wales to cartoon American Catholic bishops rescuing the Cincinnati archdiocese from financial ruin. In portraying (without explanatory text) Arthur in drag with a leaking "Arthur Boom" barrel as a Danaid, a daughter of Danaus doomed for eternity to filling a perforated vessel, Graetz posed an honest challenge to the cultural literacy of *Puck* devotees. With irony worthy of the gods and goddesses of Olympus, scrawny Peter Cooper was parodied as Atlas, a bloated Victoria as Venus, and Irish machine kingpins Kelly of Tammany, Hughie McLaughlin of Brooklyn, and McManes of Philadelphia as "The Three Dis-Graces," a ribald burlesque of the famed "Three Graces" statue of Aglaia, Euphrosyne, and Thalia, goddesses of beauty and charm.[25]

Rarely was the compelling imagery of Dante exploited by *Puck* and *Judge* artists, and equally puzzling in light of the genre's potential and the affinity for opera shared by Keppler and several peers is the dearth of cartoons utilizing operatic themes. Along with some *Carmen* takeoffs, Keppler's 1887 parody on Wagner's *Ring of the Nibelung* portraying Cleveland as "Siegfried the Fearless in the Political Dismal Swamp" provided an exception. Key literary figures exploited often were Cervantes' Don Quixote, Bunyan's aged ogre, Swift's Gulliver and Goethe's Faust and Mephistopheles. A splendid Goethe effort was Keppler's 1877 "The Erl King (New Version)," featuring Erl King Hayes riding through a swamp filled with macabre figural Stalwart rotting trees. Equally superb was Bernhard Gillam's 1889 *Judge* Tennyson parody "The Mugwump Elaine—The Dead Steered By the Dumb," portraying Cleveland poling the dead Curtis up Salt River on a civil service funeral barge above suitably bastardized Tennyson stanzas. Dickensian referents included Pecksniff, Fagin, Oliver Twist, and the Micawbers. Shakespeare yielded a rich harvest of referents. Keppler drew John Bull and Hancock as Hamlet, Butler as Shylock demanding of Uncle Sam his veterans' pensions pound of flesh, and in his excellent 1881 "A Grand Shakespearean Revival" Arthur as King Henry IV rebuking former cronies Conkling and Platt for their unseemly familiarity. Opper invoked the same theme in his 1889 "Going Back on the 'Blocks of Five' " cartoon featuring Harrison as Richard III spurning as Buckingham Indiana Republican kingpin W. W. Dudley, infamous for allegedly voting in "blocks of five" illicit nonresident "floaters." Bernhard Gillam's Shakespearean efforts included *Puck* portrayals of Gould as Shylock and Kelly as Henry V eating the leek of repudiation and *Judge* centerfolds starring Cleveland as Falstaff, Julius Caesar, and a lackey of sinister Shylock John Bull.[26]

On other occasions color cartoons drew inspiration from serious art [fig. 13]. Bernhard Gillam's renowned June 4, 1884 *Puck* centerfold "Phryne Before the Chicago Tribunal," featuring Whitelaw Reid undressing the tattooed Blaine to exhibit to party leaders, parodied the 1859 Jean Leon Gerome oil *Phyrne Before the Tribunal* featuring Athenian orator Hypereides defending the lovely courtesan Phyrne on the sole basis of her pulchritude. Keppler's 1885 inaugural salute "Cleveland's Entry Into Washington" reprised the 1878 Hans Makart work *Entrance of Charles V Into Antwerp* and his 1885 "Harmony and Envy" featured

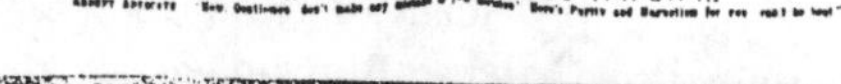

Figure 13. Among the parodies on paintings by European masters were these Bernhard Gillam centerfolds "Phryne Before the Chicago Tribunal" and "The Political Angelus," the former as shocking to Blaine Republicans as it had been to Parisians and the latter a parody of a painting so popular that *Judge* offered copies as subscription premiums.

Reid, Blaine, and John A. Logan as the envious monks in Charles Garnier's *Jour de Fete*. Several 1885-1889 Gillam centerfolds parodied the works of obscure European artists known mainly, it would seem, through cheap lithographed prints of their paintings. His 1885 "The Tribute to the Minotaur" parodied an identically titled work by Gendron and his 1887 "The Democratic Henry VIII Makes Love to Anne Boleyn (Spoils System) to the Disgust of His Mugwump Cardinal" exploited a popular painting by Piloty to savage Cleveland and Maryland Senator Arthur P. Gorman. In 1889 he drew Cleveland and Randall as Zamacois' *The Rival Confessors,* drew Cleveland as a scandalized friar watching Hill court Miss Democratic Party on a park bench in "Shocking!," and satirized free-trade attacks upon McKinley tariff initiatives in a parody of Gilbert Gaul's *Bringing Up the Guns.* Gillam's 1890 "The Political 'Angelus' " featuring Cleveland and Hill as a peasant couple sewing seeds of sham reform in a barren winter field to the tolling bell of village church bells parodied Jean Francois Millet's 1859 *The Angelus,* a work *Judge* was making even more familiar to its devotees by giving lithographed reproductions as premiums for subscription renewals.[27]

That *Judge* did so does much to shed light on a key dilemma posed by color cartoons demanding what we would regard today as an extraordinary level of cultural literacy. Clearly, cartoons predicated upon an immediate, widespread recognition of the works of Millet and Zamacois, the legends of Canute and Gambrinus, the evil of Moloch and the Minotaur, and the travails of Tantalus, the Daniades, and the gallant Rizpah either mirrored faithfully the prevailing cultural heritage of the day or failed as political cartoon art through elitist obscurity. Weighing against the latter hypothesis were press runs in six figures per issue, the resulting fortunes accumulated by Keppler and Arkell, and the absence of a compelling motive to spend a dime for the feeble humor and ads in the thirteen pages surrounding the cartoons! To be sure, cartoonists frequently "fudged" by providing reams of explanatory text. Nast especially did so, although he avoided such hedges as often as not and in instances where his art came encumbered with encyclopedic copy he was probably only indulging a characteristic affinity for the type of caption derided by *Puck* as "a chapter from the Patent-Office reports."[28] Culturally challenging allusions were less frequently given explanatory notation in *Puck* and *Judge* cartoons, and there seems to have been littler correlation between the use of didactic text and the obscurity of a referent. As cases in point, no such guidance was provided for Gillam's "A Sop to Cerberus," Graetz' study of Arthur as a hapless Danaid or his "Between Syclla and Charybdis," or Keppler's "Tantalus" and the only verbiage explaining his tribute to Sarah Bernhardt as "The Modern Rizpah" came in the editorial notes fourteen pages distant.

Such cartoons can tell us much about American culture during a remarkable generation when, to judge from the graphic art of political criticism, the traditional, essentially elite cultural heritage of our ancestors still competed upon an equal footing with the newly aborning phenomenon of contemporary popular culture and that it did so with the same creative, imaginative exuberance we commonly associate with pop culture. For Keppler, Gillam, and their compeers, the heritage of classical mythology, of Shakespeare and Scripture, and of Dante and Dickens was not some dry-as-dust medicine to ward off the atrophy of Western

Civilization, but rather a living legacy rich in dynamic parallels to the political world they satirized. For those who lament the eclipse of this heritage or construct cultural equivalents of Gresham's Law, there are lessons to be learned.

Notes

[1]Quoted in Alan F. Westin (ed.), *Getting Angry Six Times a Week: A Portfolio of Political Cartoons* (Boston, 1979), 38.

[2]See Paul Conrad, *Pro and Conrad* (San Rafael, Calif., 1979), 23, 27; and Charles Brooks (ed.), *Best Editorial Cartoons of the Year, 1975 Edition* (Gretna. La., 1975), 61.

[3]Mike Peters, *The Nixon Chronicles* (Dayton, Oh., 1976), 48, 137, 150; Doug Marlette, *Drawing Blood* (Washington, 1981), 57, 157, 172; Pat Oliphant, *Ban This Book!* (Kansas City, 1982), 28, 122.

[4]Peters, *Nixon Chronicles,* 54, 56; Charles Brooks (ed.) *Best Editorial Cartoons of the Year, 1983 Edition* (Gretna, La., 1983), 112; Carew Papritz and Russ Tremayne (eds.),*Reaganomics: A Cornucopia of Cartoons on Ronald Reagan* (Seattle, 1984), 65; Minneapolis *Star & Tribune,* March 5, 1982.

[5]Ed Salzman and Ann Leigh Brown (eds.), *The Cartoon History of California Politics* (Sacramento, 1978), 110; Charles Brooks (ed.), *Best Editorial Cartoons of the Year, 1974 Edition* (Gretna, La., 1974), 43; Marlette, *Drawing Blood,* 12, 150; Doug Marlette, *It's A Dirty Job...But Somebody Has To Do It!* (Charlotte, N.C., 1984), 30; Duluth (Minn.) *News-Tribune & Herald,* September 10, 1985, 12B; *Newsweek,* March 17, 1986, 15.

[6]Salzman and Brown, *Cartoon History of California Politics,* 134-135; Papritz and Tremayne, *Reagancomics,* 93, 104; Peters, *Nixon Chronicles,* 96; Minneapolis *Star & Tribune,* May 7, 1987, 17A.

[7]Marlette, *Drawing Blood,* 71; Brooks, *Best Editorial Cartoons, 1974,* 7, 21; Newsweek, June 1, 1981, 22; Peters, *Nixon Chronicles,* 92, 105; Carew Papritz (ed.), *100 Watts: The James Watt Memorial Collection* (Seattle, 1983), 45.

[8]Charles Brooks (ed.), *Best Editorial Cartoons for the Year 1972* (Gretna, La., 1973), 52; Marlette, *Drawing Blood,* 55, 128; *Newsweek,* April 4, 1983, 21, June 13, 1983, 19, and January 21, 1985, 25; *Target: The Political Cartoon Quarterly,* 10 (Winter, 1984), 13.

[9]*Newsweek,* February 27, 1984, 22; Minneapolis *Star & Tribune,* January 25, 1987, June 5, 1987, and July 3, 1987; Minnesota *Daily* (University of Minnesota), May 15, 1984, 6; Papritz and Tremayne, *Reagancomics,* 9.

[10]*Puck,* June 4, 1879, 194,208.

[11]See Morton Keller, *The Art and Politics of Thomas Nast* (New York, 1968), 52-55, 57, 60, 62-63, 66, 90, 145, 202, 208, 286-287, 335, 340.

[12]*Ibid.,* 70, 85-86, 96-97, 131, 149, 163, 184, 250, 336-337.

[13]The definitive study of Keppler and his art is Richard Samuel West, *Satire on Stone: The Political Cartoons of Joseph Keppler* (Urbana, Ill., 1988). See also Stephen Hess and Milton Kaplan, *The Ungentlemanly Art: A History of American Political Cartoons* (New York, 1968), 102-117, and Charles Press, *The Political Cartoon* (East Brunswick, N. J., 1981), 254-259.

[14]See Hess and Kaplan, *The Ungentlemanly Art,* 78-79.

[15]For representative examples, see *Puck,* January 6, 1886, 304, and September 28, 1887, 65, and *Judge,* December 18, 1886, 1, June 18, 1887, 8-9, May 26, 1888, 101, December 15, 1888, 166, July 13, 1889, 225, and October 26, 1889, 42-43.

[16]*Puck,* May 9, 1883, 152-153, September 26, 1883, 49, October 24, 1883, 120-121, January 23, 1884, 328-329; *Judge,* May 7, 1887, 8-9, April 7, 1888, 1.

[17]*Puck,* March 17, 1880, 32, July 5, 1882, 284-285, July 19, 1882, 316-317, April 2, 1884, 65, July 2, 1884, 288, and April 25, 1888, 137; *Judge,* November 1, 1884, 16, April 2, 1887, 8-9, January 14, 1888, 8-9, September 22, 1888, 379, March 30, 1889, 416 and August 30, 1890, 336-337. For Senate responses to Wales' "15-14-13," see Hess and Kaplan, *The Ungentlemanly Art,* 104-105.

[18]*Puck,* March 26, 1879, 40-41, June 2, 1880, 219, November 22, 1882, 184-185, May 23, 1883, 177, August 27, 1994, 416, January 21, 1885, 321, and November 2, 1887, 156-157; *Judge,* March 26, 1887, 1, December 10, 1887, 8-9, August 25, 1888, 322-323, February 16, 1889, 304-305, November 9, 1889, 67, and November 30, 1889, 124-125.

[19]*Puck,* October 23, 1878, 16, February 4, 1880, 782-783, September 5, 1883, 8-9, April 16, 1884, 104-105, November 5, 1884, 160, March 31, 1886, 72-73, September 29, 1886, 72-73, August 31, 1887, 8-9, and April 10, 1889, 104-105; *Judge,* January 8, 1887, 8-9, October 8, 1887, 8-9, October 22, 1887, 8-9, October 29, 1887, 8-9, December 3, 1887, 1, July 28, 1888, 264, November 24, 1888, 108-109, and November 23, 1889, 116. For an informative account of the tattooed man series, see Samuel J. Thomas, "The Tattooed Man Caricatures and the Presidential Campaign of 1884, *Journal of American Culture,* X (Winter, 1987), 1-20.

[20]*Puck,* November 7, 1877, 1, April 11, 1883, 88-89, May 6, 1885, 152-153, February 1, 1888, 368, and October 24, 1888, 131; *Judge,* November 22, 1884, 16, April 30, 1887, 8-9, August 27, 1887, 1, November 12, 1887, 8-9, and August 10, 1889, 281.

[21]*Puck,* May 2, 1877, 8-9, October 16, 1878, 16, November 12, 1878, 588, September 1, 1880, 456-457, August 19, 1885, 400, July 21, 1886, 336, November 30, 1887, 232, February 29, 1888, 1, April 11, 1888, 112-113, July 10, 1889, 328-329, October 9, 1889, 106-107, and June 4, 1891, 232-233; *Judge,* April 2, 1887, 1, April 9, 1887, 1, May 26, 1888, 108-109, and September 7, 1889, 345.

[22]*Puck,* March 28, 1877, 8-9, April 21, 1880, 112-113, June 30, 1880, 306-307, August 18, 1880, 424-425, September 15, 1880, 24-25, September 22, 1880, 40-41, November 10, 1880, 168, December 29, 1880, 290, January 5, 1881, 300-301, August 31, 1881, 436-437, and March 18, 1885, 40-41; *Judge,* April 26, 1884, 8-9, July 5, 1884, 1, and August 10, 1887, 8-9.

[23]*Puck,* September 4, 1878, 8-9, September 18, 1878, 8-9, February 11, 1879, 1, November 30, 1881, 200-201, January 4, 1882, 284-285, May 10, 1882, 154-155, October 11, 1881, 88-89, October 18, 1882, 112, November 29, 1882, 200-201, September 19, 1883, 33, March 5, 1884, 8-9, May 14, 1884, 161, November 16, 1887, 190-191, and November 21, 1888, 193; *Judge,* August 2, 1884, 16, September 6, 1884, 8-9, November 8, 1884, 8-9, November 29, 1884, 8-9, July 9, 1887, 8-9, September 24, 1887, 1, December 3, 1887, 16, January 7, 1888, 8-9, April 21, 1888, 24-25, October 6, 1888, 426, and December 14, 1889, 168.

[24]*Puck,* May 17, 1882, 163, August 30, 1882, 412-413, May 14, 1884, 176, February 18, 1885, 392-393, July 15, 1885, 320, November 26, 1885, 208, December 2, 1885, 216-217, and March 7, 1888, 26-27; *Judge,* February 4, 1988, 8-9, and June 19, 1895, 280-281.

[25]*Puck,* August 22, 1877, 1, January 23, 1878, 8-9, July 17, 1878, 16, August 7, 1878, 1, April 2, 1879, 64, December 1, 1880, 203, April 9, 1884, 81, September 17, 1884, 48, October 8, 1884, 88-89, November 26, 1890, 209, and December 10, 1890, 269; *Judge,* April 14, 1888, 1.

[26]*Puck,* April 18, 1877, 1, May 23, 1877, 8-9, May 30, 1877, 16, June 13, 1877, 8-9, October 3, 1877, 8-9, October 31, 1877, 8-9, January 14, 1880, 727, August 25, 1880, 448, May 18, 1881, 179, October 5, 1881, 72-73, October 19, 1881, 112, September 27, 1882, 49, February 6, 1884, 353, November 12, 1884, 168-169, January 7, 1885, 296-297, June

17, 1885, 248-249, October 20, 1886, 122-123, December 28, 1887, 276-277, March 27, 1889, 72-73, January 8, 1890, 350, February 26, 1890, 8-9, and August 27, 1890, 1, 8-9; *Judge,* March 12, 1887, February 18, 1888, 8-9, September 22, 1888, 386-387, October 27, 1888, 40-41, February 2, 1889, 272-273, and May 14, 1892, 328-329.

[27]*Puck,* June 4, 1884, 216-217, March 4, 1885, 8-9, July 8, 1885, 296-297, and December 2, 1885, 216-217; *Judge,* November 12, 1887, 8-9, August 14, 1889, 320-321, November 23, 1889, 108-109, December 14, 1889, 160-161, and January 18, 1890, 236, 244, 245.

[28]*Puck,* June 4, 1879, 194.

Pink Flamingoes: Symbols and Symbolism in Yard Art

Anthony Synnott

Pink Flamingoes: some love them, some hate them. They are pretty, elegant and inexpensive lawn decorations to their admirers, but to their detractors they are merely kitsch, tacky and in poor plastic taste; either way, they are big business: nearly half a million pink flamingoes were sold in North America in 1985 (*Harpers,* June 1986:13), which makes them a multi-million dollar industry. Yet it is hard to tell what pink flamingoes mean, and what they symbolize, apart from Florida, and maybe kitsch.

Why do some people have pink flamingoes on their lawns, while others have deer or lambs, and still others have lions "guarding" their homes? What does it mean that some have statues of Our Lady while others prefer gnomes, or antique ploughs or simply rocks? Are the Christmas lights merely decorative? People work hard on their front lawns, weeding and trimming, planting flowers and shrubs and perhaps putting in a fountain or a working wind-mill. One researcher estimated that there are 25 to 30 million homes with lawns in the United States, and their owners spent $1.3 billion on lawn care per annum (Kron, 1983: 189). Why?

The distinguished social geographer J. B. Jackson has noted that "Front yards are a national institution" with various social and climactic uses; but, he suggests, "the true reason why every American house has to have a front yard is probably very simple: it exists to satisfy a love of beauty" (1951:3). This may well be; but there are other reasons. People care for their yards, and decorate them according to their own sense of beauty and taste for beauty's sake no doubt; but also to keep up with the Joneses and, this is not unrelated to the others, to present themselves to the world in a favourable, indeed beautiful, light. Kron puts it well: the home is "an important vehicle for the expression of identity"; and "our homes are as much messages to ourselves about ourselves as communication to outsiders" (1983: 53, 56).[1] Yard art, therefore, like dress, hair-style, personal jewellery and also domestic art, is one aspect of the presentation of the self, and a symbol of the self (Goffman, 1959).

Despite the psychological and sociological significance of the home, there has been little research in this area. Gans has observed that "Popular culture is not much studied these days" (1974: vii). High art is researched more than folk art, and museums more than front yards. Yet I would make the case that the minutiae of everyday life deserve our attention; the micro-concerns of the normal round do not make the front pages, but I would hazard a guess that

the "trivia" of life, the small things, are probably of more interest to most people most of the time than the macro-concerns of international politics and economics. Pink flamingoes matter!

This research was conducted in two stages. First I observed and made an inventory of the yard art in the town of Chateauguay, Quebec, a dormitory suburb of Montreal. Then, since this proved interesting, I extended the survey to other parts of Quebec, and to Maine, Vermont, and upper New York state. This permitted some analysis of regional, occupational and socio-economic differences in artistic tastes and styles. The second part of the study involved drawing up a typology associating different types of art and associating them with the symbolic presentation of the self and the family. The main point is that the family with two deer on the lawn is sending a very different message about itself than families with a statue of Our Lady, or two fierce lions, or a large, spiky, stainless steel sculpture.

Yard Art

Most houses in downtown Montreal and in the suburbs do not have lawn ornaments or yard art; thus in this paper we are considering a minority of home-owners. The most common form of decoration (apart from flowers, etc., which are not considered here) is a rock, or rocks, which may be decorative, but can hardly be described as art. In Chateauguay, where I began this study, I was told that the local developer had offered to leave a large rock, free of charge, if the purchaser so desired. Many did so desire. One can only speculate why. The next most common form of decoration is a cedar-pole fence, followed by a pair of lions symbolically guarding either the front door or the drive-way. Altogether I counted 30 different types of yard decoration including 12 different species of birds and mammals, pink flamingoes being the most popular. These included wishing-wells, driftwood, swans, cherubs, pumps, cartwheels, spinners, cooking-pots, windmills, deer, mermaids, milk-churns, eagles, butterflies, fountains, bird-baths and, in single items only, a wheel-barrow, a pair of stone guard dogs, a donkey, a semi-clothed lady, a plough, gnomes, a raccoon, a squirrel, a woodpecker, a pelican, and a Black livery boy leading a donkey.

Some houses, as might be expected, have more art than others, the most contradictory being one with lions at the gate and deer on the lawn. Indeed some streets have more ornaments than others. Also types of art tend to be clustered; thus one may find "ghettos" of pink flamingoes: four houses within a hundred yards of each other have a couple each, for example. It seems therefore that both the frequency and the type of yard art may be an indirect measure of the degree of solidarity or individualism in the community: solidarity being indicated by imitation and agreement in taste, and individualism being indicated by deviations from the norm. One family has a densely populated yard with a bird-bath, a wishing-well, a pelican, a squirrel and a woodpecker; no other family had these last three animals.

The extension of these observations to Montreal and to rural areas meant the discovery of still more art forms, and the clarification of class, occupational, urban-rural, and regional differences. There are antiques: carriages, buggies and sleighs; old farm implements; sculptures, often by the home-owner; many more species of birds, including families of ducks, hens, pheasants, robins, bluebirds,

Canada geese, and the wing-flapping, wooden Daffy-ducks; also far more animals including a pair of goats, cats, families of skunks, chipmunks and rabbits. Statues of Our Lady, the Sacred Heart and Saint Anthony, often in a grotto of flowers, are not uncommon in rural areas; as are statues in stone, wood, or plastic of everything from Michelangelo's David through mermaids to the Seven Dwarfs. Silvered reflecting balls on a pedestal are also common. A bronze Japanese dragon lies coiled in a Japanese garden far from home. But the most bizarre decoration I saw was a cemetery for boots, complete with crosses, whimsically named Boot Hill, in New York State.

Class differences are apparent in the value and/or status display of some yard art. One expensive house in the city is guarded by *four* lions. Another has a four-wheeled carriage on the enclosed lawn: which beats the suburban cart-wheel by four to one. There are also clear urban-rural differences. Very few houses downtown have ornaments other than flowers and lawns; this may reflect differences in taste but more likely I think it reflects a different crime rate. Pink flamingoes, and other removable art forms, would not last overnight in a front yard in downtown Montreal. Rural farms, on the other hand, often have families of ducks and chickens and rabbits all over the yard.

Occupational differences can also be seen. In the granite quarrying town of Graniteville, Quebec, granite art is favoured. These occupational differences coincide with regional differences: in Maine, lobster pots, coloured buoys and inflatable Canada geese are popular decorations; whereas old ploughs and harrows, tractor tires, and families of ducks and chickens are more popular in the rural farming communities of Quebec, Vermont, and upper New York state. Such ornaments perhaps serve both to express and to reinforce, to symbolize people's identities as quarry-workers, fishermen and farmers.

Art and the Symbolism of Self

Our suburban and rural landscapes are densely populated and richly decorated with a large cast of animal and bird life, maidens and gnomes, wishing-wells and wind-mills, fountains and rocks, carriages and driftwood, sculptures and statues, tractor-tires and cart-wheels, ploughs and lobster-pots—a sort of universe in miniature, with spinners. There are therefore many varieties of yard art and yard decoration. But what do they mean? Some clues are provided by regional, occupational and status differences; in style; they symbolize different realities: they state who we are. This suggests that different "types" of yard art may symbolize different "types" of self.

All these varieties of decoration and yard art can be broken down into six basic categories, I suggest: protection ornaments (lions, eagles, guard dogs, etc.); religious art; old farm implements and rural artifacts; small animals; sculptures, cherubs and antiques, etc.; and, finally, rocks. These forms of decoration give messages to outsiders about "who lives here". They symbolize externally the internal and invisible reality of the family.

Each of these forms of yard art and their symbolism will be discussed in turn.

Protection Ornaments: Home as Castle, Family as Unit

"A man's home is his castle", it is said; and to judge from the symbolism, this is the most common aspect of home in the Montreal region. Castles are essentially defensive positions to which one may retreat in case of attack; and indeed homes are not infrequently defended militarily, like castles, against the intrusions of police, bailiffs, riot squads and other forces defined as hostile. Such homes may be protected by signs that say "Trespassers will be Prosecuted", "Keep Out!", "Beware of Dog", "Visitors not Permitted", and so on. They may also be protected by alarm systems and dogs, guards, high walls, fences, tall bushes, and other devices of a security-conscious age.

But homes may also be symbolically protected, and the most common form of such protection is a pair of lions at the garden gate. The King of the Beasts and the King of the Jungle, the archetypal symbol of bravery, symbolically expresses all the other defensive measures mentioned above. Lions are not the only aggressive animals displayed; some families have eagles, the kings of the air; and one family had two stone alsatians with yellow eyes, guarding the house. Such creatures symbolize the concept of the home as castle, and the common value of self-defense, as well as the occasional reality of violence in defense of the home.

Lions and eagles are also royal symbols (Kings of beasts and birds) and national symbols in both England and Scotland and also the United States,

Poland and Austria. Thus the two creatures convey overtones of royalty and superiority. Such overtones are congruent with and reinforce the castle image.

Lions and eagles also imply, however, that if the home is a castle, then the family is the defending force, and a (quasi-military) unit. The emphasis is on the *unit,* rather than the quasi-military, but people do join the two together as one. This is clear in such phases as the need to "defend the family name or honour", the need to "stick by one another", and in the famous remark "It's you and me against the world, babe!". The idea of unity is articulated in the marriage ceremony: "they shall be one flesh" (Gen. 2:24) and in the idea of a couple as no longer two individuals but one, and in the idea of a family as one, a concept which transcends the individualities and idiosyncrasies of its constituent members. The integration of the two ideas of defense and unity can be seen in the three musketeers' slogan in Dumas' novel, "all for one and one for all"—which expresses both a military and a family ideology.

The concept of home as castle, and the sense of withdrawal from others into the safety of the immediate family was well expressed by a Mr. Yule on a new English estate (Young and Willmott, 1965:148):

> We don't mix very well in this part of the estate. At first I used to lend every Tom, Dick or Harry all my tools or lawn mower or anything. Then I had 20 pinched from my wallet. Now we don't want to know anyone—we keep ourselves to ourselves. There's a good old saying—the Englishman's home is his castle. It's very true.

One house had four lions and a snoozing pekingese guarding the front door. Certainly lions convey a very different concept of the home than a statue of Our Lady.

Religious Art: Home as Sanctuary, Family as Religious

Convents, monasteries, and the residents of priests, nuns and religious usually have symbols of Christianity prominently displayed, indicating that the area is consecrated ground, holy and a religious sanctuary. However, few private residents in the city or in the suburbs display similar holy symbols. In the countryside, however, statues of Our Lady, the Sacred Heart, and the Saints are more common, especially in the largely Catholic Quebec.

The message being conveyed is that the family is a religious community, and that the home is a religious sanctuary, a place of God, heaven. Both Saint Augustine and Wordsworth expressed the idea of God as home, which is reflected here. In his *Confessions* (Bk. 1, ch. 1), Saint Augustine stated: "Thou hast created us for Thyself, and our heart cannot be quieted till it may find its repose in thee". Wordsworth was equally lyrical in his *Ode: Intimations of Immortality:* "trailing clouds of glory do we come/from God, who is our home". Finally, when Cardinal Newman was asked how he was feeling as he lay dying, he replied "like a schoolboy going home for the holidays". The statues remind the family that we come from God and will return to God, but they also symbolize the religious values of the family to others.

This does not mean, of course, that other families do not define themselves as religious; it merely means that not everyone chooses to make their values public. We are concerned here with the analysis of public symbolism, not so much with private reality, which would require other methods of research.

Rural Art: Home as Country, Family as "Natural"

Many of the ornaments displayed hark back to the country life and the agricultural economy of a bygone era, and to what we call "nature". These decorations include ploughs, wheelbarrows, milk churns, cart-wheels, water pumps, antique cooking pots, driftwood and "purely decorative" cedar fences. The "Back to Nature" ethos which seems to be reflected in this choice of symbolism implies surely not only an assertion of the value of the rural-agricultural life-style, however that may be perceived, but also a rejection of the urban-industrial way of life. Thus the home is portrayed as country, in contrast to the artificial, even perhaps alienating, town; and the family is a place where one is "natural" and "at home". Veblen (1953: 101) described the "make believe of rusticity" which the leisure class erect in their parks and grounds: "The rustic fences, bridges, bowers, pavilions and the like decorative features". The money is made in the town, but it is spent, or some of it is spent, on trying to create a peaceful rural country in which the family can live a "natural" life.

Raymond Williams has remarked that the ideas and images of both city and country have changed over time, but nonetheless they have usually been polarized (1975:9):

> On the country has gathered the idea of a natural way of life: of peace, innocence, and simple virtue. On the city has gathered the idea of an achieved centre: of learning, communication, light. Powerful hostile associations have also developed: on the city as a place of noise, worldliness and ambition, on the country as a place of backwardness, ignorance, limitation.

Neither idea is entirely attractive as a symbol of home; but he observed that "the pull of the idea of the country is towards old ways, human ways, natural ways. The pull of the idea of the city is towards progress, modernization, development" (1975:357). In a suburban situation with, usually, an urban job, the attractiveness of country symbolism is perhaps understandable. Oddly enough, rural farm families do not usually have these ancient farm instruments on their lawns; they have plastic farm animals. It is the suburbanites, or non-farming rural families, who tend to have the old harrows, ploughs, pumps or cart-wheels.

Animal Art: Home as Eden, Family as Loving

Deer, chipmunks, raccoons, pheasants, squirrels, lambs, rabbits, donkeys, ducks, and geese can all be seen on suburban lawns, but the favourites by far are swans and pink flamingoes. All these animals or birds are relatively non-aggressive or non-violent (or are perceived as being so) in contrast to lions, eagles, and guard dogs characteristic of the home as castle concept. And in our popular imagination they are seen as particularly beautiful (swans) or cute (chipmunks, raccoons, lambs, deer) and cuddly or even tame (squirrels, ducks, sometimes donkeys). Some exceptions do not fall easily into these categories: the pelican, goats, the skunks and perhaps the ubiquitous pink flamingoes. Missing from this list of species, however, is not only the "aggressive" animals but also the

"nasty" ones: spiders, rats, snakes, crocodiles and other horrors, but also some "friendlies" like elephants (Babar) and bears (Teddy, Pooh, Paddington).

The popular species however are easy for us to feel anthropomorphic about. We identify with some more than others. Consider Daffy Duck, Larry the lamb, Woody Woodpecker, Eeyore the Donkey (A.A. Milne), Brer Rabbit, Peter Rabbit, Flopsy, Mopsy and Cottontail (Beatrix Potter), Squirrel Nutkin (also Beatrix Potter), Chip n' Dale the chipmunks. Mickey and Minnie Mouse are classic examples; but cats (Sylvester, Heathcliff, Garfield) and dogs (man's best friend, Lassie, Pluto) are conspicuously absent, perhaps because they are alive and inside and are therefore not required in stone or plastic outside. The symbolic animals are therefore the ones that are the stuff of children's books, comics, and Walt Disney cartoons and such television series as Sesame Street.

Homes with these sorts of animals and birds are therefore presented as wildlife reserves or as Gardens of Eden, where all creatures (or many of them) are at peace. The buffalo may not roam, but the deer do play. The home is a paradise, where, as Isaiah (11:6-7) described it: "The wolf shall also dwell with the lamb, and the leopard shall lie down with the kid; and the calf and the young lion and the fatling together...and the cow and the bear shall feed; their young ones shall lie down together: and the lion shall eat straw like the ox".

The art therefore symbolizes a family that is, or wishes to be, loving and animal-friendly; their love encompasses and nurtures not only the immediate family but also, symbolically, all creatures and all creation. Despite Isaiah, this love is not necessarily grounded in religion or faith. Certainly the family with two lambs on the steps or deer on the lawn is making a statement quite different from the family with four lions or a sculpture.

Pink flamingoes may or may not belong in this typology. They certainly do not fit with the lions and eagles yet nor do they seem to be at home with the cartoon characters in Loony Tunes either. They are, however, often at home with them in suburban gardens, and this seems a sufficient reason to assign flamingoes to their company in Eden. Yet they are more than Disney creatures: They have become a fad. Bars, cocktails and even corporations are named after them; and birthdays and anniversaries are celebrated with an appropriate number of the plastic creatures stuck in the lawn. Perhaps they just symbolize "fun," with or without tongues in cheeks.

This animal art, presenting the home as Eden and the family as loving, is not all that different from the previous type: Home as Country, Family as "Natural"; after all Eden was country, and Adam and Eve were "au naturel". The difference, as I see it, is only that this family prefers life-forms while the other prefers agricultural artifacts. In practice, of course, many families have both. The typologies are not mutually exclusive, and are only intended to be indicative, not conclusive.

"High Art": Home as Gallery, Family as Artist

Some people have works of art in their front yards: iron or aluminum sculptures ("high" art), statues, usually of cherubs or maidens, or fountains, with or without mermaids. These objects are meant to be looked at, admired and enjoyed. The cherubs and so on are usually turned towards the street, rather than the house; so they are intended for the public, not directly for the owners. At Christmas some streets are a blaze of coloured lights, plastic Santas everywhere, with candles glowing and even reindeers leaping over balconies; some homes are dark, but others are locally famous for the light displays and the designers are interviewed on television and reported in the press. This is the home as art gallery, I would suggest, and the family is defined as artistic, creative and, as public benefactors, both charitable and socially conscious.

Some examples: one family has three rather large sculptures on its rather small lawn. The family is somewhat notorious locally since not everyone likes the works of art. Another family has a Botticelli-type Venus arising from a large sea of flowers and shrubs. The whole picture must require an enormous amount of work to maintain and no doubt the family is very proud of the creation. When I complimented the man of the house on its beauty he apologized, explaining that the garden was not looking at its best in September; I should have seen it in July. This illustrates the importance which some people attach to the presentation of their homes which, in turn, are presentations of themselves. The realization that people do go to time and trouble simply to please other people with their beautiful creations (of sculpture, lights, flowers, etc.) or to impress other people with their taste (if one follows Veblen's theory) was reinforced the same day when I was photographing a swan in the garden, and the lady of the house came out to apologize, again, that the garden was not looking its best.

Gardens may be more or less well-cared for and pleasing, and it is difficult to draw hard and fast lines between gardens as galleries and non-galleries. In a sense all gardens are galleries, for they can be looked at. Yet some front lawns are designed to be looked at, they shine, they are exceptional; and these, I would say, better symbolize the home as gallery and the gardeners as artistic, creative, charitable and social.

Rocks: Home as Foundation, Family as a Rock

The most common ornaments in Chateauguay, and very common throughout the Montreal area, are rocks. Why? Surely because they symbolize solidity; "as solid as a rock" is proverbial. The rock of Gibraltar. "Thou art Peter, and upon this rock I will build my church" (Matthew 16:18). And we are told to build our house on rock, not on sand (Matthew 7:24-27). The rock as a symbol of solidity and as a foundation of church and home is rooted deep in Judaeo-Christian culture. The choice of a rock as an ornament may serve to reinforce symbolically the idea of a solid home, a solid family structure, and solid people. Frazer's concept of sympathetic magic may be appropriate here.

There is, as always, a danger of over-interpretation. Geologists or lapidarists may choose rocks because they like them. People may choose them because the rocks were free, or because they might be fun for children to play on, or because they could make an attractive centerpiece for a flower arrangement. The decision may indeed have nothing to do with concepts of family or of home.

Nevertheless, it is a fascinating hypothesis that the choice to accept or reject a rock may reflect, among other things, the attitudes towards the home as the foundation of one's life, and towards the family as rock-solid; or perhaps it may reflect the wish for a solid marriage. These decisions may be made at the conscious or subconscious levels. People do have such attitudes and wishes, no doubt, but the degree to which they are publicly symbolized is a matter of empirical verification.

Symbols and Symbolism

This typology of yard art does not exhaust the total range of varieties of decoration, of course; and the degree to which the art symbolizes the reality of the yard artist or decorator is surely a variable. Nonetheless, yard art is, I suggest, like hair style or dress, a symbolic presentation of the self.

Yet there are anomalies and difficulties. Gnomes proved to be unexpectedly rare. One house had one, another had a group of over a dozen. It is difficult to know what, if anything, they are *intended* to convey or what they *do* convey. Perhaps they fit in best with the cute Disney-type animals and the concept of home as Eden. Also, some artifacts may symbolize many realities. Wind-mills and wishing-wells seemed to me to symbolize a "rural self"; but equally they are "fun", and might symbolize a "fun family", or a "fun self": a public expression of the view that "the family that plays together, stays together". Also fountains and bird-baths, depending on their size, might symbolize the nature-lover, or the artist, creating a home as a gallery. Finally, fountains, bird-baths, reflector balls and especially pink flamingoes would be interpreted quite differently within a Freudian theory of symbolism than within this theory derived from Goffman (1959).

Four points should be noted, however. First, the types are not mutually exclusive and do not exist in water-tight compartments, not least because families may have two or more types of ornaments in their gardens. Secondly, not all the ornaments seen are included in this typology; some, like Boot Hill and the Japanese dragon are too idiosyncratic to include and their symbolic meaning is unclear. Thirdly, decorations may, on occasion, totally misrepresent the self. One couple told me that they bring out a "hideous" bird-bath which an aunt gave them, whenever she arrives, and remove it when she leaves. Thus the aunt is happy, but the ornament does not symbolize the couple in any respect; quite the contrary. Also, ornaments may be there because they came with the house, like a pair of lions or a rock, and are too difficult to remove; yet, on the other hand, people are presumably more likely to buy a house which they feel symbolizes them, than one which they find antagonistic to them. Finally, not all homes have these decorations; indeed most do not; thus this typology only applies to those families who have chosen to "present themselves" in these public ways. However, an absolute mess in the front yard presents the family as clearly as does beauty and artistry; and some may find beauty in the mess.

Conclusion

Yard art and lawn decorations are no doubt matters of personal taste, as are other art forms. Yard art, however, is public rather than private; personal taste is displayed for the universe, and in that sense the entire family is also displayed for the universe, to see and to judge, to praise or condemn, to envy or to laugh at.[2]

The first sociologist to discuss lawns was Thorstein Veblen (1857-1929). His most famous work, *The Theory of the Leisure Class* (1899), was a brilliant and ironic commentary on the norms and values of the leisure class. Unlike the great "founding fathers" of sociology, he thought about such simple things as flowers, houses, parks and gardens, even pets and lawns. He argues (1953:98) that people commonly equate beauty with expense, even in flowers:

> it comes about that a beautiful article which is not expensive is accounted not beautiful. In this way it has happened, for instance, that some beautiful flowers pass conventionally for offensive weeds; others that can be cultivated with relative ease are accepted and admired by the lower middle class, who can afford no more expensive luxuries of this kind; but these varieties are rejected as vulgar by those people who are better able to pay for expensive flowers and who are educated to a higher schedule of pecuniary beauty in the florist's products; while still other flowers, of no greater intrinsic beauty than these, are cultivated at great cost and call out much admiration from flower-lovers whose tastes have been matured under the critical guidance of a polite environment.

The same logic, he said, applied to houses and gardens. Houses, gardens and flowers not only express the taste of the family, but they also symbolize the pecuniary power of the family, which in turn facilitates comparisons between families trying to achieve mobility. In this way they become "weapons" in a sort of Hobbesian economic war of all against all. This economic competition is rooted, Veblen believed, in human nature: "With the exception of the instinct for self-preservation, the propensity for emulation is probably the strongest and most alert and persistent of the economic motives proper". It is "of ancient growth and is a pervading trait of human nature" (1953: 85, 84).

These psychological traits and their economic expressions or consequences are evident in the types of social interaction among neighbours (1953: 71):

> The exigencies of the modern industrial system frequently place individuals and households in juxtaposition between whom there is little contact in any other sense than that of juxtaposition. One's neighbours, mechanically speaking, often are socially not one's neighbours, or even acquaintances; and still their transient good opinion has a high degree of utility. The only practicable means of impressing one's pecuniary ability on these unsympathetic observers of one's everyday life is an unremitting demonstration of ability to pay.

This process of "keeping up with the Joneses", or passing them, and of status display, has been observed very clearly on a new suburban development outside London; the process is described as follows (Young and Willmott, 1965: 159-69).

> To begin with, the first-comers have to make their own way. The later arrivals have their model at hand. The neighbours have put up nice curtains. Have we? They have got their garden planted with privet and new grass seed. Have we? They have a lawnmover and a Dunkley pram. What have we got? The new arrivals watch the first-comers, and the first-comers watch the new arrivals. All being under the same pressure for material advance, they naturally mark each other's progress.

Indeed many of the residents commented unfavourably on the circle of emulation; but it still persisted. On the other hand, Whyte reported that the social ethic in the suburbia of *The Organization Man* is that: " 'there's no keeping up with the Joneses here'—the job, then, is not to keep up with the Joneses. It's to keep *down* with them" (1956:346. Emphasis in the original). Whyte emphasized that these Pennsylvania suburbanites do have strong impulses towards egalitarianism, but that the norms are always changing. The competitive neighbours are regarded as deviants, as are those who are too slow to change. Uniformity is all, but it is a constantly changing uniformity as what constitutes "the good life" is constantly revised upwards (1956:345-64).

The settled community of Bethnal Green in London displayed a similar community solidarity (Townsend, 1977:23):

> Neighbours often imitate each other. In one street is a row of six houses with an aspidistra in each front window, rarely found elsewhere; in another a line of four alsation dogs and, in a third, a succession of curtains of a particular hue, dark blue, rose pink, yellow ochre.

Practices therefore seem to vary from competition to imitation, keeping up to keeping down, perhaps depending upon the socio-economic status or the "age" of the community. Both patterns are found in the United States and

England. Either way, however, the home and the yard remain a symbol of the economic self *and* of the community relations.

Sometimes it is the cleanliness and style of the home, however, which are of prime symbolic value; not the yard art, if any. Hoggart, describing working-class life in Northern England in the thirties, observed that "the window ledges and doorsteps scrubbed and yellowed with scouring-stone...establish that you are a "decent" family, that you believe in "bottoming" the house each week" (1962:34-5). And Martin makes a similar point, that the front of the house and the garden are the face that the family presents to the outside world. It may be clean, cheerful, with a well-kept lawn, bright flowers, and fresh paint, with polished brass or neatly arranged lace curtains, or a mess (1983:57; cf. Uris, 1978:91).

The rich, however, as F. Scott Fitzgerald insisted, are different; and Lundberg's well known study *The Rich and The Super-Rich* (1969:844) makes this almost painfully clear:

> What unquestionably first strikes the most indolent observers about the personal lives of the rich compared with the non rich is the opulence of their residential settings. These lush habitations, contrary to many hurried commentators, have more than a titillating value for outsiders. They are, I submit, deeply symbolic of a self-conception and of actual objective social status. They are, contrary to the eagle-eyed Veblen, more than an exercise in ostentatious display and conspicuous consumption. They are, in fact, a dead giveaway of what it is all about.

The compounds, estates and mansions of the rich and the super-rich are not means to an end, weapons in a struggle to "keep up": they are an end in themselves.

The decoration of one's property, therefore, may be as trivial a phenomenon as sticking a flamingo in the front yard or as grand as landscaping a park; for most of us it is probably something in between. But it is, surely, a valid area of sociological research.

It is beyond the scope of this paper to discuss the standards of artistic taste, or to define art; nonetheless, we have seen that yard art reflects the economic base of the community: agricultural, fishing or quarrying; it reflects the socio-economic status of the family, as Veblen discussed (e.g. an antique buggy versus one cart-wheel); it reflects the age and solidarity of the community, as the Pennsylvania and London studies suggest; and it symbolizes also, I think, the values of the family, not just their artistic taste.

One final word: in interpreting symbols there is always the danger of over-interpretation. Freud is said to have remarked on the subject of phallic symbols that "sometimes a cigar is just a cigar". Quite so. And the same logic applies to other such symbols. Nonetheless this typology does offer explanations, at least in part, for why we choose to decorate our front yards with a lion or a lamb, a rock or Our Lady, a farm implement, a fountain or even a pink flamingo.[3]

Notes

My thanks to John Jackson, Jon Jones and Joseph Smucker.

[1]There is some research on this topic; cf. Goffman, 1959: 22-30; Duncan, 1973; Duncan and Duncan, 1976; Cooper, 1976; Martin, 1983; Douglas, 1978; Rybczynski, 1987).

[2]A friend of mine, hearing me hold forth on these matters, dismissed it all as nonsense. But his hobby is carving and painting beautiful, and very expensive, decoy ducks for display *inside* the home—a form of art essentially similar, in symbolic terms, to the less expensive, and plastic, ducks and flamingoes made for display *outside* the home. Both art forms, the high and the popular, the expensive and the relatively inexpensive, in the living-room and in the front yard, surely symbolize the self-albeit different selves.

[3]In the Detroit area, according to People Magazine (8.7.87:p.123), the latest trend in yard art is water sprinklers in the likeness of Pope John Paul II, with coming attractions including Jim and Tammy Bakker, Liberace, Elvis and Moses. In Montreal, however, the latest style is large, wooden black or brown and white cows grazing the lawn. It seems unlikely that any of these new forms of yard art have deep symbolic significance. To paraphrase Freud: sometimes a cow is only a cow.

Works Cited

Cooper, Clare. "The House as a Symbol of the Self", in Harold M. Proshansky, William H. Ittelson and Leanne G. Rivlin (Eds.), *Environmental Psychology*. New York: Holt, Rinehart and Winston, 1976:435-8.

Douglas, Mary. *Cultural Bias*. London: Royal Anthropological Institute, 1978.

Duncan, James S. "Landscape Taste as a Symbol of Group Identity: A Westchester County Village." *Geographical Review*. Vol. 63, No. 3. July 1973: 334-55.

Duncan, James S. and Nancy G. Duncan. "Housing as Presentation of Self and the Structure of Social Networks", in Gary T. Moore and Reginald G. Golledge (Eds.), *Environmental Knowing*. Stroudsberg, Penn.: Dowden, Hutchinson and Ross, 1976: 247-253.

Gans, Herbert. *Popular Culture and High Culture*. New York: Basic Books, 1974.

Goffman, Erving. *The Presentation of Self in Everyday Life*. New York: Doubleday Anchor, 1959.

Harper's Magazine, June 1986.

Hoggart, Richard. *The Uses of Literacy*. Penguin Books, 1962.

Jackson, J. B. "Ghosts at the Door", *Landscape* Vol. 1, No. 2, Autumn 1951: 3-9.

Kron, Joan. *Home-Psych: The Social Psychology of Home and Decoration*. New York: Potter, 1983.

Lundberg, Ferdinand. *The Rich and the Super-Rich*. New York: Bantam Books, 1969.

Martin, Bernice. *A Sociology of Contemporary Cultural Change*. Oxford: Blackwell, 1983.

Rybczynski, Witold. *Home: A Short History of an Idea*. Penguin, 1987.

Townsend, Peter. *The Family Life of Old People*. Penguin Books, 1977.

Uris, Jill and Leon. *A Terrible Beauty*. New York: Bantam Books, 1978.

Veblen, Thorstein. *The Theory of the Leisure Class*. New York: Mentor Books, 1953 [1899].

Whyte, William H. *The Organization Man*. New York: Doubleday Anchor, 1956.

Williams, Raymond. *The Country and the City*. London: Paladin, 1975.

Young, Michael and Peter Willmott. *Family and Kinship in East London*. Penguin Books, 1965.

Deaths, Wakes, Funerals: Italian American Style

J. Michael Ferri

He looks nice for a man who was down to 97 pounds. The undertaker did a good job.

Are they taking 'places' here?

Look at that flower pinned to her dress. Do they think she's going to a wedding?

Remarks Overhead at Wakes

Introduction

In 1966, Alfred Smith wrote: "Culture is a code we learn and share, and learning and sharing require communication. And communication requires coding and symbols which must be learned and shared. Communication and culture are inseparable."[1] Each culture has systems of communication in which particular verbal and nonverbal symbols teach a person values such as success, failure, fair play, or hard work; determine attitudes toward nonverbal behaviors such as dress, appearance, time or space; and teach aesthetic or artistic concepts such as truth, beauty or ugliness. The person within the environs of his/her culture communicates cognitive and emotional meanings through symbols.

A symbol is an "instrument of thought"[2] which represents realities, values, feelings and attitudes and which may be verbal or nonverbal. The symbol may be simple and act as a sign or stimulus for something else, or it may be complex and act as a "vehicle for the conception of an object."[3] The symbol becomes a concept of an idea with a group or culturally agreed-upon meaning and with an individual or private meaning. Suzanne Langer notes: "A concept is all that a symbol really conveys. But just as quickly as the concept is symbolized to us, our own imagination dresses it up in a private personal conception."[4] Symbols, therefore, to have meaning are coded and decoded according to the group shared concept and to the individual interpretation affected by past experiences and associations.

A symbol and its meaning are a product of the integration of collective and individual perceptions and the use of symbols is, therefore, grounded in the environs of group and individual associations. The individual to function in human communication and society has to perceive the self as an integral part of a group. He or she uses symbols and perceives messages within the context of the group. Group as defined by Singer is "a symbiotic relationship that exists between a group as a whole and the individuals who comprise the group."[5] The individual has a group memory of "unique, learned, group-related perceptions stored in the memory of each individual's data-storage bank."[6] It is a group memory which defines ethnic minorities, for through the use of a relatively unique symbol system the individual may be identified as a North American, Hispanic, Italian, Irish or other ethnic minority.

While a common or mass communication system of symbols has increasingly dominated the North American consciousness, distinct and significant minority subcultures continue to exert a power influence upon everyday communicative interactions. Italian Americans—strongly influenced by their close ties to the nuclear and extended family as well as their origins with the Italian culture—function as a relatively discrete but powerful symbol-using culture in the United States.[7] And many of these people retain direct use of subculture symbols which affect personal, social, religious and family day-to-day experiences.

Italian American writers begin the history of the Italian in America with its "discovery" by Columbus in 1492. However, until the 1870s there were, perhaps, only fifty thousand Italians in the United States. In the 1870s and continuing for two decades, nearly five million Italians left unemployment, low salaries, poor medical care, no schooling, rigid class structure and exploitation, and semi-starvation in Italy for other countries. Of that number, it is estimated that one in four came to the United States. Between 1900 and 1920, another ten million left Italy.[8]

Many of the Italian American immigrants settled in the northeastern part of the United States. Carl Cecora, the former President of the Italian American Civil Rights League, estimates that one third of all Italian Americans now live in New York State, another third in Massachusetts, Pennsylvania, Rhode Island, Connecticut and New Jersey.[9] This would leave the remaining third distributed in places like Chicago, Cleveland, Denver, San Francisco, Los Angeles and Miami. In the 1970s, Richard Gambino estimates that there are twenty million Italian Americans in the United States.[10]

For this study, participant observation and recall (author introspection) were the techniques used to collect data. The information was unsolicited, spontaneous and selectively perceived. Observations were made in three cities: Providence, Rhode Island, Boston, Massachusetts, and Philadelphia, Pennsylvania. "Italian Americans tend to live close to family members and to be more residentially stable than people of other ethnic backgrounds."[11] Therefore, each city has its specific area which is heavily, if not exclusively, populated by Italian Americans. In Providence, it is Federal Hill, or, as natives refer to it, "The Hill"; In Boston, it is the North End; in Philadelphia, it is "South Philly". It was to those urban areas the Italian immigrants came, for their compatriots were located there.

Basically, the economic level of the observed people varied little from city to city, for, as with most subcultures, one may find in the specific area blue collar, white collar and professional workers in the nuclear and extended family units. The educational level was fairly predictable: grade school drop-outs, high school graduates, college and professional school graduates. In these specific areas were the poor and the wealthy, the literate and the illiterate sharing life experiences. And, most important, these people were establishing an ethnicity—through the use of shared symbols—which may be called the Italian American subculture. All Italian Americans do not share all of the recorded nonverbal patterns of behavior—social class, age and ethnic identification affect the appearance or nonappearance of these traits. However, a commonness articulates itself and allows one to infer the presence of a definite ethnicity.

Nationalist factions claim that a changing of the linguistic symbol system will result in a loss of identity or culture; however, a culture does not preserve itself "...predominantly through the conventional use of speech symbols."[12] That language is a major communication system or that a subculture may have a linguistic identity will, of course, not be denied. But, in addition to this particular system of communication, one must add the nonverbal communication systems as means of identifying ethnic groups.

Ethnicity may be preserved through nonverbal communication systems which create social meanings for the members of a group and perpetuate a unique identity. And that will be the focus of this study—the nonverbal communication interactions that have created and given identity to an Italian American subculture.

Deaths, Wakes and Funerals

Except for ritual and small talk, there is little verbal communication at Italian American deaths, wakes and funerals. At this period of sorrow, Italian Americans are traditionally bound to rituals and to fixed patterns of behavior. Nonverbal elements—touch, dress, space, time, objects, silence—reveal this group's social and economic status, its relationship to the deceased, and its evolution as Americans with an anchor in its Italian heritage. It should be noted that all of the following nonverbal behaviors are not exclusive to the Italian American; other ethnic groups may share some of these nonverbal behaviors during this period of sorrow.

Silence: Since Italian and Hispanic families tend to have a greater frequency of intergenerational interaction, to live in close proximity to family members, and to exchange help,[13] a death in an Italian American family brings relatives and neighbors rushing to the home of the survivors. After initial expressions of sympathy, the sexes will segregate—women in the dining area and men in the family room or on a porch. There is little, if any, conversation: just the physical presence and the mental aura of one's family and neighbors help to ease the sorrow and pain. Silence functions to comfort and to console, and it is a dominant element on the first night of the death.

Dress: Almost completely vanished from the Italian American environs is the woman who, when a loved one died, put on her black dress and was never seen out of it. Today, wardrobes of most Italian American women, over forty years old, contain at least one black garment to be worn for the traditional three-day wake and funeral period. Until the 1950s, women wore mourning—black dress, stockings and shoes—for a period ranging from one week to one year depending on the age of the woman and on her relationship to the deceased. Up to the 1940s, the Italian American male wore a black arm band and a black tie. Later the arm band was discarded and only the tie was worn. In the 1980s, the wearing of mourning clothes is restricted to the woman, almost exclusively reserved for members of the nuclear family,[14] and used for the three-day period.

Objects: Before the general public is allowed to view the deceased, the survivors select the clothing, the casket, the "family" floral arrangements, and the rosary beads, if the deceased was a Roman Catholic. The survivors will also provide any articles that the deceased may have requested before death.[15] The remains are shown to members of the nuclear family, and after the family inspects and approves, the remains are displayed. Even in sorrow, the Italian Americans are greatly concerned with the appearance of objects.

Floral arrangements can reveal the relationship of the sender to the deceased. In the 1980s, flowers are often color-coordinated; family members and close friends will be advised as to which colors to select and, sometimes, as to which florist to order from. Certain designs—a blanket of flowers to cover the lower part of the body, a heart-shaped arrangement, an arrangement of flowers containing the outline of a clock with the time of death indicated, a cross-shaped design—are traditionally provided by members of the nuclear family. If any one of these floral designs is not on display, there will be speculation as to which family member did not fulfill her/his obligation. Friends, business associates and professional organizations will send floral arrangements. If a "No Flowers" notice is given, contributions to a specific charity or spiritual bouquets will be made by mourners.

Death is one happening that is not recorded on film by Italian Americans.[16] Yet, an Italian American would like some record or object for this event; therefore, small cards are printed and distributed to family and friends. On one side is a pictorial representation of Jesus, the Blessed Virgin or a patron saint; on the reverse side are prayers or verses from the Bible, the name of the deceased and her/his birth and death dates.

For many years, mourners at Italian American wakes put a "place," a contribution to defray funeral expenses. The donor's name, address and the amount of the "place" were recorded on lists, so an equal contribution could be made at the time of the donor's wake. In the 1980s, more affluent and more Anglicized Italian Americans will not take any "places" at their family wakes. However, they realize that most Italian Americans have fixed patterns; therefore, they substitute the "place" with a request for spiritual bouquets (Memorial Masses dedicated to the deceased) or for contributions to a specific charity. Many Italian Americans reveal their economic and social status and their generation when, at a wake, they ask if "places" are being taken.

Spatial Arrangements: At the wake, all seats have an unobstructed view of the casket—the focal point. To the right of the casket, the survivors will be positioned according to their relationship to the deceased and according to their age. A hierarchy with members of the extended family in secondary position is established. A mourner may pass a member of the extended family and not express her/his condolences. However, she/he would never pass anyone in a primary or major position. If a mourner is not acquainted with the primary position people, someone will leave her/his place to make introductions.

The funeral and the burial will take place on the third day. Family and friends will assemble at the funeral home where their names and license plate numbers are taken by the funeral directors. When their names are called, the mourners approach the casket for a silent prayer and a final view of the deceased. Some will touch the deceased for the last time. The first people to leave the funeral home and assume final or end positions in the funeral procession are acquaintances and business associates. Spatial positioning, again, reveals one's relationship to the deceased. The nuclear family members will leave last to take front or primary positions in limousines and cars directly behind the hearse, the flower cars and the pallbearers' car.

Time: The frequency and the length of visits to the funeral home indicate the mourner's relationship to the deceased. The more time spent and the more visits made, the closer was the relationship. Less time spent and only one visit made, the more distant was the relationship. For example, family and close friends will attend every visiting period and stay for the entire period while acquaintances will attend one time for a fifteen to thirty minute period.

Burial: After church services, the funeral procession will proceed to the cemetery. Here, procedures may vary, for each cemetery has its own rules for burial rites. St. Anne's in Rhode Island, the place with which this writer is most familiar, has constructed a chapel where brief services are held and where the casket is left.[17] If the family wishes to accompany the casket to the burial site, arrangements are made for the undertaker to transport the body and extra fees are charged. Services at the chapel and/or the burial site conclude with an expression of appreciation to the mourners by the funeral director on behalf of the family. And the formal three-day period of mourning is completed.

Postscript: Friends and family members may be invited to attend a funeral breakfast or lunch at the survivors' home. Once again, the sexes segregate. Younger Italian American males and females will bridge this separation and move freely from all-male to all-female groups. Youth permits mobility to these younger adults. Now there is much conversation as some relatives renew family ties which may be only nourished at births, weddings and deaths. Conversation is directed away from the events of the last three days, and attempts are made to re-channel thoughts to rather mundane topics.

Sandwiches, coffee, soft drinks, Italian cakes and pastries are served. If alcoholic beverages are served at the funeral breakfast or lunch, Italian American households provide cordials and/or liqueurs, e.g., brandy, creme de menthe, amaretto, anisette or creme de cacao. Most Italian Americans associate alcoholic beverages with celebrations of life, and, regardless of sermons telling of rebirth and of future meetings with the deceased, death is a sad and shocking event. It has caused not only the loss of a loved one, a family member, but also a break in the continuity of the Italian American life experience and is, therefore, a threatening and painful confrontation.

Conclusion: By its distinctive functioning on the nonverbal level, the Italian American has identified itself as a separate subculture. The linguistic symbols of its origin are no longer utilized by the Italian American. The linguistic communication system has been lost, but the nonverbal has been kept. The main question generated by this study is: Will the subculture continue to retain a discrete symbol system?

Today, most Italian Americans are second, third or fourth generation, with only a small percentage being foreign born. Like other immigrant groups—Swedish, German, French, Chinese, Greek—the Italian slowly accepted the North American linguistic symbol system. There was no bilingual education law or program to protect the language of the Italian. For survival—economic, educational and social—the Italian yielded his/her linguistic symbol system. English became the language of the subculture.

The Italian American identity was preserved through the non-linguistic systems available. Some systems have been taken over by the North American culture. For example, what were once "Italian" foods are now American foods—pizza, lasagna, salami, ravioli and parmesan cheese. And television commercials scream at the North American that Wednesday is the day for "Prince Spaghetti." The "Up Yours" finger gesture now has obtained almost universal meaning. The "Gucci" bag or shoe is a status symbol. The horn medal hangs on Italian American and non-Italian American necks. Frequently used Italian-derived words include "confetti," "motto," "lava," "dilettante," "pasta," "volcano," and "terra cotta."

As many verbal and nonverbal communication symbols have been assimilated by the North American and other cultures, will all the distinctive aspects of the Italian American subculture be either taken over or lost? Will "Joelle," "Mia," "Jason," "Jennifer," "Brian," "Mindy," and "Elaine" (popular names given to children by the under forty Italian American parents) be able to retain the nonverbal symbol system of the Italian American ethnic group?

Talia Coppola Shire said: "Recently, I made my baby 'pastina,' the little letters, and I literally was remaking what my mother had given me. The Italian I am is the Italian who probably died 80 years ago, because the rituals my family holds onto belonged to my grandfather. We've held them like little sacred jewels, while Italy has evolved. We're pretty much frozen in that period from which our grandfathers came. I think this may be common with Italian American families. You evolve as American, but your anchor is the Italian heritage."[18]

The Italian American may retain ethnicity only if she/he has an "anchor" in the Italian heritage.

Notes

[1]Alfred G. Smith, *Communication and Culture* (New York: Holt, Rinehart & Winston, 1966) 1-3.

[2]Suzanne Langer, *Philosophy in a New Key* (Cambridge: Harvard U. Press, 1942) 63.

[3]Langer 61.

[4]Langer 71-72.

[5]Marshall R. Singer, *Intercultural Communication: A Perceptual Approach* (Englewood Cliffs: Prentice-Hall, Inc., 1987) 53.

[6]Singer 53.

[7]Edward J. Miranda, "The Italian American: Who, What, Where, When, Why," *Identity Magazine* (January 1977) 11-16.

[8]Gary Null and Carl Stone, *The Italian-Americans* (Harrisburg, Pa.: Stackpole Books, 1976) 4.

[9]Null and Stone 8.

[10]Richard Gambino, "La Famiglia: Four Generations of Italian Americans," *White Ethnics*. Joseph Ryan, ed. (Englewood Cliffs: Prentice-Hall, Inc., 1973) 44.

[11]Frances E. Kobrin and Calvin Goldscheider, *The Ethnic Factor in Family Structures and Mobility* (Cambridge: Ballenger, 1978) 187-180.

[12]Frank E. X. Dance and Carl E. Larson, *Speech Communication* (New York: Holt, Rinehart & Winston, Inc., 1972) 125.

[13]Andrew M. Greeley, *Why Can't They Be Like Us?* (New York: Dutton, 1971) 77.

[14]Relatives and friends are expected to wear conservative colors.

[15]Objects such as eye glasses, snuff, rings, jewelry, photography, bus tokens, "space" shoes, and wedding gowns have been placed in caskets.

[16]Italian Americans enjoy taking photographs of people, happenings and occasions. Birthdays, graduations, weddings, anniversaries, and family reunions are captured on film, placed in ornate or formal frames and displayed.

[17]After rumors that a commercial fork-lift truck was used to transport the casket to the burial site, many Italian Americans refused to allow their loved ones to be picked up like cargo and requested funeral directors to take the casket to the site.

[18]Bill Wassirziehar, "Talia Coppola Shire: A Profile," *Identity Magazine* (March 1977) 61.

The Food Habits of Italian Immigrants to America: An Examination of the Persistence of a Food Culture and the Rise of "Fast Food" in America*

Harvey A. Levenstein
and Joseph R. Conlin

In less than a generation, "fast food" has revolutionized the eating habits of North Americans. A people who once "ate out" only on signal anniversaries now hands fully one meal dollar in four across the greaseless aluminum counters of McDonald's, Burger King, Kentucky Fried Chicken, and other franchise chains, and within minutes or even seconds walks dinner to a table in styrofoam casket and cardboard tub. Indeed, the golden arches and Colonel Sanders' benign physiognomy are to be seen on the Ginza, the Champs Elysées, and at the bottom of the Spanish Steps, as well as in Fresno, Waukeegan, and Calgary: America's gift to the world.

The hamburger and fried parts of chicken are the staples of the fast food revolution, of course. Too often overlooked, perhaps, is the fact that the upheaval in North American foodways has also popularized foreign, traditionally non-Anglo-Saxon dishes among a people who, until very recently, have been oblivious or hostile towards any cuisine but that which, over three centuries, they adapted from the cultural Mother Country.[1] No one would call the United States or Canada Anglo-Saxon nations; but until the last generation, the multifarious ethnic groups that have transformed both countries have left only minor traces of their influence on the mainstream cuisine. Assimilation, among other things, meant embracing meat and potatoes.

There was an exception. In the first half of the twentieth century, one immigrant cuisine survived with its integrity intact, and won aficionados beyond the ethnic group that brought it to the western hemisphere. This was the cuisine (or, rather, *cucina*) of southern Italy, in particular the cookery of Naples in the region of Campania. Under the rubric "Italian food," *cucina napoletana* has been incorporated into the North American diet and has become Americans' favourite foreign food. Infiltrating American fancy first in the form of pasta, usually spaghetti and a tomato sauce, "Italian Food" in the form of pizza and even more elegant regional Italian dishes is almost universally known in the United States and Canada. Pizza, sold by the piece in small restaurants, often with counter-service only, is popular in the most isolated towns. Almost everywhere, a North American may have one delivered by a heated truck in an insulated box. Whether individually-owned and operated or part of giant chains such as "Pizza Hut," pizza is everywhere. Regularly polls to ascertain America's favorite food result in pizza the runaway winner.

In this paper, we will show that the link between *cucina napolitana* and fast food does not stop there. We shall also argue that the North American taste for starchy foods smothered in tomato sauce and melted and grated cheese opened the path for the rise of what now appears to be the fastest-growing sector of the fast food industry: the purveyors of "Mexican food," particularly "tacos" and "burritos," now challenging even pizza and the native hamburger as North America's favorite quick meal.

First, however, we shall trace the story of how "Italian food" survived on the generally hostile American culinary scene. The story revolves around the stubborn persistence of Italian immigrants to North America in clinging to their foodways long enough so that their cuisine was able to influence that of the dominant culture. This has not been the case, as least not to such a degree, with the foodways of any other ethnic group in North America.[2]

For millions of immigrants over the years, America has represented a land of abundance, and nowhere more so than at the table. Although their dreams of streets paved with gold often proved to be nightmares of concrete and steel, few immigrants were disappointed in the quantities of food available in a land that had never known famine or even serious food shortages. So satisfied was the largely foreign and first-generation American working class reputed to be with its diet that socialists lamented the truth in the statement of the German sociologist Sombart: "On the reefs of roast beef and apple pie, socialist utopias of every sort are sent to their doom."[3] But while such assessments may have been valid in their emphasis on abundance of food on the workingman's table, they are misleading about the reaction of immigrant toilers to the nature of North American food. Between about 1880 and 1921, the ethnic character of the working classes of the United States shifted dramatically. Instead of being native born of British stock and Irish and Germans sharing much the same culinary heritage, the new working class was a polyglot menage of southern and eastern Europeans. The new immigrants did not happily and automatically embrace roast beef, steaks, and apple pie. On the contrary, and much to the chagrin of social workers and public health officials, most immigrants clung tenaciously to their old eating habits.

None were more tenacious than the Italians. In the face of the powerful assimilationist pressure of twentieth century North America, they shrugged off the suggestions of dieticians, home economists, social workers, and settlement house reformers through three and four generations. Except for the Chinese who for racial reasons were rarely proselytized by assimilationists, the Italian immigrants and their Italian-American descendants were almost alone among the new immigrants in this. They provide an impressive and instructive case study of how foodways can persist in a new and often hostile material and social environment.

Any analysis of Italian-American food habits must begin with the observation that there was and is no such thing as "Italian food." The Italy of the era of massive emigration was unified politically, but culturally it was just "a geographical expression." Gastronomically, Italy was a mosaic of regional, provincial, and even *parochial* cuisines. Wheaten pasta was consumed throughout the country, albeit in radically different forms and in varying quantities. Maize was grown throughout Italy, but was a staple, in the form of *polenta,* almost exclusively in the North. For most of the peasantry of the South, or *Mezzogiorno,* the staple was neither pasta nor corn meal mush but bread. If there was a meal that was universal among the poorer peasantry, it was bread and *minestre,* vegetable soups which themselves varied widely with region and season.

The relatively small number of Italians who emigrated to the United States before 1880 originated primarily from the North. However, while northerners continued to emigrate in even greater numbers over the ensuing forty years, they were swamped numerically after 1880 by the vast exodus of people from the *Mezzogiorno,* making Italians the single largest component of the massive new immigration. Between 1880 and 1921 more than five million Italians came to and remained in the United States, 75 percent of them from regions south of Rome.[4]

The first problem Italian immigrants faced in preserving their foodways in the New World was material: many of the ingredients which were basic to their cuisine were either unobtainable in the United States or extremely expensive. This was not the case with bread, of course. While the bread sold in non-Italian bakeries was normally unacceptable to Italians—Americans had already abandoned loaves with hard crusts—"Italian bread" could be baked easily enough from the good wheaten flour which was universally available and cheap. Archaeologist Julia G. Costello has discovered that Italian gold miners living in isolated camps on the western slope of the Sierra built stone ovens like those they knew at home: no indigestible saleratus biscuits for them.[5] The Italians of Tampa, Florida apparently did the same thing. In the 1890s every house in the Italian district was reported to feature an igloo-shaped brick and concrete bread oven in its backyard.[7] One of the first signs of the expansion and growing permanence of the Italian population of a given city or town was the opening of small bakeries, in basements or storefronts, to serve the seemingly insatiable appetite for white bread.

Italian-style pasta, however, was not produced commercially in the United States or Canada until the 1890s, despite the fact that the northern plains states and the Western provinces were becoming the world's greatest producers of the hard wheat from which the best pasta is made. Small macaroni factories had made their appearance in a number of "Little Italies" by the late 1890s[7], but until well into the twentieth century the large majority of immigrants purchasing manufactured pasta preferred imports from Italy. This pasta was made from durum wheat originating mainly in Russia and was expensive.[8] Nevertheless, and despite their frugality in other spheres, Italian-Americans paid the price. It was the same in Canada. In 1912 nationalist sensibilities were bruised in Toronto and the municipal treasury threatened by the apparent refusal of Italian immigrants working for the city of Toronto to eat any but Italian-made macaroni.[9]

Olive oil, the preferred cooking fat of southern Italians, was also very expensive in North America. It was relatively well-known, but mainly as medicine, prescribed as a laxative and for other esoteric purposes. Americans bought it in tiny bottles, quantities laughably inadequate for cooking, at very high prices. Even when imported in large containers for Italian culinary use the cost remained very high, particularly for working class budgets.[10] In the early years of the century some Eastern merchants began carrying California-produced olive oil, but it sold for about the same as the imported variety and, by 1915, had disappeared from Eastern shelves.[11]

Neither could America come up with acceptable substitutes for Italian hard cheeses, used mainly for grating and, in small quantities, indispensable to most Italian meals. By 1905, the import trade was sufficiently regularized so that Parmesan and Romano sold for only slightly more than imported Swiss cheese, but it still cost almost as much as Roquefort, a cheese eaten in North America only by the cosmopolitan upper class. It represented so substantial a cash outlay for a working class family that, had material forces been the criteria of foodways, it would not have been eaten at all.[12]

Italian wine had been imported into the United States long before the immigration of 1880-1921, but at prices comparable to those of French and German vintages, far above what working class immigrants could easily have paid.[13] The native American grapes of the Eastern United States provided no substitutes, for the "foxy" taste of the wine produced from them outraged all palates weaned on *vinifera*. California wines had not yet attained their present quality and, as in the case of olive oil, California wine was little less expensive in the Eastern metropolises than imported wine.

Even when an American "substitute" was excellent, it was disdained. Carolina rice, long-grained and delicate, perfect for fluffy rice dishes, was inferior to the short-grained *arborio* rice of Italy for preparing the sticky *risotti*, rice-puddings, and rice desserts favored by Italians. Perhaps most striking, corn meal, so plentiful in the hemisphere in which maize originated, was usually imported by Italians. The American variety was regarded as suffering from various disabilities preventing it from making good *polenta*.

Fresh, raw fruits and fresh vegetables were consumed in such large quantities in the *Mezzogiorno* that some investigators suggested that the poor of Naples lived on them alone during the summer months. In Canada and the northern two-thirds of the United States, however, the growing season was too short to provide them in the quantities Italians preferred. Even in the Southeast and California, where the growing season was comparable to that of the *Mezzogiorno*, and garden farming was well-established, American growers did not plant many of the varieties favoured by Italians. Among the vegetables "not commonly regarded as foods in America" which the immigrants wanted in quantity were: hot peppers, mushrooms, eggplants, melon and sunflower seeds, and chick peas.[14] Despite recurring scares that raw vegetables caused cancer or other afflictions, by the turn-of-the century most Americans had ceased to regard tomatoes, essential to southern Italian foodways, as poisonous or morally dangerous aphrodisiacs. Still, they were disdained as possibly dangerous and overly-expensive. ("In unit cost tomatoes rank almost with champagne," wrote one expert.) Garlic, the *sine qua non* of Campanian cooking and an important enhancer in most southern Italian cuisines, was not widely available. It was regarded with a mixture of awe and revulsion by old-stock Americans when they had the misfortune to confront it.[15]

The immigrants, in turn, were contemptuous of those vegetables and fruits which were available. A New York street sweeper, interviewed in 1906, declared himself proud of his new homeland but he lamented that American meat and vegetables lacked the "flavour and substance" of those he had eaten in Italy.[16] An Italian woman interviewed by a researcher in Waterbury, Connecticut, looked at inferior American ingredients from a somewhat different perspective. Brimming with emotion, she described the house and abundant garden she had abandoned on the outskirts of Naples. "Food and beauty," she reportedly said, "is not so plentiful in this country; but there are not so many witches and that is better."[17]

Waiting for his execution, the anarchist martyr, Nicola Sacco wrote that not only had work been less hard in Italy than in America, but that the food was more "genuine." In America the rich ate good food, but not the working class, for in Italy labourers could eat more and fresher vegetables.[18]

The first waves of post-1880 immigrants were dominated, not merely by Italians from the South, but by "sojourners" or "birds of passage" who regarded their stay in America as temporary.[19] Many of these laborers migrated seasonally between Italy and the United States, an extension of a well-established intra-European pattern. These sojourners faced an even more serious problem in preserving their food traditions than immigrants who intended to stay. They were overwhelmingly male[20] and from a culture where the preparation of food was unquestionably the province of *la mamma* or *la moglie*. The taking of meals was the central, reaffirming ritual of *la fammiglia* in a society with extraordinary strong family ties. In North America, *la fammiglia* was 8000 to 13,000 kilometers away.

Although no substitute for family was possible, the sojourners managed remarkably well to resist American foodways. The *padrone* system, whereby Italian-American labor contractors assembled gangs of Italian immigrant workers to be hired out to work in the mining, construction, and other pursuits, saved many thousands of men from having to face the "American" food they feared so much. The owners of the mining and other companies usually gave up or sold the right to run labor camp commissaries and dining tables to the *padrone,* who stocked their stores with pasta, sausage, tomatoes, and other foods congenial to their employees. While there were many complaints of cheating, overcharging, and rotten food lodged against the *padrone,* and some *padroni* actually forced laborers to purchase a certain amount of food from them per month, the fact was that, at least, the food was *Italian.*[21]

There was an interesting discrepancy in criticisms of the food service of the *padrone*. While both the workers and American reformers attacked the *padrone* for cheating and overcharging, only the native-born critics condemned the quality of the food. In 1893, for example, a critic of the *padrone* system described a group of new recruits for the labor camps assembling apprehensively to be shipped off, clutching tin boxes of food on which they had spent their meager resources in order to avoid purchasing the "rotten sausages of the *padrone* at outrageous prices." Yet his characterization of the food they took with them as "stale bread and loathsome cheese and sausage" would lead one to suspect that he and others of his kind regarded all the hard, spicy *salsiccia,* the strong cheeses, and the coarse breads of the *Mezzogiorno* as rotten, loathsome, or both.[22] By way of contrast, the complaints of the laborers almost always involved the price, or the character of the food the *padrone* provided. Indeed, for many of them it represented a distinct qualitative and quantitative improvement over what they were accustomed to in the old country. An Italian government study concluded that inferior as the food of the *padrone* might seem, "the feeling of Italian manual laborers is that it is more abundant, varied, and rich in the United States than it is in our native land. The immigrant, generally speaking, is not used to consuming in Italy the food he acquires daily at the *padrone* commissary."[23]

The difference that likely most impressed Italian investigators was the greater quantity of meat, particularly pork sausage, that the migrants consumed.[24] American observers did not notice these things because meat consumption was universally high in the United States. Likewise, while American critics condemned some *padroni* for serving at 4:00 a.m. a breakfast that consisted only of a cup of coffee,[25] Gino Speranza, an Italian-American who himself fought the *padrone* system, pointed out in another regard that "many a Sicilian peasant feels that he has risen in life by the mere fact that he drinks coffee in the morning, for he associates coffee-drinking with the aristocracy."[26]

Another cultural institution which helped preserve old country eating habits was the Italian boarding house. Almost invariably, immigrants without relatives who could house them searched for a boarding house run either by *paesani* or, at least, an Italian from their own province or region. Such a person could be relied upon to serve the kind of food to which the newcomer was accustomed and determined to have. In Toronto's boarding houses "Calabrese boarded with Calabrese, and Abruzzese with Abruzzese. Sicilians and Friulians did not mix at all with mainland Southern Italians."[27] In some cases, especially where most boarders were sojourners, fifty, sixty, and as many as one hundred men would board in the same dwelling, making it more like a residential hotel than the kind of boarding house familiar to Canadians and Americans. Some would serve meals to non-lodgers, becoming in effect boarding restaurants specializing in the food of one region of Italy.[28]

In most cases, however, *la padrona* and her family would minister to the needs of from three to fifteen men. In such instances, food was of the utmost importance. Its ingredients and mode of preparation, along with the language and daily contact with boarders of the same origin, was a daily reassurance in the sojourner's struggle to insulate himself from cultural change. The boarder was able to maximize savings at the same time as he enjoyed ample and hearty food from his own experience. "He refused to sacrifice fully his *ambiente* and culture by eating food prepared in an 'English' or North American style."[29]

The major alternative open to sojourners, or to male immigrants who intended to send for their families, was to share rented rooms with others like them and to cooperate in the preparation and consumption of food. They too tended to live with *paesani* and preserve the food patterns of the old country. Contemporary descriptions of this kind of arrangement often speak of sausage and bread as the staples. The diets of four young Italian day-laborers living together in Chicago in 1896 appear to have been typical. Each consumed five cents worth of sausage and one pound of bread for breakfast and lunch, and three boiled eggs or what the investigator described as "head cheese" (likely *mortadella* sausage) for supper.[30] Although a frugal diet by American standards, for Italians of the late-nineteenth century this was almost a luxurious regime.

The "birds of passage" were notoriously frugal when living in America. They had to be in order to pay annual steamship passage and bring enough money back on which to live in Italy during the winter. After about 1890, there was an increase in the number of sojourners who remained semi-permanently in the New World. Even then, however, Italians seemed to spend as little as possible on subsistence so they were able to send money back home. "Habits of too great economy" were the major part of what one Italian writer called "such a supine resignation to misery, such a cynic indifference to the enjoyments of life to be found, in worse degree, only among the Chinese."[31]

In many cases, the dependents of the sojourners joined them in North America, by stages becoming permanent immigrants. While it can be assumed that the presence of *la mamma* and the wives of the men resulted in even closer clinging to traditional foodways, Italian-American frugality was not allayed. In a country in which 40 to 50 percent of a workingman's salary usually went to buying food, Italians economized on food. A Chicago social worker told of a family which managed to reduce its expenditures to $3.35 a month.[32] In order to work such a miracle, Italians turned to a dish which was common in parts of northern and southern Italy, a variation on *minestrone* called *pasta e fagioli.*

Pasta e fagioli consisted of dried, commercially-manufactured pasta—(usually tubular and purchased broken for much less than unbroken macaroni) cooked with beans in a tomato and salt pork sauce. For those able to splurge, grated hard cheese was sprinkled sparingly on top. *"Pasta e fagioli tutti giorni"* was the slogan of the frugal in Buffalo's Italian community.[33] A young man who immigrated in 1898 and worked alongside his father building a road outside of Philadelphia attributed their feat of living on $2.40 a week to the fact they subsisted on macaroni and beans which they cooked in their shanty by the construction site.[34]

Regardless of the advantages of *pasta fazool,* as *pasta e fagioli* was sounded in some dialects, few individuals, let alone families, could in fact subsist on it *tutti giorni.* Italians remaining in America were forced to adopt a host of other strategies in the struggle to preserve traditional foodways. The most obvious expedient was to buy foodstuffs imported from Italy. So great was the demand for imported Italian ingredients such as canned anchovies, oil and pasta that it is no wonder that food stores specializing in the food, not merely of Italy, but of specific Italian regions, became the social, cultural, economic, and political centres of many Italian neighborhoods.

Still, imported foods were too expensive to constitute a major part of the working class diet. "American" substitutes were often necessary. For example, while lard was a poor second choice to olive oil as a cooking fat in the *Mezzogiorno,* it was commonly used in Italian-American kitchens because, in the United States, it was so much cheaper. Corn oil, uncommon in Italy, later came into widespread use among Italian-Americans.[34] Nevertheless, while these substitutes were employed in dishes in which long cooking time or pungent ingredients obliterated the taste of the cooking fat, olive oil was still used for dressing fresh vegetables and in other dishes where its unique qualities were essential to the Italian palate.

Cheesemakers in the American midwest had begun experimenting with the manufacture of Italian-style hard grating cheeses by the turn of the century. In the eyes of the immigrants, their product did not begin to approach imported parmigiana and romano in quality. As in the case of olive oil, the immigrants continued to use the import but in diminished quantities. In the Italian immigrant communities increased consumption of imported hard grating cheese was a clear indication of improving economic status.[35]

If imports from Italy, consumed in small quantities, could keep olive oil, grating cheese, anchovies, canned tuna, and similar products with long storage lives in Italian-American kitchens, the immigrants needed to turn to local supplies of the fresh fruits and vegetables which were so important a part of the Italian diet. Rather than look to "American" sources of these foods (which in any case were not abundant), Italian immigrants took this matter into their own hands. The infusion of Italians into garden farming, both for personal consumption and in the form of intensive, commercial farming, was apparent even to old-stock Americans who otherwise paid little attention to immigrants. The "Italian Gardener" was a benign stereotype, the Italian fruit and vegetable peddler a humorous figure. Wherever an urban Italian colony of substantial size developed, Italians seized the opportunity to set up small farms in the surrounding countryside to supply the tables of their countrymen with fruits and vegetables. Immigrant Italian farmers created a large complex of farms around Hammonton and Millville, New Jersey, exploiting the location of these towns convenient to both New York City and Philadelphia. Of the 60,000 Italians in California in 1900, about half were engaged in garden agriculture, most of them on the outskirts of San Francisco, where they supplied restaurants and hotels, as well as the city's Italian-American community.[36] Not all the gardens were in the immediate vicinity of the communities they served. The vegetable growers of New Orleans served not only the local Italian population, but via railroad, supplied the large "Little Italy" of Chicago as well.

Between the growers in the countryside and the patrons in the "Little Italies," a sometimes complex network of middle men developed. The most visible of these were the ambulatory vendors with their "push carts." Most of these peddlers purchased their fruits and vegetables from wholesalers, but because of their Italian customers' concern for quality and freshness, they often pretended that their connections with the farm itself were more direct. Italian customers liked to hear the cry *"Roba dalla mia ferma,"* "stuff from my own farm." They knew it was a ruse, but still assumed that Italian peddlers sold fresher, higher quality merchandise than did non-Italians.[37] Indeed, non-Italians came to assume the same thing and the Italian pushcart vendors found a ready market in "American" neighborhoods. By the 1920s, the Italian fruit vendor was so well known that a popular song playing on the words of Italian-American dialect, "Yes, we have no bananas, we have no bananas today," could sweep the nation's fancy.

Just as striking as Italian prominence in commercial growing and vending of fresh produce was the widespread practice of home gardening among Italian immigrants. Even on the rooftops and in window boxes in the most crowded tenements in the most congested city centres, Italians seemed to have cultivated every inch of available earth. "Owns his own home and has an extensive garden and vegetable plot" was a stock-phrase in social worker surveys of Italian-Americans.[38] The Sicilians of Tampa introduced a number of previously unheard of vegetables to Florida, including artichokes, endive, and eggplant.[39] Italian factory workers in Waterbury, Connecticut, moved to the outskirts of the city, increasing the time it took to get to their jobs, because in the suburbs they could garden. A government researcher, impressed by the bounty they harvested, reported that plots were "cared for on weekdays entirely by the women" and "might well serve as models for intensive cultivation." Each house, whether it was a shack or a modern house, had its own plot of ground, usually defined by a stone fence or a well-kept hedge. Each garden had at least a few grape-vines and there were several vineyards located on the hillside.[40] The availability of free land to cultivate was also one of the major factors impelling many Italian workers in Montreal to move out from centre-city to the suburb of Jean Talon.[41]

The Italians cultivated their urban and suburban vegetable gardens amidst a culture which by no means regarded such activities highly, for the British-American tradition regarded well-clipped lawns, shrubs, and trees as the proper surroundings for a house. Joe Vergara's father terraced the backyard of his small city lot as he had in Calabria, but in deference to his American neighbors he left some grass in his front yard even though he had "a colossal distaste for lawns." Like many Italians he thought of dandelions as salad greens while, to his "American" neighbors, nurturing their lawns, dandelions were weeds. Vegara disliked trees too, for they shaded his crops from the sun.[42] Gino Speranza, a wealthy Italian-American, told of a Calabrian employee in his country home who, when it went up for sale, would emphasize what he regarded as its most attractive feature to prospective Anglo-Saxon buyers: "There isn't another place in the country," he would tell them of its lawn, "where, in the springtime, you can pick so much dandelion salad."[43]

One of the problems with gardening in North America was the comparatively short growing season, particularly in the industrialized Northeast of the United States, where most Italian immigrants settled. This problem was solved in part by preserving foods over the winter and spring. Rare was the Italian immigrant household which did not indulge in an orgy of canning, pickling, bottling, drying, salting, and fermenting in the fall as the abundant harvests of vegetables and fruit poured in from their own gardens and those of their compatriots' truck farms. Some Italians, even those who lived in congested city centers such as New York's Mulberry District, actually kept animals for food. New York City's tenement house inspectors were appalled by the large number of birds, chickens, goats, and even pigs in Italian residences.[44]

Urban animal husbandry was all the more striking because the most profound material change in the dietary circumstances of Italian immigrants was the abundance in North America of "butcher's meat." Even when a *contadino* of the *Mezzogiorno* moved from village to city within Italy, the increased consumption of purchased meat which normally resulted from the move was considered a symbol of improved status. In the United States and Canada, thanks to the recent opening of western rangelands by the railroad, meat slaughtered in mass production factories, particularly high status beef, was unbelievably cheap.

Italian immigrants responded enthusiastically to the availability of meat, consuming what would have been considered enormous quantities of viands in the old country. "Here I eat meat three times a day, not three times a year." exclaimed one immigrant affirming the wisdom of his move.[45] A dietary survey of 14 Italian laborers, 20 to 35 years of age, in turn-of-the century Chicago showed four of them regularly consuming one pound of beef steak each for breakfast and lunch. Others consumed one pound of pork chops or sausages for breakfast and lunch and then enjoyed beef for dinner.[46] A study of the diets of two Italian families living in the poorest parts of Philadelphia showed one, consisting only of a mother, father, 3-year-old and infant, living on $7.00 a week, consuming 3 1/2 pounds of beef, 2 1/2 pounds of mutton, and two pounds of pork chops in an average week. The other household—a 60-year-old mother and her daughter—still managed to consume 2 1/2 pounds of beef, 5 pounds of beef tripe, 1 pound of pork sausage, three pounds of fresh whitefish, and one pound of oysters per week.[47] By 1923, dieticians were criticizing Italians for spending too much on meat and eggs, while noting that, "strangely enough" consumption of these items "seemed to decrease slightly with the increase in income"[48]

If Italians took to eating almost as much meat as Americans, they did not necessarily eat it in the same way. American workers commonly disdained soups and stews as "pig-wash." They like their meats grilled or roasted. Italian immigrant families, however, did not sit down to dinners of roast beef, roast potatoes, and popovers. American "steak and chop houses," specializing in meats grilled in the British fashion, were not to be found in the Little Italies. When Italians cooked beef at home, or ate it in a *trattoria,* it was sauteed as veal cutlets, or stewed in any number of modes. Cuts from the round were often rolled and stuffed with chopped garlic and other ingredients to make *bracciole.* The tomato sauce in which they were stewed was used on pasta or rice. Thus, immigrants were able to overcome shortages of native ingredients while taking advantage of the relative abundance of foods which were high status items in the old country, integrating them into their native styles of cooking—eating as the better-off Italians ate in Italy—rather than adopting the "American" methods of preparation they abhorred.

The first generation of immigrants generally strove to preserve the regional cooking style of their *campania.* This was made easier by the propensity of immigrants to cluster in neighborhoods and towns with their *paesani.* The informal network by which American-born girls were instructed in traditional cookery by mothers, aunts, *nonne,* and female neighbours was abetted by grocers and other food retailers who specialized in the products of the ancestral region. In large "Little Italies," an Italian-American had no difficulty finding bakeries, butcher shops, *salumerie,* and grocery stores bearing names like "Palermo," "Calabria," and "Abruzzi." Not only did such proclamations indicate that the owner spoke the right dialect and would look sympathetically upon extending credit to *paesani,* but that he also baked the right kind of bread, cut the meat and made sausages the right way, stocked the *vino tipico,* or sold cheese, canned, and processed foods from the right part of Italy. Even in 1921, as the first generation was being displaced by their native-born children, two outside observers noted that one could tell from what locality the people of an Italian immigrant neighborhood hailed by the kinds of foodstuffs carried in the markets.[49]

Already by the 1920s, however, regional variations in the immigrants' foodways were being challenged by the emergence of what Americans came to call "Italian food," a modification of *cucina napoletana.* Why should "Italian food" have been *à la napoletana,* not Ligurian, *bolognese,* or *à la romana?* Genovese were the most numerous regional group among the Italians who came to North America *before* 1880: they were the "founders" of American "Little Italies." Bologna was already recognized as the home of Italian haute cuisine. Rome was the capital of the nation that, after 1922, Benito Mussolini idealized in messages to overseas Italians as well as to the citizens of the new fascist state.

At this time it is possible only to suggest some explanations.[50] First, although Ligurian modes of cookery did continue to characterize "Italian food" in areas where *genovese* immigrants continued to dominate the Italian-American population into the 20th century, for example, in the fishing ports of California, the immigration from the Campania was so massive after 1880 that Campanians were immediately the majority in almost all of the "Little Italies" of American metropolises. Consequently, they were more numerous in the petit-bourgeois occupations such as shop-keeping. The essential ingredients of *cucina napoletana*—pasta, tomato paste, and oregano—were more readily available than, where they differed, the main ingredients preferred by people from other regions, such as, for example the ginger of Basilicatan cookery.

When, after 1910, Sicilians displaced Campanians as the most numerous regional group in the Italian immigration, Campanian grocers, bakers, butchers, and other retailers of foodstuffs were too well-established to be displaced. In the oft-noted American pattern, they were "pushed up" from below and further entrenched in the position as provisioners to Little Italy, while the most recent immigrants moved into the lower *niches* of the food provision industry as small-time *fruttovendori,* selling their wares from push-carts or tiny stores. It is almost symbolic of the fact that Sicilians dominated only the final wave of Italian immigration to North American that the most notable Sicilian contributions to "Italian food" in the United States and Canada were desserts: Sicilian *cassate* and ice creams.

The numerical dominance of the Campanians also had its impact when, despite the best efforts of parents to marry their children within the regional groups, second-generation Italian-Americans crossed regional lines to find their spouses. With new husbands demanding the *cucina* of their mothers' *paesi,* and wives prepared to cook in the style of their mothers, both the male domination of the Italian family and the woman's control of her own kitchen worked in favour of the *cucina* of the dominant group.

Not only did *cucina napoletana* possess positive advantages in the creation of "Italian food," the other regional *cucine,* particularly those from the North faced formidable obstacles. In a culture where time was money, *polenta* was much more difficult to cook than pasta, requiring, at one stage, at least one hour of constant stirring. Moreover, while pasta was a higher status item in the North than *polenta, polenta* was rock-bottom on the southern scale, almost universally despised. How much easier it was for northerners or married couples of mixed southern origin to reverse the actual order of rural Northern Italy and serve pasta and bread as the weekday staples, perhaps reserving *polenta* for the occasional Sunday dinner as a memento of the ancestral culture. Cooking with *pesto,* characteristic of Ligurian food, meant waiting for the crops of basil that matured far later than at home and lasted for a much shorter time in America. Why bother to walk halfway across town to a *salumeria* which stocked the coarse, hard sausages of Sicily, Calabria, or Abruzzi when every butcher seemed to carry fresh Neapolitan-style sausages? There was no need for the second generation to search out the many regional cheeses of Italy when there was more than enough ricotta and mozarella, cheeses of the Mezzogiorno, with which to do what Campanians did with cheese: put it on or in pasta? In the 1920s and 1930s then, at the same time as Italian nationalism was sweeping the Little Italies for other reasons, a common concept of what constituted "Italian Food" was emerging as well. It was, for the most part, the essentially Campanian tomato, garlic and olive oil-based cuisine which reigns in most Italian-American homes and restaurants down to the present.

The tendencies working towards the homogenization of Italian food emanating from within the Little Italies were reinforced by outside forces, for in the years following 1917 the attitudes of native-born Americans towards Italian food underwent a profound change. Because of the discovery of vitamins and pressures to conserve meat during the World War, nutrition experts completely reversed their earlier contempt for Italian immigrant eating habits as unhealthy and uneconomical. Now, consumption of fruits and vegetables was to be encouraged; pasta was a nutritious staple, and recipes for spaghetti and tomato sauce became standard fare in women's magazines. Domestic producers of pasta, canned tomatoes, and grated parmesan cheese expanded their production rapidly in the 1920s, promoting the popularity of pasta and tomato sauce in American homes in a number of ways. Canned spaghetti sauce became a favourite "convenience" dish for housewives, quick, economical, and easily prepared. Even more convenient was canned spaghetti and tomato sauce itself.

Meanwhile, pasta and tomato sauce proved to be an ideal dish for the new self-serve "cafeterias," the most dynamic sector of the restaurant industry in the 1920s. Whether canned or prepared in their own kitchens, the concoctions were versatile, highly profitable, and ideal for "makeovers" using leftovers.

The growing popularity of pasta and tomato sauce in non-Italian circles enabled many Italians to open "spaghetti houses" catering to the "American" trade in cities across the nation. By the end of the 1920s, Italian restaurants were by far the most popular "foreign" restaurants in cities of the United States.

The Depression of the 1930s and the recurring meat shortages of the 1940s highlighted pasta and tomato sauce's economical qualities. Canned and bottled tomato sauce made home production even simpler and visits to restaurants with names like "Roman Gardens" became common features of city and town life. The pasta dishes featured in these restaurants were variations on an already-familiar theme: spaghetti or some other manufactured pasta covered with a Neapolitan tomato sauce or a "meat sauce" consisting of the tomato sauce and ground meat. Meat and poultry courses almost invariably consisted of meat balls (the smaller version of which constitute one of Italian-American cooking's major variations on the Campanian theme), veal cutlets, or chicken in the same tomato sauce.[51]

With American and Italian-American tastes so well-attuned to Neapolitan-style tomato sauce, and melted and grated cheese, it would seem almost inevitable that the first of the "foreign" fast foods to sweep America was pizza, which took America by storm in the 1950s. In its most common American incarnation pizza consists of white bread dough, kneaded flat after rising, topped with tomato sauce, melting cheese, (usually American mozarella), and grated cheese (usually American "Parmesan"). Conservative though they might have been about trying "foreign" foods, it was but a small step for Americans of every ethnic background to acquire a taste for tomato sauce and cheese applied to bread dough rather than pasta.

At present, the pre-eminence of "Italian food" as the favoured foreign food of Americans and Canadians appears to have met a serious challenger from "Mexican food," now seeping up from the southwestern U.S. It is significant, though, that the version of Mexican food which is by far the most popular, the tacos and burritos served in franchised chains such as "Taco Bell," bears little resemblance to what Mexicans, with their richly varied regional *cocinas,* would call their own. In the United States and Canada, "Mexican food" consists of imitation *tortillas* (wheat or corn meal pancakes) rolled around a stuffing of suspiciously Neapolitan-style tomato sauce and grated or melted cheese. Beans heated with the same tomato sauce and melted cheese topping normally accompany the more elaborate preparation. The result is not so unlike a pizza, or spaghetti as served in "Italian restaurants," or other Americanized versions of *cucina napoletana,* that most American palates would be offended. Indeed, the influence of the distinctively Mexican ingredient, chile peppers, is studiously muted or omitted in the "Mexican food" Americans and Canadians know and distinctive Mexican cooking methods, impractical or uneconomical for "Fast food" operation, are avoided, replaced in large part by Italian-style seasonings and preparations. Whether the millions of Italian immigrants who stubbornly resisted the pressures to abandon their food habits would regard the success of the Taco Bell, or even Pizza Hut, as part of their lasting endowment to American Culture is another story.

Notes

*A French version of this appeared as "Les habitudes alimentaires des immigrants italiens en Amérique du Nord: Etude de la persistance d'une culture culinaire et de la montée du 'fast food' en Amérique du Nord" in *Culture/Technique,* No. 16 (1986).

[1]Waverley Root and Richard de Rochement, *Eating in America A History,* (New York, 1976).

[2]This includes the Cantonese Chinese. Although the "Chinese" or "Chinese-American" or "Chinese Canadian" restaurant is very common, very few North Americans prepare anything approximating Chinese food at home and the "take out" volume in Chinese food is minuscule compared to pizza. It may be significant that the largest firm purveying what purports to be canned and frozen "Chinese" food, Chungking Foods of Minneapolis, Minnesota, is Italian-American owned.

[3]Werner Sombart, *Why No Socialism in America?,* trans. and ed. Patricia Hockings and C. T. Husbands, (New York: Macmillan, 1976) 106.

[4]Absolute precision in enumerating the Italian emigration is not possible. The figures of the U.S. Commissioner-General of Immigration and the *Italian Dirizione Generale della Statistica* differ significantly, the Italian figures being considerably the lower before 1902, and the American figures somewhat lower after that year. In his still invaluable study of the subject, *The Italian Emigration of Our Times* (Cambridge: Harvard University Press, 1924, reprinted New York: Arno Press, 1969) 10-15, Robert F. Foerster explains why a great many emigrants did not apply for passports before 1902, when they became mandatory of emigration, while many who took out the *nulla-osta* (which the Italian

government counted) after 1902 did not, in the end, depart. For aggregate figures, therefore, we have relied on American statistics, the annual *Reports* of the Commissioner-General of Immigration; U. S. Department of Commerce, Bureau of the Census, *A Statistical Abstract Supplement, Historical Statistics of the U. S. Colonial Times to 1957,* and *Statistical Abstract of the U. S., 1963,* 100; U. S. Department of Justice, Immigration and Naturalization Service, *Annual Report of the Immigration and Naturalization Service* 1962, 4.

Although it now houses an enormous population of immigrants from Italy, Canada was not nearly as popular an objective as the United States for pre-World I immigrants. Because of the high proportion of sojourners and their tendency to move seasonally between Toronto and Montreal and the railway, mining and forestry jobs of the interior accurate population estimates are impossible. However, a rough estimate that there were about 15-20,000 Italian-born people in Montreal and about 8-10,000 in Toronto in 1915 might not be far off. They were overwhelmingly from the South and formed the same kind of "Little Italies" revolving around communities of *paesanos* as their counterparts in the United States. Robert Harney, "Toronto's Little Italy, 1885-1945," and Bruno Ramirez and Michele Del Balzo, "The Italians of Montreal: From Sojourning to Settlement," in Robert Harney, and J. Vicenza Scarpaci, eds., *Little Italies in North America,* (Toronto: Multicultural History Society, 1981) 63-104.

[5]Julia Costello, "Gold Rush Archaeology: Excavating the Mother Lode," *Archaeology* (March-April): 27-34.

[6]Anthony Pizzo, "The Italian Heritage in Tampa," in Harney and Scarpaci, *Little Italies,* 131.

[7]John W. Briggs, "Italians in Italy and America: A Study of Change within Continuity for Immigrants to Three American Cities, 1890-1930," Ph. D. dissertation, University of Minnesota, 1972, 205. Those noodle manufacturers who did operate on a large scale were mainly German-Americans catering to the preference of the Central European and American markets.

[8]In the mid-1890s, it sold on the New York City wholesale market for 8 cents a pound, or about 16 cents a pound in New York shops and considerably more inland, a significant expense for working people, who generally earned less than $7.00 a week. *American Grocer* (November 13, 1895).

[9]Robert Harney, "Boarding or Belonging" Thoughts on Sojourner Institutions, *Urban History Review,* 2-78, (1978), 28.

[10]Imported bottled olive oil, like "Rae's Lucca," wholesaled for $6.75 a gallon in 1895. The two gallon cans which immigrants preferred wholesaled for $4.50. *American Grocer* (September 25, 1895).

[11]*Ibid.,* May 10, 1895, September 15, 1915; F. Romeo & Co., Wholesale Price list [1905], Gino Speranza Papers, Manuscript Division, New York Public Library, New York City, N.Y.

[12]*American Grocer,* May 10, 1905.

[13]Lacrynma Cristi, for example, not by far a fine or expensive wine, wholesaled for $7.00 a case in 1895, the same as Hungarian wine and almost as much as Scotch whiskey, at $9.50 a case. Chianti sold for somewhat less, but was still in the same middle class price bracket as an unexceptional Bordeaux.

[14]Phyllis Williams, *Southern Italian Folkways in Europe and America,* (New Haven, 1938), Wilbur Atwater, *The Chemistry and Economy of Food,* U. S. Department of Agriculture, Office of Experiment Stations, Bulletin No. 21, (Washington, 1895), 174.

[15]See Harvey Levenstein, "The American Response to Italian Food," *Food and Foodways,* 1, 1, (1985) for examples of American attitudes towards tomatoes, garlic and other Italian favorites.

[16]John F. Carr, "The Flower of Her Peasantry," *The Outlook,* (February 24, 1905).

[17]U. S. Children's Bureau, *Infant Mortality in Waterbury, Ct.,* Mortality Series No. 7, (Washington, 1918) 37.

[18]Niccola Sacco, *Letters of Sacco and Vanzetti.*

[19]Between 1892 and 1896, for example, for every 100 Italian immigrants arriving in America, 43 returned to Italy. Between 1907 and 1911 an average of 73 immigrants repatriated for every 100 who arrived. Thomas Kessner, *The Golden Door: Italian and Jewish Immigrant Mobility in New York City, 1880-1915,* (New York, 1977) 28.

[20]About 80 percent of all Italian immigrants from 1880 to 1900 were male. *Ibid.* 30.

[21]For some of the complaints about the food and a description of the food commissary system see Gino Speranza, "Report on Italian Labor Conditions in West Virginia," n.d. [1903]; C. B. Phipard to Eliot Norton, December 5, 1905; Memorandum, C. B. Phipard to Speranza, September 8, 1904, Speranza Papers, Box 12. A generation later, during the Great Depression of the 1930s when New York social workers asked unemployed Italian-Americans why they would not allow their sons to take jobs in the forestry camps run by the government's Civilian Conservation Corps, the principal reason turned out to be that "they would find the American diet unpalatable." Williams, *Folkways* 35.

[22]S. Merlino, "Italian Immigrants and their Enslavement," *Forum,* 15: 4, (April, 1893) 185.

[23]Kingdom of Italy, Commissariato dell Emigrazione, *Emigrazione a Colonie,* III (Rome, 1908), cited in Humberto Nelli, *The Italians of Chicago, 1880-1930,* (New York, 1970) 62.

[24]However, the immigrants' increased consumption of pasta which, in the impoverished parts of Southern Italy was mainly a Sunday dish, was also prominent in Italian reports.

[25]Nelli, *Italians of Chicago,* 61.

[26]Gino Speranza, "The Influence of America on the Italian Immigrant", typescript ms. [1908?] in Speranza papers, Box 35, Folder "I".

[27]Harney, "Boarding" 37.

[28]Joseph Conlin discusses the boarding restaurant phenomenon in *Beans, Bacon and Galantine Truffles: Food and Foodways in the Gold Rush and on the Western Mining Frontier,* (Reno, 1985).

[29]Harney, "Boarding" 27.

[30]U. S., Commissioner of Labor, *Italians in Chicago,* Special Report of the Commissioner of Labor, (Washington, 1897) 47.

[31]G. Giacosa, "La coloni Italiene di New York et di Chicago," *Nuova Antologa,* August 16, 189.

[32]I. W. Howerth, "Are the Italinas a Dangerous Class?" *Charities,* III (1984): 149.

[33]Virginia Yans-McGlaughlin, *Family and Community: Italian Immigrants in Buffalo, 1880-1930,* (Ithaca, 1977) 157.

[34]Frances E. Clark, *Our Italian Fellow-Citizens,* (Boston, 1919) 175-76. The adoption of lard may have been facilitated by exposure to Northern Italians in the United States for it was commonly used in Piedmont, Lombardy, and Emiglia-Romagna. Waverly Root, *Food of Italy,* (New York, 1977) 21, 147, 188, 271.

[35]*American Grocer* (July 24, 1895).

[36]Liciano Iorizzo et Salvatore Mondello, *The Italian-Americans,* (New York, 1971) 112-13.

[37]Williams, *Folkways* 64.

[38]Paul Radin, *The Italians of San Francisco: Their Adjustment and Acculturation,* (San Francisco, 1937) 71.

[39]Some of the vegetables they grew, such as *cardone* and *fico d'India,* are as rare today as they were in the 1880s. Pizzo, "Italian Heritage in Tampa" 131.

[40]Children's Bureau, *Infant Mortality in Waterbury, Ct.,* 72.

[41]Ramirex, "Italians of Montreal" 75.

[42]Vergara 31-36.

[43]Gino Speranza, "The Bright Side in the Life of Our Immigrants," typescript ms., Speranza Papers, Box 35, Folder A-H.

[44]George E. Pozetta, "The Mulberry District of New York City: The Years before World War One," in Harney, *Little Italies* 23.

[45]Gary Mormino, "The Italian-American Community in St. Louis," in Harney *Little Italies,* 144.

[46]Commissioner of Labor, *Italians in Chicago* 47. The beef round steak was most likely veal cutlets.

[47]The latter items also represented a divergence from the old country, where fresh water fish were not particularly common. U. S., Department of Agriculture, Office of Experiment Stations, *Dietary Studies in Boston and Springfield, Mass., Philadelphia, Pa., and Chicago, Ill.,* (Washington, 1903).

[48]Gertrude G. Mudge, "Italian Dietary Adjustments," *Journal of Home Economics,* 15: 4 (April, 1923) 184.

[49]Michael Davis and Bertha Wood, "The Food of the Immigrant in Relation to Health," *Journal of Home Economics* 13:2 (February, 1921) 68-9.

[50]The authors hope to provide a more definitive answer in a book on the subject, tentatively titled *The Food and Foodways of Italian Immigrants to America.*

[51]For a more detailed analysis of the change in American attitudes and the rising popularity of Italian food see Levenstein, "The American Response to Italian Food."

Contributors

Marc Baldwin, after his tour of duty on the car lots, Baldwin taught high school English for ten years. He currently teaches the art of composition to college freshmen, while working on his PhD in English, at the University of South Florida in Tampa. His wife is wonderful, his two daughters darling, and his Buick a bargain.

Ray B. Browne is Distinguished University Professor of Popular Culture and Chairman of the Popular Culture Department, Bowling Green State University. He was founder of the Popular Culture and American Culture Associations, founder and editor of *Journal of Popular Culture* and *Journal of American Culture*. He is the author and editor of more than forty books on various aspects of American and popular culture.

Kevin O. Browne is a practicing Counselor in Madison, Wisconsin. A member of the Popular Culture Association, he is co-editor of *Contemporary Heroes and Heroines* (1989).

John G. Cawelti is Professor of English at the University of Kentucky and in 1989-90 Walt Whitman Professor of American Studies in the Netherlands. He is author of *The Six-Gun Mystique, Adventure, Mystery and Romance, The Spy Story*, and other books on American literature and popular culture.

James Combs is currently a Professor of Political Science at Valparaiso University. He is currently at work on a study of political propaganda. He is known to haunt one of the ultimate representational symbols of American culture, Wrigley Field.

Joseph R. Conlin is Professor of History at California State University, Chico. His most recent book is *Bacon, Beans, and Galantines: Food and Foodways on the Western Mining Frontier* (Reno and Las Vegas: University of Nevada Press, 1986.)

Gary Edgerton is Associate Professor and Chairperson of the Communication Department at Goucher College. He has published extensively on media and culture issues in such journals as *Journal of Popular Culture, Journal of American Culture, Journal of Popular Film and Television*, and *Journal of Regional Cultures*. An earlier version of this chapter appeared in the Winter 1982 issue of *Journal of Popular Film and Television.*

J. Michael Ferri, PhD, is a Professor of Rhetoric and Communication at the University of Puerto Rico—Rio Piedras Campus. Ferri has been co-editor of *Puerto Rican Voices: Oral History in Print* and has published and presented studies in rhetoric and public address, non-verbal communication, intercultural communication, and mass media.

Roger A. Fischer is professor and head of History and American Studies director at the University of Minnesota-Duluth, and a specialist in American political popular culture.

Marshall W. Fishwick has written and spoken widely on American Studies and Popular Culture. Recent books include: *Common Culture and The Great Tradition, The Godpumpers, Symbiosis: Popular Culture & Other Fields* (co-edited with Ray B. Browne). He is a professor of Communication at Virginia Polytechnic Institute and State University.

Mary Catherine Flannery is a professor of English at the University of Louisville and a specialist in Anglo-Irish literature. She is author of *Yeats and Magic,* and is currently writing a book on Yeats and women.

Tom Juravich is Assistant Professor of Labor Studies and Industrial Relations at Penn State University and coordinates a worker's education program in Philadelphia. The author of *Chaos on the Shop Floor* (Temple, 1985), he has published in a wide variety of areas in labor studies and industrial relations. Also a folk and labor musician, his latest album *A World to Win* was released by Flying Fish Records.

Elizabeth Atwood Lawrence, a veterinarian as well as an anthropologist, received her A.B. degree from Mount Holyoke College, her V.M.D. degree from the University of Pennsylvania School of Veterinary Medicine, and her Ph.D. in cultural anthropology from Brown University. She is an associate professor in the Department of Environmental Studies at Tufts University School of Veterinary Medicine, where she teaches and carries out research in the field of human-animal relationships. Dr. Lawrence is the author of three books: Rodeo: *An Anthropologist Looks at the Wild and the Tame, Hoofbeats and Society,* and *His Very Silence Speaks,* as well as numerous journal articles dealing with human-animal interactions.

Harvey A. Levenstein is Professor of History at McMaster University in Hamilton, Ontario, Canada. His most recent book is *Revolution at the Table: The Transformation of the American Diet* (New York: Oxford University Press, 1988.)

Richard Peterson, a free-lance writer, has graduate degrees in human behavior and sociology. His book, *Electric Sisters,* contains profiles of nationally-known women in televangelism (religious radio and television).

Sam G. Riley is a Professor of Communication Studies at Virginia Polytechnic Institute & State University. Though all his books are in the area of mass media history, he has written humor columns for roughly a decade and has taught courses in humor writing and performance.

Michael Aaron Rockland has written widely on mobility in such books as *Homes on Wheels* and *Looking For America on the New Jersey Turnpike.* He is the author of the novel, *A Bliss Case.* Rockland is professor and chair of the American Studies Department at Rutgers University.

Harold Schechter and Jonna Gormely Semeiks have collaborated on a number of textbooks, including *Patterns in Popular Culture* (Harper & Row, 1980) and *Discoveries: Fifty Stories of The Quest* (Macmillan, 1983). They are members of the English Departments of Queens College and C.W. Post, respectively.

Anthony Synnott studied at the London School of Economics and the University of Western Ontario, and is now in the Department of Sociology and Anthropology at Concordia University in Montreal. His pink flamingo was stolen from his back yard.

Philip G. Terrie teaches English and American Studies at Bowling Green State University. He is the author of articles on environmental literature and history and *Forever Wild: Environmental Aesthetics and the Adirondack Forest Preserve* (Temple University Press, 1985).